Get What You Need

The pervasive and common thread among the countless books dealing with the issue of relationships is the way they often lack an effective means of really helping us evolve. They all seem to offer a quick and pithy fix—*how to walk away from it without leaving yourself behind—how to tell someone you love them when you can't say the words I LOVE YOU—how to add more zip to your sex life in only 60 seconds a day.*

In the galactic scheme of things, this is like stacking sandbags around the earth in hopes of preventing a gigantic meteor from hitting it ... no chance. Most often, these books tell us that we've made a mistake. Yet they don't tell us why we keep making the same mistake over and over again. This suggests that most books on relationships are not often engaged with things to do with the Soul. Indeed, how many books on relationships address the evolution of the Soul, its past history, or its needs in this lifetime?

Pluto: The Soul's Evolution through Relationships presents a profound understanding of the purpose of relationships. Author Jeffrey Wolf Green's lucid vision exemplifies that you can't always get what you want, but you do get what you need. Green illuminates the simple yet often ignored reality that in the process of a relationship, you must deal with your limitations ... and then and only then can you evolve.

When I translated Jeffrey's counseling in Germany using the ideas and the karmic concepts of this book, every client said "Yes, that's exactly how it is," and nobody used the words "sounds nice, could be like that." These concepts are touching a deep inner truth. When in 15 years most astrologers will follow Jeffrey's way of thinking, you won't be able to imagine how their current interpretation of relationship dynamics could have been considered essentially correct.

Klaus Bonert

About the Author

Jeffrey Wolf Green is a world-renowned astrologer who has combined his deep spiritual insights with the vast experience gained by counseling over 16,000 clients into a significant new science called Evolutionary Astrology. He is the author of the bestselling *Pluto, Volume I: The Evolutionary Journey of the Soul* and *Uranus: Freedom from the Known*, contributed to *How to Personalize the Outer Planets* (ed. Noel Tyl), and was the astrological advisor to John Hogue's bestselling book *Nostradamus and the New Millennium*.

Green's life experience is practically as wide as his vision. He saw service in Vietnam, spent two years in a Vedantic monastery, studied in a matriarchal temple in Nepal, and was initiated by a Navajo peyote master in the high desert of New Mexico. He has been an astrologer for over twenty years, has lectured throughout the United States, Canada, Europe, and Israel (including being a faculty member at most of the world's major astrological conferences), has hosted a radio show in Seattle, and has published numerous magazine articles in various countries.

Green currently lives in Boulder, Colorado, with his wife and fellow astrologer Martina and his three children.

To Contact the Author

If you wish to contact the author, would like more information about this book, or would like information about the School of Evolutionary Astrology, a professional course of study designed by the author, please write in care of Llewellyn Worldwide, and we will forward your request. Llewellyn Worldwide cannot guarantee a reply to all letters, but all will be forwarded. Please enclose a self-addressed, stamped envelope or $1.00 to cover costs. If outside the U.S.A., please enclose an international postal reply coupon. Address your correspondence to:

Jeffrey Wolf Green
c/o Llewellyn Worldwide
P.O. Box 64383, Dept. K333-6
Saint Paul, MN 55164-0383, U.S. A.

Llewellyn Worldwide does not participate in, endorse, or have any authority or responsibility over any private business transactions between our authors and the public.

Pluto

Volume II

The Soul's Evolution Through Relationships

Jeffrey Wolf Green

1997
Llewellyn Publications
St. Paul, Minnesota, U.S.A. 55164-0383

FIRST EDITION
First Printing, 1997

Cover design: Anne Marie Garrison
Project management: Ken Schubert

Library of Congress Cataloging-in-Publication Data

    Green, Jeffrey Wolf, 1946-
      Pluto.
      Contents: vol. 1. The Evolutionary Journey of the Soul—
vol. 2. The Soul's Evolution through Relationships.

      1. Astrology. 2. Pluto (planet)—Miscellanea.
3. Horoscopes. I. Title.
BF1742.2.P4G74 1997 133.5'3   85-45290
ISBN 0-87542-296-9 (vol. 1)
ISBN 0-87542-333-6 (vol. 2)

Printed in the United States of America

Llewellyn Publications
A Division of Llewellyn Worldwide, Ltd.
P.O. Box 64383
St. Paul, MN 55164-0383, U.S.A.

Dedication

I would like to dedicate this book to my sweet wife Martina Wolfiana Green, to my children Luke, Deva, and Cheyenne Green, and to Peter, Wolfgang, and all those who have unconditionally supported me over the years.

A child is born on that day and at that hour when the celestial rays are in mathematical harmony with his or her individual karma. The individual's horoscope is a challenging portrait, revealing the unalterable past, and its probable future results. But the natal chart can be rightly interpreted only by men or women of wisdom: these are few.

Swami Sri Yukteswar

Endorsements

This book is an absolute must for those who are seriously interested in Evolutionary Astrology. Upon reading this book, your consciousness becomes so heightened that the big picture naturally presents itself to you, and allows you to evolve through awareness instead of getting stuck in the pain of trauma. Jeffrey's book contains excellent methodology, very concise and easy-to-follow ways to employ this information. Using the methodology uncovers the core dynamics of an issue, the understanding and the reasons surrounding the issues, thus allowing for great healing and evolution to a greater place. Integrate what you have read, use it, and you will be doing humanity and yourself a great service.

Mary J. Connoly

The profound significance of this classic work is staggering. Pluto's job in Scorpio would not have been complete without having revealed these last nuggets from her most secret places.

Jeff Green embodies the potent truth of Pluto in Sagittarius as he leads us through the terrifying shadowlands of our heritage. We zoom in from the perspective of earlier generations who set our stage, right to the core of the individual's birth chart.

Startling revelations abound from the natal Mars/Venus phase, especially in the composite chart. Clarification on relationship types, Soul Mates, evolutionary states, Mars and Venus through the signs, and the composite Pluto message add to the rare treasure you are about to read.

The in-depth case studies may seem unnecessarily severe, but unfortunately the scenarios discussed are far too common! But in claiming our darkness we reclaim our power—the Plutonian power to re-create, refreshed and redeemed.

If one drop of blood can give us AIDS, dare we turn our heads too quickly from our own connection to all this? The time for denial is over! The time for acceptance and healing is NOW.

I am convinced that Jeff Green was destined to write this book because his life has catapulted him through more intensities of Light and Dark than most of us could even imagine, let alone survive. His experiences and integrity of purpose combine to bring us a voice that speaks to our Souls.

We have no choice but to listen.

Sandy Hughes

Table of Contents

Foreword

Sharing the Soul-Wind

Relationships are never simple. Anyone who has tried it will tell you so! Examining your relationships through the natal chart explains the energy patterns in your current life partnerships. Adding the dimension of previous lives gives a deeper meaning to any relationship, whether love, friendship, or business.

In this book Jeffrey Green shares his lifelong, direct experience and deep knowledge of how to graph your deep-rooted partnership needs in this lifetime, through any natal and composite horoscope, as Jeffrey himself puts it, "by embracing all these ideas, you come to understand what all of us attract exactly what we need, even if we do not know we need it!"

Some people have a hard time embracing the idea of previous lives together. I myself belong to this category. Before meeting Jeffrey, I always thought that reincarnation was a logical rational, coherent, sensible, and intelligent way to explain human existence. My analytical brain accepted the idea of reincarnation fully—but my heart felt nothing.

It was only after meeting Jeffrey that my intellectual understanding has to give way to a deep emotional acceptance and inner recognition of previous lives. Jeffrey's ability to transform his insights, and to transmit and teach them in a very personal and direct way, just through his presence, was simply too convincing to deny. It is this special quality of Jeffrey's presence that this book clearly transmits.

This book has repeated and deepened my own knowledge and acceptance of reincarnation, and I know it will do the same for almost any reader. Through this book runs a strangely familiar and well-known insight to which you can immediately connect. This book is like a mirror placed in front of you—and you have to be very hard-hearted and hard-eyed not to recognize yourself and your relationships in it.

Through its magic mirror this book shows you that astrology is not something you learn by assimilating information, but that it is something you rediscover in the most unconscious and hidden corners of your mind. The astrology in this book gives to you, and helps you learn, the language of communicating with others what you, on a Soul level, already know.

How would you explain the beauty of a special summer day, the dismal face of the Moon moving over a mountain range, the trickling sound of a stream headed for the ocean, the calm movements of a diving whale, the quiet hissing of the wind in the brown leaves of a tree in autumn? We cannot see the wind. Out mind can reason that it is there, but all we see are the physical effects of its invisible presence. This book gives you a glimpse of the disguised soul-wind within you, and in your partners—the wind that moves you toward any person and the wind that moves that person toward you.

With each breath we share the air and wind with everything living. You cannot remain sane in this world without relating. We need each other. We need to know that we are not alone. We need to know why we can share our inner reality, our Soul-wind, with some people, but not with all people.

Sometimes, when walking down a street in a strange city, you look in another person's eyes, and you feel the wind. You quietly nod, like saying, "I've been there," and the stranger nods and agrees. Then you know.

If you have ever looked across a room and suddenly felt a gale of love hit you, or experienced how a brief encounter on a stormy railway station can change your life ... you know.

Life is not merely a repetition of old patterns, but the discovery of new ways to handle and use something very familiar to you. When you realize this ... you know.

Jeffrey's writing mirrors the eternal reality of your Soul, as you read this book you will feel the Soul-wind that brought you to this world,

gave you a body, and made you share your current physical life with the most meaningful people in your world-in your closest partnerships.
We will meet again.
Read on, and you will know!

Christian Borup, Director
The Irene Christensen Astrological Institute
Copenhagen, Denmark

Preface

Pluto and the Soul's Journey

Every practicing astrologer has heard many times from clients, "My Goodness! It took my therapist months to get to that, and here it comes up right away in the horoscope!" Such an observation about a spiritual need, a subtle force in relationships, a creative connection between past and present is a compliment to the incisiveness of astrology and the astrologer. It is also a suggestion of how much is frequently lacking in the therapeutic processes that exist in our society to help us. And it suggests that existing or "common" therapeutic processes in our society often lack an effective means of really helping us evolve.

This comment suggests that therapists are not often engaged with things to do with the Soul. Indeed, how many therapists concern themselves with the journey of a Soul, with its evolution, its past history, or its framework of needs in this lifetime? The current wisdom is, "If we don't really know what the Soul is, how can we talk about it?"

Yet things are changing. It has been most edifying to see the works of psychotherapist Thomas Moore—*Care of the Soul* and *Soul Mates*—top the best-seller lists. Moore himself told me that over one million copies of *Care of the Soul* have been sold! This lucid writer, who is most sympathetic to astrology, deals poetically and practically with the archetypal references personified in Greek myths. People everywhere respond to this work.

We can cite as well the works of Scott Peck—T*he Road Less Traveled* and *Further Along the Road Less Traveled*—as helpful books about the human condition, framed in decidedly holistic dimensions. The Soul is alive and well, though not everywhere to be seen.

Jeffrey Green fits in easily here. While his lens is explicitly astrological, it is burnished with an empirical, psycho-sensitive polish and a courageous presence. Psychotherapists could enrich their work and help others more if they would take even a few pages of Jeffrey's work to heart (let alone several semesters of astrological study). How about understanding the purpose of relationships, for example? Can you imagine a therapist pursuing the fundamental, all-pervasive concern: "What purpose does your present relationship serve in your development in this life?" Yet, that concept alone can help set us free. Coming to grips with this issue can ameliorate the nagging feelings of unconnectedness with past, present, and future that so many people have.

Green says that the purpose of relating is to encounter and experience "our personal limitations." He takes this precept quite a distance—a "journey" indeed. Throughout the route he reiterates the fact that relationships are complementary situations, not structures we create to please ourselves. Relationships are situations that involve self-recognition only secondarily and only through others, in ways that help eventually to make us whole. We find ourselves outside ourselves and need others to help, just as night needs day, and the Moon needs the light of the Sun.

Seeing relationships through Green's special vision reveals that we are not being victimized by some chicanery of fate, as some pop psychologists (and even some astrologers) would have it; rather, "You get what you deserve." In other words, we are linked necessarily with what we need. And in the process of relationship, we accomplish "the metamorphosis of our limitations ... and we evolve."

I read all this filtered through my own decades of astrological experience, and still this book shines another respectful light upon the miraculous process of the human condition as it is revealed through astrology. Green keeps returning to the thought that there is simply no way to go it alone in life, so essential are relationships. Relationships demand that we look outside ourselves (the polarization of astrological archetypes) and that we listen in order "to learn equality." This is the heart of Green's refurbishment of the Libra archetype, and I think it is the core of his book. That's why I'm repeating myself—as astrologers, it is very important to know this and to pass it on to others who trust us to be helpful.

I recall studying long ago at college a definition of "maturity" offered by the celebrated psychologist Gordon Allport. He suggested that maturity has three steps to it: The extension of self; self-objectification from this new vantage point; and only then a return to self through a unifying philosophy of life. Green takes us on just such a journey through the horoscope: Out of ourselves into relationships in which we see our personal growth and are thereby refined and strengthened. And then, as Allport and Green say, we are unified. We get it together.

Astrologers see Pluto as the symbol of empowerment and, to the extent that empowerment embraces outcome as well as stimulus, I've suggested in my own work that Pluto is the symbol of perspective. One way or another, astrology's theorists and practitioners say that Pluto embodies an ultimate concern, a potential that is formidable. But it is all too clear in reality that normal people living normal lives don't all set records with personal achievement or fulfillment as measured by our society. Commonly, the power implodes instead (often problematically), or never even touches a life experience suggested by a particular Plutonian configuration. I think Green explains this with many indications that reveal Pluto not to be a point of power but, rather, a synthesis of identity strength. It is not an isolated quantum focus, but development power spread around—it is *evolutionary*. We tap into it purposefully to one degree or another as our journey requires.

Pluto permeates the horoscope not only in terms of personality invigoration (empowerment) but in terms of time, as our ultimate symbol of awareness, and in terms of sequential personality development. When Green uses the word "karma" he avoids the misconception of retribution and punishment, using it properly as the accumulation of balance within successive growth times, within lives in series.

So the Soul is constantly changing and evolving on a journey through time. It is energized by Pluto in part, and it is synthesized into networks of manifestation among the other planets. All of this is acted out in relationships—thus, the composite chart and synastry are so important to Green's analytical presentation. And because this subject manifests naturally in socio-sexual expression, Green devotes a lot of thought to Venus and Mars, their occurrence in the natal horoscope and their transits.

And it is thought well spent: I have yet to encounter in astrological literature such real, emphatic insights into socio-sexual dimensions as Green presents, with courage and grace—and extraordinary applicability. Insights like these would have been impossible in astrology even twenty-five years ago. Astrology, in its own journey of development, has grown conspicuously toward maturity. Green certainly is helping us all make the trek—extending ourselves, looking back, putting a philosophy together. The pages about Venus and Mars should be given to your favorite therapist!

Please don't think that the word "Soul," so prominent in this book, or even the sense of "spiritual" that so often accompanies the mention of Soul, automatically relates to religiousness. It just isn't so, and religiousness is certainly not what this book is about, as Green points out. The much-loved Isabel Hickey, in one of our many conversations some years ago, said, "Noel, people have to learn that spirituality is not an end in itself; it's a means of getting somewhere."

Spirituality describes how we live, not why we live. A soldier on the battlefield can be just as spiritual as a priest saying mass. "Onward Christian Soldiers" is not an oxymoron!

This preface is intended to prepare the reader for the fine book that follows. To be complete, I want to add one more thought: Green's verismo should not shock us. His realism vividly defines the amorphous (the Soul) with the guideline of hard experience.

In his case studies, Green shows us people who are working out their wholeness—their *Soulness*—within essential relationship, within a living, pushing, shoving, giving, taking, society. He shows the spiritual grit it takes to understand this life. Remember, in hunting treasure, we move big rocks and dig deep in the sand to find the gold.

For this map, Jeffrey, thank you!

Noel Tyl
Fountain Hills, Arizona
December 1995

Acknowledgements

There are so many people to thank that it is impossible to name everyone. I would like to give special thanks to my wonderful wife Martina for her total support of me, and for her counsel and advice in writing this book. She is an excellent astrologer in her own right. I want to thank my children Luke and Deva for giving up their time with "papa" while this book was being written. I would also like to extend a special thanks to my friends Noel Tyl, Christian Borup, Sandy Hughes, and Klaus Bonert for taking the time to read my manuscript, and for writing the Preface, Foreword, and reviews for this book. A very special thanks to Tom Bridges who also read my manuscript and offered very critical and necessary advice, and to my special friend Mary Connolly for her comments, advice, and support as she read through this manuscript as it was being written. A big thanks to Nancy Gavin who appeared in my life at a critical time, and who supplied financial support that allowed our lives to be sustained. And, lastly, a big thank you to all of you that I have met in my lecture travels in America, Europe, Canada, and Israel and who have encouraged me in the work that I do. You know who you are.

God Bless,
Jeffrey Wolf Green

Introduction

It has been quite a few years since *Pluto: The Evolutionary Journey of the Soul* was first released. The response to the first volume has been overwhelming. In it I invited people to write to me with their observations, questions, and feedback. I have since received thousands upon thousands of letters from all over the world. The support for the work reflected in those letters has truly touched my Soul. And, of course, many have asked and wondered about the planned second volume of *Pluto*. Well, because of your encouragement, here it is!

The intention in this volume is to focus all the ideas about Pluto and the Nodal Axis of the Moon, first presented in the original volume, upon the dynamic of relationships. All of us are in relationship to others all the time. From the great mass of people on the planet we all choose certain people to be intimate with, and to be friends with. We have different kinds of relationships with those that we work with, and we have a relationship with our parents in one way or another. We have relationships with our children, and so on. The intention of this book is to show the evolutionary and karmic causes, reasons, and prior life backgrounds that determine the types of relationships that we have, and with whom.

Within the book, a precise astrological methodology is presented that will allow you to determine what the prior life-orientation has been between two people, where the relationship left off, where the two people re-begin their relationship, and what the current evolutionary next step is—the specific reasons or intentions for being together again.

Composite charts and traditional synastry charts are used to understand this. The key difference between the synastry chart and composite chart is explained. Many case histories are used to exemplify and illustrate these core ideas. There are chapters on the natures and functions of Mars and Venus. A chapter is devoted to explaining the eight primary phases of the Mars/Venus phasal relationship, and the aspects that take place within those phases. The same study is applied to Mars/Pluto. Another chapter is dedicated to defining the primary archetypes of the composite chart Pluto in each sign and house, and relative to the natural evolutionary conditions for any given Soul—the consensus state, the individuated state, and the spiritual state.

There is a chapter that discusses the different types of relationships that can exist between people. Within this, I explain the differences between Soul Mates, Karma Mates, Twin Souls, etc., and how to determine them. In addition, I devoted a chapter to the study of one of the greatest dark secrets that can exist between life-partners—the sado-masochistic relationship. An explanation of the Garden of Eden Myth precedes and sets up this discussion, and an extensive case history is used to illustrate it. Some of you may be offended by this because the instinctual reaction to these words, and archetypal dynamic, is repulsive in most. Yet it permeates individual and collective reality in a way that most can no longer ever recognize. My intention in doing this is to put the light of consciousness on this archetype so that, hopefully, a little change can begin, which will purge this archetype from our consciousness.

As in *Pluto: The Evolutionary Journey of the Soul,* I encourage you to read this book very slowly so as to be able to integrate it. If you have not read the first volume yet, I would strongly encourage you to do so. A deeper and fuller understanding of the material presented in this volume will then occur. This is not an astrological "cookbook." Accordingly, it is important that you read this book from the first page to the last if you are to have any real understanding of the dynamics and archetypes presented within it.

Thank you to all who have taken the time to write to me, and to all the people I have met in my lectures in America, Europe, Canada, and Israel who have been so encouraging and supportive.

Jeffrey Wolf Green
Boulder, Colorado
Winter, 1996

Chapter One

The Nature of Relationships

The intention of this chapter is to hopefully generate an understanding of the nature of relationships. The entire nature of the manifested Creation is in relationship to Itself, interrelating and interacting. The interrelationships and interactions of all forms of the Creation generates evolution and change *because* of that interaction and interrelationship. Nothing within the Creation, including an individual's sense of self, can be known or understood unless it is related to something else.

In this chapter, we will focus on two primary themes or dynamics that totally condition our approach, orientation, attitude, and psychology towards relationships in general, and those that are closest to us specifically, such as parents, lovers, children, and/or our closest friends. The first theme or dynamic will be based on the possibility of past life connections to others. Those we have had past life connections to will reflect experiences, understandings, orientations, and attitudes that have come before this life. These dynamics in combination will subconsciously condition how we relate with each other in this life in ways that will sometimes defy any rational explanation or cause from just this life's point of view.

The second theme or dynamic will be based on our relationship to our early parental environment, and, through extension, our relationship to social/cultural and religious imprinting. The nature of this imprinting or conditioning contributes just as strongly as past life dynamics to our attitude, orientation, and psychology of how and why we generally relate to others as we do, and specifically in the ways we relate to those that are closest to us.

The deeper question becomes this: Why did we choose, on a Soul level, the specific type of our birth environment (including our parents), and, through extension, the type or nature of the country, society, or tribe in which we grow up? The core answer is that these current life conditions, our early environment and country of birth, serve to foster our next evolutionary step. In addition, our evolutionary and karmic requirements typically create conditions in which the prior life dynamics between a child and his or her parents is not finished or complete. The parents' subconscious memories that condition their own behavior towards one another will obviously impact or imprint upon the child. The subconscious memories that the child shares with each parent and each parent with the child will also impact and condition the behavior of all concerned. The current life conditions of each parent's own childhood environment, and the past life conditions impacting on their relationship with their own parents, also serves to condition their own psychology towards relationships in general, and with those closest to them specifically.

So we meet again, eh? Yes, we do. Many, many times. Why do we do this? The answer is very complex, yet can be boiled down to this: Souls evolve over great lengths of time by desiring to experience a variety of necessary experiences, dynamics, behaviors, circumstances, values, and beliefs that ultimately allow the Soul to be reunited with the Source of Creation through an exhaustion of all possible experiences that generate or create the appearance of being separated from, or separate from, the Source.

Certain dynamics that dictate the need for specific kinds of experiences generally take more than one life to work through. Because we evolve by focusing on certain dynamics for a period of time in order to focus on other dynamics at another period of time, we tend to keep re-creating circumstantial realities in life after life that reflect those key dynamics. In so doing we create relationships with people whose nature reflects the dynamics that we are working on, or are defined by. Thus, we re-meet those people, and they us, for many lives until those dynamics are exhausted and evolved beyond.

WHY RELATIONSHIPS?

For all the possible ways for the Creation to have created Itself, why relationship? It is because the Manifested Creation is in relationship to Itself. This is so because of the sheer act of projecting Itself in the causal act of creation in the first place. That which has been projected is the totality of the Creation in all its possible forms and images which appear as separate phenomenal forms apparently unrelated to anything but themselves. But, in truth, all images and forms, all structure, are interrelated and interacting because of the Creative Act of projection. Projection is the ultimate law of motion, and motion generates magnetism, electricity, and gravity. These laws in combination generate evolution, transformation, and metamorphosis as all forms of the Creation interrelate and interact upon themselves. Again, the totality of the Creation is in relationship to Itself which is forever changing, yet is always the same.

As human beings on this tiny, out-of-the-way planet, we are in relationship to the projected Creation because we are part of it. We are in relationship to our planet, Gaia, or the totality of Nature. We are in relationship to other human beings, and we are in relationship to ourselves. We are governed by the law of motion (projection), magnetism (vibration), electricity (positive and negative charge), and gravity (the condensation of pure energy into form). Thus, we are governed by the law of change (evolution) which created the law of transformation and metamorphosis. In essence, it is because of the law of relationships that we evolve. We evolve through forming relationship to something or someone that seems to represent something that we desire or need in order to grow, something that we sense or perceive that we do not have. By forming such a relationship a Plutonian osmosis occurs through which we *become* that which we have formed a relationship to. Through this type of relationship we confront, or become aware of, our preexisting limitations which are defined by our current state of being or reality: our beliefs, ideas, values, understandings, emotional patterns, etc. By forming a relationship to that which we perceive we need or desire in order to grow or evolve beyond these preexisting limitation, a transformation or metamorphosis occurs—and vice versa. The union of two apparent, separate forms allows for a mutual osmosis in which the two separate forms become more than they were prior to the union in which the mutual osmosis took place.

IN THE BEGINNING

The law of relationship and evolution was set in motion at the moment that the Creator projected Itself outwards from within Itself. This simple fact is the basis of the apparent law of appearance or duality—out of nothing there was One. The unmanifest *created*, giving rise to Yin and Yang, night and day, hot and cold, etc. By projecting

Itself outwards, the Creator generated the apparent law of separation and individual form. Yet, because all form is part of the total Creation, the law of relationship and union with the Creator was also set in motion. Thus all forms of the Creation simultaneously reflect the appearance of distinct individual form that appears to be born, grows, and dies, and the law of return or union in which all the forms of Creation are interrelated, interactive, and cannot exist except through relationships to other forms or structures of the Creation. In essence, all forms can appear separate and distinct, yet reflect and contain the essence of total Creation or the Creator. All forms then reflect the law of re-creating or procreating themselves through the apparent law of separation—to procreate life just as the Creator has. Yet, for any form or structure to recreate itself it must form a relationship to another form or structure which allows for a merging or union to occur. The merging or union generates an osmosis through which the perception or experience of separateness is suspended for a time. In this suspension generated through osmosis or union all forms re-create or procreate themselves through an exchange of their essence of energy. As the physicists have pointed out, energy can never be destroyed; it can only change form.

The appearance of distinct form and duality is sustained through the laws of motion, magnetism, electricity, and gravity. These laws are, again, governed by the ultimate act of the Creator projecting Itself outwards from within Its own Center. The evolution of separate forms is dependent on those same forms forming a relationship to other forms of an opposite polarity, i.e. masculine and feminine. The union of these differing forms generates, through osmosis, a metamorphosis of form that allows for the evolution of form to occur.

THE HUMAN BEING

Focusing these thoughts to the human being brings us to the idea of the Soul. The Soul can be simply defined as an immutable consciousness or energy. This means that the Soul cannot be destroyed or die—it can only change form. The evolution of the Soul is ultimately based on the simple laws of separation from the Source, and returning, reuniting, or remerging with that Source—the perception and experience of separateness no longer existing. The evolution of the Soul is based on a dual desire archetype inherent within the Soul: one desire is to separate from its Creator, the other is to return or reunite with It. The evolution of the Soul is thus based on a progressive elimination of all separating desires, and the dynamics and experiences that this desire generates. By progressively exhausting all separating desires over great lengths of evolutionary time, the desire to return or reunite with the Creator progressively begins to dominate the consciousness within the Soul. Until their ultimate remerging with the Creator is realized, the Soul is dependent on forming relationships with other Souls in order to evolve, to re-create, or procreate itself in new ways.

All Souls are simultaneously male and female in essence just as the Creator is. In the act of Creation the Creator simultaneously projected the law of duality, or opposite electrical charges that we call male and female. Through the law of appearance (form) the Soul can appear male or female. Through the law of separation the Soul must form a relationship with its opposite in order for its evolution to proceed. By forming a relationship to its opposite the Soul forms a union in which it "osmoses" its opposite into itself. The male takes in the female, and the female takes in the male. Over great lengths of evolutionary time the Soul that appeared as male will, at some point, appear as female and vice versa—the symbolic matrix of the *I Ching* will illustrate this upon consideration. This reflects the ultimate intention of the Creator to reunify or remerge Its projection back unto Itself. Thus, in human form, for the Soul to eliminate all separating desires that create the experience and perception of separateness is to return to the Source. At the Soul level this means, in evolutionary terms, to merge or unify equally its maleness and femaleness. In psychological terms, this means to achieve a state of androgyny. In essence, the dance of opposites through the law of separation continues until each form within the Creation evolves to the point where it is able to merge within itself the relationship between its own inner opposites of male and female which allows for an absolute return and merging with its Creator.

Chapter Two

Evolutionary Astrology

At this point, it may be useful to review key astrological principles and methods that correlate to the evolutionary nature and progression of the Soul, as developed in *Pluto: The Evolutionary Journey of the Soul.*

PLUTO

The evolutionary principle itself correlates with Pluto. For our purposes, Pluto specifically correlates to the Soul and its evolution. The Soul can be defined as an immutable consciousness or energy that cannot be destroyed—it can only change form. The archetype or dynamic of desire is the causal factor or driving dynamic that generates the Soul's evolutionary progression from life to life. Within the Soul, there is a dual desire archetype. One desire is to separate from the Source of the Soul. The other desire is to return to the Source of the Soul. The evolutionary progression of the Soul is based on taking action on all separating desires over great lengths of time until, finally, the Soul exhausts itself of these types of desires to the exclusion of the only desire that can remain—the desire to reunite its sense of identity with the Source Itself. This simple archetype of the dual desire nature of the Soul is the basis of what is called free will or choice-making. This simple truth can be validated by all of us independent of astrology. Is it not true that all of us can have a myriad of separating desires—i.e., the new possession, the career promotion, the new lover, etc.? We may have the ability to actualize that which we are desiring of a separative nature, and when we actualize this type of desire we will have a sense of satisfaction. But this sense of satisfaction is soon replaced with a sense of dissatisfaction, and a sense of needing something more. It is this sense of dissatisfaction that echoes the ultimate desire, within the Soul, of returning and reuniting with its own Source. This is a universal experience among all peoples everywhere.

In the first volume of *Pluto* it was stated that the natal position of Pluto, by house and sign, correlates with the types of desires, or evolutionary intentions, that the Soul had before the current life. For example, a Ninth House Pluto would have typically defined its core sense of identity in religious, metaphysical, philosophical, or cosmological terms. Because the Soul would have spent many lifetimes developing this structure of self-definition before coming into this life, it will naturally gravitate to that same orientation. This is because of the need for security based on self-consistency. Pluto, again, correlates with the sources of our deepest, unconscious, sense of security. This is why Pluto correlates with compulsions, obsessions, feeling threatened, being defensive, emotional complexes of all kinds, manipulations, etc. The evolutionary next step is determined by Pluto's *opposite* house and sign relative to its natal placement in the birthchart. By evolving towards this point a metamorphosis or evolution of the natal placement of Pluto naturally occurs.

In composite charts, the house and sign placement of Pluto will correlate with what the core prior life dynamics or evolutionary intentions were between two people who were in some kind of relationship. Like the individual, the coupled unit will naturally gravitate to those prior life orientations in this life. As in the individual chart, the next evolutionary step for the couple is determined by the opposite house and sign relative to the placement of Pluto in the composite chart.

Synastry charts, where one person's Pluto is located somewhere in another person's chart, and vice versa, correlate with how each other's core sense of self-definition impacts upon one another. This impact has a generational as well as an individual application. Generational, because the entire generation's Pluto will, through synastry, be in the same house and sign as an individual's natal Pluto, forming a sense of generational identity. Individually, because each of us will form relationships of a personal nature with others of our generation. However, because of the concurrent desire within the Soul to separate, each of us will also attempt to separate, in our own ways, from our generation in order to define our own sense of identity. This separating desire leads an individual into his or her next evolution-ary step via the opposite house and sign of the natal position of Plu-to. Thus, the impact of our generational influence serves to stimulate this separating desire in order to actualize our next evolutionary step. The individual relationships that we form with those within our gen-eration also serve to do this, yet in much more personal terms.

Again, Pluto correlates with the principle of evolution at every lev-el of reality. There are two primary ways that evolution occurs, and these are reflected in how the Soul also evolves. These two ways of evolving can be called *cataclysmic* and *uniform.*

Cataclysmic evolution is based on a very intense event that leads to and creates metamorphic change—a rapid acceleration of evolu-tionary needs. In nature, this can be an earthquake, volcanic eruption, destructive storm, etc. For human beings, this can be things like the sudden, unexpected loss of a loved one, violations of trust that lead to an intense experience of betrayal and/or abandonment, the enforced loss of social position or power (such as the forced resignation of the U.S. President Richard Nixon via the Watergate episode), the experi-ence of rape or any type of sexual violation, and cataclysmic physical trauma such as AIDS, cancer, etc.

There are two causes for cataclysmic evolution. One is based on resistance or resisting evolutionary necessity. Resistance generates tension or stress, like a piano wire being wound tight to the point that it snaps. At that critical point, the person generating the resistance can no longer withstand the forces of evolutionary necessity. The real question becomes this: why resist evolutionary intentions or purposes at all? The answer is based in our need for *security.* Security for most people is based on the need for self-consistency. Self-consistency is based on known and familiar ways of being or reality—that which has come before, the past, which perpetually leads to and defines every current moment. And yet the moment is also being defined by evolu-tionary forces, progression, which reflects the future: that which has not come before. It is in this dynamic tension of the past and future as experienced in the moment that each of us has the power (Pluto) of choice or free will to embrace our evolutionary necessity, or to resist it because of a fear of the unknown. This fear impacts on our sense of security. How many of us like to feel insecure? Thus, many of us tend to resist making the choices that facilitate our evolutionary require-ments. At key junctures this resistance generates cataclysmic events in order for the evolutionary purposes to proceed.

The other cause of cataclysmic evolution is karmic. Karma is, again, the simple law of every action having a proportionate reaction. If, for example, I have betrayed someone's trust, then is it not possible that I may also experience the betrayal of my trust at some point? If I have abandoned children at some point, is it not possible that I must experience being abandoned? And so on.

By contrast, uniform evolution is slow, progressive change without cataclysmic events. It is simply the ebb and flow of life that equals progressive change and growth. For most people this type of evolution is the main and primary way that they evolve; it is the balance of the lifetime with a few cataclysmic events mixed in. On balance, this is how evolution occurs most of the time.

THE SOUTH AND NORTH NODES OF THE MOON

In the first volume of *Pluto*, it was stated that the South Node of the Moon, by house and sign, was used by the Soul as a vehicle, a mode of operation, that allowed the evolutionary intentions and desires of the Soul to be actualized in a conscious way. Just as the natal position of Pluto, by house and sign, symbolized what those desires and intentions were before this life, and, as a result, where the Soul naturally gravitates to in this life in order to define itself (we always pick up where we left off), so too with the South Node of the Moon.

Another way of putting this is that the Soul always creates the conscious personality or ego that it needs in each lifetime to facilitate and actualize its evolutionary intentions. The Moon correlates with what we call the ego. The ego is quite analogous to a lens in a movie projector. The function of the lens is to focus the images in the film upon the screen. Without the lens the images are simply diffuse light. Thus, the Soul creates an ego that is conscious of itself by generating a focused self-image. By having an egocentric self-image the Soul has a defined identity. One has a name, a personality, and so on. The ego is a vortex of concentrated energy that allows for an integration of the conscious personality that the Soul creates. And just as the Soul evolves, so too does one's ego and sense of identity.

Thus, whereas the natal position of Pluto by house and sign symbolized the nature of its evolutionary intentions and desires before this life, the bottom line so to speak, the South Node of the Moon, by house and sign, symbolizes the type of ego that it created in order to actualize those intentions and desires—to create an identity, personality or ego that was defined by those core desires and intentions. And because Pluto and the Moon correlate with our need for security, so most of us come into life unconsciously gravitating to these dynamics as our primary sense of self-definition, as displayed in our current birthchart. The evolutionary next step for the Soul is determined by the opposite house and sign of the natal Pluto, actualized *in tandem* with the North Node of the Moon—the evolving ego, sense of identity, etc.

The future can only be known from the point of view of the past as perceived in the moment. The present moment is defined by both the past and the yet-unknown future. This situation will create various degrees of evolutionary stress depending on specific circumstances. The dynamic stress between past and future is reflected in a conscious way at the egocentric or personality level by the South and North Nodes of the Moon. The *natal* Moon in a person's birth chart symbolizes the immediate, conscious personality or ego that experiences this dynamic tension of the past and future *in each moment.* It is the element of our consciousness that registers this evolution, and allows for it to be integrated by giving it form and personal identity.

In composite charts, the South Node of the Moon correlates with the personality or ego of the couple, a vehicle or mode of operation that the couple has used before this life to actualize the core evolutionary intentions and desires that defined their relationship before this life—the house and sign position of the composite Pluto. The South Node in combination with Pluto, by house and sign, will correlate to how their union had been defined and actualized before this life, and where it was left off. As a result, these symbols will correlate with where the relationship is picked up in this life.

The next evolutionary step for the couple is determined by the opposite house and sign of where the composite Pluto is located. And this is actualized, in a conscious way, by the North Node of the Moon in the composite chart by its own house and sign placement.

In synastry charts, where the South and North Nodes of the Moon occur in each other's charts correlates with specific past life dynamics. The South Node placement shows what we may have shared with another individual, and how past life dynamics subconsciously influence our overall response or reaction to another. The placement of the North Node correlates with how we can move forward or beyond those past life dynamics in this life.

By utilizing both the composite and synastry charts, a detailed analysis can be made of the prior-life dynamics of the couple, and what the current life intentions and purposes are. The composite chart, again, correlates with the dynamics that exist between two people as a unit—a third entity, so to speak. And yet each person in the unit, or couple, is their own person. This is why it is important to not only analyze the composite chart relative to Pluto, its polarity point, and the South and North Nodes, but also the synastry charts with respect to the mutual Pluto and nodal placements in each other's charts.

THE PLANETARY RULERS OF THE MOON'S NODES

The planetary rulers of the South and North Nodes of the Moon, by house and sign placement, are used as facilitators by the South Node to actualize itself, and by the North Node to actualize itself.

In essence, the natal position of Pluto has used the South Node of the Moon to actualize its prior life evolutionary intentions and desires, and the South Node has used its planetary ruler, via its house and sign placement, to actualize itself—the self-defining egocentric structure of the personality the Soul needed to actualize its intentions and desires. The polarity point of the natal Pluto, its opposite house and sign, is developed through the North Node of the Moon and the North Node of the Moon is developed or actualized through the house and sign placement of its planetary ruler.

PLUTO CONJUNCT THE MOON'S NODES

When Pluto is conjunct the South or North Node of the Moon, or square the Nodal Axis of the Moon, special evolutionary and karmic conditions apply. When Pluto is conjunct the South Node, one of three possible conditions exist. The first two conditions are extreme; the last condition is most common. These conditions are:

- The individual has totally avoided the evolutionary steps and lessons reflected in the house and sign position of the South Node, Pluto, and the location of the planetary ruler of the South Node by its own house and sign. As a result, the individual is forced to completely relive those conditions and lessons in this life. The North Node (the way out of those conditions) is denied access until the past life conditions, and the lessons involved, are complete. Generally, the relief of those conditions does not occur until the second Saturn return at roughly fifty-six years of age.

- The individual has so thoroughly developed and learned those evolutionary lessons, and the intentions and motives have been so pure, that the individual is in a karmic condition of fruition:

they have some special gift, knowledge, or ability that they will bring with them into this life that will generate some kind of recognition. This individual, too, can feel the frustration of being locked into this condition, of wistfully desiring to actualize the North Node as a way out of those conditions. The reason for the frustration is that such an individual has thoroughly developed the conditions of the house and sign placement of the South Node, Pluto, and the location of the planetary ruler of the South Node, for so many lifetimes, that they want to get on with something else, as shown by the North Node, and the location of its planetary ruler by house and sign. Again, generally speaking, the release point is around the second Saturn return.

- A condition in which there is an element of reliving certain past life conditions in this life, and of karmic/evolutionary fruition. This condition is the most common effect of Pluto's conjunction to the South Node of the Moon. Again, the release is around the second Saturn return unless other significant conditions are indicated.

In relationship analysis, when you find these astrological signatures in the composite chart, these conditions will apply to the couple or unit. The specific houses involved that symbolize the past life conditions are what the astrologer should focus on in order to help the couple understand what is happening, and what specific areas of their lives are involved. When you find, through synastry, that Pluto or another planet conjoins the South Node, then a situation exists in which there is a specific karmic or evolutionary situation or condition that is being brought forward into this life in order to resolved—a condition or situation between the two people which will be indicated by the specific nature of the house and sign that the South Node is in, the nature of the planets that are conjuncting the South Node of the other person, and the aspects that they are making to important points in the other person's chart.

When Pluto is conjunct the North Node, a special evolutionary condition exists. This symbol means that the individual has already been working on the area of evolution symbolized by the house and sign placement of the North Node, its planetary ruler by house and sign, and Pluto's conjunction to the North Node prior to the life being lived. As a result, this individual is meant to continue working in those areas in this life—there is no polarity point for Pluto in this case.

When you find this condition in the composite chart, it means that the couple who has it has been working together in those areas, and meant to continue in those areas again in this life. When you find Pluto or another planet conjunct someone else's North Node through synastry, then that person has either been helping the other achieve or develop the dynamics, issues or new orientation symbolized by the house and sign location of the North Node and its planetary ruler by house and sign, prior to this life, or can be a key person for the other in this life to help him or her develop those areas in this life. In order to understand which is which, remember that when one person has a planet conjunct their own South Node, and another person has a planet conjunct that other person's North Node, then the person who has the planet conjunct the other's North Node has served to help that person develop those lessons prior to this life.

PLUTO OR OTHER PLANETS SQUARING THE NODAL AXIS

When Pluto and/or another planet is square the Nodal Axis, then a karmic/evolutionary condition exists that I have called "skipped steps." This means that such an individual has been fluctuating back and forth between the areas indicated by the house and sign positions of the North and South Nodes, and the locations of their planetary rulers; and the house and sign of Pluto itself, and its polarity point. By fluctuating back and forth like a see-saw, the individual has not developed any of these areas or lessons completely. There has been, and will be, a resistance to the complete development of these dynamics, issues, and lessons. In order for the evolution to proceed, the individual must recover the skipped steps. Typically, these people feel that their past is their future, and that their future is their past; all at the same time. So the question becomes: What is the way out of this box? The answer, astrologically speaking, is to understand what dynamics, what issues, what area of life must be *consistently* developed and actualized in order for the skipped steps to not only be recovered, but integrated in a new way. This can be determined by understanding what Node Pluto or any other planet is applying to. The simplest way to know this is to determine which Node last formed a conjunction to Pluto, or the planet(s) squaring the Nodal Axis, keeping in mind that the mean motion of the Nodes of the Moon is retrograde. It is this Node, by house and sign location, and the location of its planetary ruler, that must be consistently developed. In this way, the polarity point of Pluto can be developed in a new way.

In composite charts, when you see this symbolism, it means that the couple involved has skipped some evolutionary steps in terms of the development of their relationship. The nature of what those skipped steps are will be symbolized by the houses, signs, and aspects of the Nodes and Pluto, or by a planet squaring the Nodes and the relevant houses and signs of each. By understanding which Node Pluto or other planet is applying to, and thereby the dynamics, issues, and lessons that must be consistently developed, then you can help them not only to recover those skipped steps, but also to move forward, evolutionarily speaking.

In synastry charts, when Pluto or another planet is squaring the Nodal Axis of another person, an evolutionary and karmic condition exists wherein those two people have had prior life connections in which something has occurred that has caused a separation to occur between them. Thus, the relationship has been interrupted—it has not come to completion. The actual nature of what has occurred to cause the separation can be determined by the houses and signs of the Nodal Axis, and the house and sign of Pluto or the planet that is forming the square to the Nodal Axis. The intention in this life is to repeat those conditions or situations in this life in order for the relationship to move forwards—to evolve and resolve.

POLARIZED PLANETARY RULERS OF THE MOON'S NODES

There can also be variations of these principles. These variations exist when the planetary ruler of the North Node is conjunct the South Node, when the planetary ruler of the South Node is conjunct the North Node, or when the planetary ruler of the South Node is conjunct the North Node *and* the planetary ruler of the North Node is conjunct the South Node.

When the planetary ruler of the North Node is conjunct the South Node, then one of the three karmic/evolutionary conditions listed under Pluto conjunct the South Node will apply. In this case, the polarity point for Pluto will be actualized only to the extent that the karmic and evolutionary conditions reflected in the house and sign placement of the South Node, and the location of its planetary ruler by house/sign and aspects to other planets, are fulfilled. This situation applies to composite charts as well.

When the planetary ruler of the South Node is conjunct the North Node, then the dynamics, issues, situations, and conditions reflected in the house and sign placement of the South Node are being reexperienced in this life. The difference in this condition is that those conditions that are reflective of the past are being *released* in the current life. Thus, instead of being blocked by the necessity of perpetually re-living past life conditions with no way out, the reliving of past life conditions will be released relative to the archetypes inherent in the house and sign position of the North Node. This is like being in a room that has a doorway to another room, the new room being the house and sign position of the North Node). Pluto's polarity point, by house and sign, is the *causal* factor in actualizing the "new door" symbolized the North Node. This condition applies to composite charts as well, with the new door being symbolized in the composite North Node which is actualized by Pluto's polarity point.

When the planetary ruler of the North Node is conjunct the South Node, and the planetary ruler of the South Node is conjunct the North Node, then a very unique karmic/evolutionary condition exists where-in the past and the future are experienced at the *same time*. The future will seem like the past, and the past will seem like the future. This is like being in a continuous loop in which the past and future are perpetually *recycled*. It is in the process of recycling the past and future as they interface in the immediacy of the moment that a metamorphosis will take place through time that allows new insights, understandings, and realizations to take place that progressively promotes an evolution. It is the polarity point of Pluto by house and sign that is the *causal* factor in this metamorphosis of the past and future as they recycle and interface in each moment. In essence, the polarity point of Pluto is that which moves the individual or couple—the composite chart—forward by promoting the new understandings, realizations, and insights that can only occur by recycling the past and the future symbolized by the house and sign placements of the South and North Nodes, the planetary nature of their rulers, and the aspects that these two planets are making to other planets.

PLUTO'S ASPECTS

The number of aspects that Pluto is making to other planets in the horoscope correlates with the degree of evolutionary metamorphosis that the Soul intends to accomplish in any given life. Any planet that Pluto is in some kind of aspect to has been, and is, in an evolutionary condition in which the preexisting structure, orientation, dynamics, and the resulting behavior associated with the nature of the planet must be metamorphosed in an intensified way in order for a new cycle in evolutionary development of the planet to occur. The amount of aspects that Pluto forms to other planets simply correlates with how much metamorphosis the Soul has desired for itself in any given life. An individual, or a couple, who has six or seven aspects from Pluto to other planetary dynamics will have a fundamentally different experience than an individual or a couple who has two or three aspects.

It is very important to remember the core archetype throughout this book and life: *Evolution.* When Pluto forms an aspect to a planet, the principle of active or accelerated evolution has been and is taking place. The type of evolution is reflected in the kind of aspects that Pluto is making. Stressful aspects generally will correlate with cataclysmic evolution because the nature of stressful aspects is *stress.* Stress here implies some existing resistance, like on a fault line, that is impeding a necessary change or metamorphosis of the dynamics linked with the nature of the planet involved. The cause of the resistance is fear—a fear to change because of the insecurity attendant to such change. When the Soul reaches a point in time, evolutionarily speaking, in which the change can no longer be resisted, then a cataclysmic event will occur in order to remove the cause of the resistance. Again, this type of evolutionary development produces great leaps in evolutionary growth even though the experiences created in order to do this are typically very difficult and painful. Rarely does the individual or couple understand the meaning of what is happening when the actual events are occurring. Understanding will occur some time after the cataclysmic event, though sometimes the understanding does not occur within the actual lifetime of the event. This is typically very difficult for the person or couple because a feeling of resolution does not occur. The necessary understanding will occur in another life, however, because the Soul will re-create the event (or the dynamics that have led to the necessity of the event) until understanding and resolution does occur. When Pluto forms stressful aspects to another planet, the probability of several cataclysmic events associated with that planet, and the house that it is in, does exist.

The nature of these cataclysmic events can also have karmic causes. For example, it is not uncommon for an individual who has Pluto in opposition to Mars to have had a least one premature death through violent causes. Or when a composite chart has Pluto in opposition to Mars, it is common for the couple to have experienced a premature ending to the relationship. In synastry charts, when one person has Pluto in opposition to another's Mars, it is not uncommon for the Pluto person *and* the Mars person to have caused very violent, and potentially life-ending, events to each other for a variety of reasons.

Since Pluto and Mars can be quite vindictive, this cycle of causing each other great difficulty will *karmically* continue until they can finally forgive one another or they become so exhausted from this dance over many lifetimes, that at least one of them stops the insanity.

The challenge to the astrologer is to be able, by playing astrological detective, to uncover and understand what the karmic dynamics are that lead to the necessity of cataclysmic events. Again, the key will be found in focusing on the actual houses and signs that are involved between Pluto and the stressful aspects(s) to the planet(s). This can be done individually, and in composite and synastry charts.

Non-stressful aspects between Pluto and other planets generally correlate with uniform evolution—slow yet progressive change of a steady accelerated nature.

It is also important to understand that Pluto aspects to other planets continue to evolve over many lifetimes. When you observe a Pluto aspect to another planet, in all likelihood that planet has come under the influence of Pluto before the life being lived. The simplest way to illustrate this point is this: Let us assume Pluto is at 5° of Leo, and Venus is at 5° of Scorpio. Not too many astrologers would disagree that an exact square exists between these two planets. Now let's put Venus at 25° of Libra. Relative to a 10° orb, a square between Pluto and Venus exists also. Now let's put Venus at 15° of Scorpio. A square can still exist between these two. A square is a square, right? Wrong. Between 25° of Libra and 15° of Scorpio, relative to Pluto being at 5° of Leo, an evolutionary arc exists that reflects the progression or development of the metamorphic intent of Pluto squaring Venus—one that correlates with the progression of a metamorphosis over many lifetimes. A couple who has Pluto square Venus in their composite chart when this aspect is "new," i.e. 10° before the absolute aspect (90° is the absolute or exact square) will have a fundamentally different experience than a couple who has Pluto square Venus in the last degree of this square, i.e. 10° past the absolute aspect.

This is because the first couple will be experiencing the metamorphic intent of the aspect for the first time, whereas the second couple has experienced this intent over many lifetimes, and are thus used to it. The responses will be fundamentally different. A simple analogy can apply to this, which we can all understand. If I go into a department store and buy a new pair of pants, when I first put them on they will feel new and uncomfortable. After I have worn these pants for many years, they will then feel very comfortable and familiar. In the same way, Pluto aspects evolve over many lifetimes. This, again, is very important to know. When you are analyzing Pluto aspects in this way, you now have a vital piece of knowledge that will help you and your clients understand exactly the evolutionary dynamics involved.

It is very important to understand that specific aspects only have their meaning relative to the phase that they take place within. We all know that there are 360 degrees. There is a progression, an evolution within the entire circle. Within this circle there are key or critical transition points that correlate with what I call evolutionary gates. These gates occur at 0°, 45°, 90°, 135°, 180°, 225°, 270°, and 315°. These gates will correlate with the eight basic lunations: New phase, Crescent phase, First Quarter phase, Gibbous phase, Full phase, Disseminating phase, Last Quarter phase, and Balsamic phase. Within these phases, specific aspects exist that represent gates within the phases. Each in its own way is an evolutionary transition. By understanding the great circle in this way in general, and with the Pluto aspects in mind specifically, you will have a deeper knowledge and insight into the actual nature and meaning of aspects from an evolutionary point of view. For more specific information about Pluto's aspects to other planets please refer to the first volume of *Pluto: The Evolutionary Journey of the Soul.* Later on in this book I will discuss and describe the eight primary phases, and the aspects within them.

PLUTO'S EFFECTS ON ITS EVOLUTIONARY REQUIREMENTS

There are four ways that Pluto affects its evolutionary requirements. Two of these ways are cataclysmic, and the other two are non-cataclysmic. The four ways are these:

- At certain key points in the evolutionary journey of the Soul, when increasing resistance to evolutionary necessity occurs, events associated with emotional loss, betrayal, violations of trust, or events that have the effect of totally changing the individual's life will occur, with or without the cooperation of the individual. These are typically cataclysmic in nature.

- The formation of key new relationships. Forming a relationship to something or someone symbolizes something that we think we need which in our own estimation we do not currently have. By forming a relationship to that "something," an osmosis occurs in which we extract into ourselves the quality or essence of that which we have formed a relationship to. In this way, a metamorphosis of our preexisting reality occurs. Simple examples of this are the re-lationships that we form to other people, or the fact that all of you became interested in astrology at some point in this life. By form-ing a relationship to the knowledge system of astrology, you "os-mosed" it into your consciousness in such a way as to metamor-phose your preexisting understanding of phenomenal reality. Generally, this way of evolving is non-cataclysmic.

• At crisis points in our evolutionary journey, we can become in-creasingly aware that we are stagnating—that the very meanings we have given to our life, the nature of our reality, are becom-ing progressively meaningless. The awareness of the stagnation does not imply an awareness of the *cause* of the problem. When this occurs, our consciousness will naturally withdraw from our circumstantial reality in order to look inward for the causes or reasons of this increasing lack of meaning or stagnation. Pro-gressively, this withdrawal or introversion leads to a core de-tachment from our outward or circumstantial life. This effect will increase until the awareness of the cause occurs. When the awareness does occur, it will necessitate a fundamental change in our life orientation and circumstantial reality. For most, this type of evolution is cataclysmic because it requires a radical shift from the past in order to embrace the future. In worst-case sce-narios, this unresolved condition will produce catatonia.

• At critical evolutionary times, we can experience a release of con-tents from our unconscious, or Soul, into our consciousness that reflects latent abilities or capacities that we were previously un-aware of. By embracing these latent capacities and acting upon them, an evolution of the preexisting conditions occurs. This is typically non-cataclysmic for most people.

The four natural ways in which Pluto affects its evolutionary require-ments can be interactive. For example, a person may become aware of latent abilities, and desire to embrace and act upon them, but in so doing may become aware of some preexisting condition that blocks or undermines the development of the latent capacity. Therefore, a non-cataclysmic evolutionary cause can induce a cataclysmic cause *if* the individual resists or is afraid of acting upon the latent ability.

THE FOUR NATURAL EVOLUTIONARY STATES

It is very important to understand that, in accordance with the principle and natural law of evolution, all Souls evolve in ways that are completely unique to them. This is why "cookbook astrology" is totally irrelevant and a disservice to astrology. It is essential to grasp and embrace this principle so that your understanding of the symbolic nature of astrological correlations can reflect the natural law. Thereby, your understanding of each client will be much more precise and will reflect their actual reality, not the reality that you may believe if you are dependent on some astrology book that tells you that Venus in Virgo means such and such, and you think every client who has Venus in Virgo must be like what you have read.

There are four natural evolutionary states, or gates, that all Souls evolve through over great lengths of evolutionary time. Each state has specific psychological archetypes that are intrinsic and unique. Each state *conditions* the consciousness of the individual. This natural conditioning factor of the four evolutionary states thus determines each individual's orientation to their life experience. In addition, each of the four natural evolutionary states has three levels or stages of development within them that reflect the Soul's evolution through them. The four natural evolutionary conditions for the Soul are as follows:

The Consensus State. This state embodies the majority of all Souls on Earth. Roughly 70% of all people, in all lands, are in this evolutionary condition. The consensus state is a state wherein the individual Soul is utterly defined by the norms, customs, taboos, religion, laws, rights and wrongs, and morality of the consensus society that he or she is born into. There is no ability to stand outside of such a society or reality, or to separate him or herself from it. For example, if the majority of people consider astrology to be bogus, a pseudo-science, then each individual within the consensus state will carry or reflect this opinion. This state reflects the desire to *conform* in order to feel secure—the safety in numbers syndrome.

In the first stage of this condition, individual Souls will reflect a very rudimentary consciousness that is analogous to the worker bees within a beehive. In the second stage of this condition, the Soul will reflect an emphasized desire for positions of status within their society. As a result, their consciousness progressively evolves because it must become "educated" in the ways that society dictates in order to succeed. In the last stages of this condition, individual Souls can evolve to the station of political leaders, or positions of leadership in a variety of occupations. This is because they have learned how the system works. As a result, this could very well be the origin of the saying "the blind leading the blind." On the other hand, as evolutionary necessity dictates, every once in a while a political leader will emerge that truly reflects a vision that has the effect of fundamentally altering or restructuring the existing system or society so that it to can evolve. Such leaders will be individuals who have begun the process leading to the next evolutionary condition or gate—the individuated state. Typically, as such leaders attempt to implement their ideas or vision, they are met with various degrees of resistance, confrontation (Pluto), and opposition by various factions within society who are invested in maintaining the existing status quo.

The Individuated State. Generally, 20% of Souls will be in this evolutionary condition or state. These are individuals who have evolved beyond the consensus state—to individuate. The first stage of this condition will reflect persons who have begun the process of independent questioning and thinking, who have rebelled against the consensus and the pressure to conform. Uranus, the archetype of rebellion intrinsic to consciousness, is a common denominator in these Souls. These individuals have begun the process of separating themselves from their specific societies—to stand outside of them, so to speak. This psychology of detachment allows for an objective awareness of reality in all its relative forms. In this perception of relativity, the individual realizes that there is much more to "reality" than any consensus-based view can offer. This condition thus allows for an expansion in consciousness in which the individual begins the process of understanding the nature of reality in increasingly larger frames of reference, which then begins the process leading to the next stage or evolutionary state. In the individuated state, if the individual was told that astrology was a bogus science, he or she would independently investigate to see whether this was true or not. Classic psychological symptoms of this state are cultural alienation, a feeling of not fitting in to the comfortable ways of living that most people do, psychological and emotional isolation, but also a feeling of undefined freedom to do or become whatever they so desire. Yet in this first stage of development, the individual typically compensates for the inner feeling of being different. This compensation manifests because the inner feeling of being different creates a real feeling of social insecurity— of not knowing where to fit in. Thus, since most of us do not want to feel insecure, the individual at this state compensates by adopting the external appearance of "normalcy." This causes the individual to create an external and circumstantial reality that appears "normal." Yet, because of the inner feeling of being different than the very circumstances that they have created, the individual has now effectively created a living lie—the difference between who they are inwardly, versus the circumstantial reality that they have created through the act of compensation.

In the second stage of this evolutionary state, in varying degrees of intensity, there can also be a core feeling of anger at "the system," of a core feeling of pessimism or futility that does not permit the individual to integrate in any way into the consensus based society, and of a desire to destroy either themselves, the system, or both. The second stage of this evolutionary state is perhaps the most difficult of all evolutionary conditions. This is because the dynamic of *detachment* has been progressively emphasized and developed within the Soul's consciousness. By embracing progressively larger frames of reference in order to understand "reality," the Soul can now perceive the repetitive cycles of human history. It is in this perception of repetitive cycles that the psychology of futility and pessimism are born. It is difficult, because the evolutionary challenge to the individual, in this second stage of development, is to learn how to integrate its individuality, in fact, within the consensus society in order to advance it. A latent fear in such people is that if they do attempt to integrate themselves within the consensus society that their individuality will be lost or absorbed by society in such a way as to lose that individuality. Once the individual realizes that this fear is only a fear—that their individuality cannot be lost, and that the "value is in the effort," then they will evolve to the third and final stage within the individuated state.

At the third stage of this condition, individuals will or can evolve to the point of being the geniuses of their times. They are the inventors and innovators who manifest a new vision, who break new ground, who can transform the very nature of consensus reality. These people are utterly secure within themselves, and they have realized what the great Einstein has pointed out: "When genius interacts with mediocre minds, expect violent opposition." It is in exactly this realization that they will successfully integrate themselves individually and within society. Their consciousness has begun to evolve in such a way as to begin to embrace the transcendent perceptions of Ultimate or Timeless reality. Thus, they are not *attached* to the outcome of their efforts. They make the effort for the effort's sake, realizing that at some point these efforts will succeed.

The Spiritual State. Roughly 5% or so of all Souls will be in this final state of evolution. Spiritual here does not mean religion! Religion is for those in the consensus state ("We are right, and they are wrong") which becomes the basis of religious wars, ethnic "cleansing," and genocidal holocausts. Spiritual in this context means an absolute openness to the relativity of all spiritual teachings—that many spokes lead to the same goal. The nature of these individuals' consciousness will be utterly defined by the teachings of their spiritual system of choice. As a result, they will embrace a universal and transcendent reality that is simultaneously beyond time and space, yet living within it. The consciousness of detachment that began in the individuated state is now fully developed in such a way that the very center of gravity within consciousness will progressively shift from the ego to the Soul. As a result, these individuals progressively experience themselves inwardly in a dual fashion. On the one hand, they experience their specific ego and individual identity; yet also how their ego and individuality are emanations from the Source of all Things—God.

In the first stages of this evolutionary state, the individual is defined through the psychological dynamic of humility. This occurs because the ego is now utterly aware of the universal—of a transcendent reality that seems so large that the ego is but a speck of sand on a very large beach. In this stage, individuals become the spiritual seekers of a devotional nature who seek out various spiritual teachers and teachings through which to define their inner and outer reality. Many will have an active desire to be of service to a larger whole, and will orientate to forms of work that directly benefit other people.

In the second stage of this evolutionary condition, an inherent danger exists for the ego—to think that one is more "enlightened" than one actually is. These are people that become spiritually full of themselves, so to speak, and run the risk of great spiritual delusions of egocentric grandeur. They present themselves as spiritual teachers and healers who somehow have a unique toehold on "the truth." This situation sets the stage for all the "false prophets" throughout history. In our times, unfortunately, there have been, and are, many such people as the the spiritual yet dangerous clown Rajneesh, Clair Prophet, Ramtha, the reverend Moon from Korea who pretends to be the incarnation of Jesus Christ, etc., etc., etc. Many who purport to be "channelers" reflect this same egocentric delusion. Thus, in this second stage, the ego must be finally destroyed in the sense of just identifying with itself. Consequently, the Soul will actually "program" itself to experience inner and outer circumstances that create absolute humility of the ego so the final stage of this evolutionary condition or gate can be realized. These circumstances will be associated with crises, the very essence of which will reflect the evolutionary necessity of moving beyond the delusion of egocentric spiritual grandeur.

In last stages of this evolutionary state, the Soul evolves progressively from a "true" spiritual teacher to a guru, and finally to the condition that is known as an *avatar*. Remember this simple fact: truly God-Realized Souls only point the way home, not to themselves!

The Dimly Evolved State. The Souls in this state are either evolving into human consciousness from other forms of consciousness, or are forced into this type of consciousness through karmic causes. In the first case, these Souls will be characterized by a dim sense of self-awareness, a basic sense of occupying time and space. Their gaze will be dull, and they will typically be quite innocent and happy because they know no other reality. Modern terminology that describes this condition are words like *mental retardation, cretinism, Down's Syndrome*, etc. Evolutionarily, such Souls will evolve through this evolutionary condition by progressively becoming ever more self-aware which will lead them into the consensus state.

The second group will be very conscious from within the limitations of their condition. Their gaze will have a brilliant point of white light emanating from the pupil of the eye. Instead of being innocently happy, these types will typically be angry in various degrees, even violent to themselves and others. This is because they know different—they have had a different consciousness in other lifetimes, and have been forced through karmic causes to be in this highly restricted condition. Roughly 5% of all Souls will be in the dimly evolved state, with around 3% being of the first type, and 2% of the second type.

These natural conditions exist in all lands, with all peoples. In understanding the composite and synastry charts, as in the individual chart, it is essential to know and understand what evolutionary state or condition that people are within. And you cannot know what condition or state people are in by looking at the birthchart, composite chart, or the synastry charts. The very essence of astrology is a science based in observation and correlation. It is a natural science reflecting the natural laws of correspondence. Accordingly, you must observe the people you are doing astrological work for to determine, through observation, just what evolutionary condition they are in. Once you make such a determination, you can then understand how each evolutionary condition naturally conditions the individuals in question. As a result, you will be able to interpret the astrological symbols in any kind of chart correctly. Venus in Virgo manifests differently within the consensus state than it does in the individuated or spiritual state. Each state is unique to itself, yet evolution proceeds through each state. The necessary observations can be illustrated in this way: If a client comes to me and asks when to expect the BMW, and another client comes to me and asks when to expect enlightenment, there is an observed difference! Thus, my own orientation to the client, the language and approach that I use, is adjusted to reflect the client's reality, not mine.

Chapter Three

So We Meet Again, Eh?

In this chapter, we will focus on the theme of prior-life connections and dynamics that we may have had with other people, in order to understand not only how these dynamics and connections may be influencing how we are relating to those people in this life, but also, and most importantly, what the current life purposes and evolutionary intentions are for this life.

In order to do this, we will be employing the astrological principles and methods that were explained in the previous chapter and defined in the first volume of *Pluto: The Evolutionary Journey of the Soul*, which I would recommend reading or rereading for a deeper and more comprehensive understanding. Our purpose is to understand the evolutionary and karmic progression of two people who have been in relationship to each other before this life, and understand the next evolutionary and karmic step for these two people in this life. In order to do this, we will employ the use of composite and synastry charts between two people.

Composite and synastry charts are both necessary to our purposes because they reflect different dynamics. The composite chart symbolizes the dynamics that existed, and still exist, between two people *as a coupled unit.* Synastry charts symbolize the dynamics that existed, and still exist, between two people as *distinct individuals.* To illustrate this key difference in traditional synastry, consider this simple example: Person A has Pluto square person B's Venus. A quick analysis would suggest that Person A, from a prior-life point of view, had attempted to manipulate and control Person B's sense of values, needs, and inner sense of the meaning of his or her life in very compulsive ways. Person B perceived and sensed that person A was very compelling, convincing, and omnipotent in such a way as to find it hard to resist the overall impact of what was being suggested or told to them concerning what they should do, what they needed, etc. Any effort to resist these manipulations would be met with an increasing intensity by Person A as he or she attempted to reinforce a position of control and total power within the relationship. This one simple dynamic would constitute subconscious memories in each of these two people as they met again in this life.

These subconscious memories would, in their own way, determine how they related to each other in this life, person to person. Because of the nature of the squaring aspect between Pluto and Venus, from an evolutionary point of view, Person B is beginning the process of separating away from Person A's influence in order to establish their own sense of meaning, values, and needs on his or her own terms. Thus, Person B would have an attraction/repulsion reaction to Person A *in this life* because of the prior life dynamics. Attraction in the sense that Person A once represented so much to Person B from the prior lifetimes point of view. Yet, through evolutionary necessity, Person B is desiring to grow independently of Person A's influence—thus, repulsion. This repulsion would be created because of the current life evolutionary intentions, and would manifest subconsciously within Person B as he or she would experience a fear of being absorbed by Person A's power and dominance. Person A, on the other hand has subconscious memories of being able to manipulate and control Person B, and has used Person B to fulfill all kinds of hidden or ulterior emotional agendas relative to his or her own needs over many lifetimes. Thus, Person A will have a hypnotic attraction to Person B because of these memories.

In this life, these preexisting dynamics can become very difficult because of Person B's need to actualize independently of Person A. The resistance of Person B to Person A's compulsive need to control, dominate, or manipulate will become increasingly intense as the relationship evolves in this life. The resistance by Person B will be met by Person A's increasing sense of anger or emotional rage as he or she begins to realize that they can no longer control Person B. This will continue until one of two dynamics evolves: Either Person A realizes the need or requirement to encourage the independent actualization of Person B, or Person A continues to manifest through repetitive compulsion towards Person B in the ways that he or she always has until Person B finally breaks off the relationship completely. The emotional shock of this turn of events would hopefully produce the necessary realizations in Person A *after the fact.* In either scenario, the evolutionary intent has been accomplished.

Let us contrast this with a composite chart. The couple has Pluto square Venus in their composite chart, representing dynamics that exist within the unit as a couple. A simple interpretation could be this: These two people acting together, through expression of independent desires and needs, chose to be in relationship with each other in order to explore and understand the deeper meaning of life beyond those prescribed by consensus opinion or expectation. Through mutual consent, choice, and desire they could have been drawn together in order to facilitate an understanding and healing of each other's' emotional wounds through intense discussions of a psychological and emotional nature. *Both people would be manifesting the Venus and Pluto roles.* This would occur simultaneously at times, and at other times one person would be in the Pluto role, while the other was in the Venus role, and vice versa. In synastry, again, Person A was always in the Pluto role, and Person B was always in the Venus role.

From a prior-life point of view, this unit or couple developed a deep, penetrating, mutual reliance on one another that was based on psychological/emotional understandings and realizations. The square aspect not only demonstrates the intensity of this dynamic and mutual reliance, but also that there has been an excessive focus and reliance on that dynamic as a way of maintaining the security (Pluto/Venus) of that relationship. In effect, each has made the other indispensable through excessive proximity to one another, and an exclusion of other people from the secretive bubble of the relationship.

These dynamics would be operative in this life because that is how they have been before. A current life intention for this couple, as viewed through the composite chart, would be to evolve into psychological and emotional independence (Pluto square Venus) from one another without changing the core commitment to the relationship as it evolves beyond being the entire and total meaning of each others lives. This current life evolutionary intention would not necessarily be easy to achieve, because of what the prior life dynamics were. Either partner could fear abandonment or betrayal, or could experience a permeating insecurity as one or the other, or both, attempted to actualize this intention. In the worse-case scenario, a break-up of this couple could occur in order to achieve this purpose.

WHAT IS A COMPOSITE CHART?

A composite chart looks like an ordinary birth chart, but actually combines two charts into one. It is based on the near planetary midpoints of two natal charts (the halfway points between the same planets in the two charts), for example, the two Venuses. Its houses are based on the near midpoints of the Ascendant, Midheaven, and other house cusps. A composite chart, in essence, is produced through two people acting as a unit.

A second method for combining two charts, called the Davison or midpoint-in-time chart, is based on the exact halfway point in time between two individuals' birth data—time, day, month, and year of birth, as well as the midpoint of their respective longitudes and latitudes of birth. I have found that the Davison method, for evolutionary purposes, has no applicability whatsoever. Astrology is essentially a natural science that is based on correlation of the planetary patterns taking place at the point of observation. Based on my own experience of counseling over 15,000 people I would recommend that you use the near-midpoint method.

Let us now use a simple example to apply these principles to a composite chart (see Chart #1).

This signature demonstrates a couple who has come together before this life in order to confront the nature of learned patterns of emotional behavior, psychological imprinting via the parental and societal environment, fears of abandonment, betrayal, violations of trust, being manipulated controlled, or dominated by others, sexual wounds and misuse of sexual energy, and negative self-beliefs or images that have the effect of generating many forms of personal crisis.

These are two people who have committed to each other long before this life (South Node in the Eighth House in Libra), and who have equally and mutually (South Node in Libra) played the role of helper, healer, psychologist (Pluto in the Sixth House square Venus in Scorpio in the Tenth House) through intense discussions and emotional/sexual exploration. Their mutual roles have had the intention of realizing and understanding the dynamics that have lead to self-defeating psychological and emotional patterns generating a state of perpetual crisis (Pluto in the Sixth House, South Node in Libra in the Eighth House,

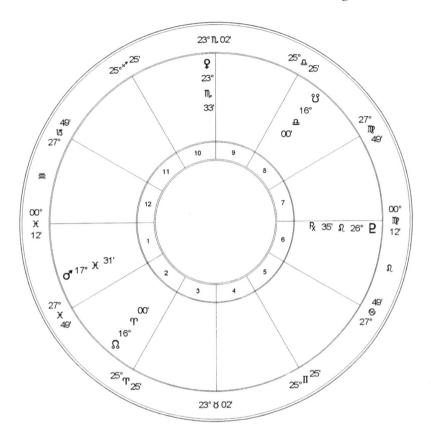

Chart #1
(*Not All Planets Shown*)

Venus in Scorpio in the Tenth House). Their intentions have involved coming up with strategies dealing with self-improvement and healing of those dynamics (Pluto in the Sixth House). These two people have bonded together many times because they have already learned to trust one another, to rely on one another to the exclusion of most other people (Pluto square Venus). Yet the compulsion and habit of their Souls being together is one of having their relationship defined within the dynamic of crisis. There is always something wrong (Pluto in the Sixth House) in such a way that these two people compulsively and perpetually keep recreating their roles of mutual saviors (Pluto in the Sixth House via the South Node in Libra; via Venus in Scorpio in the Tenth House). They are addicted to their roles, which generate security for each of them. These roles are the counterpoint to their mutual fears of abandonment, betrayal, "no one else will understand us," trust, and so on. As a result, there is an excessive co-dependency. The fear of losing each other or separating from each other will constitute much of their mutual subconscious memories and associations coming into this life.

With the polarity point of Pluto in the Twelfth House and Aquarius, relative to the North Node in Aries in the Second House with its planetary ruler Mars in Pisces within the First House, the next evolutionary step is for this couple to liberate themselves and become free from the subconscious memories that generate the compulsion and addiction to co-dependency. Also, the intention is to become aware of the reasons for these dynamics and how these dynamics have defined their relationship before this life, and to stop being mutual saviors for one another (Pluto's polarity point in the Twelfth House in Aquarius, which is actualized through the Aries North Node in the Second House, which itself is actualized through its planetary ruler Mars in Pisces within the First House).

In addition, these symbols of the next evolutionary step demand that this couple learn how to be together without the compulsion to create and re-create crisis, to learn how to identify and supply their own needs (North Node in Aries in the Second House demands learning a fundamental self-reliance), to learn how to actualize their own identities, values, and beliefs from within themselves, to learn how to be together without expecting that the partner will always meet their needs, and to embrace a transcendental philosophy that will allow them to objectify themselves, and thus their relationship. This would allow them to form a relationship with a higher principle or dynamic that would allow them to solve their problems in a new way, a way that is very different than just looking to each other to solve the problems. In essence, the evolutionary next step is symbolized by totally breaking free from the prior life dynamics, and to establish a brand new way of being together that will serve them well not only in this life, but the next few lifetimes to come.

In synastry charts, the location by house and sign of the planetary rulers of the South and North Nodes in one another's charts correlates with additional and specific past life dynamics (the South Node by house and sign, plus its planetary ruler by house and sign) that we may have shared with another that constitutes subconscious memory associations conditioning our response or reaction to that person, and the North Node by its house and sign location, plus its planetary ruler by house and sign location, that reflect how the next evolutionary step in this life is to be accomplished.

Additionally in synastry analysis, there are other dynamics to look for so that a complete and total analysis can be affected that will uncover past life connections. Understanding the total picture will allow you to more fully grasp and understand what the next evolutionary step is, and to help understand what strategies to create in order for this step to be taken. The additional dynamics to look for include:

- Planets in one's chart conjunct to or forming some other aspect to the other's South Node, its planetary ruler, or both. Planets in aspect to the South Node will also be in aspect to the North Node, meaning that the person who has the planet in aspect to the other's Nodal Axis has served, in some way, to jump-start the evolutionary dynamics symbolized by that person's North Node at a time prior to the current life.

- Aspects between each other's nodal axis.

- Aspects between each other's planetary rulers of the South Nodes.

- Planets in one's chart are conjunct the other's North Node, its planetary ruler, or both. This condition only applies when other conditions, as above, are met, or when the person whose planets conjunct the other's North Node, or its planetary ruler, are in aspect to the planetary ruler of the other's South Node, or in opposition to a planet that is conjunct the other's South Node. When these conditions exist, these two people will re-create past-life conditions in this life in order to resolve, or bring to completion, issues or dynamics that were not completed or resolved prior to this life. The nature of the aspects, the specific houses and signs that the Nodes are in, and the nature of the planets will describe what these dynamics and issues are.

- The planetary ruler of one person's North Node in aspect to the planetary ruler of the other person's South Node. This situation correlates to two people who have had a relatively brief and initial meeting before this life. The circumstances or conditions of what brought these two people together before will be described by the location of these two planets in each other's horoscopes, the nature of the planets involved, and the type of aspect that they are making to each other. The circumstances or conditions that existed before this life that brought the two people together will be *re-created* in this life because the intention is to reestablish their connection and move forward with it.

• Pluto in some kind of aspect to the other's personal planets.

These are the key dynamics to look for. Once you have deduced that there has been prior life contact via these dynamics, then, of course, there are other synastry connections of the planets (i.e., Saturn square Venus) that will fill in the entire picture. The nature of the synastry aspects is also very important to consider. Stressful aspects indicate stressful conditions that have preceded the current life—conditions that are not resolved or finished. They can also indicate difficult or problematic karmic conditions in which the element of retribution may be a theme in some way. The non-stressful aspects tend to indicate non-stressful conditions—conditions that promoted some positive circumstance beneficial to both people.

Let us now refer to Charts #2 and #3, where we create a simple example to illustrate some of these points. You will notice in these two charts that the planetary ruler of Chart #2's South Node, Jupiter, is square the South and North Nodes of Chart #3's Nodal Axis, and conjunct its Neptune, which is itself square the Nodal Axis. Chart #3's Jupiter is conjunct the South Node and square to Chart #2's Jupiter. Chart #3's Jupiter, in addition, is sextile Chart #2's South Node, and trine its North Node. Chart #2's Pluto is conjunct Chart #3's North Node, square its Neptune, and in opposition to its Jupiter which is, again, conjunct the South Node. Chart #3's Pluto forms a square to Chart #2's Nodal Axis, and is sextile to its Jupiter. Chart #3's South Node in Aquarius is in Chart #2's Third House, and its planetary ruler, Uranus in Virgo, is in its Tenth House. Charts #3's North Node is in Chart #2's Ninth House, and its planetary ruler, the Sun in Capricorn, is in its Second House. Chart #2's South Node in Sagittarius is in Chart #3's First House, and its planetary ruler, Jupiter in Scorpio, is in its First House. Chart #2's North Node is in Chart #3's Seventh House in Gemini, and its planetary ruler, Mercury in Scorpio, is also in Chart #3's First House. Referring to the rules above, you will notice many conditions apply that demonstrate past life dynamics and issues that will be brought into this life for an intended resolution through evolution.

Before an accurate understanding of synastry or composite charts can occur, the astrologer *must* have a firm and total understanding of each person's natal chart. If we confine ourselves to just the symbols

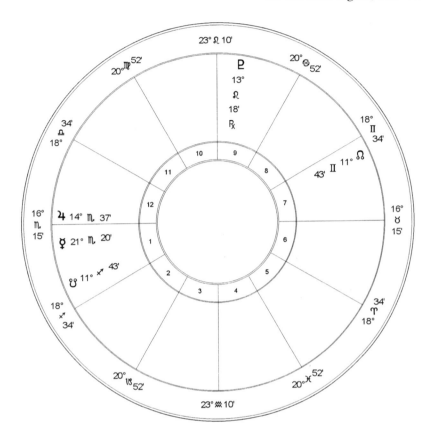

Chart #2

presented, for the sake of simplicity at this point, we notice that Chart #3 has Pluto in the Tenth House in Virgo, conjunct Uranus in Virgo, which is the ruler of the South Node in Aquarius. Pluto is inconjunct the South Node and Jupiter in Aquarius in the Third House. Jupiter is square Neptune in Scorpio on the Ascendant, and Neptune is square the North and South Nodes. The North Node is in Leo in the Ninth House, and its planetary ruler, the Sun in Capricorn, is in the Second House. Starting with the first step in any chart analysis, an understanding of Pluto, the Tenth House Pluto in Virgo will correlate with an individual who has been atoning for causes of guilt over many lifetimes. The causes of guilt can be of two types depending on the individual. One cause is based on specific past-life actions, intentions, motivations, etc., and the other cause is based on being made to feel

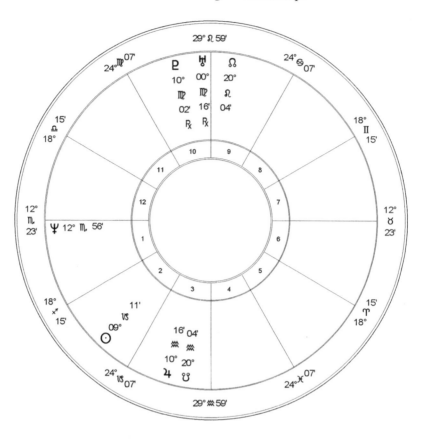

Chart #3

guilty through a variety of conditioning factors— learned guilt. An example of this second cause could be being born into a family/societal dynamic that expected the individual to conform to being certain way. If the individual deviated in any way from these expectations,then a resulting guilt would occur via the judgments that would be issued from the family or society.

Because Jupiter and the South Node are in Third House Aquarius, inconjunct the Tenth House Pluto in Virgo, we can clearly see that this individual has needed to rebel against the ideas, beliefs, values, and norms of not only the immediate family, but against the whole of various societies or cultures that he or she has been born into. Because the ruler of the South Node (Uranus) is also in the Tenth House, this rebellion, and the problems it generates, has occurred before this life.

In the deepest sense, it is a rebellion against laws created by human beings, manmade laws, versus natural law, or the laws of Nature. Natural Law is an archetype that correlates to the Ninth House, Sagittarius, and Jupiter. The act of rebellion against the immediate family and society has caused the individual great crisis, the nature of the inconjunction and Pluto being in Virgo. Again, this dynamic is compounded because of the planetary ruler of the South Node being present in the Tenth House. It is compounded because, karmically speaking, the individual will have parents in this life that have been the parents to the individual before this life. Each of them will have subconscious memories to this effect which will condition their reactions and responses to each other from the very moment of the individual's birth in this life.

The crisis is one of feeling a core isolation from the immediate parental environment, an environment that could also be psychologically and physically abusive to the extent that he or she did not conform to the expectations of the parents. The physical abuse can be symbolized by the connection of Pluto to the First House Neptune which, again, is connected to the Nodal Axis and Jupiter. It is a crisis leading to a negative self-image, of feeling that there must be something wrong deep within the individual, and a crisis of induced guilt.

This type of psychological imprinting would create an individual who, on the one hand, would try to conform to the parental and societal expectations in order to feel some acceptance and love, and, on the other hand, who lived a deeply secretive life of inner isolation in which he or she could "think for themselves". This duality of realities would create cyclic confusion (Neptune square the Nodal Axis) of a personal identity nature (Neptune in the First House) that would be based on the individual's experience that most people do indeed conform to, and are defined by parental and societal expectations of what to think and believe, how to live, what is right and wrong, etc. (Pluto in the Tenth House). Yet, because the individual desired to independently question and think about the nature of reality, to try to understand the nature of life and their own sense of identity in ways that were and are not culturally or parentally prescribed, the resulting confusion would occur.

It is important to remember that all children naturally expect to be nurtured and accepted for who they are, and for what they inherently need. When this does not occur, the child creates displaced emotion. These emotional dynamics that are not resolved in childhood are brought forward into adult life at a subconscious level.

Thus, this individual would bring his or her own displaced emotions into adult life in such a way as to attract adult partners that would mirror the inner duality of his or her childhood. On the one hand, the individual could re-attract parental figures who would expect him or her to conform to their realities—to more or less be vicarious extensions of their reality. To the extent the individual did conform in order to feel love and acceptance, this love would be extended. If the individual began to rebel against this at some point within the relationship, then the abuse experienced in childhood would likely be repeated in the adult relationship. On the other hand, the individual could also attract someone who mirrored his or her own inner rebellion—an adult partner who empowered and encouraged real self-expression in order to actualize an identity and overall reality that was in harmony with the person's true nature.

Evolutionarily speaking, this individual has been going back and forth between this duality for many lifetimes (Neptune square the Nodal Axis and Jupiter). The Soul's intention is to entirely break free from parental and societal expectations to conform, to establish an identity and reality that is true to the actual essence of their Soul, to learn to stand as a group of one if necessary, and to establish a core security from within themselves (the polarity point of the Tenth House Pluto is the Fourth House). This will be accomplished through embracing a spiritual teaching that is defined by Natural Law, not man-made law (North Node in Leo in the Ninth House relative to Neptune squaring the Nodes and Jupiter). With the planetary ruler of the North Node being in Capricorn in the Second House, the individual must learn a fundamental self-reliance which is defined (Capricorn) through his or her own values which reflect the principles of natural law. In this way the individual's own voice and authority are creatively actualized (North Node in Leo) in such a way as to finally break free the displaced emotions of childhood which cause the two extremes in the individuals psychological behavior.

Examining the nature of Chart #2, we notice that it has a Ninth House Pluto in Leo which is trine the South Node in Sagittarius, and sextile the North Node in Gemini. The South Node is the First House, the North Node is in the Seventh House, and Pluto is squaring the Twelfth House Jupiter in Scorpio, ruler of the South Node, which is inconjunct the North Node in Gemini. The planetary ruler of the North Node is Mercury, which occupies Scorpio in the First House, and which is also conjunct the Twelfth House Jupiter.

With Pluto in Leo in the Ninth House trine the South Node in Sagittarius in the First House, we have an individual who has desired to understand their sense of identity, and the nature of reality in general, in cosmological, philosophical, or metaphysical terms in a prior life or lives. Because the South Node is in the First House, and in Sagittarius, this individual has had the courage (First House) to be an independent thinker, an individual who has already learned to ask and answer questions for oneself, and from within oneself. These symbols correlate with an individual who is a true individual in the sense of being a person who has been totally self-dependent. This is an inherent loner who is very comfortable being alone. With the planetary ruler of South Node, Jupiter, being in Twelfth House Scorpio, this is also an individual who has investigated *and* experienced the inherent natural laws that are the basis of consciousness and reality. This has been done through a variety of natural disciplines such as Tantra, Shamanism, the Occult, etc. Jupiter in Scorpio requires proof through experience before it can have belief in anything. In combination, these symbols produce a natural teacher and healer, who has a natural knowledge and wisdom built up over many lifetimes. This knowledge is a result of direct and personal experience.

Because the North Node in the Seventh House Gemini is inconjunct the Twelfth House Jupiter, and its planetary ruler Mercury in the First House Scorpio is conjunct Jupiter, this is not the first life that the evolutionary lessons or progression reflected through the Seventh House has been attempted. This linkage correlates with this progression or evolution being in progress—it is being carried forward in this life from the last few lifetimes. Again, the nature of the inconjunction, archetypally, is to create crisis. Crisis thus becomes the specific experience through which the individual comes to understand what the evolutionary lessons are. In this case, the nature of the crisis has been, and will be, based on the evolutionary requirement to open up to intimate relationships (Seventh House) and to share with others the knowledge that he or she has gained over many lifetimes of being alone. The crisis is one in which the individual must learn to speak in ways that are understandable to most people, from the intuitive principles of Sagittarius and the Ninth House, to the logical/deductive method of Gemini. It is a crisis based on knowledge which is outside of the existing knowledge norms or consensus of the current society or country, and the necessity to challenge these norms or conventionally held beliefs. The necessity to challenge is reflected in Pluto forming a square to the Twelfth House Jupiter.

In addition, it is a crisis of disillusionment, because the Twelfth House Jupiter is defined through idealism—the way things should ultimately be. With the individual's South Node ruler being in the Twelfth House, it correlates with a person who is naturally innocent. There is a natural kind of purity, and an expectation that everyone else is pure, too. Sagittarius, Jupiter, or the Ninth House can overly generalize by thinking that its truth or reality is everyone's truth and reality. Combined with Sagittarius, and the Ninth House Pluto, this is an individual who is naturally honest, and will expect all others to be just as honest. Because this is part of the individual's nature, he or she can perceive the essence, spirit, or Soul of another, and then expect the other to reflect or be the essence. The crisis is one disillusionment when the individual experiences the reality that not all other people are like this. With the North Node in Gemini in the Seventh House inconjunct Jupiter in Scorpio, which, again, is also conjunct Mercury in Scorpio, the individual is fated to experience people whose natures are emotionally manipulative, dishonest, defined by ulterior motives or agendas, who can create emotional betrayal and abandonment. The individual can be used as a scapegoat by others relative to their own inability to be responsible to their own dynamics. In a larger sense, this same pattern can create large-scale persecution and misunderstanding by social and societal systems who perceive the individual to be a threat (Pluto square Jupiter) to its most cherished beliefs. The intention of the Soul in creating these kinds of experiences is to expand its consciousness to embrace the totality of reality—not just the portion of truth or reality that the individual has already learned. This is reflected in the Ninth House polarity of Pluto being the Third House, and the South Node in Sagittarius evolving through the North Node in Gemini.

Because these experiences would have preceded the current life, this individual will be born with these memories at a subconscious level, and a natural resistance to the ongoing evolutionary requirements. The tendency will be to be a loner who lives in a kind of spiritually narcissistic reality. Yet because of the intentions of the Soul, these requirements, lessons, and experiences are fated to occur until the individual learns what it must. Karmically, the individual will reexperience   relationships, intimate and otherwise, with others who have been in relationship to the individual. Now we can begin to apply the principles of synastry to these two charts. In both cases Pluto is linked to the Nodal Axis of each other's charts. Chart #2 has Pluto conjunct the North Node in Leo in the Ninth House of Chart #3, in opposition to its Jupiter and

South Node in Aquarius in the Third House, and serves to ignite the natal T-Square between Neptune and the Nodal Axis. Chart #3 has Pluto and Uranus squaring the Nodal Axis of Chart #2, with Pluto and Uranus in Chart #2's Tenth House. What could this mean?

By grasping some of the core dynamics in Charts #2 and #3, we can now understand, through synastry, that the Chart #2 individual has already acted in Chart #3's prior lives to encourage and teach him or her to embrace their own natural truths—to learn how to trust and understand that these truths originate from the intuition. This has been done, at times, in very forceful ways, and at other times in very gentle ways. In both ways, the intention (Pluto) has been to teach Chart #3 to take charge (Leo) of their own life, and to rebel against (South Node in Aquarius conjunct Jupiter in the Third House, inconjunct the Tenth House Pluto) the ideas, opinions, beliefs, rights and wrongs, morality, norms, customs, and taboos of the consensus of society and parents. Remembering that Chart #3 has had an inner duality because of the compensatory behavior learned in childhood in order to feel love and acceptance, which has conflicted with their desire to question freely the nature of things, Chart #2 has tried to teach these things in order to resolve the identity conflict reflected in Chart #3's Neptune squaring the Nodal Axis and Jupiter.

As a result of this, Chart #3 will and has perceived Chart #2 as a natural teacher. This dynamic is repeated in the fact that Chart #2's South Node is in Sagittarius within Chart #3's First House, and Jupiter is conjunct Neptune. These symbols correlate with teaching Chart #3 natural spiritual laws of an experiential nature, and to help in healing the wounds of abuse that have occurred when Chart #3 has rebelled against the parental environment, and later against adult partners who expected the individual to conform to their reality. The influence of Chart #2 has been to help liberate and break free from all external conditioning—a message of self-empowerment and self-actualization.

If you allow yourself to intuitively feel the nature of these synastry symbols, you can understand that these two people have had lifetimes of intense discussions of a psychological and metaphysical nature. With Chart #3's Pluto and Uranus squaring Chart #2's Nodal Axis and falling in its Tenth House, you can also understand that, at times, Chart #3 has resisted, negatively judged, and rebelled against Chart #2's teachings and intentions whenever Chart #3 felt too challenged, stretched, or inadequate (Virgo) by the evolutionary demands of Chart #2. This has had the effect of stopping or ending the relationship at various times (Pluto square the Nodal Axis). This is restated by Chart #3's South Node and Jupiter in Aquarius landing in Chart #2's Third House (rebellion against this type of communication), and Uranus landing in Chart #2's Tenth House acting out the displaced emotions of childhood on Chart #2 via critical statements and judgments.

Conversely, these very same symbols have helped Chart #2 learn the lesson reflected in the Seventh House North Node in Gemini—to learn how to speak and communicate in ways that are acceptable and understandable to most people, as well as to learn how to integrate into society (Uranus and Pluto landing in Chart #2's Tenth House) in such a way that the knowledge that Chart #2 has can be disseminated on a large scale versus living a reality of spiritual narcissism. Thus, Chart #3 has served as a motivational force (Pluto) to do this.

In addition, Chart #3 has had, and will have, the effect of helping chart #2 understand the nature of reality as most people live it. This has fostered and will foster Chart #2's ongoing evolutionary intentions of bursting the idealistic world reflected in this South Node ruler, Jupiter in the Twelfth House Scorpio, inconjunct the North Node Gemini in the Seventh House. These two people will pick up where they left off in other lifetimes. Chart #3 will reembrace Chart #2 in this life via Pluto conjunct its North Node, and Chart #2 will reembrace Chart #3 via its Pluto and Uranus squaring the Nodal Axis. It is fated when Pluto is involved in this way.

Chapter Four

Social, Cultural, Parental, and Religious Imprinting

Just as it is important to understand the past-life dynamics that contribute to the subconscious conditioning via memory association with people that we form some kind of relationship to, it is just as important to understand the impact of social, cultural, parental, and religious conditioning on our orientation to relationships.

Every group of people living together as a socially organized unit, through all time in all places, develops psychological attitudes based on beliefs of how people should be in relationship to themselves in all kinds of socially interactive situations. These consensus-based attitudes and beliefs condition every individual within the socially organized unit regarding what is expected of them in every possible socially interactive situation. This then allows the social group to live together in a state of organization versus anarchy. On the one hand, this is obviously necessary. On the other hand, this consensus expectation inhibits the actualization or development of individuality, if that individuality conflicts with the consensus expectations.

Because most people want to feel secure and included in socially interactive groups, instead of excluded and thus insecure, the socially implied pressure to conform conditions our orientation to reality in general, and to our relationship formations specifically.

Relative to the purposes of this book, we will confine ourselves to how this conditioning factor impacts on our primary relationships—those between spouses or intimate partners, a child's relationship to its parents, and the parents' relationship to their child.

Let's illustrate an example of religious beliefs that has conditioned men and women for at least the last 2,000 years in their mutual attitudes toward one another, and how these conditioned attitudes have more or less dictated the roles men and women have played out in their relationships.

We are talking about the Garden of Eden myth. In this religious myth, women are presented as the temptation leading to man's spiritual downfall. The temptation is rooted in sensuality—the life of the senses. The first implication in this myth is that the flesh is in some intrinsic conflict to the life of the spirit. The second implication is that man is superior to woman. As a result of the implications within the myth, we have some resulting psychological consequences that have defined the nature of men and women's relationship to each other and to themselves since the origin of the myth itself. These consequences have, in a large sense, defined the most basic structure of civilization itself. These consequences are:

- Women have been made to feel guilty because they have served as man's spiritual downfall. Thus, they are inferior to men. Men embody spirit, and women embody sensuality—the world of the senses—and guilt is associated with the senses and the flesh.

- Because spirit and flesh have been presented in the myth as mutually antagonistic, and because woman embodies the world of flesh, women must *atone* for the guilt associated with man's spiritual downfall. Inferiority, linked with guilt and the need to atone, produces the psychological consequence of *masochism.*

- The psychological consequences to men are just as distorted, because the myth also makes them feel guilty for succumbing to the temptation of flesh as embodied in women—for choosing flesh over spirit. Since the myth teaches that men are superior to women, the reaction to the guilt is the opposite of atonement. It is a reaction of *anger,* an anger at women which is really a reaction from within themselves, at themselves. This produces the psychology of *sadism.*

- The root consequence for both men and women is guilt. Yet, because women atone for the guilt, and men are angry because of the guilt, the combined consequence produces the archetype of sadomasochism. The underpinning of this entire myth, reflected in the psychological consequences, is that spiritual growth, or any real growth or gain, can only occur through suffering—the senses must be *denied* in order for spirit to grow.

The archetype of sadomasochism, which is a consequence of the religious myth, is thus the fundamental or core conditioning factor that, like branches emanating from the trunk of a tree, conditions the very behavior we act out at every level of reality. An example of this point is this: The dynamics of inferiority and superiority generated in the myth connect to related dynamics that we call dominance and submission. I would encourage you to take a few moments and simply meditate on the consequences, at all levels of reality, of the psychology of dominance and submission.

Is it not true, for example, that the integrity of the natural world is now in peril because of this psychology? Is not the atmosphere of our planet suffering because it has been forced to submit to the dominance of the human species? Is it not true that women have been expected to submit to man's will and to be a vicarious extension of man's reality? With Pluto transiting in Scorpio relative to Neptune and Uranus moving through Capricorn (its polarity being Cancer) as of this writing, is it not true that all the psychological and sexual abuse of so many families is becoming known to the collective consciousness via the printed and visual media? What is the causal factor of needing to abuse anyone or anything, or to let oneself be abused? Clearly, an answer lies within the nature of the Garden of Eden Myth.

Again, every group of people living together as an organized unit has had, and will have, belief systems that explain the nature of phenomenal existence in order to have a sense of meaning and purpose for the life experience. The nature of the specific belief systems, as in the Garden of Eden Myth, will dictate the nature of the specific psychological consequences to the men and women who are conditioned by them. These consequences will thus dictate the attitudes that men and women have toward one another, and these attitudes will thus dictate the roles that occur within the relationships between men and women. The social conditioning and its impact on the individual can not be underestimated. It has the effect of inhibiting and suppressing the actualization and expression of the inherent individual law or nature in each of us. The consequence to this suppression or inhibition is itself tremendous.

For example, women born in the 1930s had Pluto in Cancer with Uranus in Aries forming a square to Pluto. The inherent structure of such a symbolism is for the individual to liberate (Uranus) themselves through an actualization of their will to be free and in charge of their own lives (Aries). And yet, via Pluto in Cancer, the entire generation of these women has not only been subjected to the prevailing social conditioning of confining their lives primarily within the home and raising the family, but also to the larger archetypes symbolized in the Garden of Eden myth.

The consequences to such women of suppressing the Uranus in Aries call to freedom and liberation from such conditioning can be severe. This is because men were also born at this time who have, obviously, the same astrological pattern between Pluto and Uranus. Just as women were basically conditioned to be vicarious extensions of their men—weaker and inferior to them, and subject to their will—men were conditioned to be "supermen" who had stoic control of their emotions, were not permitted to be weak, were conditioned to always be in control, and were taught to protect and safeguard everyone in their sphere of influence. Their very image of masculinity was rooted in this conditioning. So for a woman of this time to desire to break free from this conditioning, to step out on her own and take control of her own identity, needs, and life, was to threaten the very social fabric defined by men via their own conditioning. And the consequence to men who also desired to break free from their own conditioning, to access and experience their emotions, to actualize the fact that they can feel insecure too, to rebel against the very nature of the roles that were dictated by social and religious imprinting, was to make them something less than men. So even though the intention in each of them is to break free from this conditioning, they, like most other men and women in this generation who have this astrological symbolism, will not succeed because of the *additional* fact of the natural conditioning factor reflected in the four natural evolutionary states or gates.

Again, 70% of all people are in the consensus state. If one is in this state or condition, and yet has this symbolism, then why have this symbolism at all? The answer can only be seen in evolutionary terms. The answer is this: To experience such a core frustration—*because of these conditions*—that the experience and psychology of frustration, which is born of limitation, will generate deep inner thoughts that *do* reflect the intention of the Pluto/Cancer square Uranus/Aries. In other words, to experience that these conditions are too limiting, and that there must be another way. This deep inner rebellion and examination thus sets the stage for not only their personal evolution in lifetimes to come, but also the stage for the millions of Souls who share in this astrological signature who will now carry these thoughts, *en masse*, into generations of people yet to be born.

It is important to consider this: *When the expression of natural law is conditioned or suppressed by manmade and religious laws, that which is suppressed becomes distorted.* Link this fact to the men and women who had the Pluto/Cancer square Uranus/Aries via the Garden of Eden Myth, and perhaps you can now see the causal factor in the psychological and sexual abuse that permeates our times. In fact, this abuse has been going on since the origin of the myth itself. Both the man and woman above feel limited and confined by the nature of the conditioning that they have been subjected to. In the man, this will create a deep anger that is displaced because he does not consciously know why he feels limited or angry. And, of course, he will blame the women for his conditions, frustrations, anger, and sadistically take it out on her. And the woman, of course, will somehow masochistically blame herself for his problems, frustrations, and anger. The stage is now set, via the Garden of Eden Myth, for the sadomasochistic roles to be played out in some way.

The impact of parental imprinting is also an extremely strong factor that must be considered. If a child grows up in an environment in which he or she experiences the father being abusive to the mother, what are the logical consequences, psychologically speaking, to him or her? How would this childhood experience condition their orientation to relationships when they become adults? If a young girl is taught by her mother to submit to the man, what is the likely orientation to relationships that she will carry with her into adult life? If a boy is sexually abused by his mother, and then psychologically abused because of the sexual abuse, what imprint does he carry into his adult life that will dictate, via displaced emotion, the types of women he will be attracted to? If a child is born into a family that teaches the equality of gender, what will be his or her orientation to the opposite sex as an adult? If a young girl is born into forms of Islamic culture that authorize the cutting off of her clitoris and the sewing up of her vaginal opening, what is going to be the impact to not only her body and her self-image as a woman, but to men—when at the same time her mother passes on the teaching that "women are not to feel pleasure, only men can feel pleasure through our bodies"?

The point of all this is to impress on you the importance of social and religious conditioning and how strongly it impacts on our sense of individual identity specifically, and our orientation to reality generally.

When doing astrological counseling, it is most important to understand these dynamics, because it will help you in understanding the actual and existing reality of the people in front of you. Again, astrology only reflects life. It does not cause it. And astrology only correctly operates relative to the observed context of its application. Thus, a couple who has a composite Pluto in Virgo within the Tenth House, who has grown up in Iran or Iraq and been conditioned by Islamic religious beliefs, and who are both within the consensus state, will have an entirely different orientation to that symbol than a couple who has grown up in Los Angeles, California, U.S.A. during the 1960s and '70s, and are well within the individuated state. For those who wish to read more deeply and extensively on the impact of social conditioning from an astrological point of view, I would recommend the book *Synthesis & Counseling in Astrology* by Noel Tyl.

THE TRANSITION FROM MATRIARCHY TO PATRIARCHY

Most of the psychological and behavioral problems that occur in relationships are traceable to the original transition from the matriarchy to the patriarchy. Throughout the matriarchy there is no evidence of any wars or sexual violence to women, men, or children. It is clear that the matriarchy lived in absolute and complete harmony with Nature, and the natural laws therein. The people who lived in that time understood all of nature to be interrelated, interdependent, and conscious. They understood human beings to be part of the totality of Nature, and all were equal within the totality. They understood the inherent and natural truths of phenomenal reality. Their belief systems were derived from observing Nature, especially the life of animals and plants. These observations became the basis of how men and women patterned their own interactions. As a consequence, there was no nuclear family, no monogamous relationships, children were raised communally, and men and women played out their natural gender roles as defined by natural laws. Accordingly, men and women were coequal in every way. There were no hierarchies as we know them. This natural orientation thus precluded the psychologies of jealousy, possessiveness, ownership, insecurity, attachment, dominance, and submission.

The matriarchal society understood what we now call God as the Earth itself, or Gaia. There were no "sky gods"—an invention that occurred during the patriarchal transition when men needed to control and subjugate women. The cause of the transition from matriarchal to patriarchal society is quite interesting. In matriarchal society, neither men or women understood that men had an equal contributing role in conceiving babies. Thus conception was thought to be a magical occurrence, directly caused by the Creator. This fact is the historical basis of all Goddess religions and myths. It is also the reason adult women throughout the matriarchy initiated pubescent boys into the mystery of sexual life—to have direct contact with the Creator in this way, and to teach them the right attitudes towards sexuality. Thus, women or children were not subjected to sexual violence in any way.

Once men began to realize that they coequally contributed to conceiving babies, the transition to the patriarchy began. For some yet-to-be-explained reason, this awareness created a sense of power in men. Men only wanted to have more power, more control, and more dominance. Accordingly, men realized that land and possessions symbolized power. To maintain power, men had to transfer their power (status, land, and possessions) to "their" children. To know who their children were created a need to know who the mothers were, and a need to control these specific women. This became the basis of paternity, which in turn became the basis of the nuclear family. Progressively, the patriarchy created new beliefs and religions that were "man-made" and in direct contradiction to natural laws. As these new beliefs evolved, there was a progressive creation of "sky gods" which symbolized the patriarchal creation of an intrinsic conflict between spirit and flesh, wherein women symbolized the world of flesh (sexuality), and man symbolized the world of spirit. As these beliefs took hold in he collective psyche, the way the nature of phenomenal reality itself was "interpreted" also changed.

Progressively, a women was given two essential choices. On the one hand, the woman could declare herself to be a "good woman," which meant to become married. Once married, she was then expected to live in the man's house, rarely allowed to come out of the house, was not allowed to be educated in any way, was not allowed to own possessions, and was expected to produce babies which were hopefully male. And, of course, she was expected to remain monogamous to her husband even while the husband gave himself the right to "sleep around." The other choice the woman could make was to legally declare herself to be a prostitute. If she made this choice, she was then allowed to educate herself, own possessions, and have some essential freedoms not allowed the "good women." And, of course, she could have sex with whomever she pleased.

Of course, the intention of these new patriarchal beliefs was for men to be able to justify their new way of being. The motivation for controlling women was so that male dominance could be assured and sustained. Many Creation myths were generated in order to rationalize this—the Garden of Eden myth being but one example. The progressive suppression of Natural Law in favor of manmade law and religious injunctions and doctrine continues to cause the psychological, emotional, behavioral, and sexual distortions that exist to this day—not only between men and women, but also between the human species and Nature. As a result of these distortions, the patriarchy became responsible for the manifestation of wars, different classes of people, ownership, and sadomasochistic pathology. Male supremacy has engendered the psychologies of distrust, betrayal, manipulations, jealousy, attachment, dominance and submission, and sexual and psychological violence to men, women, and children. And, of course, the progressive dominance and rape of Nature Itself.

From an astrological and evolutionary point of view, this historical transition is quite fascinating. The original matriarchy gestated during the last Age of Pisces, and was firmly established during the last Age of Aquarius. The transition from the matriarchy to the patriarchy began during the Capricorn sub-Age of the Age of Cancer—roughly around 6500 B.C.E. We have now entered a five-hundred-year process of mutation wherein the Age of Pisces is culminating, while at the same time the Age of Aquarius is just beginning. Progressively there will be a necessary involution (the destruction of existing forms) that allows for an evolution of new forms or paradigms to manifest. In essence, this is like having a giant galactic return, just as an individual can have a solar return chart for any given year. Most fascinating is the fact that almost every human being on the planet has the South Nodes of the planets Saturn, Pluto, and Jupiter in Capricorn, with the resulting North Nodes in Cancer, and that every human being on the planet now has the South Node of Neptune in Aquarius, and the South Node of Uranus in Sagittarius. From an evolutionary point of view, this means that all of us have had prior lifetimes not only when the transition from the matriarchy to the patriarchy began, but that all of us have our ultimate spiritual root going back to the original matriarchy— the South Node of Neptune. And with the South Node of Uranus being in Sagittarius, all of us have had prior lifetimes in quite nomadic tribes all over the Earth that were living in direct harmony with Nature, and its self-evident natural laws. So why is this group of collective

Souls on the planet now? We are all on the planet now in order to begin the process—the transition of the Ages—that will lead us back into a situation of living in direct balance with Nature, and its inherent laws. The North Node of Neptune being in Leo means that the generation who has Pluto in Leo becomes the generation to begin this process.

A simple review of recent history will illustrate this point. During the middle to late 1960s, there was a progressive rebellion by this generation against the prevailing norms, customs, moralities, and religions of the consensus societies of that time. This included a total rebellion against how men and women were expected to relate to themselves, including the institution of marriage. There was a total "sexual revolution" as a result. Within this, there was an active search of information or knowledge systems from other cultures and times, and there was a strong focus on expanding consciousness through the use of drugs and various Eastern spiritual systems as well as forms of Western Magic and Wicca. Environmental issues emerged as many wanted to reembrace the sacredness of the Earth. This all occurred as the planet Neptune transited Scorpio, causing a transiting T-Square to its natal South and North Nodes in this generation's birth charts. At the same time, this Neptune transit was squaring this generation's natal Pluto in Leo, while transiting Pluto was in Virgo. This transit thus created a T-Square to the natal South and North Nodes of this generation's Uranus. And if this were not enough to trigger this generational rebellion, the transit of Uranus was in Libra, conjuncting the natal position of Neptune for the entire generation, resulting in total rebellion against gender assignment, and the roles within relationships that this reflects. The women's movement began at this time.

Since that decade, the movements that it spawned have increased to the point of creating a collective awareness of the issues related to the environment, as well as the dissolving of the barriers between races and classes of people. Women's and children's rights issues remain in the forefront, and a progressive return of women to positions of power has begun. This has even included the election of women to run countries like Turkey, Pakistan, Norway, and Iceland. During the time that Neptune and Uranus have been transiting Capricorn relative to Pluto in Scorpio, all the hidden dark secrets of women's and children's sexual abuse have been revealed. The "wounded child" became a buzzword in therapeutic circles. This occurred as the transits of Neptune and Uranus conjuncted all of our South Nodes of Pluto, Jupiter, and Saturn in Capricorn!

This all means that since the 1960s, both men and women have been trying to liberate (Uranus) themselves form patriarchal conditioning in one way or another. All of us have the South Node of Uranus in Sagittarius, the archetype of Natural Law leading to natural living. Thus all of us, in one way or another, have intuitive knowledge and awareness that Nature Itself is the real teacher. And because we all have the South Node of Neptune in Aquarius, our ultimate spiritual root lies within the original matriarchy. As Pluto moves into Sagittarius, and with Neptune and Uranus moving into Aquarius, we can anticipate a progressive confrontation of all patriarchal beliefs that still determine how we are interpreting the nature of phenomenal reality, and the behaviors that this interpretation generates. We can anticipate a progressive confrontation of gender-specific roles defined by patriarchal beliefs. These confrontations reflecting the transition of the Ages will manifest as external events that will gradually become more cataclysmic to the human population. These progressive cataclysms will finally lead to a situation wherein the human species has no choice but to change. These changes will not occur through some sudden event of "collective enlightenment," but through circumstantial necessity. Later in this book I will write more specifically about the nature of these collective events. However, I will state now that the *intent* of these changes as it pertains to human relationship is to remove the patriarchal beliefs that have caused the pathology of sadomasochism, dominance, and submission, based on the idea of the superiority of men and the inferiority of women. A return to natural gender roles will be the result.

Chapter Five

Relationship Types

In this chapter, we will be discussing relationship types. There are five primary, archetypal forms that define a relationship between two people. By understanding the dynamics inherent to each type and linking these archetypes to the conditioning nature of past-life dynamics, the four natural evolutionary conditions, and the conditioning impact of societal, parental, cultural, and religious imprinting, you will increase your astrological ability to help a couple seeking guidance. The five primary relationship types are:

- Co-dependent

- Counselor/counselee

- Student/teacher

- Sado/masochistic

- Self-sufficient

There are also four special variations that can exist or occur *within* the five primary types. They are:

- Karma Mates

- Soul Mates (with an additional sub-type of Same Soul)

- Twin Souls

- Souls in different evolutionary states

CO-DEPENDENT

The most common of all relationship types is the co-dependent condition. The co-dependent relationship is one in which both people are dependent on one another for their lives to be sustained. In this condition, each person will project their needs upon the other in such a way as to expect each other to perpetually meet those needs. This then becomes the basis of mutual projection, wherein each person "out-pictures" their inner reality upon one another. This projection of inner realities upon each other creates a situation wherein neither person can see clearly, if at all, the actual reality of the other. As each person expects the other to perpetually meet their needs, the stage becomes set for conditional love—"I will love you if...."

In this way, each person can progressively lose sight of their own identity because of their co-dependent needs. The two people become so hopelessly enmeshed that the normal boundaries that generate a healthy relationship, in which each other's individual lives can blossom and thrive, becomes non-existent. In the worst cases, each person in such a relationship will feel that they simply cannot live without the other person, and will do whatever is necessary to maintain and sustain the relationship. In effect, each person makes the other person their very reason for living as if each were *de facto* gods and goddesses to each other. If, for any reason, one of the partners is removed from the relationship—death occurs, for example—or one of the people decides to change the dynamics because of the enmeshment and co-dependency, then the other person will feel like they are dying, that they cannot live without them. The psychological state this will lead to is truly tragic and problematic. Some will contemplate (or actually commit) suicide.

COUNSELOR/COUNSELEE

The next relationship type is the counselor/counselee condition. This is a relationship condition in which one person feels that another person has some vital knowledge or information of a psychological nature that they need—knowledge or information which they themselves do not have. The other person will feel that they do indeed have this information or knowledge to offer the other person. The person who feels that they have this knowledge will typically seem quite mature and integrated, and will present themselves to almost everyone as very adept and "together." They can appear as quite insightful and reflect a wisdom that is attractive to many people.

Yet underneath this persona will be a person who is highly insecure at an emotional level. This type of person will typically have an emphasized emotional fear of loss, betrayal, abandonment, fears related to violations of trust, and fears of persecution if they reveal too much about their actual inner reality. Through the psychological dynamic of compensation, they will attract those who appear more needy than themselves. The key word is *appear.* This is because they are just as needy, perhaps more so, than those who are in touch with their needs. This compensatory act of attracting those who appear more needy than themselves is created in order for them to feel secure in a relationship. By presenting themselves as someone who can help another understand themselves in psychological terms, they think they are guaranteeing their emotional security through being in a position of emotional/psychological control. They feel: "I am secure because this person needs me."

These people have a knack for keying in on the weakest psychological/emotional link in the other person in such a way as to present themselves as the person who will help them out of that situation. Yet, if the other person actually begins to heal, or begins to understand things for themselves, then the counselor type will feel threatened and insecure. Consequently, this person can be very manipulative in quite covert ways in order to maintain their position within the relationship, since their emotional security is at stake. In the worst case, this person, who once seemed so nice and helpful, becomes abusive and vindictive as their deepest fears of emotional loss, abandonment, and their perception of betrayal become played out yet again.

Conversely, the counselee in this type of relationship will present oneself as someone who needs the counselor. In the beginning of the relationship, the counselee will feel, again, that the counselor symbolizes or represents something that they need which in their own estimation they do not have. In this way, they give their power up to the counselor who is all too happy to take power, for it serves their need for emotional and psychological security. The inherent problem is that the counselee will only maintain the relationship for the duration of the needs that brought them into the relationship in the first place. And once these needs are satisfied or met, they will then want to terminate the relationship, either because they have begun to learn how to satisfy their own needs, or because they will uncover another set of needs that the existing counselor/partner cannot meet. Thus, they will become attracted to another counselor type who now represents or symbolizes the ability to satisfy these new needs.

For both the counselor and counselee, the karma of manipulation can exist or occur for reasons that are unique to each. Both are dependent on their roles in order to feel secure. Typically, this type of relationship reflects an inherent imbalance, wherein the counselor does most of the giving, and the counselee does most of the receiving. Generally, the counselor is all too happy to give, for this makes him or her feel secure. But underneath this apparent happiness, the counselor is not really so happy because the counselor's core needs are not being met—the core needs of getting in touch with their own fears of loss and betrayal, and to examine the causal factors and reasons for these fears. This is why the counselor will unconsciously re-create loss, violations of trust, and the perception of betrayal via this type of relationship. By repeating this dynamic through the psychology of repetitive compulsion they will, at some point, become emotionally and psychologically honest with themselves. Of course, when this occurs, the counselor may become the counselee!

STUDENT/TEACHER

The next relationship type is a variation of the counselor/counselee. This is the student/teacher type of relationship. Many of the same dynamics that are present in the counselor/counselee type of relationship exist within this type. One of the core differences is that in this type of relationship the content is not specifically psychological. It has much more to do with teachings that reflect life itself in a broad sense. Depending on the evolutionary states of the people involved, these teachings can be anything from the spiritual and metaphysical to just the nuts and bolts of how to live in order to survive.

Whatever the case may be, the core dynamics still exist of a relationship defined by inequality of roles, and the emotional investment in those roles for security purposes. A high probability for manipulative behavior in order to sustain those roles also exists. Both the counselor and the teacher must realize that, by playing their roles, they are also using their partners to fulfill their own security needs. And the arrangement is in no way foolproof—just as the counselor can experience being used and then left, so too can the teacher.

SADOMASOCHISTIC

The next, and perhaps the most difficult relationship type, is the sadomasochistic relationship. Difficult, because it has so many forms and expressions that many people do not recognize it for what it is. For example, it can be as simple as a man and woman doing the same kind of job, yet the woman makes less money. In one form or another, this type of relationship seems to permeate the interrelationships of men and women—even gay men and women.

The archetypal dynamics that generate and lead to this type of relationship were detailed in our study of the Garden of Eden myth, which again is a reflection of the distortions born during the transition to the patriarchy. Let's reiterate the resulting dynamics: A permeating guilt that leads to atonement or anger, dominance and submission, along with roles and feelings of inferiority and superiority. Within these dynamics is the implicit teaching that flesh is antagonistic to spirit, and that suffering is a prerequisite for any real growth or gain to occur.

In a masochistic pathology, there will always be three messages, or thought patterns, that permeate the subconscious of such individuals. These underlying thought patterns will condition, control, and create the circumstantial realities of the masochistic type of person. These three thought patterns are:

- I deserve pain, punishment, crisis, suffering, humiliation (enforced humility), and denial, and I do not know why. In addition, the dynamic of denial/avoidance expresses itself as a suppression of the truth that is causing this to occur in such a way as to make excuses that will always sound like rational reasons in order to justify such conditions. And within this the related thought: there must be something wrong with me.

- For my needs to be met, I must hurt, suffer, or sacrifice first.

- I am essentially worthless, while intellectually knowing better.

In essence, a masochistic orientation to reality will create a circumstantial reality that is defined by personal crucifixion—to compulsively sacrifice oneself in a myriad of ways. When atonement is linked with guilt, the behavioral manifestation can only lead to pain and crisis. Self-sacrificial behavior, pain, and the creation of inner and outer crisis generates a type of consciousness wherein analysis linked with crisis, etc., produces self-knowledge. In effect, a masochistic type can only learn about oneself through the creation of crisis and the analysis of self that this will produce. Crisis also has the affect of removing the psychology of denial and avoidance of the truth because of the repetitive nature of crisis formation in the masochist. At some point, the masochist will simply become totally exhausted from the cycle of repetitive crisis and desire to change. When this occurs, the blinders of excuse-making will come off. Reality will set in. They can change.

In relationships, the masochist compulsively and habitually attracts one of two types of people. One type is what I call the "emotional wounded birds" of this world. This type needs extensive emotional and psychological healing or repair. They are quite typically very narcissistic, and have no real capacity to acknowledge the actual needs or identity of their masochistic partner. Typically, they are so deeply insecure that they will create an idea or image in their minds of who their masochistic partner is, and then expect that partner to *be* that idea or image. Consequently, the masochistic partner is left feeling totally misunderstood and invalidated, no matter how many confrontations or pleas for recognition occur. In this situation, the masochistic person does almost all the giving, and is constantly putting out the emotional brush fires that the "wounded bird" is creating. The masochistic partner might as well walk around the house with a white uniform on, red cross on the shoulder, and a name tag on the breast!

The other type that the masochist will attract is what I call the "silver-tongue-devil type." This is the type who knows how to present themselves—they know what to say in order to "hook" the masochistic type. Yet, once the masochist bites on the hook and makes the decision to be in the relationship, the actual emotional and psychological agenda or reality of the sadistic partner becomes revealed—and this reality has nothing to do with their original presentation of themselves. At this point, the masochist becomes totally disillusioned, and another crisis is at hand. The "silver-tongue-devil" will then often adopt an air of great concern and sincerity, and promise to change in order to resecure the relationship. Yet once it is resecured, they revert to the old patterns. And, of course, these two types that the masochist can attract can be combined in the same person.

The masochistic person reflects a natural kind of innocence that creates naiveté and gullibility. They see the spirit of *potential* in an individual, and then expect the person to either *be* the potential that they perceive, or to actualize what their spirit reflects. Rarely, if ever, will their partners do either. Then disillusionment sets in, and more crisis. Masochists have a need to be needed—they live for it.

In the sadist, anger is linked with guilt instead of atonement. This pathology will also make excuses sounding like rational reasons as a way of avoiding/denying the truth of what is actually happening. As a result, the subconscious messages or thought patterns become these:

- I have been made to feel guilty and I am angry because of it, so I want to hurt others and make them feel as guilty or as bad as I do. And I will hurt others *first*, before I myself get hurt.

- I want to make others atone for their mistakes or sins. I want to humiliate others so that I will humiliate myself.

- By punishing others for their imperfections, mistakes, or sins, I am punishing myself.

These three thought patterns will create a circumstantial reality that is defined, in essence, by dominance/submission, master/slave, superior/inferior, and victor/vanquished orientations to reality. In men, this dynamic is projected upon women, due to an underlying or latent fear called the "castration complex." For women, who can also be sadistic, the castration complex also applies. This complex is psychological, not literal! The essence of this complex is the fear or feeling that the opposite gender will disempower, undermine, capture, enslave, or in some undefined way destroy you. Consequently, the sadistic person will desire to hurt another first, to attack first, to destroy first, to "get even" first, before it allows itself to get hurt. For individuals who are defined by this sadistic pathology, there is always an underlying feeling that someone or somebody is out to get them, to attack them, to hurt them, and to victimize them. And instead of feeling that they deserve this, as the masochist does, they will feel victimized. The masochist also feels victimized, but the masochist feels that they deserve to be a victim. The sadist feels only anger because of feeling victimized in this way, and this anger can only be used to destroy or hurt others. They are compelled to punish others for the underlying guilt that resides in their own psyche or subconscious. In some people, the sadistic and masochistic pathology operate together—the manifestations of each pathology depend on specific circumstances. In classical psychology, this is known as the passive/aggressive type.

The sadomasochistic relationship type has a wide range of behavioral applications. This dynamic is easily recognized by any of us. The most overt forms, of course, are the classical forms of sadomasochistic sexual practices that most people have some awareness of—the whips and chains, the leather costumes, the spiked heels, all the equipment that creates sexual/emotional torture, and so on. The operative psychological/emotional dynamic in such overt forms is intense pain, and the *release* from such pain. Intense suffering leads to a sense of freedom when the release from the suffering occurs. In recent modern history, the most gross, yet most recognizable, person who embodied the darkest and most distorted dimensions of this archetype was the Marquis de Sade.

In his time, the sadomasochistic archetype was actually given a fancy philosophical name by the "noble" class that practiced it. It was called the "libertinage" philosophy. The implied teaching of this philosophy was "In order to be free, to liberate, one must suffer." The first premise in this philosophy was that God is inherently evil, and that to do God's work one must consent to embrace evil and "to confound the laws of nature, to turn the laws of nature upside down." As ridiculous as this may sound, try to understand that such distorted thinking directly emanates from the equally distorted religious thought embodied in the Garden of Eden myth—that flesh is in conflict with spirit. The implied guilt linked with flesh thus distorts the life of the flesh or senses because of suppression via religious injunction. The effect of this teaching existed long before de Sade—for example, the self-flagellation of so many pious monastic Christians during the 1400s and 1500s, which is still seen today among some of those in the Islamic world. During the Crusades, it was a common practice, under the banner of the cross, to sexually torture and mutilate men and women (mostly women) in unspeakable ways in an effort to extract confessions about their "immoral" life practices, and to force them to turn in other people who were also living "immorally." The sadomasochistic dynamic also emerges among Jewish teachings, where to be especially "chosen" or favored by God requires persecution by others.

It also exists in other races. For example, certain American Indian tribes perform the Sun Dance in which metal is pierced into the nipples of an individual, and the metal is attached to ropes tied to a pole. The Sun Dancer then will progressively suspend himself so that the body is only held up by the metal attached to the ropes. The pain and suffering experienced is meant to induce visions from on high.

The point that I am making is that this sadomasochistic archetype permeates the collective psyche of millions of people living today, and most do not know it. Yes, the most overt forms can be recognized by almost all of us. And in this recognition, we recoil in shock and horror—"How could anybody be like that, do such things, allow oneself to be such a way"— and so on. In our times, this dynamic is most easily understood by us as the battered wife syndrome, the abused child syndrome, and the like. All we have to do is turn on the television set and observe the next set of people on the increasingly popular talk shows discussing their childhood abuse to understand how extensively this S&M archetype permeates society. But how many of us can recognize the less overt forms of this archetype? And what are these less overt forms?

Again, can it not be seen in the man and woman doing the same job and the woman makes less? Can it not be seen in a man or a woman who withholds their emotional or sexual attention from their partner as a form of punishment? Can it not be seen in various forms of perpetual criticism from one partner to another? (This form can also be linked with "teasing" when it has the motive of humiliation.) Can it not be seen in the man who expects the woman to be merely a vicarious extension of his reality, whose only purpose is to serve his needs? The thought that the woman is inferior to him—a second-class citizen at best—is this not a form of the dynamic of dominance and submission? And why is it that when a woman wants to fully actualize herself that she is considered, consciously or unconsciously, as wanting to be "like a man"? From a man's point of view, is this not an example of the castration complex? And why is it culturally acceptable in every society for a man to flaunt his sexuality, to brag about his conquest, to talk about women in the crudest terms, but not OK for a woman to do exactly the same? Is this not traceable to the original archetype of the Garden of Eden myth wherein man is now "getting back" at women for the original temptation? Here is the root of the unconscious rationale for the rape of a woman—an act of power and rage linked with the castration complex generated in the Edenic myth.

More commonly, we have the situation of a man who can be emotional and placating to the woman in order to have sex with her, and then, when the act of sex is over, he is suddenly emotionally remote or disdainful of the woman—sometimes even angry at her. Why? Because he has given in to the temptation! If you can understand this, then you will understand why so many women feel that they must be *pure* for their men—the unconscious desire to atone for their responsibility for the "Original Sin."

It is very difficult to overstate the degree to which this archetype permeates the minds of millions of people. Just as the nature of the seed that is planted in the ground determines the shape and form of the plant that we can see, so too does this seed of the Garden of Eden myth, residing in the collective unconscious, determine the shape and form of the interrelationships between people—particularly between men and women—and, by way of extension, to how human beings interrelate with the rest of Nature.

Astrologically, the sadomasochistic archetype correlates with the signs of Virgo and Pisces. From around A.D. 0 until now, we have been living in the Pisces Age. Many years ago, for example, I did a research study of people who consciously defined themselves as masochistic or sadistic. This was done in the context of a specialized group of people who were members of an S&M "church." Of all the people studied, ninety percent had an emphasized Twelfth or Sixth Houses, a stellium of planets in Pisces or Virgo, and/or the South and North Nodes of the Moon in the Sixth or Twelfth Houses. This should not be surprising when we consider the birthchart of Jesus of Nazareth, who ushered in the Pisces Age for Western peoples. The chart that I use, the one that makes most sense to me, was a chart that was rectified by the theologian/astrologer Donald Jacobs. In this chart, Pluto is conjunct Mars in Virgo (which are both retrograde in the Ninth House), and in opposition to the Sun, Moon, Venus, Jupiter, Uranus and Saturn in Pisces within the Third House. Neptune, the ruler of Pisces, is conjunct the South Node in Scorpio. In essence, the life of Jesus was a life of "suffering for our sins," of trying to absolve our guilt through absorbing our karma through the act of sacrificing his own life, of "Father forgive them, for they know not what they do," and also of an attendant guilt based in *imperfection* which is reflected in his own words: "Father, take this cup from me." This means: "Lord, I am weak and not perfect enough for the job that you have given to me; please let me go." The implication here is that if one is pure enough, perfect enough, good enough, then that which we are given to do will simply occur. But perfection, in this context, can only be linked with a God that is conceived as perfect, and the human being is something less than this because of the temptation that was succumbed to in the Garden of Eden—the commission of original sin. So human beings in general, and women in particular, are never good enough, never perfect enough, to do what is given to one to do. This archetypically conditioned psychology thus sustains and perpetuates guilt relative to the God that is conceived as perfect.

The bottom line in all of this is that the sadomasochistic archetype will be sustained until and unless the Christian and Islamic doctrines that conceive God in this way are changed. As an example, these doctrines state that what is called God is the origin of all things. If so, then wherein lies the origin of imperfection? Wherein lies the origin of evolution? Wherein lies the origin of anger? Guilt? Sexuality? The list goes on and on.

If we can confront these questions, then we can see that what is called God is also an *evolving force* seeking to perfect itself. If God is understood in this way, love and compassion will replace guilt, and the self-hate and anger that guilt generates. Natural law will become that by which the human being understands life, not manmade laws that distort natural law. It is only in this way that the sadomasochistic archetype will no longer exist. Until this occurs, the sadomasochistic acts, on a large scale, such as the Holocaust against the Jews and Gypsies that Hitler fomented, the "ethnic cleansing" insanity that now engulfs what was once Yugoslavia as of this writing, or the dark forces of Russia who wish to return Russia to a state of domination via purging non-Russians from its borders, etc.,will continue. As we move toward the Aquarian Age, the transition necessary that will allow an embracing of natural law as opposed to manmade law is under way. The intention of Pluto in Scorpio, relative to Neptune and Uranus being in Capricorn, is to accelerate this transition. This acceleration will only increase as Pluto moves into Sagittarius (a fire sign) and Neptune and Uranus move into Aquarius (an air sign). The last time this occurred, the transition to Humanism began during the Renaissance in the West.

Astrologically speaking, we all have the signs Virgo and Pisces in our horoscope somewhere. The question becomes this: Where and how is this archetype of sadomasochism operating in your life? The house positions of those signs and planets associated with them reveals exactly where you are most susceptible to this archetype via the impact of the Garden of Eden myth, and its permeation into the collective unconscious—the seed in the ground!

SELF-SUFFICIENT

The next relationship type is what I call the self-sufficient type. The self-sufficient type of relationship is an archetype in which both individuals have learned how to identify and meet their own needs. The resulting attitude of such people becomes one wherein each will feel that they are in the relationship simply because they want to be, not because of what the other can do for them. The element of compulsion and projected needs is entirely eliminated. Such people are simply free from within themselves to be with another person. As a result, such individuals have the evolved capacity to see their partners clearly and objectively. The feeling of being threatened or insecure because of each other's individual needs or desires to actualize in the ways that each requires is eliminated. Instead, each person will encourage and facilitate the individual development of one another. This allows for an unconditional love—"I will love you always, no matter what." This is totally different than the conditional love that manifests in every other relationship type thus far discussed.

The self-sufficient relationship type does not mean that each person does not have needs—everyone has needs in a relationship. The difference is that each person has learned how to meet their own needs without projecting those needs on the partner. Such individuals are fine whether they are in a relationship or not. Because this type of person does not project needs upon his or her partner, the partner, paradoxically, is all too happy to meet those needs. Evolutionarily speaking, it takes a long time to arrive to a condition of self-sufficiency. As a result, this relationship type is not common—in the West, roughly fifteen percent of all relationships will be in this condition.

The nature of cultural and religious conditioning promotes dependence on external factors in order to feel secure. From a religious point of view, this is reflected in a God who is somehow *outside* of the individual. From a cultural point of view, women have been more or less controlled by the nature of patriarchal societies. Thus, women have been conditioned to be dependent on men, and men have been conditioned to have women dependent on them. Men are dependent on women's dependence on them—a typical man's egocentric sense of maleness is *reinforced* by having a woman dependent on him. Women, in turn, seek out a strong provider figure, a "bread-winner," whose desires and activities will dominate the relationship. It is for such reasons that the self-sufficient type of relationship is not common.

Astrologically speaking, the archetypes that correlate to self-sufficiency or self-reliance are Taurus, the Second House, and the inner side of Venus. Remember, Venus has a dual rulership–Taurus and Libra. The Libra side of Venus reflects a person's needs that are projected upon a partner—co-dependency. It also reflects our capacity to give to and receive from a partner. The Taurus side of Venus reflects the inner awareness in all us of what our needs are, needs that must be met in order to live and survive. It also reflects our inner relationship to ourselves. Thus, all birth charts will have a sign on the Second House, and the planetary ruler of that sign will be located somewhere in the birth chart.

This planetary ruler will be making aspects to other planets. The sign Taurus will also be somewhere in the birthchart, and Venus will be in a house and sign, making its own aspects. In combination, these symbols correlate with how an individual can learn this vital lesson of self-sufficiency. In a composite chart, the couple will have a sign on the Second House, it will have a planetary ruler located somewhere, Taurus will be somewhere, and Venus will be somewhere. In combination, this is how any couple can learn to be self-sufficient together.

It is interesting to note, with Pluto transiting through Scorpio since late 1983, that the buzz words in relationship counseling have been "enmeshment," "the wounded child," and "establishing your boundaries." Remember that the opposite sign of Scorpio is Taurus, indicating that, evolutionarily speaking, Pluto's intention within the collective Soul is to destroy excessive dependence on any external situation for security reasons. The evolutionary enforcement of learning self-reliance and self-sufficiency is at hand. This is why so many relationships have simply been blown to pieces—relationships that were once so close, so loving—and yet too co-dependent. New relationship models are in the process of evolving. Evolution is always preceded, in varying degrees of intensity, by involution. Involution means to undo or destroy something that currently exists. Evolution then follows this involutionary change. One of these new relationship models will be, in a common sense, the self-sufficient type that we have been discussing.

KARMA MATES

We now come to the four special variations that can exist or occur within the five primary relationship types. The most common of these is what I call Karma Mates. Now that you have gotten this far in the book, it should be fairly clear to you what karma mates are—two people who have had past-life connections and experiences that are not finished or resolved. A past-life connection is a very inclusive and broad situation that can be simple or complex depending on the two people in question. Karma, again, is the simple, natural law of every action having a proportionate reaction. Karma includes effects from 100% positive to 100% negative. In synastry charts, karma can exist between two people as distinct individuals, and in composite charts, karma can exist within the relationship as a unit. As exemplified before, the couple who had Pluto square Venus in the composite chart could have excluded other people from their life completely because of their excessive co-dependency relative to their fears of emotional betrayal by other people. This was a mutual choice (Pluto square Venus in the Composite Chart) that could create mutual karma in which they, as a unit, experience being excluded by other people at some point after they made their mutual decision to do so for themselves.

The natural tendency in all people who feel that they have been taken advantage of by another, or have been purposely hurt, used, manipulated, had their trust violated or betrayed, or experienced someone else creating these situations for someone they love, is to be vindictive. They need to get back or even at someone, to create a sense of justice in an otherwise perceived unjust situation. This natural tendency in all of us correlates with Pluto, Scorpio, and the Eighth House. This natural tendency can be controlled within our own consciousness as it naturally exists, and it can be controlled or modified by conditioning patterns of a cultural and/or religious nature. Examples of this include "God will take care of it;" "Let the justice systems work;" and so on. Acting on the impulse to get even with someone, whatever the specific nature of the situation is about, is a causal factor in specific karmic conditions of a personal nature that can exist between two people. This type of karma, rooted in the desire to get even, will always be of a difficult or negative nature.

It is very important to understand this point, because when we act upon this impulse to get even, to right a wrong, the karma that is created, or is pre-existing from other lifetimes, will or can be sustained for an incredibly long time—many, many lifetimes. This is so because not too many people have a consciousness that has evolved to the point of being able to see or understand the original cause or reason for any currently existing condition or situation. Acting upon the tendency to get even can perpetuate whatever the karmic situation or condition is about, because most people's orientation to and perception of reality is limited to the life that they are currently living.

If a person experiences emotional betrayal by another person in the life that is currently being lived, then that person most commonly will want to get even with the betrayer because the betrayer is perceived to be the cause of the emotional pain. For example, what if the one who was betrayed in this life did in fact betray the other in another life? And, in that life, the one who is now the betrayer felt exactly the same as the one who was betrayed in this life—the need to get even. So on it goes, cycle after cycle—a karma that is sustained over many lifetimes. A modern example that can illustrate this point, one that we can all recognize, is the example of psychological or sexual abuse that occurs within families over generations, the abuse being perpetuated through cause and effect from parent to child. When the child who has been abused becomes an adult, he or she will have the tendency to abuse their own child. At what point does or can this cycle of karma (cause and effect) between such family members stop? And how can it stop? What is necessary to stop it?

For many of us it can be very difficult *not* to act upon the inherent Plutonian desire to get even, to create relative justice, to right a wrong. Obviously, this is a very complex and difficult dynamic in life to truly understand, let alone *knowing* what the right thing is to do in any given situation. For those who do have an expanded consciousness that is able to "see" beyond the life that is currently being lived, allowing for a knowing or perception of the original cause in any given karmic situation, the "right" thing to do can be seen. Great. But most of us do not have such an expanded consciousness. So then what? Perhaps the simplest answer lies in the axiom: Two wrongs do not make a right. So in the illustration of the abuse that was passed down from generation to generation of family members, at some point one of these family members will break the chain of karma by acting on this axiom. In many situations this will require a conscious act of courage to do so, and require a tremendous act of will (Pluto) to resist the natural tendency to get even.

And yet, karma can also be very positive. Many people today who try to understand the complexity of karma tend to think that karma is generally negative. Positive karma always results from a purity of desire to do that which is inherently the right thing to do. The key here is purity of desire. For example, if I desire to help someone in some way, yet my motivation (desire) in doing this is to reap some reward for myself, then the desire to help is not pure—the desire has an ulterior motive. Conversely, if this desire to help another is motivated by the intention to help for its own sake, because it is the inherently right thing to do, then the purity of the desire speaks for itself. Yes, there is an inherent right and wrong from an ultimate point of view. But this inherent right and wrong has nothing to do with religions. It simply exists in and of itself, and is part of our consciousness as naturally created. In consciousness as naturally structured, the awareness of what is naturally right and wrong is reflected in our sense of conscience. If we do something that is inherently wrong, then our conscience creates a feeling of guilt. This type of guilt is instinctual and natural to consciousness. Not many of us would disagree, for example, that it is inherently wrong to sexually abuse a child, to emotionally betray another person, or to cheat, lie, purposely hurt another, and so on. Conversely, if we do something that we know is an inherently right thing to do, then our conscience knows it to be so at an instinctual level.

Again, astrologically speaking, difficult karmic situations generally exist in synastry and composite charts when stressful or hard aspects exist between planets. Favorable or positive karmic situations generally exist when non-stressful or harmonious aspects exist between planets. As most astrologers know from looking at many charts, most synastry and composite charts have both stressful and non-stressful aspects between planets. Thus, most of the relationships that we have with other people reflect a combination of positive and difficult (in varying degrees) karmic conditions.

Karma can also be confused with evolutionary necessity. To illustrate this point, we see that an individual may have spent many past lifetimes denying or avoiding emotional reality—for example, by trying to embrace a transcendent reality reflected in some spiritual teaching, and isolating themselves in some kind of religious or spiritual environment such as a monastery. At some point in this person's evolutionary development it would become necessary to create a life or lives in which what had been avoided or denied could no longer be so. Consequently, through evolutionary necessity, the Soul of such an individual would create one or more lifetimes in which emotional dynamics would be the very essence of the life being lived. And because of the prior life resistance to this, the nature of the life in which the emotional dynamics were experienced could be very difficult. The circumstances of such a life would be one of *enforcing* the emotions to be experienced. The Soul could create a continuing chain of emotionally laden events offering no way to avoid the emotions. These circumstances would include people whose actions or behaviors created difficult emotional conditions or situations for the individual—for example, being born into a family in which the mother tried to murder the individual as a child. The point I am making is this: It is evolutionary necessity that has dictated this situation. There is not any pre-existing karma to explain it, nor any specific prior-life dynamics that would account for it. Yet the temptation for many who embrace the precepts of the law of karma is to think that, if this individual is experiencing such difficult situations, then he or she must have done the same or similar things to the people who are now doing this to the individual.

At this point it may be useful to remember that all of us, at a Soul level, simply create the conditions necessary to facilitate our evolutionary progression, and to work out the difficult aspects of our karma, personally and with other people, in the ways that we do. *We are all responsible for our own actions.* From the largest point of view, an ultimate point of view, there are no victims.

SOUL MATES

The next specialty type is the infamous Soul Mates. Within this type there exists a subtype—the same Soul. In the last decade or two, it seems that a great many people have been consumed by the desire to find their Soul Mate. Much of this has been fueled by the appearance of many books on this subject, complete with guidelines and instructions of how to attract and secure such a partner. For those of you who have been doing astrological counseling for a period of time, you probably have had the repeated experience of yet another client racing through the door, with yet another chart in hand, and with the exasperated plea: "Is this my Soul Mate?"

Unfortunately, the conceptual basis of what a Soul Mate actually is has been horribly clouded and confused by a diversity of opinions from too many sources. So, I will share my opinion of what a Soul Mate is, gleaned from the teachings of many God-realized Souls such as Jesus of Nazareth and others. It is simply this: Soul Mates are two people who have independently acted on their desires to embrace a spiritual or transcendent reality, and the real purpose of the union with one another is *to continue their individual spiritual development because of and through the relationship.* In spiritual terms, this is called the path of the householder, in contrast to the path of the monastic.

This does not mean that these two people are perfect. It *does* mean that they both have embraced a transcendent or spiritual principle to guide both their individual lives and their relationship. There is a common spiritual (philosophical) foundation upon which the relationship is built and based. As a result, there is a larger point of view to refer and defer to. This then allows for unconditional love and support for one another, as opposed to conditional love. Conditional love is one of the primary breeding grounds through which difficult karmic situations or conditions can be created. Unconditional love is one of the primary breeding grounds through which harmonious or positive karmic situations or conditions are created. Thus, true Soul Mates only have positive karmic conditions or situations that are mutually supportive and beneficial to each other. The state of Soul Mates, evolutionarily speaking, is a condition that is evolved into from the most common of relationship unions—Karma Mates.

Same Soul

A subtype within Soul Mates is the phenomena of the Same Soul. What this means is that in certain states of advanced evolution, the spiritual state defined earlier, a Soul can manifest itself in more than one body/personality/ego at a time. In essence, the Soul, in order to accelerate its evolution through the progressive elimination of all separating desires, can manifest itself in what appears to be different people who exist at the same time and place, at the same time in different places, or both. These different people can look very different or the same, can dress very different or the same, can have very different life experiences or experiences that are remarkably similar with key variations, come from the same or different cultures, be the same or opposite sex, and so on.

The classical or archetypal feeling in each of the egos or personalities that the Soul has created in order to accelerate its evolution in this way is one in which there is a deep, permeating sense of not being complete—that there is a great inner void. Even when everything else in their life is full, including a rich and experiential spiritual life, the different "individuals" who emanate from the same Soul have an inner feeling of something missing that haunts their sense of self. Archetypally, the reason for this feeling is that, at some point, the Soul who has splintered itself in these ways must merge back into itself the different components of itself that took on the *form* of distinct and separate people. This is no different than the Ultimate Source of Creation projecting the totality of Itself into what appears to be the distinct and different forms of the manifested Creation. The act of Creation is an act of expansion. Through the natural law of polarity, expansion is met by contraction; like the rhythm of a heartbeat. And just as the Ultimate Source, God, calls back to Itself that which It has created (reflected as the transcendent impulse in the human being, for example), so too does the Soul who has splintered itself for evolutionary reasons call back to itself the different components of itself that have manifested as different people.

These different people that emanate from the same Soul are reflections of a complex of different desires. Each person that is created by the same Soul acts out these desires in an accelerated way. In other words, instead of the Soul creating just one life at a time in order to act out the myriad of separating desires that exist within it, the Soul has now evolved to a point where it can create simultaneous lifetimes in order to accelerate the elimination of separating desires.

Again, the Soul must be quite advanced, evolutionarily speaking. The Soul must have evolved to the Spiritual state, as defined earlier. Since this state only embraces 5% or so of all people on the planet, the situation wherein the Soul meets itself in the form of people who appear separate is not common. And it is not common for another reason. Generally, the complex of various separating desires that the Soul is acting.out, in an accelerated fashion, by manifesting itself in "different" people at the same time are relatively compatible. Therefore, the Soul is able to integrate the lessons and realizations that the various desires and evolutionary intentions create without needing to actually meet itself in the form of the different people that it has created. The spiritual state of evolution allows for this. However, in some Souls at this level of evolution, there can exist certain conditions that will create a situation wherein the Soul will meet itself in the form of what appears to be different people. The intention of this situation is the same—for the Soul to call back to itself its different components in order for a integration to occur within itself, which then allows for a total integration with God to occur.

So what conditions lead to a situation of the Soul having to meet itself in the form of the different people it has created? The primary condition is one wherein the Soul has separating desires of an antithetical nature—desires that are in opposition to themselves. An example would be a Soul who had desires of a sexual nature that, if acted upon, would conflict with other desires of a purely spiritual or transcendent nature. Of course, the apparent conflict only exists because of the teaching that spirit and flesh are antagonistic. The Soul who has accepted this teaching would thus have this conflict, and the desires of a purely spiritual or transcendent nature would judge the desires of a sexual nature as wrong or impure. Yet the evolution of the Soul is based on the elimination of all separating desires, whatever those desires are, and that which is desired must manifest into empirical reality for it to be acted out and eliminated.

The intensity of the inner conflict within this Soul would thus create different people who each embodied a nexus of desires that were in conflict to themselves within the Soul. In this way, they are acted out simultaneously in an accelerated fashion. The purpose of the different people who would actually meet in "real" life, again, is for the Soul to merge back to itself its different components: desires. This allows for total integration of the Soul to occur. For this purpose to be achieved, the Soul must necessarily confront itself in the form of these different people. By confronting itself in this way, the original cause creating this situation is also confronted. In this example, it is reflected in the types of desires that are antithetical to themselves because of the accepted teaching that spirit and flesh are antagonistic. The purpose of the confrontation that the soul is posing for itself is one of changing the basis of the judgment generating the original conflict—in this case, to realize that spirit and flesh are not antagonistic.

This is a really interesting dynamic because when these different people meet in actual life, it is as if the Soul is confronting itself through the dialogues that would occur between these people. And because these people emanate from the same Soul that had a conflict relative to the nature of its different desires, the nature of these dialogues could be quite confrontational. Conversely, since these different people do emanate from the same Soul, there is an overwhelming sense of recognition of one another when they do meet. And when these people do meet, because the Soul intends to merge back to itself its different components—desires manifesting as different people—the process of reunion begins.

In the beginning of this reunion, they can manifest a resistance to one another. The reason for this is: The ego in each person has defined itself as a separate individual. This is a reflection of the separating desire inherent to the Soul. Thus, for the ego to let go of itself, to merge back to the Soul that created it, is to simultaneously ignite the fear of personal dissolution. So, in the beginning of such a dynamic, there is attraction and repulsion. Over time, such fears will subside. As they do so, the different people that the Soul has created will become even closer to one another. The last stages of this process will manifest in such a way that the different people will finally commit to one another in a marriage type of dynamic. When this occurs, it will be a relationship within the special variation called Soul Mates. When this evolutionary process culminates, the manifestation of the different people will no longer exist. The merging of the Soul's different components, reflected in antithetical desires as the different people, has occurred. Thus, the soul is now fully integrated, and ready to begin the conscious merging of itself back to its own Source—God.

TWIN SOULS

The next specialty type is called Twin Souls. Twin Souls are simply Souls that were created by God at exactly the same point in time, and who have been evolving through time and space at exactly the same rate. Twin Souls, as a result, have had almost identical lifetimes, acting upon the types of desires that are unique to nature of the Souls themselves. Thus, life after life, the types of lives the Twin Souls create are essentially identical. Twin souls look alike whether they are male or female, they will generally wear the same kinds of clothes, have the same kind of dreams, fears, thoughts, perceptions, and be psychologically and philosophically orientated to phenomenal reality in the same ways. Twin Souls are not the Same Souls as just discussed. They are separate Souls, yet Souls that are essentially identical.

Twin Souls rarely meet themselves. The reason for this is that the very purpose of relationships is to encounter or experience the nature of our personal limitations. By experiencing and confronting our limitations as they interface with another person, a metamorphosis of those limitations will occur. Thus, we evolve. Since Twin Souls are essentially identical there is no evolutionary need, requirement, or purpose for such Souls to actually meet; or to be in a relationship with one another. In all the years that I have been counseling people through astrology, which now totals over 15,000 people, I have fifteen documented cases of Twin Souls who have actually met. And out of those fifteen cases, only one set of these Souls actually tried to live together. After a short period of time, after the original fascination and amazement wore off, this couple separated because there was not any real reason to be together. They got bored always looking in the mirror, so to speak!

Of the documented cases that I have studied, what has emerged is the astrological fact that these people have almost exactly the same birth charts! In all fifteen cases, the place of birth was the same and the birth time was within minutes.

SOULS IN DIFFERENT EVOLUTIONARY STATES

The last special variation is that of Souls in different evolutionary states. It is very common for two people who are in a relationship to not be at precisely the same state of evolution. Most of the time, the difference in two people's evolutionary condition who are in an intimate relationship is not that large, and the resulting challenges and problems are minimal. Basically, the one who is evolutionarily ahead of the other person can feel like they are pulling the other person forward all the time. Nonetheless,, the other person will generally balance the relationship in other ways.

But in some cases, the difference can be quite large. This will be a big problem when this situation is also linked with the primary relationship types of the counselor/counselee or the student/teacher. When this condition exists, the one who is more advanced evolutionarily will feel quite dissatisfied because of the obvious imbalance within the roles of the relationship—yet the responsibility for this imbalance lies within the individual who is more evolutionarily advanced, because of dynamics or reasons for being in this kind of relationship type as discussed earlier under those types.

Chapter Six

Essential Relationship Needs

A key to understanding essential relationship needs is to understand the inherent archetype in the horoscope between the Second, Seventh, and Twelfth Houses. If you examine the inherent symmetry between these houses, you will notice that the Second and Twelfth Houses form inconjunctions to the Seventh House, and the Second and Twelfth Houses are in a sextile relationship to each other. Thus, there is an inherent Finger of God (Yod) aspect pattern pointing to the Seventh House. What does it mean that these houses are tied together in this way, and why should we utilize this archetype to understand the inner and outer relationship dynamics, including sexual dynamics, at all?

The answer is that the planet Venus naturally rules the signs Taurus and Libra, and that Neptune, the planetary co-ruler of Pisces, is the higher octave of Venus, Thus, since the natural zodiac has Taurus on the Second House, Libra on the Seventh House, and Pisces on the Twelfth House, there exists this natural archetype that correlates to our relationship dynamics, including our sexual dynamics. So, the first step is to understand the nature of this archetype.

To understand this archetype is to understand the inherent nature of each of its components first. The first component we will examine is the Second House and Taurus. The core archetype that Taurus or the Second House correlate with is one of *survival*—one of the deepest instincts in all human beings. Within the human being, anatomically speaking, this instinct manifests from what is known as the primary brain, which regulates all the instinctual functions of the human being. The instinct to survive has many applications and manifestations. One of these manifestations is the instinct within the human species to perpetuate itself. Thus, Taurus and the Second House correlate with the sexual instinct to procreate the species within all of us. And, yes, the sexual instinct emanates from the primary brain.

The actual reason for the human species to procreate through the act of sexual intercourse, as opposed to asexual reproduction wherein a cell simply clones itself, is a biological act of survival. Because the main danger to the integrity of the human organism occurs through viruses, bacteria, and parasites which mutate and evolve very quickly, it was and is essential that the human organism be able to evolve its own immune system in order to survive these types of assaults. In the case of asexual reproduction, the immune system remains static and fixed. To procreate the species through sexual intercourse is necessary because it allows for an ongoing evolution of the immune system through combining the genetic structures of two people into a third person. This constant evolution of the immune system thus allows for the survival of the human organism. The immune system in astrology correlates with Neptune, Pisces, and the Third House. The survival need of the species as a whole is reflected in each individual, and each individual determines the selection of a partner based on attraction. This natural selection is largely determined through a subconscious reaction to the secretion of pheromones, which emit a scent. This reaction will be either positive or negative, and thus serves as a basis of who has intercourse with who. Through this biological cue, we select partners who will produce offspring with an evolved immune system that is better able to defeat disease and infection. This, in turn, helps to guarantee the survival of the species. Pheromones are astrologically associated with Taurus, the Second House, and the inner side of Venus.

Another manifestation of the survival instinct is one of identifying what is *needed* in order to survive. This can have many applications, including identifying what resources we already have or possess in order to survive. This duality of what we already possess, combined with identifying what we need (i.e., what we do not already have) for survival to continue or be sustained thus generates the following paradoxical crisis for the human being.

On the one hand, identifying what we already have in order to survive correlates with the archetype inherent to Taurus or the Second

House—the archetype of self-reliance, self-sustainment, and self-suffi-ciency. This archetype is one of inner awareness and focusing. On the other hand, identifying what is needed (that which we do not already have) for survival to continue correlates with the archetypal awareness within consciousness that looks outside of itself in order to gather or attract that which is needed. Long ago, the human being learned that it was much easier to survive individually by forming relationships to other human beings who could live together as an organized unit. Thus, the human being, in many ways, became dependent on other human beings for survival to occur. This is not to say that the human being cannot survive completely alone. Of course, this can be done. But how many people do you know of that live in absolute isolation, surviving only through their own capacity?

The paradoxical crisis of survival is rooted in that which is already possessed within the individual, and that which is perceived to be need-ed that is outside of the individual. Astrologically, this paradoxical cri-sis is reflected in the natural inconjunct between the Second and Sev-enth Houses. It is also reflected in the inner nature of Venus (Taurus) and its outer or projected nature (Libra). Thus, psychologically speak-ing, it becomes the paradoxical crisis between the need for self-re-liance, and our dependence on others (relationships) in order to sur-vive—the procreational instinct combined with the awareness of what we do not currently have, and yet what is needed in order to survive.

Another manifestation of the instinct to survive is one of values. Why? Because whatever it is that correlates with what is needed in order to survive, or that which correlates with the resources that al-ready exist in order for survival to occur, will be *highly valued.* And that which is valued will correlate with how much *meaning* we give to it. Thus, the Second House and Taurus correlate to the meaning that we give to life, in the broadest sense. In an immediate sense, the archetypes of Taurus and the Second House correlate with the mean-ing we give to *ourselves* and, through extension, the meaning we give to other people. This, of course, is dependent on how much we val-ue both ourselves and others.

Astrologically speaking, the sign on the Second House cusp, the lo-cation of its planetary ruler by house and sign, plus the aspects that planet makes to other planets, will condition how the archetype of the Second House is oriented to and actualized by any individual. In ad-dition, the location of the sign Taurus in the horoscope and its natur-al ruler Venus by its own house/sign, plus the aspects that it is making to other planets, will condition the archetypes inherent to those hous-es with the archetypes intrinsic to Taurus. In composite charts, these same principles apply to how the couple orients to actualizing these archetypes. Later on, when we discuss an actual case history, these principles will seem more clear.

The next component of this archetype is the Seventh House and Libra. The core archetype of the Seventh House and Libra is of the *initiation of relationships* with other human beings. The initiation of re-lationships has as its casual factor the projected need for survival that emanates from the Second House and Taurus. The projection of these needs from the Second House and Taurus to the Seventh House and Libra occurs through the inconjunction that links these archetypes. Through the Seventh House and Libra we initiate relationships with a diversity of people in order to discriminate (inconjunct) between those people who reflect what we need, versus those people who do not. Once the individual determines which people can best meet what it needs, needs that are now projected, the basis of expectations simul-taneously occurs. That which we expect from other people, and they from us, in order for the projected needs of each to be met, is the causal factor for conditional giving, sharing, or love.

The inconjunction also teaches the human being that it must also learn to give to others in order to secure or receive what itself needs. In order to give others what they need, the human being must learn how to *listen*. Venus (the co-ruler of Libra and Taurus) correlates with the psychology of hearing, whereas Mercury rules the anatomy that exists within the ear. By learning how to listen, the human being learns how to objectify itself—to experience itself and others objec-tively. In this way, the human being is learning *equality*. The Seventh House and Libra teach the human being to equally give and receive. When the balance of giving and receiving within relationships is dis-proportionate, a crisis (inconjunct) within the relationships will occur. The crisis created in this way is necessary in order for the relation-ships that we form to become adjusted. In this way, we achieve a state of balance, and the roles become equal.

The inconjunction between these archetypes will also create a cri-sis when the individual either becomes too dependent on others, or when others become too dependent on the individual. When exces-sive dependence occurs in this way, crisis occurs within the relation-ship in order for an adjustment to happen. The effect is to enforce ac-tualization of the Second House and Taurus archetype of self-reliance.

The inconjunction that links the Second House and Taurus to the Seventh House and Libra has another primary function—to define a person's individual identity. This occurs as a person compares or evaluates him or herself through interrelating with other people. In essence, it is through social interaction that people become aware of who they are as individuals. Through comparison and evaluation, people become aware of that which is unique and individual about themselves. In the same way, they also become aware of that which is unique and individual about other people. In this way, they become aware of their roles within the relationships that they form, and the function of the relationship.

The function of the relationship describes the reason for the relationship—the *purpose* of the relationship. The function, reason, and purpose of the relationship restates the expectations that we have for it, the roles that are created for those expectations to be met, and the relative dependence that is generated in order for the needs and expectations to be met.

In the individual chart, the sign on the Seventh House cusp, the location of its planetary ruler by house and sign, along with the aspects that planet makes to other planets, will condition how the individual actualizes the Seventh House archetype. In addition, the location of the sign of Libra in the chart, the house and sign locality of its ruler Venus, and Venus' aspects to other planets will condition the inherent archetypes of those houses relative to the archetypes of Libra and Venus.

In composite charts, the nature of the signs and houses that these archetypes are conditioned by, along with the sign and house locality of Venus and the aspects that it is making to other planets, will describe how the couple understands and actualizes the reason, function, and purpose for their relationship. The archetypes symbolized by the composite chart will reflect how each of the individual's needs (symbolized in their natal horoscopes) *combine* in a relationship. By combining the individual needs in a relationship, the needs of the relationship itself are symbolized by the sign on the composite Seventh House cusp, the location of its planetary ruler, and the aspects that it is making to other planets. These symbols will correlate with the relationship's capacity to fulfill each individual's needs. In addition, these archetypes will show how the couple defines their roles within the relationship in order for their mutually projected needs to be met, along with the relative balance or imbalance in these roles. The inherent inconjunction between the Seventh House sign and the Second House sign, and the locality of the planetary rulers for those signs by their own house and sign placement, will correlate with what types of crises could occur, and what the causes may be. This inconjunction also correlates to the creation of a crisis within the relationship when the relationship cannot meet the individual needs of one or both partners.

The last component of the inherent archetype being discussed is the Twelfth House, Pisces, and Neptune. The core archetype here is one of *transcendence*. Transcendence of what? No less than the confines of time and space or place. This archetype reflects the desire in all human beings to search for or embrace an ultimate purpose or meaning for life itself. Anatomically, this desire or impulse emanates from the pineal gland within the brain. Astrologically, this gland correlates with Neptune. This gland secrets a hormone called melatonin. This hormone is responsible for many things including sleep, dreams, imagination, creativity, revelations from on high, insanity, and, from an evolutionary point of view, the spiritualization of consciousness. Psychologically, this archetype reflects the intention or motivation inherent within consciousness to search for the higher or ultimate meaning for the totality of what we call life. This is especially true when the human being experiences cataclysmic evolutionary or karmic events.

Because this archetype correlates with transcendence or the search for ultimate meaning or purpose, the linkage to the Seventh House or Libra via the inconjunction correlates to the person's conscious or unconscious ideals that are projected into its relationship needs. This projection becomes the basis of idealistic expectations that we have in the relationships that we form—the desire for the "perfect" relationship. In addition, unless or until an individual truly acts upon the transcendent impulse for him or herself, this archetype explains why so many people unconsciously or consciously make their partners *de facto* gods and goddesses. In essence, they project the ultimate meaning that the Twelfth House, Pisces, or Neptune correlates to upon the partner. When projected through the Seventh House, Libra, or the projected nature of Venus (not the inner nature of Venus) in these ways, a crisis will result at some point. The nature of such a crisis is one of *disillusionment*. One realizes that the partner is not perfect, the partner is not a god or goddess, the projected ideals manifesting as unrealistic expectations not being realized, the partner is not who they seemed to be at the beginning of the relationship, and so on.

The crisis of disillusionment is necessary in order for the human being to readjust the focus within its consciousness. Instead of projecting the Twelfth House, Pisces, or Neptune's search for transcendence or ultimate meaning upon the partner, each or us, at some point, will focus and act upon this desire and need from within ourselves. The inherent sextile from the Twelfth House and Pisces to the Second House and Taurus correlates with the intention, evolutionarily speaking, within the Soul to relate to itself in a transcendent way, and to establish a relationship with the Ultimate Source of All Things from within itself. Thus, that which is valued, and the meaning we give to that which is valued through the Second House or Taurus, changes. It changes from the temporal (time and space equaling the immediacy of what we need in order to survive) to that which is transcendent or ultimate. When this occurs, each of us will relate differently not only to ourselves, but also to other people.

Instead of trying to make our partners into gods and goddesses, we will realize that each human being has innate divinity within him or herself because all of us have been created by the Ultimate Source of All Things. Instead of projecting our ultimate ideals upon a partner, we will actualize those ideals for ourselves. Instead of seeking our ultimate sense of meaning in our partners, we will discover this meaning from within ourselves by embracing a spiritual teaching or path. When the crisis of disillusionment manifests one too many times, the necessary adjustment that will lead to this shift of focus within our consciousness will create a vibrational shift in our emotional, mental and physical bodies.

Then effect of this, in essence, will be that instead of projecting the search and desire for ultimate meaning outwards, the projection is now inward—toward self-reliance. The inner nature of Venus now actualizes its higher octave, Neptune, to create a vibrational shift from within the human being that will allow it to attract (Venus) other people who have achieved this shift for themselves. The shift is also reflected in the natural linkage between the Second and Twelfth Houses because of the natural planetary rulers of each being Venus and Neptune.

It must also be remembered that the Twelfth House, Pisces, and Neptune all correlate with the potential for sadomasochistic psychological behavior in relationships. The root of this, again, is reflected in the Garden of Eden myth, or any religious teaching that pretends that man is superior to woman, or that woman is the cause of man's spiritual downfall through the "temptation" of the flesh.

In an individual's chart, the sign on the Twelfth House, the location of its planetary ruler by house and sign, and the aspects it makes to other planets will correlate with the ultimate ideals that he or she projects onto other people through the Seventh House. The types of experiences that will lead to a necessary disillusionment in order to readjust the individual's focus will also be described in these symbols. Pisces and its ruling planet Neptune will condition the inherent archetypes of the houses and signs that they occupy. In composite charts, these same symbols will correlate with what ideals the relationship has for itself, what constitutes the sense of ultimate meaning for the relationship, how this is actualized, and what kinds of unconscious projections may occur in order to readjust the focus of the relationship.

A NOTE ON RETROGRADES

A retrograde archetype also serves to accelerate the evolution of the Soul. It does so by rejecting or rebelling against the consensus expectation of how the planet that is retrograde should be actualized. A planet that is retrograde will feel disconnected from the consensus—it does not fit. Thus, the experience of feeling disconnected promotes a psychological withdrawal from the consensus, and a feeling of isolation results. But the positive function of this process is this—by internalizing the function of a planet that is retrograde, a natural *individuation* of the planet begins. The person with the retrograde planet is required to experience and define the planetary archtype personally. This evolutionary process of individuation promotes and accelerates the evolutionary progression of an individual.

The Soul will manifest the retrograde archetype at key points in its evolution, and this will occur in all four natural evolutionary states over a series of lifetimes. This is so because it typically takes the Soul more than one lifetime to fully individuate and actualize the intention and nature of the planet that is retrograde. Once this has been accomplished, the function of that planet will then become stabilized, and manifest in a direct way for a series of lifetimes. This evolutionary process of planets going back and forth between retrograde and direct extends to all the planets, at all levels of the four natural evolutionary conditions or states, until the last stage of the spiritual state of evolution is finally realized.

On a behavioral level, a planet that is retrograde reflects an instinctual impulse to rebel against or disengage from existing conditions in order to continue the individuation process. The retrograde archetype emphasizes individual development and that which is needed in order for this to be accomplished. As a result, an individual may initiate many situations or conditions that are not necessarily followed through or completed. This is precisely why the retrograde planet can reflect reliving or repeating past life conditions in the current life. The intention is to finish or resolve such conditions or dynamics—otherwise, they will continue to be repeated until they are resolved.

A NOTE ON INTERCEPTED SIGNS

Classical or traditional astrology has presented the phenomena of intercepted signs as archetypal qualities that are deeply buried in the unconscious of the individual, and that normally remain dormant or unmanifested. However, at key points in the individual's life, these unconscious archetypes will become activated and developed by transiting planets moving through these signs, by progressions of planets activating the planetary rulers of the intercepted signs, by transits of the planetary rulers of the intercepted signs, by transits to planets in the intercepted signs, or by having the intercepted signs rising on a current solar return chart.

But what classical astrology does not mention is that, in many cases, there can also be evolutionary reasons that signs are intercepted. From this view, the main reason is that those archetypal qualities or dynamics have been so thoroughly developed prior to the current life that they not longer need active development. The Soul now intends to emphasize other archetypal dynamics or qualities that it needs to develop in order for its evolution to proceed. This is no different than having the elements water, fire, earth, or air unemphasized—zero earth, for example. Classical astrology would say that zero earth would correlate to a person who has no intrinsic capacity to be responsible, honor their obligations, lacks self-determination, is unable to accept the responsibility for their own actions, and so on. And yet many individuals who have zero earth are the very essence of those dynamics. They are born with these abilities highly developed at birth.

Classical astrology has clearly missed something. Once we embrace the evolutionary view of life, then this missing piece is rapidly understood. The real question becomes this: How do we know, in evolutionary terms, who is who? How can we determine, astrologically speaking, which individuals have already developed the archetypal dynamics or qualities symbolized in the intercepted signs, or elements, and which have not? There is a way.

In the case of intercepted signs, determine the condition of the planetary rulers of the signs intercepted. If these planets are highly emphasized through many aspects from other planets, then the archetypal dynamics or qualities symbolized by the intercepted signs have been developed prior to this life. If they are lightly aspected and not conjunct a major angle in the chart, then those dynamics or archetypal qualities symbolized by the intercepted signs have not been emphasized prior to the current life. At various points in the current life they will become worked upon, as stated above.

In addition, examine the natural houses of the signs intercepted. For example, in the case of the woman we will be studying in the next section, Aquarius is intercepted in the Second House, Leo is intercepted in the Eighth House, and the planetary ruler of the South Node (Neptune) is located in her Eleventh House. This would demonstrate that the Eleventh House or Aquarius archetype has obviously been actualized prior to the current life. And with her Sun, the planetary ruler of the intercepted Eighth House Leo, forming a trine aspect to the Eighth House Pluto, an inconjunction to the North Node (which is linked with her past via its planetary ruler Mercury being conjunct the South Node), and a square to her Capricorn Moon, the Leo archetype has been clearly actualized prior to this life.

In the case of lacking elements, zero earth for example, simply determine if the houses which naturally correlate with the elements are occupied by a planet or not. If a person had zero earth, yet the natural earth houses in his or her horoscope is occupied by some planet, then this would demonstrate that the Earth archetype has been developed to some degree prior to this life. If not, then the classical understanding would apply.

AN ASTROLOGICAL CASE STUDY

At this point, it will be useful to embark on a sometimes harrowing case study of the most destructive of the relationship types in order to illustrate the principles thus far discussed. The birthchart (Chart #4) we are now considering has the following astrological signature:

- Capricorn is on the Second House cusp, with the sign Aquarius intercepted within it. Because of Aquarius being intercepted, this house will have *two* archetypes that condition the natural archetype of the Second House, and two planetary rulers to consider: Saturn and Uranus.

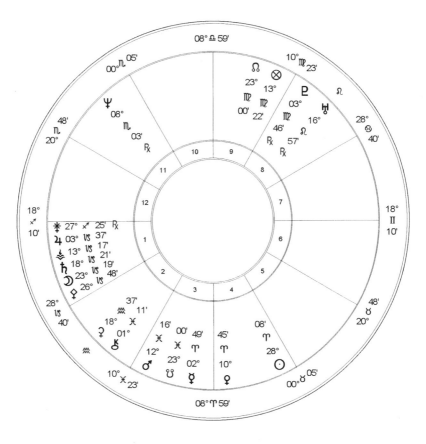

Chart #4

- Saturn, the planetary ruler of Capricorn, is located in the sign Capricorn in the First House, conjunct the Capricorn Moon. Saturn is making the following aspects: Quintile to Eleventh House Neptune retrograde in Scorpio; quintile to Third House Mercury in Aries; inconjunct to Eighth House Uranus in Leo; and a sesquiquadrate to Eighth House Pluto retrograde in Virgo.

- Uranus, the planetary ruler of Aquarius, is retrograde in the sign Leo in the Eighth House, and is making aspects to the following planets: Inconjunct to Third House Mars in Pisces; trine to Fourth House Venus in Aries; sesquiquadrate to Third House Mercury in Aries; sesquiquadrate to First House Jupiter in Capricorn; inconjunct to

First House Saturn in Capricorn; and square to Eleventh House Neptune in Scorpio.

- Gemini is on the Seventh House cusp.

- Mercury, Gemini's planetary ruler, is in Aries in the Third House.

- Mercury is making aspects to the following planets: Conjunct Venus in Aries in the Fourth House; square Jupiter in Capricorn in the First House; inconjunct Pluto retrograde in Virgo in the Eighth House; and inconjunct Neptune retrograde in Scorpio in the Eleventh House. Thus, Mercury is the focus of a Yod or Finger of God involving Neptune and Pluto. It is also forming a sesquiquadrate to retrograde Uranus in Leo in the Eighth House.

- Scorpio is on the Twelfth House cusp.

- Pluto, Scorpio's planetary ruler, is located in the Eighth House in the sign Virgo. It is making the following aspects: Trine to First House Jupiter in Capricorn; opposition to Third House Mars in Pisces; and opposition to Second House Chiron in Pisces.

Before we being to analyze this pattern, it is important to understand a few things. This is a birthchart of a woman who was born in the United States, but who was raised primarily in Germany by parents who were stationed there in the United States Army. She was subjected to strict religious upbringing of a Roman Catholic nature, and was sent to religious schools of this type. Evolutionarily speaking, she was in the third stage of the individuated state or condition. Racially speaking, she was Caucasian. These factors, again, are very important to consider before you attempt to analyze the chart, or any other chart.

From my point of view, the understanding of any birthchart must start by embracing the past life dynamics that have lead to or "set up" the current life. The core evolutionary/karmic foundation in this chart is symbolized first by retrograde Pluto in Virgo in the Eighth House, forming the aspects as defined above, and second by the South Node in Pisces in the Third House, and its planetary ruler Neptune, which is retrograde in Scorpio in the Eleventh House. Neptune is trine Mars in Pisces in the Third House, inconjunct Venus in Aries in the Fourth House, and quintile to the Moon in Capricorn in the First House. The South Node is making a conjunction to Mercury in Aries—the focus of a Yod or Finger of God aspect pattern. Since Mercury is the planetary ruler of the North Node (Virgo in the Ninth House), yet is conjunct the South Node, a special evolutionary and karmic condition exists. Past life conditions, dynamics, and situations are being relived in the current life. Since Mercury is the planetary ruler of the Seventh House, these will obviously involve key relationships with people she has known in other lives.

This reliving of key relationships can also be seen by the fact that Mercury is the focus of inconjunctions from Neptune and Pluto, which are retrograde. Evolutionarily speaking, a planet that is retrograde correlates with repeating or reliving past life conditions in order to resolve those conditions in the current life.

Our analysis will start by an understanding of the past life dynamics and evolutionary intentions that have lead her into this life, and the reasons for repeating those past life conditions in this life. With Pluto retrograde in Virgo in the Eighth House, relative to the third stage of the individuated state or condition, she has had past life desires to experientially understand the essential truths, laws or reason for the basis of life itself. Why life, why death? These two questions have motivated her to explore a diversity (Third House South Node) of knowledge systems of a transcultural nature (South Node in Pisces, relative to Neptune retrograde in Scorpio in the Eleventh House) in order to answer these questions in the fullest possible way.

With Pluto being retrograde in Virgo, her Soul structure is defined by that which it lacks. It creates the feeling of an existential void that needs to be filled up with something. Because this is occurring in the Eighth House, relative to the South Node being in the Third House, this slack or void is filled up with information or knowledge of an Eighth House nature. Both Virgo and the Third House correlate with the mental body, and the Eighth House correlates with the emotional or sensation body. Thus, she has investigated ideas or knowledge system intended to intensely develop or actualize her emotional or sensation body. This could include reading about the lives of other people, learning about psychology, intense discussions with individuals who symbolized something that she was interested in or needed, investigating and thinking about the nature of sexuality or sexual energy, investigating various forms of magic or occult laws, and so on.

With the South Node in Pisces, she would also have desired to understand and investigate the nature of spiritual law in order to develop the spiritual body. With the South Node's ruler being in Scorpio in the Eleventh House, she would have found herself very attracted to other people who were social iconoclasts—others who felt they did not fit into the "system," just as she did not. In this evolutionary condition, the South Node in Pisces has felt persecuted by the system. With its ruler being in the Eleventh House, this would have also created lifetimes in which she sought out communities of people who also felt persecuted—communities that were formed by "like-minded" individuals who could then feel safe enough to explore "alternative" ways of living, and investigating the nature of life itself.

Because her Soul is defined by what it lacks, her Eighth House Pluto retrograde in Virgo has attracted powerful people who symbolized the knowledge and experiences that she was seeking. Yet the intention of the Eighth House retrograde Pluto has been for her to also actualize her own power and knowledge, as discovered from within. This intention can be seen by Pluto's trine to Jupiter in Capricorn in the First House, its inconjunction to Mercury in Aries in the Third House, and its opposition to Mars in Pisces in the Third House. In effect, this creates a paradox at the Soul level. On the one hand, her Soul is defined through what it lacks, which creates a compulsion to join with other people who can bring her the knowledge, information, and emotional/sexual experiences that she thinks she needs. On the other hand, she will rebel against this as she desires to empower and actualize herself from within. As a result of this paradox, she has created a pattern over many lifetimes in which she has used and manipulated people for her own purposes, and others have used and manipulated her for their own purposes. The basis of this pattern is reflected in Pluto's opposition to Mars in Pisces in the Third House. In essence, her soul has had desires for self-actualization that have been so diverse and contradictory in nature that it is deeply conflicted within itself.

The basis of this inner split or conflict is caused by the nature of her desires. The essence of these desires is to experience the totality of herself. This is seen in Pluto trine the Sun, trine Jupiter, in opposition to the third house Mars in Pisces, and in the South Node in Pisces in the Third House relative to its planetary ruler Neptune in Scorpio in the Eleventh House. The Sun equals totality and creative self-actualization. The Third House equals diversity of life experience and the restlessness born because of the need for diversity. The Eleventh House equals the desire to rebel against any restriction of personal freedom. Neptune in Scorpio in the Eleventh House equals the desire to know or understand the mystery of life and herself in the fullest possible way.

How we interpret life is based on our beliefs. Beliefs, astrologically speaking, correlate with Jupiter, Sagittarius, and the Ninth House. With her Jupiter in Capricorn linked through a trine to Pluto in Virgo, the nature of her beliefs is conditioned by dogmatic, strict, and negatively judgmental religions that try to control or suppress the life of the body or flesh. To deviate from these beliefs, to explore and experience desires that conflict with these beliefs, is to create guilt and negative judgments upon herself.

Yet her Soul also desires to rebel against being controlled by anyone or anything. The South Node's ruler is in the Eleventh House, Aquarius is intercepted in the Second House, retrograde Uranus in Leo forms inconjunctions to Mars, Saturn, and the Moon, and is at the apex of a Yod. In addition, Venus, Mercury, and the Sun are in Aries, and the Moon, Jupiter, and Saturn are in the natural Aries House (the First). In effect, her Soul has desired to lose control of itself, to be free to experience her totality, to surrender (Mars in Pisces, South Node in Pisces, Pisces ruled by Neptune) to any source of power that would allow her to discover herself through the act of surrendering to it. And yet this very desire has created the fear of losing control, of being overpowered, of the ego dissolving into nothing. This fear manifests from Pluto's opposition to Mars, Jupiter, Saturn, and the Moon being in the natural Aries House, and her Venus, Mercury and Sun being in Aries. This inner paradox and conflict has defined her Soul for many lifetimes, and generated two alternating and unpredictable behavioral patterns that have created a pattern of suffering, intense pain, and turmoil for herself and many other people.

Thus, there are two paradoxes in her Soul. The first is her drive to self-empowerment and independence versus the feeling of inner lack that compels her to seek powerful, controlling people. The second is the desire to actualize her totality through surrendering to all her desires versus the desire to control and suppress those desires because of the fear of losing control.

One pattern or cycle would find her in an absolutely hedonistic orientation to life, and the other cycle or pattern would find her in an absolutely austere and repressed orientation to life because of the guilt and desire for atonement that was created in the hedonistic cycle. Because of the fear of losing control which simultaneously exists with her *desire* to lose control, she has cyclically been attracted to religions that were control-oriented and that would offer rituals (Pluto in the Eighth House) that would allow her to "purify" herself and to atone for her guilt.

The inner conflict has created a situation over many lifetimes in which she has always lived at extremes. It is because of these two alternating cycles of extreme behavior that she has created a deep inner confusion about who she is, what she desires, and what motivates her and other people. By trying to control herself on a cyclic basis through external religions that negatively judge the life of the body, flesh, emotions, and sexuality, she has created the very cause of negative inner judgments when her other desires manifest. She tries to control and suppress these desires (Pluto in Virgo relative to Mars in Pisces), but when they are suppressed they become distorted at a subconscious level, and have manifested anyway in the form of the circumstantial realities that she has created, and in the form of intense relationships with people who symbolized her total desire nature.

On a cyclic basis she would be attracted to such people, and form relationships to them. The different people that she has been attracted to over many lifetimes would represent some kind of experience that she desired; yet she would not be able to accept or understand that the desire emanated from herself. Her typical comment to me when she was a client would be: "He seemed curious to me (Mars in the Third House) and I wanted to find out what was so curious about him". Or another typical comment: "He talked me into it, and I just went along with it." These types of comments illustrate the dynamics of denying the nature of her own desires, and becomes the causal factor in creating a consciousness of victimization in which she can blame others for that which emanates from herself.

Because of this inner conflict, she would only maintain relationships for certain periods of time, and would then terminate the relationships. Even in this life, when she was my client, she had many relationships; all of which she herself had terminated. She had never been left by anyone. Why has she always been the person leaving a relationship first? What kind of karmic consequences does this create?

The answer to the first question is linked to her own inner paradoxes. Because she is unable to consciously accept the nature of her total desire nature, and thus unable to understand the link between what she desires and the circumstantial realities that she has created over many lifetimes, she has attracted many people over many lifetimes who have symbolized the nature of her own desires that she is unable to "own" for herself. Thus, she would be attracted to these people for a period of time, but would then rebel against them as her guilt-ridden, anti-flesh religious conditioning took over. The cyclic termination of these types of relationships would always occur with her assuming the role of victim and blaming others for the very nature of her own desires and the behavior that these desires would create. Because these desires had been distorted through the cyclic suppression of them, the types of people that she attracted would themselves be reflections of her own inner dishonesty, psychological/behavioral extremes, and embody the very nature of her own inner distortions which had been created through suppression of her total desire nature.

This pattern or dynamic has been in place for many lifetimes. Because Pluto is in Virgo relative to its opposition to Mars in Pisces, and because Jupiter, Saturn, and the Moon are in Capricorn, she has built up a tremendous amount of guilt and rage. She feels guilty about her total desire nature, and the experiences that it has generated over many lifetimes. She also feels guilty for the many people that she has hurt and punished through the act of leaving them. This guilt is then linked with the need to atone for it. She has an unresolved anger and rage because she allowed herself to be "talked into" experiences that she would then rebel against and attempt to disown. All of this in combination creates, in psychological terms, a passive/aggressive type or, more accurately, a sadomasochist who would cyclically manifest a sadistic or masochistic pathology depending on the nature of her specific circumstances which are created by the two extreme alternating paradoxical dynamics that have occurred within herself.

Thus, she would always leave people first for three reasons. First, because of the cyclic suppression of her total desire nature. When in the guilt/atonement cycle, she would deny her sensual nature by leaving an individual who was the very symbol of her own desires. Second, because of the built-up rage and anger of "being talked into experiences." This is a reflection of a victimized consciousness that is denying the nature of its own desires, and thus creates the need to hurt or victimize others first. It is a sadistic pathology which is born out of a masochistic pathology.

The third reason is the most complex, because of her emotional paradox linked with relationships in the first place. On one side is her desire for absolute freedom in order to actualize herself without the constraints that her perception of relationships would impose. In her birth chart (Chart #4), we see Venus and Mercury in Aries forming inconjunctions to Pluto in Virgo in the Eighth House, and forming squares to Jupiter in Capricorn in the First House. Pluto forms an opposition to Mars in Pisces in the Third House.

On the other side is her desire for relationships with people who symbolize something that she feels she lacks. Pluto in Virgo in the Eighth House, again, is a Soul that is defined by that which it lacks. Relative to the Eighth House Pluto, she has used her sexual nature to seduce or attract others that represent that which she wants or needs from them. She would then leave such people once the needs and desires that attracted her to these people were satisfied.

Virgo is also an archetype that can deny the actual reality that is occurring. Thus, by denying the nature of her own total desire nature, she has been attracted to others who embody the nature of the desires that she herself denies and feels she lacks, yet actually wants to fulfill. After all, these desires are emanating from herself whether she consciously accepts this or not. But once the denial cycle starts, she would rebel against her partner and the dynamics that were occurring in the relationship This again is an inner rebellion based on cyclic denial of her total desire nature.

Karmically speaking, these dynamics create a very difficult situation. Beyond the consequential karmic requirement to repeat or relive past life connections and dynamics with individuals she has known over many lifetimes in which there are unresolved issues, the very nature of the dynamics that have defined her relationships with other people creates a very difficult karmic and evolutionary condition for herself and others. The essence of this karmic and evolutionary situation can be summarized by the following:

- A karma of manipulating and using others relative to an essential dishonesty that is based on denying the nature of her own desires, and an inability to accept the responsibility for her own actions.

- A karma of being used and manipulated by others who are themselves reflections of her own dishonesty. In other words, people who themselves are in a state of denying the nature of their own desires, or are unable to be honest about the nature of their motivations and intentions.

- A karma of blaming others for the nature of her own actions and behaviors that reflect desires that are being inwardly denied. Thus, she will attract others who will project upon her, or blame her, for that which is a reflection of their own inner denial.

- A karma rooted in betraying other people's trust and abandoning others who have become dependent on her. This karma will create a situation in which she will attract to herself individuals whom she has betrayed and abandoned, and these people will have a deep-seated need and desire to get even with her. The manifestation of this karma will have many applications as we shall see later in the book.

- A sexual karma which is based on a fundamental emotional, spiritual, and sexual dishonesty. This karma is further complicated by the fact that she has had sexual desires, over many lifetimes, of wanting to dominate and be dominated. Inherently, the desires of wanting to dominate and be dominated have no karmic implications. The karma is created through the core dishonesty of her Soul, which is unable to own or accept the nature of these desires, and thus is unable to express or relate to others in an honest way the nature of her intentions or motivations. In addition, she has commonly used her sexual nature to attract to herself other people in order to actualize what she wanted from them, leaving or abandoning them once she got what she wanted. Within this karma, she has also had desires to investigate sexual "taboos," as defined by various cultures and religions over many lifetimes. Here again, the karma is created and linked to her core dishonesty and inability to own the nature of her own motivations, intentions, and desires.

With the North Node in Virgo in the Ninth House, one of the deepest evolutionary lessons that she will bring into this life is one of absolute honesty at all levels of her spiritual, emotional, intellectual, physical, and sexual being. She will learn this through the creation of one life crisis after another, the theme of crisis permeating her very existence. The theme of crisis can be seen everywhere in her horoscope, including the Yod between Pluto, Neptune, and the Mercury/Venus conjunction; the Yod between the Saturn/Moon conjunction, Mars, and Uranus; the Pluto/Mars opposition; and Chiron in Pisces in opposition to Pluto in Virgo. The nature of crisis will always lead to analysis, and analysis linked with crisis will produce self-knowledge at some point. Her Soul's intention is to remove the psychological dynamic of the inner denial of her own total desire nature, to learn to point the finger at herself instead of other people, to evolve into a philosophy or belief system that is rooted in natural law (Ninth House) instead of manmade laws or doctrines. This will then allow her to inwardly unite the world of spirit and flesh instead of believing that they are inherently in conflict, to accept responsibility in her own actions (Moon, Saturn, and Jupiter in Capricorn), and to learn an essential self-reliance, self-empowerment, and self-validation (Pluto's polarity point in the Second House). In addition, her Soul intends to unite the emotional paradoxes that dictate her cyclic behavior, and to purge the built-up rage and anger that has occurred because of the perception of victimization that she has created in many lifetimes. When all of this occurs, she will finally evolve into a consciousness of compassion (Ninth House) for who she totally is, and she will learn to extend this compassion to not only herself, but to all others.

Now that we have begun to understand the past-life dynamics that have brought her into this life, we will focus our attention on the astrological principles and methods that will allow you to determine how all of us attract to ourselves that which we desire in relationship—even if we do not know that we need or desire it! We will be applying each of these astrological methods step by step, and illustrating each step by referring to Chart #4.

First, we will examine the meaning of Capricorn on the Second House cusp with its planetary ruler, Saturn, located in Capricorn in the First House conjunct the Moon, square the Sun in Aries in the Fourth House, inconjunct retrograde Uranus in Leo in the Eighth House, sesquiquadrate Pluto in the Eighth House, quintile retrograde Neptune in Scorpio in the Eleventh House, quintile Mercury in Aries in the Third House, and trine the North Node in Virgo in the Ninth House.

Since Aquarius is intercepted in the Second House, we will also examine its archetypal meaning and how it manifests. With its planetary ruler Uranus at the focus of a Yod, making an inconjunction to Mars in Pisces in the Third House, sesquiquadrate Jupiter in Capricorn in the First House, and trine Venus in Aries in the Fourth House, there are many archetypal dynamics to consider in the analysis of the Second House. The key principles of the Second House, again, are:

- The survival instinct, which includes the procreational instinct in order for the species to survive.

- The resources one has in order for survival to occur.

- The awareness of resources that we do not have, yet need from others in order for survival to occur.

- The resources that are needed in order for survival to occur and continue thus equals the value and meaning we give to ourselves,

• The archetype of self-sufficiency, self-reliance, and the inner relationship one has with oneself: the inner side of Venus.

Psychologically speaking, the deepest survival instinct that she has relative to Capricorn on the Second House is one of self-determination
(Capricorn). Relative to her evolutionary condition, the third stage of
the individuated state, the Capricorn archetype would create a deeply
introspective person who would develop a natural perception into the
structural nature of the society, parental conditions, and global reality
that she was born into. Based on this perception, she would understand
how "the system" worked, and would inwardly realize that she did not
fit into it (Aquarius intercepted in the Second House relative to her evolutionary condition). Therefore, her survival instinct would manifest as
not allowing her to integrate into society. In other words, to survive
means standing outside, or apart from, mainstream reality. The Aquarius interception creates a core detachment from parental and societal reality. She has learned, and is learning, to relate to herself as disconnected from reality, the way most people live and understand it.
Inwardly, she feels very different than most other people.

   With the planetary ruler of Capricorn (Saturn) located in the First
House conjunct the Capricorn Moon, these perceptions and realizations occurred early on in her life. Her father was in the military and
reflected a rigid orientation to life; a life defined by conformity to authoritarian norms, customs, laws, and procedures. Accordingly, he was
emotionally remote and unavailable to her as a child. This had the effect of driving her deeply within herself and of creating an inner compression that induced her perceptions and realizations. This was compounded by a mother who was also emotionally isolated by her father.
Accordingly, the mother was deeply emotionally frustrated and progressively withdrew from any meaningful emotional interaction with
her children. She also worked for the military and was gone during the
day, as was the father. The mother was very religious (the
Saturn/Moon conjunction is trine the North Node in the Ninth House
Virgo) and put this woman in Catholic schools. In these schools, she
was expected to conform to rigid, dogmatic, and righteous teachings
that were devoid of any inner substance.

   In fact, in this school she had one particular teacher (a nun) who
singled her out for various forms of punishment, including not being
allowed to go to the toilet when she badly needed to. She was told to
"hold and control it" until she was "allowed" to perform this natural

function. This only had the effect of igniting her core detachment (Aquarius intercepted in the Second House) from "the system," as well as a detachment from her body (Pluto sesquiquadrate Saturn in the First House, Uranus inconjunct Saturn). Because of past-life dynamics in which she would cyclically act upon all kinds of sexual desires of a "taboo" nature, and because she had used her sexuality to seduce people in order to manipulate them relative to "getting" something from them that she needed, the build-up of guilt leading to the need to atone becomes the causal factor creating the conditions of being "punished" in this life by the nun/teacher. The essence of this punishment, archetypally, was a form of "humiliation." Thus, her inner relationship to herself was based on feelings that she was not a good person. And, of course, as a child and young woman she could not know why.

This core detachment fueled the survival instinct of self-determination. She learned to stand on her own two feet early in her life as a result of these early life conditions (Saturn/Moon conjunction in Capricorn in the First House). In essence, she learned to survive in spite of these conditions, and was determined to do so. She learned early in her life that she could only rely on herself, because there was no meaningful interaction from her immediate environment.

She did not fit into "the system" and could not conform to its dictates, and was therefore made to feel guilty. With the Saturn/Moon in the First House, an Aries House, her Soul desired an absolute freedom or independence to do and become whatever she wanted to. Yet because of the past-life dynamics that we just discussed, she has cyclically needed to control and judge herself, and to suppress her total desire nature. This pattern over many lifetimes becomes the causal factor from within her own Soul that has created these early-life conditions of emotional deprivation, psychological constraint, and punishment.

As a child, she would not be aware of past-life conditions. She was only aware that she did not fit into her parents' reality, and that she did not fit into her religious school. She was born in the U.S. but taken to Germany as a child, so she did not even grow up in her own country of origin—she was displaced and detached. The nature of German society is quite different than American society. It is a highly structured society based on emotional control—at least outwardly. In fact, the German language does not even have a word for emotion that is intrinsic to the language itself. These facts are very important to understand because the very essence of this woman is emotion (South Node in Pisces, ruled by Neptune, Mars in Pisces, Venus, Mercury, and the Sun in Aries, Venus and the Sun in the natural Cancer House, and Pluto in the natural Scorpio House). As a child, she could only be aware of what was lacking in her environment based on her circumstantial conditions, as indicated by Pluto, the Soul structure, being in Virgo.

Based on her awareness of what was lacking in her early life, and because the essence of her Soul is emotion, she learned to compensate by two specific kinds of activities that further served her need to survive her environment—by extensive reading of fictional material, and by playing alone outside in the context of nature in which she could run free. These activities served to ignite her Soul's desires to understand the mystery of herself and life in general, to understand the higher purposes of life, and to keep her detached from mainstream reality in order to continue her evolution in the individuated condition. They also served to formulate what she came to value as an adult, the meaning she gave to herself and others in general, and how she learned to relate to herself and others. These two survival methods are indicated by the Saturn/Moon conjunction forming a sextile to the Third House South Node in Pisces, trine the Ninth House North Node in Virgo, forming quintiles to the Eleventh House Neptune in Scorpio and Third House Mercury in Aries, and forming an inconjunction to the retrograde Uranus in Leo in the Eighth House.

As a child, the extensive reading of fiction allowed her to live through other characters or personalities, creating a deep and active fantasy life in which she could escape from the immediacy of her environment. She learned to survive by vicariously living through self-created fantasy. In effect, she detached from her environment and her own actual inner reality and learned to relate to herself by imagining or pretending to be the identities of the people she was reading about in her books. With retrograde Uranus in Leo in the Eighth House at the focus of the Yod between her Saturn/Moon conjunction and Mars in Pisces, she "actualized" herself in this way (Leo is the archetype of self-actualization). Here again, you can see the link to past-life dishonesty, and an inability to own or accept her own reality—the nature of her own desires, motivations, and intentions. By immersing herself in Nature (outside of the structure of her home and family, away from the religious school), she was unconsciously compensating for the rigid control of her immediate environment. Also, even as a child, she had a keen perception of structure as stated above. She was trying to understand the higher meanings of life, in her own childlike way, by uniting with Nature in her outside activities. She would sit silently for long periods of time letting Nature infuse her with its life force.

When she became twelve years old, the emotional frustration that her mother was experiencing with her father led to a divorce—the natal signature of Uranus forming an inconjunction to the Saturn/Moon conjunction. The outward fracturing of the family that this created reflected itself as a deepening of her own inner fracturing and detachment from her emotional and physical reality. Her mother became attracted to another man who also in the United States Army, stationed in Germany. It should be said that the mother's psychological dynamics are quite similar to her own, and because the mother terminated the relationship with her father due to a lack of emotional/sexual nourishment, she chose to become attracted to this new man who was psychologically, emotionally, and sexually intense. He was also a sadistic type who ended up terrorizing everyone in the family. Just after this girl entered puberty, she witnessed this man forcing her mother to have sadistic sex with him. She was tied up and gagged, and was being brutally sodomized. He became enraged when he saw her witnessing this event and began to "stalk" her over the next few months. The girl was, of course, traumatized and lived in real fear for her own life. Yet, paradoxically, she was attracted to this man's power and the seductiveness of his sexuality. With her survival instinct triggered, she decided the best way to survive this situation was to give in to this man's demands.

Unconsciously, she was attracted to his intensity, power, and sexuality as compensations for her sense of emotional deprivation, and the deep inner void that she felt within herself. Unconsciously, she was desiring to feel connected in this way as compensation for her own inner fracturing and detachment from her own inner being. And, unconsciously, she was attracted to this "sexual taboo" as a reflection of her desire to be dominated in a masochistic way because of her built-up guilt over many lifetimes, and the need to atone for this guilt. As stated before, she also had built-up rage and anger towards men over many lifetimes because of the self-created perception of victimization caused by her own denial of the nature of her desires. Thus, psychologically, she also wanted to "get back" or even with men—to dominate, control, humiliate, hurt, and abandon them. As a result of all of these dynamics, she started giving this man "dual signals." It is interesting to note that this man's job in the Army was one of an interrogator of suspected spies—to find out the truth. Given the fact that this woman has been in a state of denial concerning her own desires, motivations, intentions, agendas, and thus, essentially dishonest, the attraction to this man is quite revealing as reflected in her own core life lesson—to learn to become totally honest about herself.

On the one had, she would run and hide from him in a "hide-and-seek" way, avoid him, curse him, and taunt him. On the other hand, she would "seduce" him by making him so enraged that he would run after her, the nature of her taunting words stimulating his sexual energy. This finally culminated one night when he entered her bedroom and forced her to have anal sex, threatening her as he did so. It should be stated that the anal canal, thus anal sex, correlates to Saturn, Capricorn, Pluto, and Scorpio. With Capricorn on her Second House cusp, and its planetary ruler, Saturn, in Capricorn in the natural Aries House (Mars/Aries correlating to one's sexual instinct), sesquiquadrate Pluto in the Eighth House, and inconjunct Uranus in the Eighth House, her unconscious (as a child and young woman) orientation, fascination, and attraction to this area of the body is part of her emotional/sexual nature. Within this, the Aquarius interception in the Second House correlates to a rebellion against the social/sexual norms or customs as defined by consensus society (Capricorn). Thus, this interception creates an inherent attraction to "different" forms of sexual experience. With its planetary ruler Uranus retrograde in Leo in the Eighth House, this rebellion is intensified and linked to the archetype of self-actualization or discovery (Leo). In other words, the sexual archetype of life becomes emphasized, and through it she becomes aware of the nature of her emotional dynamics, psychological dynamics, intentions, and motivations. It becomes a primary vehicle through which to act out her masochistic/sadistic desires towards those that she becomes intimate with.

Pluto in Virgo reveals her Soul structure that is defined by what it lacks, and in the current life, her early experience of emotional deprivation or nurturing. Her compensation for this is to be attracted to emotional, psychological, and sexual intensity as a way of igniting or stimulating her own Soul. This can be seen by Uranus in the Eighth House making the various aspects that it does to Mars, Saturn/Moon, Venus, and Pluto's aspects to Jupiter, Saturn, Chiron, Mars, Sun, and the Mercury/Venus conjunction.

In addition to this, she has Scorpio on the Twelfth House cusp. Scorpio's natural planetary ruler is Pluto. With Pluto in her Eighth House, her Twelfth House is brought into the Eighth House as well as the Eighth House being brought into the Twelfth House. The Twelfth House, again, is the astrological archetype that correlates with our need and desire for transcendent or ultimate reality—the archetype that dissolves the subjective ego from identifying with itself as separate from the totality of the Creation, and to align or identify the ego/Soul complex with its Creator. Thus, it correlates with our ultimate sense of ideals, and our ultimate sense of the meaning that we give to life. The operative dynamic within the Twelfth House is to surrender to the highest power or will of the totality of God. Thus, with the Twelfth House planetary ruler being in her Eighth House, her Soul desires to understand the mystery of God, herself, others, and life in general through intense psychological and sexual experiences of all kinds.

Relative to her evolutionary condition, the individuated state, she also desires to investigate occult and spiritual laws or systems that are experiential in nature. The Eighth House Pluto relative to Scorpio on the Twelfth House demands proof versus simple faith. With Pluto in Virgo, this would manifest as attractions to various methods or techniques through which her desire for proof relative to actual experience could occur. As she became older, she did indeed become attracted to various forms of yoga and mediation, and, on a cyclic basis relative to her need to atone and purify for the build-up of guilt and the need to suppress her total desire nature, to Roman Catholic rituals.

Thus, even though she was afraid and traumatized by her mother's boyfriend, she was also attracted to him because he symbolized emotional and sexual power. Unconsciously, she desired to surrender to this power in order to become emotionally, psychologically, and sexually alive, and to experience something deep within herself. Sexual power and intensity for her equals a metamorphosis of her existing and ongoing reality. Unconsciously, because of the build-up of guilt and consequent need to atone for it, she was attracted to him as a form of personal punishment and humiliation. Unconsciously, she was attracted to him because of the "taboo" nature of the dynamic. Unconsciously, she was desiring to humiliate him before and after the event through the nature of her abusive words (Pluto in opposition to Mars in the Third House Pisces, and Pluto's inconjunction to the Third House Venus in Aries). Unconsciously, she was attracted to him because of the lack of emotional interaction with her biological father (Capricorn on the Second House cusp relative to Saturn in Capricorn conjunct the Moon forming squares to the Fourth House Sun). This lack created the displaced emotions of the child that was desiring actualization through the emotional/psychological/sexual intensity reflected in her mother's boyfriend, who focused a tremendous amount of energy and attention upon her. And, lastly, she had anger linked with her mother because her mother not only divorced her father whom she loved very much, but also because she brought her new boyfriend into the house to live with them. The Moon/Saturn conjunction in Capricorn is in the First House (a natural Martial house), this conjunction square the Sun in Aries (Mars ruled), and Mars itself is the planetary ruler of her Fourth House, which is in opposition to Pluto. Thus, she was blaming the mother in such a way as to want to "get back" at her for doing these things—and she did it by having sex with her mother's boyfriend.

As stated in the beginning of this section, both the Second House and Twelfth House can be projected through the Seventh House, relative to the inconjunctions that each archetypally form to that house. She has Gemini on her Seventh House cusp with its planetary ruler, Mercury, in Aries in the Third House. Mercury forms a conjunction to the Fourth House Venus in Aries, an inconjunction to Pluto in Virgo in the Eighth House, and an inconjunction to Neptune in Scorpio in the Eleventh House (which is connected back to Pluto via a sextile). Thus, there is a Yod focused on Mercury. In addition, Mercury is square to Jupiter in Capricorn in the First House and quintile Saturn in Capricorn in the First House. It is also the planetary ruler of her North Node, and yet conjunct the South Node. Again, this pattern creates a karmic and evolutionary condition in which she will necessarily relive past life conditions in this life, and repeat or relive relationships with others she has known before.

As stated before, she experienced emotional deprivation in her early life linked with her parents, and later through her religious school. Her compensation for this was to involve herself in reading fictional material in which she could escape her conditions through fantasy and imagination. This pattern was sustained as she became older, but also manifested through her Gemini Seventh House as attractions to individuals who represented or symbolized knowledge, ideas, or information that she was attracted to. Relative to the aspects that Mercury is making, this pattern is an extremely dominant and emphasized dynamic within her. Because of the displaced emotions linked with her parents, she projected her Second House and Twelfth House archetypes through the Seventh House via being attracted to older (Capricorn on the Second House cusp) men and women who symbolized and represented the intense emotional, psychological, spiritual, and sexual experiences that she desired to have because of the inner sense of emptiness that she felt (Scorpio on the Twelfth House cusp).

This projection manifested as being initially attracted to people relative to their ideas, knowledge, information, or the "different" kinds of lifestyles that they were leading, as compared with cultural norms. These kinds of people would stimulate her intellectual curiosity to discover what made these kinds of people be the way that they were. This dynamic is an extension of her early-life reading of fiction and curiosity about the characters that would be in those stories.

Her way of projecting herself to others is dual in nature (Gemini on the Seventh House cusp). On the one hand, she would present herself as an individual who had been victimized by life. In this projection, she would seem so sweet, innocent, naive, sincere, and honest that others would inevitably want to help her and believe in her. They would have no clue that this was only a mask being purposefully worn to get something from them that she needed. This persona is caused by Mars in Pisces; Chiron in Pisces; the North Node in Virgo in the Ninth House (which is ruled by the Mercury conjunct the South Node); Sagittarius Rising relative to its opposition to Gemini on the Seventh House Cusp; and the South Node in Pisces relative to its planetary ruler Neptune in Scorpio. This mode of projection would occur when she found herself in some deep crisis or state of emotional despair that she desired to change, or be free from. Thus, she would set out to "hook" people in this way.

On the other hand, she could also project herself in such a way as to be unapproachable—to be so totally isolated within herself, so withdrawn from life, and so angry about life, that she would construct a persona resembling an emotional flack jacket: Mercury inconjunct Pluto and quintile Saturn creates this effect. The trigger for this cycle is caused within her own Soul as discussed earlier: a cycle of suppression and denial of her desire nature. Her nickname was "the Ice Queen."

After the incident with her mother's boyfriend, she was extremely traumatized. This would be obvious because she was still quite young, and could not really have any real insight into herself at that point in time. She could not talk to her mother or anyone else about what had occurred. As a result, she ran away from her home and tried to find her father who was now living in California. She actually did find him, and lived in California for one year with him. She then returned to Germany and lived with a girlfriend and her parents. Her projected victim persona induced them to want to help her. They finally made her leave their home, though, when she could not conform to their expectations. She now found herself "on the streets" with nowhere to go or live. At this point, she was not yet sixteen.

While she had been living with her girlfriend's parents, she had been taking tennis lessons. Her instructor was a thirty-year-old man. When she was kicked out of the house she was, of course, desperate and in great need of help. Thus, she affected the persona of victim with this man, and at the same time sexually flirted with him as a way of getting what she needed. He offered that she could stay in his apartment until she got herself straightened out, so she moved the things she had into his apartment. Within the first few days, he started to express his sexual desires for her as a result of her ongoing flirtations. One night, he got her drunk on wine and seduced her into having sex with him—again, her words were "He talked me into it." The next day she felt, of course, victimized by him and would not talk with him. She was now unapproachable. This enraged him, and finally a day came when he physically forced himself into her room and raped her anally. Afterwards, he picked up all her things, threw them out the window, and told her to get out.

This event was, once again, due to her core dynamics of manipulating others in order to get what she needed and desired, allowing herself to be manipulated in order for the "other" to get what he needed and desired, an emotional, psychological, and sexual dishonesty that attracted another of "like mind," and an archetypal form of being a "predator" who stalks and tracks down the "prey" that they are seeking. In her case, again, she can be both predator and prey depending on what emotional/psychological cycle she is in. The archetype of being a predator can be seen in the Eighth House Pluto, and being a prey with Pluto being in Virgo. This is intensified, in her case, by Pluto's opposition to Mars in Pisces. So in this case, she initially was a predator who sought this man out in order to get what she needed, and then became prey because of his own actual emotional/sexual agenda which was the motivation of offering to her his apartment to start with. This event also illustrates the key way that her Soul desires to learn personal honesty versus an inner denial and blaming of others for that which motivates her: the way of crisis.

With Pluto in Virgo in the Eighth House, a Yod focused on the Eighth House Uranus, and another Yod focused on Mercury (the ruler of her Seventh House and linked to the Eighth House Pluto and

Neptune in Scorpio), the nature of the types of crises that she attracts and creates for herself are sexual and emotional as acted out with other people. Again, these are people from other lifetimes that she is karmically destined to remeet in this life.

Her compensation for this trauma was to run away again. Running away, in this context, is just another form of personal denial and avoidance of her actual truth, a running away from accepting the responsibility of her own actions, as seen in the Saturn/Moon conjunction in Capricorn sextile the South Node in Pisces, trine the North Node in Virgo, and quintile Neptune. This time, she ran away to an Eastern-type spiritual center in Germany. Even though her Soul has legitimate desires to embrace spiritual reality, the desire that motivated her at this time was one of guilt and atonement, and a desire to detach from her body because of the nature of the event. With the planetary ruler of her South Node in Pisces being Neptune in Scorpio in the Eleventh House, her consciousness would naturally think in those terms. Even in this environment she was taunted and subjected to sexual innuendoes by some of the men who lived there—a karmic boomerang of taunting and subjecting others to sexual flirtations.

One of the more revealing things she told me about this time that directly correlates to Scorpio being on her Twelfth House cusp, with its planetary ruler being in the Eighth House, was that one day during a deep meditation (Scorpio on the Twelfth House cusp) she had an orgasm (the Twelfth House ruler in the Eighth House). With Capricorn on the Second House cusp, she felt "guilty" about this because of her belief that spirit and flesh do not go together—that they are in an inherent conflict. From an evolutionary view, her Soul desires to eliminate this existing belief system and to change the belief structure in such a way as to allow the spirit and flesh to be reflections of one another. This is exactly why her Soul created an orgasm while in deep meditation upon God. This evolutionary intention is seen in Pluto's opposition to Mars in the Third House Pisces—a metamorphosis of existing ideas or beliefs.

It is also interesting to note, with these astrological patterns and dynamics in mind, that while in this spiritual environment she decided to "get even" with one of the men there who had been sexually taunting her. One night she took off all her clothes, went to his room, and got into his bed. She "dared" him to have sexual intercourse with her. He was so shocked that he was unable to perform. She ended up sadistically abusing him with her words so as to totally humiliate him. The next day she broadcast this occurrence to all.

She left this place after a year. She decided to return to America, and live near her father. The actual motivation was, however, to track down a childhood sweetheart who was a good friend of her family—a man, again, much older than herself. As a child, she would often fantasize about him, wonder what it would be like to be with him. This man was now also living in America, close to where her father was living. She did indeed track this man down, and succeeded in getting him to marry her—the predator/prey archetype manifesting yet again.

Realizing he had been trapped, this man spent progressively more and more time away from home. When he was home, he was depressed, withdrawn, or verbally abusive to her. She became pregnant, but the unborn baby symbolized a commitment he was unwilling to make, and he demanded that she get an abortion. He in effect "out-pictured" her own fear of entrapment relative to a committed relationship (Eighth House Pluto intensified through its opposition to Mars; Venus in Aries square Jupiter in Capricorn in the First House; Mercury, the ruler of her Seventh House, in Aries inconjunct both the Eighth House Pluto and the Eleventh House Neptune in Scorpio), and a cyclic need to be absolutely free. She had the abortion even though she was extremely angry about it. This is quite interesting because one of her karmic and evolutionary requirements was to also recover or repeat past-life relationships with children whom she had abandoned, abused, or betrayed (the planetary ruler of her Fifth House, Venus, is also the apex of a Yod between Neptune retrograde in the Eleventh House Scorpio, and Pluto retrograde in Virgo in the Eighth House). It is as if her Soul knew that she was abandoning a child again through the act of abortion.

Her anger created a situation wherein she progressively withdrew from this man as a form of punishing him, and eventually divorced him. Not surprisingly, she was not alone for long. After a small amount of time, three to four weeks, she met yet another older man. She was nineteen at the time, and this man was in his late thirties. In many ways this relationship turned out to be the most traumatic and cataclysmic experience of her life. On the following pages, Chart #5 is the synastry chart between these two with her chart on the outer ring, Chart #6 is a synastry chart between these two with his chart on the outer ring, and Chart #7 is the composite chart between them.

They met each other in the context of her work. She was a waitress in an alternative restaurant that specialized in macrobiotic cooking.

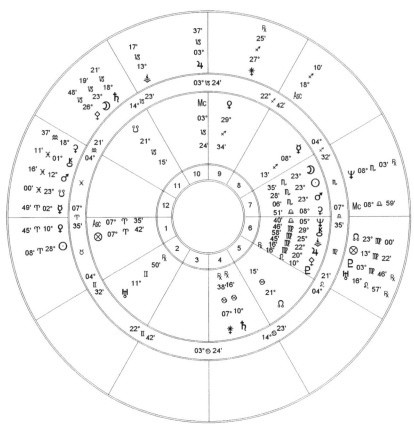

Chart #5

She enjoyed this because she was personally focused on the "purity" of this way of eating. He would frequent this restaurant often, and they struck up a friendship over time. With her Moon/Saturn conjunction being conjunct his South Node in Capricorn in his Eleventh House, the past-life dynamic or theme of starting off as friends is obvious. Meeting in an alternative restaurant can also be seen in this symbol. She was attracted to him because "he seemed so different" (the Eleventh House). And because of the displaced emotions of her own childhood linked with her biological father, this older man served as an unconscious vehicle through which she was seeking a "replacement figure" for her father. With his south Node conjunct her Moon/Saturn con-

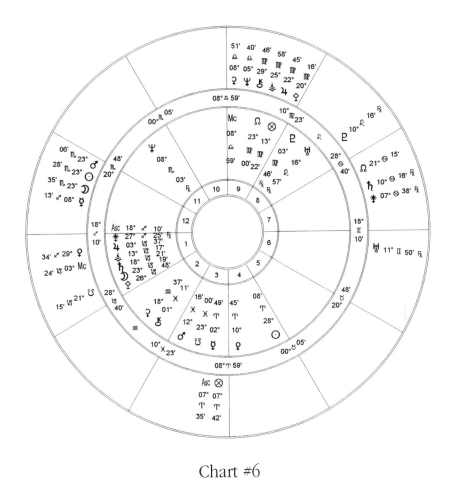

Chart #6

junction in her First House, the origin of these displaced emotions in her chart, he served this function well because he gave a tremendous amount of energy and attention.

Through synastry, her South Node is in his Twelfth House with its planetary ruler, Neptune, in his Seventh House. His South Node is in her First House with its planetary ruler, Saturn, in her Seventh House. Clearly, this is the signature of a relationship of an intimate nature that has occurred long before the current life. The themes of friendship and an intimate relationship have occurred through the obvious past-life dynamic of being in the same families together (her Moon/Saturn conjunction on his South Node in Capricorn). In addition, their Moons are

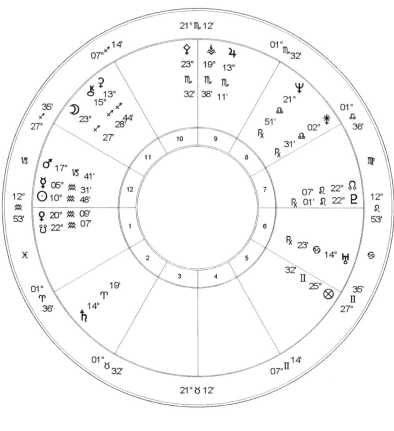

Chart #7

exactly sextile to one another, and her Venus in Aries in the Fourth
House forms a square to his Nodal Axis of Capricorn/Cancer, which
occurs in her First and Seventh Houses. Her Venus is also square his
Saturn in Cancer, and their Saturns are in opposition to one another,
from Capricorn to Cancer.

The composite chart also demonstrates this, relative to the Composite Pluto being exactly conjunct the North Node (within one minute)
in the Seventh House, and in opposition to the First House Venus in
Aquarius, which is also conjunct the South Node. Venus is the planetary
ruler of the composite chart's Fourth House. Since Taurus is also on the
composite Third House cusp, the nature of their relationship within family structures would be one of siblings (Third House). The nature of this

opposition demonstrates that this relationship has involved intense cataclysmic situations that have led to sudden separations. Thus, it is not
complete or resolved. This theme is further symbolized in the composite chart by Mars being inconjunct to the North Node and Pluto; Jupiter
in Scorpio being square the Nodal Axis, Pluto, and Venus; and the Cardinal Grand Cross between Mars, Uranus, Saturn, and Neptune.

The two themes or dynamics they shared that served to deepen
the initial connection were the reading of certain books and authors,
and a mutual interest in jogging. Jogging is a Mars activity, and with
his South Node conjunct her First House (naturally Mars ruled)
Moon/Saturn conjunction this became a natural connection. This is
also seen in the composite chart relative to Venus in Aquarius conjunct
the South Node in the First House. The books that they had both read
and had a mutual fascination with included the works of John Fowles,
who wrote many books including *The Collector*, the works of the Marquis de Sade; a book called *"O,"* which is about the life of a young
French woman who totally submitted to the will of her man who was
a sexual sadist; and the works of Frederick Neitzche, especially the
books *Will to Power*, *Beyond Good and Evil,* and *Thus Spake Zarathus-
tra*. Their mutual interest in this type of material would generate deep
psychological discussions that included the nature of their families of
origin and the different problems and issues that their families created for them. Venus, again, correlates with our inner relationship to ourselves based on what we value and meaning we give to life based on
those values, and, thus, what we value in another based on the meaning we give to another: the external projection of Venus. In this way,
Venus correlates to our inner magnetism or vibration that serves to attract others who resonate in the same way.

It will be useful and necessary at this point to examine the natal
chart of this man in order to understand his inner dynamics, motivations, intentions, and desires. Referring to Chart #8, you will see the
South Node is in Capricorn in the Eleventh House, and its planetary
ruler, Saturn, is in Cancer in the Fourth House conjunct the North Node
in the Fifth House. Saturn is inconjunct his Eighth House Mercury in
Sagittarius, which is in opposition to his Second House Uranus, which
is retrograde in Gemini. Uranus is in a semi-sextile aspect to Saturn.
Saturn is also sesquiquadrate his Seventh House Mars, Sun, and Moon
in Scorpio. The Moon, the ruler of his North Node, is thus connected
to his past via its aspect to Saturn. Pluto is retrograde in his Sixth
House and semi-sextile Saturn, sextile Uranus, and trine Mercury. His

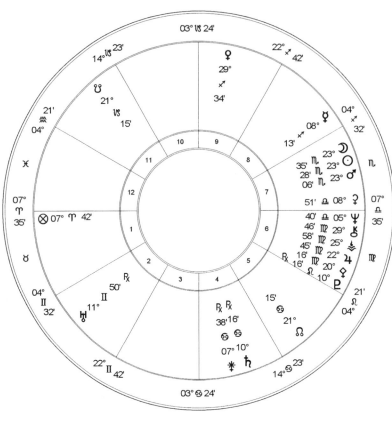

Chart #8

Sixth House is emphasized not only because of Pluto being there, but also because the placement of Jupiter, Neptune, and the asteroids Chiron, Pallas, and Vesta.

In essence, this is an individual who had tremendous power over people in many lives, and was very dictatorial in exercising that power. This can be seen in his South Node in Capricorn in the Eleventh House relative to the Moon/Mars conjunction in Scorpio in the Seventh House, which sextiles his South Node. The dictatorial application of power is seen in Moon/Mars sesquiquadrate his Saturn (the planetary ruler of his South Node). Because Saturn is in his Fourth House, his depth of insecurity is intense. Any challenge to his authority or power would create a deeply insecure condition within him. The cause of this insecurity is based in the fact that he had been born into families, in past lives, who were in positions of social control and financial privilege. The planetary ruler of the South Node in Capricorn is in the Fourth House and conjunct the Fifth House North Node, sextile Uranus in the Second House, and inconjunct the Eighth House Mercury. This pattern demonstrates someone who engages in exploiting the resources of others in order to secure those resources for oneself. With the Moon/Mars conjunction sextile to the South Node, and trine to the North Node, he would have been in a position to inherit (Scorpio) this social position and power through his family. With Mercury and Uranus linked to his Saturn, insecurity would be caused by the fact that he had siblings who could have also inherited the power and privilege that he coveted. Thus, his own siblings were perceived to be potential competitors—the causative factor in his insecurity. In addition, his biological parents would cause this insecurity by playing psychological games with him that involved threatening him. If he did not do exactly what they wanted him to do then they would leave everything to one of the other siblings. This parental behavior is a form of psychological tormenting, and is an additional cause of his insecurity relative to his self-determination (South Node in Capricorn) to inherit what he desired.

Thus, the compensation for this insecurity was to manifest a dictatorial behavior that overpowered (Scorpio) anyone who challenged, or was perceived to potentially challenge, his authority. There has been a fundamental abuse of power that has manifested in extreme ways (extremity is reflected in the Seventh House). Because this archetype of extremes is manifested through Scorpio, the nature of the abuse of power, beyond the generalized dynamic of being dictatorial, expressed itself as murdering or killing large and small groups of people (the Seventh House linked to the Eleventh House) as psychological and sexual abuse or torture, and the enslavement of people.

Enslavement is a dynamic linked with the archetype of the Sixth House. Because his Pluto in Leo is in the Sixth House and tied into Saturn (the ruler of his South Node), and Saturn is linked to the Moon/Mars conjunction in Scorpio through the sesquiquadrate aspect, a dynamic of enslaving small and large groups of people can be seen as a way for him to sustain his own power. The extremity of his acts was also caused by the intense build-up of rage and anger that was caused by his parents' dictates that he conform to their will in order to actualize his desires. With the South Node in Capricorn in the Eleventh House, his instinct to rebel against authority figures was frustrated, controlled, and crushed. His desire to do everything in his own way conflicted with his desire to inherit his parents' power and privilege. The resulting rage led him to feel victimized by his parents, as seen in Saturn square Neptune in his Sixth House, and Pluto in the Sixth House semi-sextile Saturn. Victimization is linked with the archetypes of the Sixth and Twelfth Houses, Pisces, Virgo, Neptune, and Mercury. The rage and anger over his perceived victimization by his parents became emotionally displaced (South Node in Capricorn relative to Saturn in Cancer in the Fourth House) in such a way as to act out this rage towards others as an adult—to get even with others (Scorpio).

His rage linked with victimization has also been caused by *not* inheriting the social power and privilege from the family of origin—another sibling inherited that which he coveted. Thus, he has also experienced *powerlessness* (Pluto, Neptune, Jupiter, and the asteroids in the Sixth House). This would occur when he did not, or could not, conform to his parents' dictates. These dynamics have been manifested and emphasized in many lifetimes, through many different families, as his soul is attempting to learn the right use of power and social position, and how to be an equal with other people versus the need to be superior and dominate them. The midpoint between the extremes of absolute power and powerlessness is equality—the Seventh House.

In his current life, he was born once again into a family that held social privilege and was very wealthy. However, his father was preoccupied with his career and was not emotionally available to him in any way. Psychologically, the father simply did not like his son, and was inherently repelled by the nature of the boy's personality. The mother was emotionally frustrated due to the lack of any meaningful interrelatedness with the father. Her frustration evolved into a permeating anger that was displaced and manifested at the boy. He became psychologically abused and terrorized by the mother. In essence, both parents rejected and rebelled against him. The causal factor should be clear as to why his Soul chose this condition to be born into. It is based on a build-up of guilt (South Node in Capricorn) based on the past lifetimes of misusing power in the ways discussed. Relative to Pluto in the Sixth House with Jupiter, Neptune, and the asteroids, the consequent desire to atone for this guilt becomes the causal factor in experiencing the pain and humiliation of this parental environment.

Even though his Soul is inwardly intensely tortured because of the haunting feelings and memories of other lifetimes in which he caused tremendous pain and suffering for countless numbers of people, he would not have any real conscious awareness of this as a child. All children naturally expect to be loved, accepted, and nurtured. As a child, he experienced the opposite of love and acceptance—hatred and rejection. Since most of this was actively projected onto him by his current-life mother (the father being absent most of the time), a deep psychological complex was created in him called the "castration complex"—that is, the feminine principle perceived as a force of power that symbolically cuts off the genitals of the man.

This current life parental impact only intensified the unconscious dynamics that were created in other lifetimes—the sense of being victimized through either allowing himself to be psychologically manipulated in order to actualize his desire for the inheritance leading to power and privilege, or being denied that inheritance when it was given to another sibling. Relative to the Scorpionic desire to get even with those who are perceived to be the cause of his suffering, built up over many lifetimes, and the intense rage and anger that accompanies this desire, he once again became defined through the psychological pathology of sadism. Sadism, again, is also caused by guilt, and anger because of the guilt. Accordingly, the sadist will hurt others before another can hurt the sadist. With the build-up of guilt in his Soul over many lifetimes based on his actions, there has been a simultaneous desire to atone for it, and then to be angry because of it. The atonement cycle is the causal factor in masochism—experiencing powerlessness, abuse, rejection, and humiliation. The anger cycle is the causal factor in his sadism—the desire to get even, to purposefully and consciously hurt others. Thus, both psychological pathologies of masochism and sadism are core archetypal dynamics within his Soul. Cyclically, his guilt causes him to act out the masochistic pathology which, in turn, causes him to act out the sadistic pathology.

As an adult, these core archetypal pathologies defined the very essence of his life. Professionally, he became a master hypnotherapist who invested a tremendous amount of time and money investigating and learning as much about hypnotherapy as he could. Astrologically speaking, hypnotherapy correlates to Scorpio, Pluto, and the Eighth House. Thus, with this Pluto in Leo in the Sixth House combined with Jupiter, Neptune, and the asteroids Vesta, Chiron, and Pallas relative to the Sun/Moon/Mars conjunction in Scorpio, his attraction to hypnotherapy as a profession is clear. This is further indicated through Pluto's trine to his Eighth House Mercury in Sagittarius, and the sextile from Pluto to Uranus in Gemini in his Second House. This signature demonstrates his desire to learn as much about hypnotherapy as he could, and the amount of money invested relative to this desire. The linkage of Uranus to the Sixth House Pluto correlates to his desire to do something unique or different as his personal work.

His motivations and intentions in this kind of work are complex and dualistic, as symbolized by the relationship between the Second and Eighth Houses. Gemini demonstrates the dualism while Jupiter, the planetary ruler of the Eighth House, is in Virgo and square to Venus, which demonstrates the complexity. On the one hand, his motivations and intentions in orientating to a work that is of the "helping professions" nature is linked to the atonement/guilt archetype. On the other hand, his motivations and intentions are also linked to the anger/guilt archetype—the desire to have power over people.

In his personal life, he was not only an alcoholic, but also a sexual sadist as primary orientation to his emotional/psychological/sexual life. The alcoholism was caused by the deep inner tormenting of his Soul based on not only the distant memories from other lives, but also caused by the sadistic actions in this life, which were based in the need to avoid or escape from these memories. Through his hypnotherapy practice he could do very fine work, but he also targeted certain women in which he could manipulate by way of hypnotic suggestion. His intention in this was to "capture" these women in order to make them "sexual slaves."

In his personal life, he spent a tremendous amount of time reading and investigating the writings of the Marquis de Sade, and any other writings that involved sadomasochistic sexual practices, methods, and techniques. The astrological linkage, again, between the Sixth House Pluto in Leo to his Second House Uranus in Gemini, and the Eighth House Mercury in Sagittarius relative to Jupiter (the planetary ruler of the Eighth House) in Virgo square the Ninth House Venus, correlates to this desire within him. This dynamic is caused by the "castration complex" created by his current-life mother, and the resulting desire to have power over women in order to totally humiliate them.

So when these two meet in the restaurant, all these dynamics were operative between them, as well as their individual dynamics. Their relationship became progressively deeper because of the nature of their discussion. As stated before, she was attracted to others who represented and symbolized knowledge, information, and ideas of a psychological and metamorphic nature: Gemini on her Seventh House cusp relative to its planetary ruler, Mercury, being in the Third House in Aries inconjunct Pluto in Virgo retrograde in the Eighth House, inconjunct Neptune in Scorpio in the Eleventh House, and quintile (creative transformation) her Saturn in Capricorn in the First House. Again, the Seventh House correlates to our projected needs, needs we feel we have that can only be met by another. Thus, with Gemini on his Second House cusp (resources that the individual already has), she was attracted to him because he represented what she needed. With his Uranus in Gemini in his Second House he would naturally value not only his own uniqueness, but would feel deeply different than most people. Thus, he would value uniqueness in others, others who were rebelling against the prevailing social norms. Sexually, he would value "different" forms of sexual behavior as measured against social norms. With her Aquarius intercepted in the Second House, and with its planetary ruler Uranus retrograde in Leo in the Eighth House, she vibrated and resonated inwardly in exactly the same way as he did. Each has Uranus sextile to the other's. From the current-life point of view, with her Moon/Saturn conjunction on his Eleventh House South Node, she became a perfect vehicle through which he could act out his own fractured and displaced (Eleventh House) emotions of rage and anger linked with his mother.

With Scorpio on her Twelfth House cusp, and its planetary ruler Pluto located in Virgo in the Eighth House, her Soul desired to surrender to any source of power that symbolized metamorphic change, and emotional/sexual intensity as a way of not only assuaging her sense of emptiness, but also as a vehicle to make her aware of herself. This man certainly represented such power and intensity. With Aquarius on his Twelfth House cusp, its planetary ruler Uranus in Gemini in the Second House in opposition to the Eighth House Mercury, and both planets connected through Pluto in the Sixth House, his ultimate value was to make others submit to his will—to capture, enslave, own, and possess. He desired to surrender to the archetype of dominance and submission (Pluto in the Sixth House, and its polarity point in the Twelfth House). With Libra on his Seventh House cusp, and its planetary ruler Venus in Sagittarius in the Ninth House square Jupiter in Virgo in the Sixth House, he projected himself as a "teacher" to others who were in some kind of crisis. He could "help" them resolve their crisis. Thus, he would always be attracted to others who were "weaker" than himself, relative to circumstances that reflected the other's crisis in some way.

As stated before, she had just divorced her husband. Based on the nature of that relationship, she had cut herself off from her feelings and emotions as a form of survival. As her relationship with her new man became deeper, she began to talk about what occurred in the relationship with her divorced husband. One of the things that she kept telling him was that "I cannot feel anything anymore. I feel frozen in my emotions, and in my body" (the Moon/Saturn conjunction in Capricorn in the First House). She presented herself through the persona of victimization. She felt totally defeated and crushed by life. Even though she would have these discussions of deep psychological issues, discussions about the different books and authors that they had a common interest in, and would jog together from time to time, she remained essentially aloof from him, and told him repeatedly that she "just wanted to be friends" (her Moon/Saturn conjunction on his Eleventh House South Node).

He interpreted this statement as rejection of him (his Venus square Jupiter in Virgo—Virgo correlates to rejection, and Jupiter to how we interpret phenomena). This interpretation ignited his displaced castration complex and intensified his determination to "get" her. He was very covert and careful in his well-planned manipulations of her. Over time, she began to trust him because he never put overt pressure on her for anything but a friendship. Then, finally, one night he invited her to have dinner with him at a very elegant and expensive restaurant. She interpreted this as him having great respect for her, a respect that she desperately wanted from anyone, given her past and her lack of respect for herself. She began to drop her instinctive defensiveness (Pluto in the Eighth House). After dinner, he causally suggested that they go to his house to look at some rare book that he owned. She had never been there before. With her natural defenses down at this point, she agreed to go. Once there, he began to suggest to her that he could help her "feel again." He began to relate his knowledge of anatomy and physiology, a knowledge he learned in his investigation of sadomasochistic sexual practices. Relative to her astrological dynamics, this piqued her curiosity. She asked him to explain more about the nature and purpose of the knowledge that he had. Since they already had established an intellectual connection through their common interest in the writing of de Sade, she was open to what he had to say without realizing what his actual intentions were—to capture and sexually dominate her.

After talking for some time, he finally told her he wanted to demonstrate some of these methods to "help her feel." Initially, it was a very simple method of just rubbing one spot on her skin over and over. This kind of repetition naturally begins to irritate the nerves and muscles, and his irritation causes the senses, the sensation body, to act differently. The reaction that this created in her body surprised her, yet her curiosity deepened even more. Because he was a professional hypnotherapist, he began to covertly use repetitive suggestion while stimulating her senses in this way. This repetitive suggestion was "I can make you feel," and it was said in a very low, quiet, and deep way. She began to "surrender" to him, submitting to his will without realizing that she was doing so consciously. At this point he had succeeded in his objective—she was captured.

At this point he told her "You are like a wild stallion, and I am going to break you!" What began to happen then cannot be written in this book. In general terms, I can only say that he employed everything he had ever learned about sadomasochistic sexual practices upon her, especially focusing his attentions and energy on her anal canal. His intention was to own her completely and make her his sexual slave. The physical and sexual intensity that he caused her body and Soul to experience almost caused her to die. At one point during these events, she actually had a brain seizure. (Brain seizures correlate with Uranus, Aquarius, and the Eleventh House. Thus, with Uranus the planetary ruler of her intercepted Second House Aquarius, the sexual submission that he forced her into led to this seizure.) The stimulation to her genital region was so intense, and the physical orgasms so consuming on a repetitive basis over many hours, that she lost all control of herself. Feces, urine, and vomit were everywhere.

During all of this, he kept programming her subconscious with a post-hypnotic suggestion that would be operative after the event itself. A post-hypnotic suggestion is a key word, or series of words, that triggers an automatic behavior when heard in any context. The key word that he used was "home," telling her that her "home" was in his house, with him. Think of the synastry connections, and the composite chart, and you will understand why he used his word. He also programmed her subconscious with the thought that she would remember nothing of this event, and that the only memory that she would have was that of having a night together with him. He also programmed her subconscious with the thought that she had been so humiliated, so used, so destroyed, that no other man would ever want her, and that only he loved and accepted her—and that she loved to be made to "feel" in this way, so that when she heard the word "home" she would automatically want to feel this way again with him.

The next morning, she woke up in his bed, and was afraid without knowing why. Her whole body was sore and her genital region was in fire-like pain. He was now very civil, polite, and seemed to be the way he had always been with her. She could not remember what had happened, and only felt a mounting terror and her survival instinct to run. She had no time to analyze what had occurred. She went home and passed out.

In effect, she was a victim of her own curiosity. She had been thoroughly and sadistically raped. At a Soul level, however, she desired to surrender to power of a metamorphic nature, and to others who symbolize such power as a way of awakening her Soul. In addition, she was attracted to the archetype of dominance and submission because of her own sadomasochistic pathology. In fact, she said to me "I always wanted to be had, totally taken over, but not like that." Karmically speaking, she had set the stage for this kind of event to occur. As stated before, her Soul structure learns through crisis. This was certainly a crisis. Evolutionarily speaking, this type of event occurred to make her aware of and accept responsibility for her own actions—a main lesson in her current life. Yet she spent the next ten years in a state of denial and suppression of this event, even though the memories kept bleeding through to her conscious awareness. In fact, relative to the post-hypnotic key word "home," she would automatically find herself going to his house without knowing why. Her fear of him was strong enough so that she never actually got to his house again. She would always stop herself a block or two away. Post-hypnotic words can only work for a relatively short time, and then lose their power. In her case, this only lasted for a few months. He would still call, still seek her out, but she resisted him completely. She is rightfully terrified of this man to this day.

The composite chart is most revealing in its symbolic correlations to this event. Upon examination, and deep inductive introspection, it reveals many, many levels and dimensions that would not be commonly understood in classical astrology. So let us examine this together, step by step.

As stated above, the composite Pluto is in the Seventh House, conjunct the North Node within one minute of exactness, and in opposition to the Venus/South Node conjunction in the First House. Venus is the planetary ruler of both the Third and Fourth Houses in this chart.

Uranus, the planetary ruler of the South Node, is in Cancer in the Sixth House, and is part of the Cardinal Grand Cross via opposition to the Twelfth House Mars in Capricorn and squares to the Second House Saturn in Aries, and the Eighth House Neptune in Libra, respectively.

With Seventh House Pluto in mind, they have obviously been in relationship to one another prior to this life—yet this relationship has experienced sudden and intense cataclysmic dynamics leading to separation, loss, or termination. Thus, it is unresolved. As stated before, with Venus being the planetary ruler of the Fourth and Third Houses, the nature of these past-life relationships would have taken place in the context of the same family, and that they would have been siblings within these families. This theme of being in the same family is restated by the planetary ruler of the South Node (Uranus) being in Cancer and in opposition to Mars in Capricorn. It is also restated by the fact that Scorpio is on the Tenth House cusp, and its planetary ruler, Pluto, is in the Seventh House. For those who have been researching the significance of asteroids, you will also notice that the asteroid Pallas in the Tenth House Scorpio is almost exactly square the Nodal Axis, Venus, and Pluto.

With the Moon in Sagittarius trine the North Node/Pluto and sextile the South Node/Venus, the theme of family is again seen. What is interesting here is that the Moon is deposited by the planet Jupiter which is in Scorpio, squaring the Nodal Axis. In evolutionary terms, this correlates to "skipped steps," and the requirement to recover those skipped steps in order for evolution to proceed. With Jupiter itself deposited by Pluto, the theme of cataclysmic events leading to sudden disruptions or terminations of the relationship is again linked with family issues and dynamics. Because Jupiter is in Scorpio, inheritance of wealth, prestige, and power is clearly seen as one of the dynamics that has created the cataclysmic disruptions within this relationship. This theme is restated by Saturn's placement in the Second House in opposition to Eighth House Neptune. These opposing planets are both square to the ruler of the South Node (Uranus) and to Mars, which is in opposition to Uranus. Mars is also inconjunct Pluto and the North Node. This correlates to competing (Mars) for the favored position within the family hierarchy (Capricorn) in order to inherit the family fortune and power, and the resulting crisis (inconjunct) for the one who did not win, who would then feel victimized by not only the parents, but by the sibling who did win (Twelfth House Mars). It also correlates to the resulting build-up of rage and anger, and the need to get even with that sibling.

All of these symbols in combination clearly demonstrate that there has been much hidden plotting and intrigue in order to secure the promised inheritance by the parents. This theme would have been very extreme and included trying to "remove" the other in a variety of ways in order to secure the inheritance. This removal theme would have included the purposeful invention of lies (Jupiter square the Nodal Axis) in order to make one or the other less than worthy of the inheritance, plots to have one or the other murdered (Mars in the Twelfth inconjunct the Seventh House Pluto, and part of the Cardinal Grand Cross involving the Eighth, Second, and Sixth Houses), or ways to have one or the other incapacitated through poison or disease.

Again, these themes have occurred between them over many lifetimes, through many different families. This is because each has felt victimized by the other and the need to get even with one another. Because each of them as individuals are defined by the co-equal pathologies of sadomasochism, they have effectively played out the role of victim/victor with each other over many lifetimes.

So can this cycle be broken? If so, how? It is very interesting to note that their initial level of discussion with one another involved the nature of their current-life families and the impact that those families had on them. Unfortunately, they both used their family dynamics to feel victimized yet again, and used these feelings as a rationale for their behavior. Obviously, each of them has their own need to learn to accept responsibility for their own actions—to "own" their own dynamics, desires, and natures. It is only when this occurs that they will each learn to forgive one another, which will then break this horrible cycle of victim/victor and the resulting karma. In the last analysis, this is the intention of the composite chart as reflected in the planetary ruler of the North Node (the Sun, which is also the depositor of Pluto) being located in the Twelfth House. Through their synastry charts, this is also seen with her Chiron, Mars, South Node, and Mercury in his Twelfth House, and his Mars, Sun, Moon, and Mercury in her Twelfth House. Forgiveness is the key, a forgiveness extended in the awareness that each is equally responsible for what has happened. What occurred in this life is just the latest chapter in a long book. Hopefully, it will be the last chapter of this kind.

The probability that this will happen in this life does not seem to be great. After the events that brought them together and then took them apart, he continued working as a professional hypnotherapist who would "capture" vulnerable women who were predisposed to his "methods," continued to be a professional sexual sadist, and continued to be an alcoholic. She denied and suppressed this experience for ten years, and in those ten years she gave birth to two sons by different fathers, not allowing either father any real access to these kids because, as she said, "they're mine." She called the father of the second boy simply the "sperm donor." They would plead with her to see their sons, but she would sadistically taunt them and keep them away from the children. It is interesting to note that she was "determined" not to have a second child. This second child was conceived while she was on LSD with a "pick-up" man she met in a bar on one of her "hunting expeditions." She had him wear a condom and she had an IUD in place. She even used a spermicidal jelly on top of this. She conceived anyway! This second son had four planets in Aquarius in her Second House, and a Moon in Virgo in her Eighth House conjunct her Pluto!

Chart #9 is the natal chart of this boy, and Chart #10 is their composite chart. Chart #11 is the synastry chart with her planets on the outer ring, and Chart #12 is the synastry chart with his planets on the outer ring. It is interesting to note that when this boy was two years old, he spontaneously talked of his last lifetime. In perfect German, he said that this name was Herr Burmer, and that the had been a general in Hitler's army. He said that he was a medical doctor operating in the concentration camps who performed medical experiments on the Jews, and was finally caught by the Dutch resistance and drowned in a river. At this time, he also announced to her that when he became a man he wanted to have a "giant penis." This at two years of age! It is also interesting to note that her most recent past life was as a Jew in Hitler's concentration camps, and that she was one of those who would betray her own people in order to save her own life. In this context, she assisted a doctor who performed medical experiments, as well as serving his sadistic sexual needs. Guess who this doctor may have been. Examining the natal, synastry, and composite charts between these two, it should not be hard to figure out. The man who sadistically raped her has his Mars in Scorpio in her Twelfth House—this second son also had Mars in Scorpio in her Twelfth House. It is also interesting to note that when she was a teenager in Germany, she decided to take a train to Berlin and "inadvertently" ended up on a train that took her to a town where one of Hitler's concentration camps had been located. Upon arriving at this place, the past-life memory association that was triggered created a form of catatonia that lasted almost a week. Given all of this, it

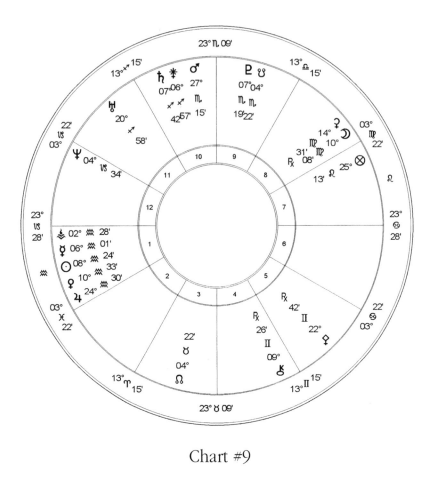

Chart #9

is not so surprising that she conceived her son in the way that she did. Considering the overall nature of the composite chart and synastry charts, what is clear is that this boy, at a Soul level, has owned and possessed her in every way, and was determined to be conceived by her in this lifetime. When he was three years old he forcefully told her "I own you, and you are mine!" Karma? The "pick-up" man had five planets in Libra in his Fifth House, and all in her Tenth House through synastry. And, yes, he was many years older than her. Within this time, she was also arrested and charged with the statutory rape of a four-year-old girl. She initiated and terminated many relationships with men and with one woman. She indulged herself with drugs and alcohol, and lived in a romantic relationship with her

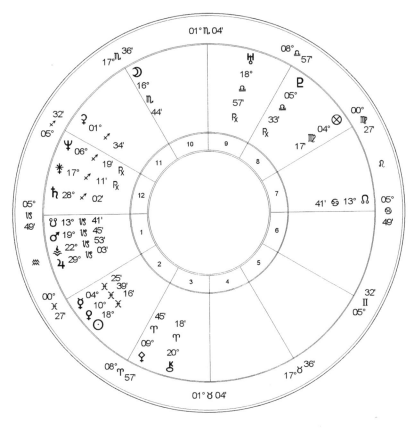

Chart #10

cousin for over two years—yet another "taboo" to be experienced. Then she left him, too.

To this day, she continues to blame everybody for everything, taking no responsibility for her own actions. With her South Node ruler in the Eleventh House, she creates new friends to fulfill her need— friends that she projects the victimized persona to, who believe in her as a result, and who thus unwittingly support her need to continue to live in a state of absolute unwillingness to look at herself as she really is. By surrounding herself with these "friends" who believe in her lies, she effectively believes in her own lies to the point that "the lies become the truth." These revolving-door friends thus serve as her current-life community of like-minded people. Despite

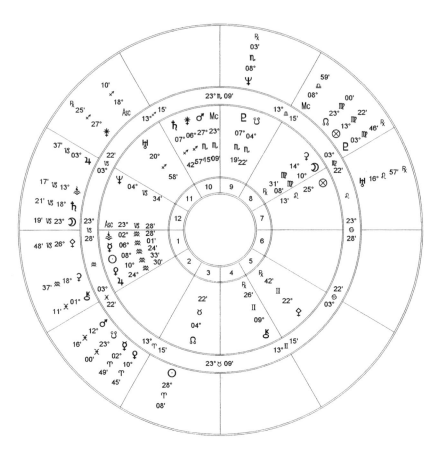

Chart #11

the intensity and traumatic nature of much of her life, she continues in her old patterns.

Given these facts, what is the probability of either one of these people changing their dynamics with one another any time soon, not to mention their individual dynamics that are the causal factors for creating the necessity for these types of life experiences? I have used this case history expressly so that an appreciation of the complexity of the dynamics that bring people together can be embraced, and to underscore why it can take more than one life to resolve those dynamics.

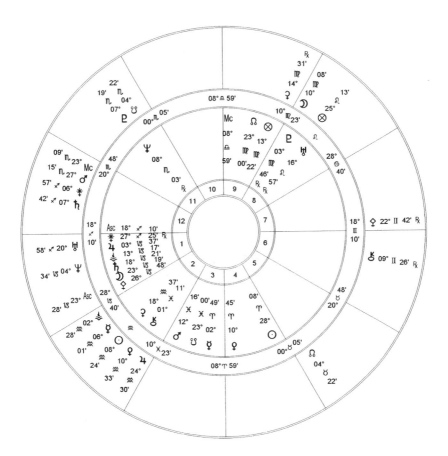

Chart #12

Chapter Seven

The Nature and Function of Venus

At this point I would like to discuss the planet Venus in light of the astrological methods that correlate to the relationship we have with ourselves, the essential needs that we have and project onto others, and how and why we attract the types of relationships that we do.

As stated before, Venus has two natures—an inner nature, and an outer or projected nature. The inner nature of Venus correlates to how we are inwardly relating to ourselves, and how we go about uniting inwardly discordant aspects of our overall nature or personality. Within this archetype Venus correlates to the psychology of *listening*—how we listen to ourselves, and, thus, how we listen to other people. Listening infers how and what we hear within ourselves, and how and what we hear from other people. Listening and hearing thus correlate to how we are inwardly relating to ourselves, and how we relate outwardly to other people. How we relate to (and thus feel about) ourselves generates an inner vibration or magnetism which attracts others who reflect or symbolize our self-relationship. For example, if a person has Venus in Virgo and is inwardly relating to oneself in very self-critical ways, feels very inadequate, and is all too aware of their shortcomings, is it illogical to conclude that this person will attract others who are very critical towards this person? If this person is inwardly listening to oneself and hearing an ongoing inner dialogue that is self-critical, then is it illogical to conclude that he or she will listen to others and hear critical comments from them?

All of us are forever "outpicturing" our own inner reality in this way without realizing this one thing—that those whom we attract into our lives are symbols of our inner reality. We project outwards that which is a reflection of our inner reality. Would the Venus in Virgo person actually be able to accept the fact that by attracting those who were very critical of him or her that this was a projection or outpicturing of how they were relating to themselves inwardly? That they needed this mirroring effect in order to learn about their inner reality? Typically, the answer would be no. The nature of the times and societies that we are living in promote the idea of collective "victimization." It is very easy to be a victim, and much harder to own or accept responsibility for our own action—to understand that the overall realities we create emanate from within ourselves according to our evolutionary and karmic requirements.

We must also remember, in terms of the time/space reality that we live within, that everything that we learn and understand occurs through polarity—night/day, yin/yang, Virgo/Pisces, etc. This is called learning through counterpoint awareness. So the Venus in Virgo person would be aware in some way of the polarity of Virgo (Pisces). He or she would inwardly "hear" the call and promise of Pisces. By hearing this call, the Venus in Virgo person must then actually listen to it in such a way as to apply what they are hearing. The polarity point correlates to the evolution of a pre-existing pattern (Venus in Virgo) to a new pattern (Venus embracing Pisces) which then allows for an evolution of the original imprint of Venus in Virgo. Again, this counterpoint learning reflects the law of the Trinity—from the original imprint to its polarity which allows an evolution of the original imprint.

In the case of the Venus in Virgo person, this would mean that he or she would have to embrace the polarity of Pisces before they could attract others who were not so critical of them. In other words, they would have to change how they were inwardly relating to themselves before any external change could be expected. Until then, the Venus in Virgo person would typically complain about why they keep attracting very critical people into their lives, at the same time wistfully wondering why they would not be with someone who would just love them for who they were. In this case, the solution would simply be a matter of the person embracing the Piscean message, "I am trying my best; I resolve to be a little bit better each day; nothing on Earth is perfect; God is not perfect, but an evolving force just as I am." By applying what they are inwardly hearing, by listening to it, he or she would evolve into and embrace a compassion for themselves and others which then allows for an entirely different attraction pattern to emerge. They would attract people who are loving and encouraging, who support this person's efforts to become a better person.

In understanding the role of Venus in the birthchart it is very important to remember the four natural evolutionary conditions discussed earlier in the book. The four natural evolutionary conditions correlate to the natural conditioning at an archetypal level in consciousness. Venus in Virgo, as in any other sign, manifests differently relative to the evolutionary condition of any given individual. In addition, by understanding the main karmic/evolutionary dynamic in the birth chart as symbolized by Pluto, its polarity point, and the South and North Nodes with their respective planetary rulers, you can then understand exactly how any planet will manifest in any birthchart. The point here is that no sign has just one meaning or orientation, but is an archetype that has a spectrum within it. Thus, by understanding the main karmic/evolutionary axis within the birth chart you will be able to understand what point within the total spectrum of any sign a planet is orientated to. It is also important to understand that the Venus function will be conditioned by other factors symbolized in the aspects to other planets. These aspects correlate, again, to a preexisting pattern at birth. Embracing the polarity point of the natal sign that Venus is in will automatically evolve or change these pre-existing patterns. In other words, the polarity point of Venus is the causal factor in changing the patterns shown in the planetary aspects.

A NOTE ON VENUS RETROGRADE

From a terrestrial view, the planet Venus goes into apparent retrograde motion every 542 days or so. Thus, it is retrograde the least amount of time of any planet in our solar system. Venus retrograde in a natal chart has very specific archetypal correlations that condition how we inwardly and outwardly relate to ourselves and other people. Consistent with the archetype of retrogradation in general, Venus retrograde correlates with a necessary rebellion or individuation of its function relative to our orientation to relationships. Thus, the Venus retrograde person will inherently rebel against the cultural conditioning of how we are expected to define ourselves in general, the meaning of life specifically, and how we are expected to be in our relationships: gender-specific roles, how children are meant to be raised, the purpose of relationship, and so on.

When Venus is retrograde at birth the individual consequently *internalizes* the Venus function. This means that such an individual is orientated to establishing an inner relationship with themselves as a primary focus in life. Consequently, there is a perpetual inner questioning of who they are, and what they need in order to actualize a life consistent with their individuality. By internalizing the Venus function, the individual is essentially defined through the Taurus side of Venus, versus the Libra side of Venus. There is a primary focus on self-sustainment, self-reliance, self-empowerment, and a desire and need to actualize individual values that correlate to the individual's sense of the meaning and purpose of his or her life. As a result, such people inwardly hear and respond to a very "different drummer." They create a very different inner vibration or magnetism that serves to attract others who are similarly vibrating or resonating, individuals who rebel against the "normal" way of living life according to the consensus of society in general, and the "normal" forms of relationship specifically.

Because of this deep internalization of the Venus function, the Venus retrograde person relates to others in a very different way. He or she is a deeply self-introspective individual that psychologists would classify as an introverted type. Being introverted, the Venus in retrograde person thus creates an aura or atmosphere around them in which there is a "buffer" that does not allow others to penetrate into their inner reality. As a result, the Venus retrograde person appears to be enigmatic or difficult to understand. This buffer creates a condition in which other people typically project onto the Venus retrograde person the realities that they represent, versus understanding their actual reality. Because this happens so often, it has the continuing effect of keeping the Venus retrograde person deeply withdrawn from the environment. This reaction to others' projections is a form of the survival instinct as embodied in the Taurus side of Venus.

In my work as a counseling astrologer, I have counseled over 15,000 clients to date, and I have observed that many Venus retrograde people naturally attract partners who have a strong Uranian emphasis in their natures, even if they do not have Venus retrograde themselves. Even in the consensus evolutionary state, which again correlates with generally seventy percent of the world population, the Venus retrograde person has either managed to uniquely define their relationship in some way so as to reflect the principle of individuation, or they have created a relationship dynamic in which they have deeply and silently withdrawn while "going through the motions" of the relationship itself. This deep inner withdrawal, when it occurs, serves the individuating function of Venus retrograde, for it creates a psychological condition of deep inner reflection, examination, and questioning that can and will be applied as some future point in such an individual's evolution. Furthermore, around twenty percent or so of the Venus retrograde individuals that I have counseled have had no relationships of an intimate nature whatsoever.

As a preexisting pattern, the Venus retrograde person has already learned, or is focused on learning, the polarity point or sign of the natal Venus in the birthchart. This is important to understand because the archetypal themes of Venus in the different signs or houses will be oriented to quite differently when Venus is retrograde. It is also important to understand that Venus retrograde individuals desire to continually grow or evolve within themselves. They are never comfortable with reaching a degree of comfort in their lives, and stopping their growth because of that comfort. As a result, when they are in a relationship, they desire a partner who also demands and needs to evolve and grow from within themselves. In addition, because the Venus retrograde person internalizes the Venus function (the Taurus side of Venus), they also desire a partner who is self-empowered, self-sustaining, and self-reliant. These qualities will be quite necessary in the partner if there is to be a successful relationship, since the Venus retrograde person typically is quite silent and withdrawn in relationships, and relates to their partner, or others generally, only as necessary. Thus, they need a partner who is self-secure, so that when these periods of silence occur the partner does not project onto them something that has nothing to do with them.

Karmically and evolutionarily speaking, the Venus retrograde person reflects a situation in which they are necessarily repeating or reliving past life relationship dynamics in the current life. The specific nature of those dynamics are reflected in the following indicators:

• The house and sign that retrograde Venus is in.

• The nature of the aspects that it is making to other planets.

• The nature of the planets that it is forming aspects to.

• The nature of the houses that these aspected planets are in.

• The nature of the houses that the signs Libra and Taurus occupy.

Venus retrograde also means that these people are karmically and evolutionarily determined to re-meet key people that they have known in other lifetimes in which something has not been finished or resolved. The intention is for final resolution of these circumstances in order for a new evolutionary cycle to begin. If you are a counseling astrologer, this point is necessary to understand because many people who have Venus retrograde can be quite frustrated because they seem to be in an ever- repeating loop of relationship dynamics with no way out. By helping such people understand the larger picture of why this is occurring, and that there will be a release from this requirement at some point, they can begin to come to terms with these karmic and evolutionary conditions in their lives.

Famous People with Venus Retrograde

Jane Roberts
Gordon Lightfoot
Jeffrey Green
Audrey Hepburn
Craig Russell (female impersonator)

At this point, I would like to provide a description of the general archetypal themes of Venus in its natal sign, which will correlate to the preexisting pattern of inner/outer relatedness. I will also address its polarity sign, which will allow these pre-existing patterns to evolve into a new way of inwardly relating to oneself. This, in turn, will change the types of people we attract into our lives. Please understand that these are general descriptions of Venus in specific signs that are not conditioned by any other factor such as aspects, the house that Venus is in natally, one of the four natural evolutionary conditions, or the specific evolutionary/karmic axis in the birthchart as symbolized the Pluto, its polarity point, or the South and North Nodes with their respective planetary rulers. These are all factors which must be considered for any complete and accurate analysis.

VENUS IN ARIES

As a pre-existing pattern from birth, the Venus in Aries person will be quite narcissistic, self-orientated, and feel within themselves that they are quite special. Inwardly, they will instinctively feel that they have some undefined special destiny to fulfill which requires a fundamental independence in order to actualize it. Thus, in a relationship these people can never fully commit themselves to another person, always keeping a deep part of their inner self isolated from the relationship. Cyclically, the Venus in Aries person can be extremely passionate and involved. They seem fully committed through displays of intense, passionate energy of a very creative nature which keep the relationship moving forward. On the other hand, the Venus in Aries person will cyclically withdraw this energy when they instinctively feel that they have become too involved, too caught up in the relationship in such a way that their need for independent actualization of their sense of a special destiny is threatened. The instinctual trigger for this cyclic withdrawal is when they feel that they have become too enmeshed with the other person. The other person will then feel totally deflated and confused, angry, and become intensely confrontational by way of projecting their own insecurities upon the Venus in Aries person.

Because these people feel inwardly that they are special, they need to be treated as special by other people. Conversely, they can make the person that they are with feel incredibly special, pumping the other person up with intense displays of love and energy. They are instinctively attracted to others who have a strong sense of self, who radiate a strong, passionate nature, who are as deeply self-orientated as themselves, and who have a strong sense of purpose in life. As a result, the relationships that the Venus in Aries person forms must have a sense of adventure, a continuing sense of ever moving forwards in life. The Venus in Aries person will instinctively reject too much comfort, and established routines that lead to stagnation or boredom. Because Venus in Aries persons will attract others who are just as narcissistic as themselves, who can make them feel that they are the most special person that they have ever been with, yet also cyclically withdraw through their own fears of losing themselves in the relationship, they will cyclically lose their sense of self-confidence, and become deeply insecure. As this point, they can become extremely aggressive, confrontational, abusive, and project an intensity of displaced anger that is disproportionate to the actual circumstances that exist within the relationship. The problem here is that the Venus in Aries person operates instinctively and is essentially unaware that they create relationships in which everyone must serve them and their purposes in some way. Thus, they attract others who have this same orientation, and are reflections of their inner reality so that, at some point, the mirroring effect will produce self-knowledge.

Because Aries is a Mars-ruled sign, these people have a strong, passionate, and narcissistic sexual nature that generates an inner vibration that manifests as an animal kind of magnetism. This operates instinctively, not consciously, and the Venus in Aries person is unaware that they appear this way until others tell them. Consequently, others are sexually attracted to them without really knowing why. Physiologically, Venus in Aries people emit very strong pheromones that chemically excite people. Thus, others can be attracted to the Venus in Aries person as sexual objects through which they can act out their own sexual desires or natures. Such sexually narcissistic types of people are primarily orientated to acting out their sexual desires through the Venus in Aries person in a very self-centered way.

The Venus in Aries person is simply aware that their sexual energy is strong, yet it is unformed. From birth, they do not know who they are as sexual beings. Accordingly, they will experiment with different ways of being sexual with other people in order to discover, through experiences over time, what their basic sexual nature is, and what they need in order to actualize it. Thus, they will be attracted to others who also radiate a strong sexual nature. The Venus in Aries person instinctively uses their sexual nature as a way of securing the attention of another person that they are interested in, or as a way of sustaining an existing relationship. Conversely, relative to their cyclic withdrawal from an existing relationship, they will withhold their sexual energy, and stop being sexual with an existing partner. This is really a form of controlling the relationship so that their need for independence is not consumed in their fear of becoming enmeshed in the relationship. Venus in Aries will also use their sexual energy as a way of renewing the relationship, of bringing it back together, especially when major problems threaten to end the relationship outright. This pattern entirely depends on how much the Venus in Aries person wants to sustain the relationship for their own purposes.

In essence, the basic pattern of the Venus in Aries person is one of narcissistic self-involvement in which everything, including other people, must serve their own purposes for self-actualization. This naturally creates an emotional paradox linked with relationship. On one side of the paradox is their need for relationship, and on the other side of the paradox is their need for absolute independence. This paradox generates an instinctual fear of becoming too enmeshed in any relationship. Thus, it is very difficult for these people to remain committed to a relationship for long periods of time because their fundamental need is to be in control of their own destiny. They instinctively use other people for whatever their existing purposes or needs are, and others can use them in exactly the same way.

In evolutionary terms, the Venus in Aries person has embarked on a new cycle of personal development. Freedom is necessary in order to discover and actualize this new cycle. The key to actualizing this new cycle in a positive way is to embrace the sign Libra, because by embracing the individual needs of a partner or friend, and encouraging the independent actualization of those needs, they will then attract others who do this for them. Thus, their fear of losing their individuality, of not being able to have their own life because of their relationship, will no longer exist. By learning to give, rather than always creating relationships in which the other must serve their needs and purposes at all times, they will learn that they will be given to in ways that are free from subjective, ulterior, self-serving motives and agendas. In this way they will learn role equality in relationship, and role interchangeability.

Famous People with Venus in Aries

George Carlin
Rita Coolridge
Charles Darwin
Adolph Eichmann
Sigmund Freud

VENUS IN TAURUS

As a preexisting pattern from birth, Venus in Taurus people have learned to deeply internalize themselves in order to understand who they are and what they need in order to have a sense of meaning in their lives. As a result, these individuals are quite introspective and self-possessed. They have learned, in the last analysis, that the only person that they can truly rely on is themselves. Thus, these people are more or less self-reliant and self-sustaining, and can be extremely resourceful and resilient in their ability to sustain themselves, even in the face of overwhelming problems or circumstances.

These people have learned to limit what they value relative to what life means to them. Thus, their sense of meaning, of what life means, determines what they value. Consequently, they can have a limited value system that is more or less fixed and static—one that works for them. In terms of relating to other people, these individuals tend to evaluate and hear others relative to their own value system. If there is no common thread between their value system and another's value system, then these people will generally be unable to relate. In other words, there is an inherent resistance to others whose values are different than their own, whose sense of what life means is at odds with their own. They simply "tune out" and do not hear what the other is saying. As a result of their intrinsic resistance to embracing other values, ideas, knowledge, or other forms of reality, these people tend to evolve or grow very slowly. In social situations as an example, Venus in Taurus people will typically remain silent and self-enclosed unless there is a commonality of values in which they can then relate to someone else. When there is a basis of relating to another through shared values, then the Venus in Taurus person can appear very warm, engaging, deep, intense, highly focused, and have an absorbing quality wherein others can feel drawn into their inner reality which now appears magnetic and solid.

Whatever the Venus in Taurus person values, including other people who they have given meaning and value to, they will want to maintain and possess. It is very difficult for these people to give up or let go of anything that holds meaning and value to them because that correlates to their sense of purpose for living. In intimate relationships, as a result, Venus in Taurus people can be highly possessive of their partners, and attempt to limit what their partners do because of their fear of losing them. Because of this they can be quite controlling in covert and overt ways, the sense of ownership or possession of that which they value generating an emotional psychology of jealousy. Unless other astrological factors are indicated, this way of controlling or limiting their partners' activities manifests as psychological withdrawal and inner isolation from the partner. Vibrating inwardly in this way, Venus in Taurus people can also attract others who are very possessive of them, and who can also feel very threatened when they manifest any interest in other people. They can attract others who attempt to limit their own development, others who unconsciously expect them to be vicarious extensions of their own reality, to have no real life of their own, to simply be a prize possession like a trophy on the wall. Interestingly enough, when the Venus in Taurus person has projected value and meaning on such a partner they will allow themselves to be limited in this way even if it means limiting their own development. This means that the Venus in Taurus person has projected too much meaning and value into such a partner, because of their need for stability in life at all costs. Over time, when this occurs, the Venus in Taurus person will create a progressive build-up of resentment towards the partner, which can lead into very explosive confrontations.

Conversely, if the Venus in Taurus person attempts to break free from the limits of a controlling and possessive partner, then that partner can manifest very explosive behavior, motivated by jealousy and the fear of losing them.

Venus in Taurus people will also have a very strong sexual instinct or nature. This is because part of the survival instinct in all forms of life, including human, is to procreate the species. Consequently, their sexual needs and desires are constant. Sexual energy, and the expression of it, correlates in a very strong way to their sense of meaning and relatedness of life itself. They have a strong, magnetic, earthy sexual energy that reflects a strong integration into their physical bodies. Whereas Venus in Aries desires strong, passionate, and relatively quick sexual expression, Venus in Taurus desires long, sustained, intense, and permeating sexual expression. This way serves to "ground" them, and serves as a way of releasing their cyclic build-up of internalized emotional and psychological energy. Sexuality will symbolize a great deal of meaning to them, and they find themselves thinking about sex a great deal of the time. It is very important for Venus in Taurus people to have a strong, positive, and ongoing sex life. When they do not, then their overall reality will seem negative and stagnated. Their psychology will be inwardly compressed and withdrawn, and their life force will be weak and heavy.

When this occurs, the Venus in Taurus person is forced to remember, or must come to understand, that the primary intention of Taurus is one of self-reliance and self-sustainment. As a result of this intention, the Venus in Taurus person can create periods of cycles in their life in which their sexual needs are not met, if those needs have become too dependent on another person. When this occurs, either the person that they are with appears to lose sexual interest in them, or there is no one in their life at certain times that they desire to be sexual with. In either case, the intention is for the Venus in Taurus person to take matters into their own hands, so to speak—to sustain themselves sexually through masturbation.

Many individuals with Venus in Taurus have a strong masturbatory instinct that manifests even when they are in a relationship with another. Sometimes this can create confusion for such individuals because of the fact that they are in a relationship with someone, yet still desire this form of sexual expression. The reason that this can occur, again, is because the primary intention in this symbolism is self-empowerment and self-sustainment. For others, this instinctual need can create confrontations with their partners when those partners feel threatened by this need. The partner can feel insecure and inadequate, especially when the Venus in Taurus person "isolates" oneself from the relationship in order to fulfill this need. Conversely, the Venus in Taurus person can attract partners who desire to masturbate even though they are in a relationship with them. The Venus in Taurus person can now feel threatened, inadequate, and so on. This condition will occur to the Venus in Taurus person for one of two reasons. Either they have become too possessive or too dependent on the partner, or they have attracted a partner who is also learning the Taurus lesson of self-empowerment which dictates this need. Because of this, many people with this symbol have learned to incorporate sexual self-stimulation within their sexual dynamics with another person. For some with Venus in Taurus, masturbation has become an art form in which they have learned to create highly erotic rituals that involve various kinds of sexual symbols and "tools" that serve the intention of self-sustainment and self-empowerment. For some, depending on their evolutionary condition, this means that they have learned to use themselves as their own vehicle or symbol of metamorphic transformation. Some with Venus in Taurus will attract partners who will encourage them to learn to do this, partners who try to teach them about the power that exists within them.

Their sexual values and orientation are primary and basic. There is not too much of a desire or need to "experiment." The Venus in Taurus person will desire to sexually possess or own their partners, and they can attract partners who want to sexually possess and own them. Because there is such a high value given to sexuality, if they are with a partner who does not honor their need for monogamy, who has sex with someone else behind their backs, then their inner relatedness will suffer. They will feel insecure, unworthy, create a negative self-esteem, become withdrawn, and compare themselves to whatever qualities or traits that their partner has been attracted to in the "other person." Even though the Venus in Taurus person inherently desires monogamy, they can involve themselves in an "affair" when their partner is not monogamous with them. The motivation is one of vindictiveness, and also to rebuild a positive self-image through making themselves desirable to someone else.

In evolutionary terms, the Venus in Taurus person desires to stabilize him or herself. To do so, they have necessarily had to narrow their focus to that which is specific to their own life's purpose, and that which supports that purpose. Any other aspect of life in general that is not relevant to that purpose is "tuned out." This creates a "frog in the well" effect—the frog can only see the segment of the sky that is observable from the bottom of the well. The frog is stable at the bottom of its well. It can control and feel secure within that well. Accordingly, there is a compressed internalization leading to a highly subjective reality that defines a pre-existing pattern of inner and outer relatedness. This creates a block to growing, learning, and evolving beyond the parameters of the well. In a relationship, this can create a polarized state between the two people. For a positive evolution to proceed the Venus in Taurus person must embrace its polarity: Scorpio.

Essentially, this means that they must learn how to listen to other people in such a way as to objectively identify what motivates other people, and learn how other people are psychologically constructed. In this way, they will learn how to evaluate others objectively which will, in turn, allow them to evaluate their own inner/outer reality in an objective way. In order to do this, the Venus in Taurus person must learn to open up to the totality of reality that lies beyond the parameters of their own "frog in the well" reality. They will then remove the bottleneck of their own inwardly compressed reality, one that generates a fixity of subjective perception and interpretation of their own and others' behaviors, motivations, intentions, and what life mans in general. By learning how to listen to others objectively, to hear what others need and desire, and to support their development, they will attract others who do this for them, and who do not want to possess, control, or limit their own development.

Famous People with Venus in Taurus
Princess Diana
Prince Edward
Cyril Fagan
Adolph Hitler
Salvador Dali

VENUS IN GEMINI

As a preexisting pattern of inner relatedness, the Venus in Gemini person hears an inner call for self-knowledge. This manifests as a deep inner restlessness, fueled by a constant inner dialogue within themselves. This inner dialogue poses a variety of questions leading to experiences of all kinds. The essence of these questions is defined by the inner question "Who am I?" which leads also to "Who are you?"

Venus in Gemini people relate to and understand themselves inwardly through a reactive process. This means that these individuals pose a variety of thought possibilities leading to potential experiences, and then react to these thought possibilities in such a way that the reaction itself produces self-awareness and self-knowledge. This is a perpetual process with the Venus in Gemini person, because Gemini as an archetype is mutable. The mutable archetype is one of unrestricted growth and perpetual expansion. Yet because we live in a time/space reality that is defined and understood through polarity, the process of expansion must, at some point, contract. Thus, Venus in Gemini people learn about themselves through cycles of contraction which are induced as a reaction to excessive expansion. In the cycle of expansion, Venus in Gemini people are inwardly considering a diversity of thoughts in their desire to understand themselves, and life in general. These thoughts are induced by exposure to life itself: "What does this mean? What does that mean? By doing this, what will I discover? If I read this, what will I learn? If I talk to this person, or take that class, what will I discover?" and so on. By initiating experiences of kind, by bringing into themselves all kinds of information from all kinds of sources, they react inwardly to this relatively indiscriminate intake of information. "Do I really believe this? What does this really mean to me? How can I apply that?" becomes a perpetual inner dialogue that is restrictive in nature as a reaction to their desire for perpetual growth and expansion.

The rhythm between expansion and contraction is ever-shifting, yet always ongoing at an underlying level. Even though the cycles of inner/outer expansion and contraction are not predictable, there is always an underlying reactive dialogue that occurs within the Venus in Gemini person. Thus, these people may enter into a cycle in which they are seeking out all kinds of experiences, taking all kinds of classes, reading all kinds of books, seeing all kinds of movies, etc. This will then induce a cycle of contraction because they will reach the limit of such expansion. They simply become exhausted and fragmented because of too much intake of stimulus of this kind. When the cycle of contraction is induced in this way, the Venus in Gemini person necessarily assimilates the meaning of the different experiences they have created relative to their desire for knowledge. So, on the one hand, there is this reactive process occurring within them even during the cycle of expansion, and, on the other hand, they cyclically withdraw from the cycle of expansion because they simply become overwhelmed and exhausted. By withdrawing from external stimuli, they are able to assimilate what they have been exposing themselves to.

Because of their deep inner restlessness and intense inner curiosity to experience as much of themselves and life as possible, the Venus in Gemini person relates to other people in a very open, friendly way. They are naturally attracted to anyone who symbolizes new experiences or knowledge. Because they are open to all the possibilities of life, they are open to, and accepting of, the differences in all people. They are color-blind, so to speak. They are able to relate to people in a very free way that is relatively devoid of prejudice. Because of their own inner curiosity as to the possibilities of life itself, the Venus in Gemini person is very adept in being able to carry on conversations with other people. They ask good questions, and are able to communicate quite well. They are quite skilled at drawing other people out of themselves. They are versatile, quick, and quite witty.

Conversely, when these individuals are in a contraction cycle, they can be very reactive in their conversations with other people. The reactive process manifests as not completing their own sentences, or allowing another to complete their own sentences. When this occurs, the mutual reaction does not allow for either one to actually hear the other. Needing to contract and stabilize thus creates a resistance to any more intake of information. This reactive process which is really a manifestation of the survival instinct intrinsic to the archetype of Venus via its natural rulership of Taurus, and thus the Second House.

The Venus in Gemini person understands their feelings through their mental body or process. Let us understand that feelings are different than emotions. Feelings are an immediate reaction to an existing stimulus, whereas emotions are a reaction to our feelings. Because Gemini is an Air archetype, people who have Venus in this sign relate to themselves inwardly through the nature of what they are thinking at any given moment. This process will induce a feeling reaction to the specific nature of what those thoughts are. In this way, they come to understand the nature of their feelings. On a projected basis, these individuals understand what and how another is feeling by approaching another through their intellect. In other words, they must engage someone's intellect or mental processes first in order to understand how that person is feeling about anything.

Sexually, the Venus in Gemini person values sexual openness in the sense of mentally entertaining all kinds of sexual possibilities.

Again, they are naturally curious, and they do not want to preclude any possibility out of hand. They will (at least mentally) consider almost any sexual possibility. Some with Venus in Gemini will have a dual sexual nature that leads to bisexuality. Thus, they can be quite sexually versatile, playful, and "sporting" because of the implied adventure of being open to all sexual possibilities. There is also a particular attraction to oral forms of sexuality, and a strong mental orientation to the sexual act that induces a detachment from it. This is necessary for Venus in Gemini because it is through this kind of *de facto* voyeurism that they learn about themselves as a sexual being, and learn about others as sexual beings. On the other hand, this kind of mental detachment can create sexual frustration because it is as if they are forever observing instead of being totally engaged at a purely emotional and physical level. It is as if they cannot get out of their heads, so to speak.

In evolutionary terms, the Venus in Gemini person desires to expand their consciousness in order to learn how to relate to themselves in a diversity of ways through the multiplicity of experience. The process of learning occurs through reactions to initiated experiences of an internal and external nature—thought and counter thought. For evolution to proceed, the Venus in Gemini person must embrace its polarity: Sagittarius. In essence, this means to continue the desire for expansion, to expand the inner and outer horizons of awareness, but in such a way that indiscriminate curiosity is replaced by conscious intention: "I want to learn this for this reason; I want to do that for this purpose; I am interested in learning this and will focus on it until I learn it thoroughly before learning something else; I am thinking about that because of this reason" and so on. In addition, the Venus in Gemini person must progressively evolve away from externally acquired knowledge into the dynamic that the knowledge they are seeking is inwardly realized through the development of the intuition. They need to transfer the center of gravity in their consciousness from the left to right brain. In this way, these individuals will learn to relate to themselves in a responsive way, versus a reactive way. They will create a deep inner center within themselves that is constant, versus an inner center that becomes cyclically fragmented. They will learn to listen to themselves in a different way, and thus how they listen to other people. In effect, they will learn to hear more deeply what is behind or within the actual spoken words and the thoughts that are occurring within their own consciousness. In this way, they will learn to communicate differently as they speak to the essence of what is being said, versus reacting to the specific nature of the words only. They will learn how to communicate their own essence in a very direct way versus a plurality of words that is trying to describe that essence.

Famous People with Venus in Gemini

John F. Kennedy
Jeddu Krishnamurti
Vivian Robson
Oliver Cromwell
Bob Dylan

VENUS IN CANCER

As a pre-existing pattern of inner relatedness, the Venus in Cancer person comes into life fundamentally insecure. This insecurity is based on, and caused by, the nature of their inner emotional reality, which is like a tornado of different swirling emotional states that seem to come and go of their own volition, that seem to be beyond the control of the individual. Inwardly, as a result, the Venus in Cancer person feels that they are standing on ever-shifting sands. These people feel deeply insecure because the nature of their emotional state and the needs that these states create cannot be inwardly controlled. The inner cross-currents of different emotions converge and combine in ways that create moments in which they can feel stable and secure in one moment, and highly insecure and unstable in the next.

The intention of Souls who have Venus in Cancer has been, and is, to inwardly know and relate to themselves as emotional beings. The knowing of themselves through the ever-shifting cross-currents of different emotional states produces an inner confusion because of the different self-images that each emotional state induces. And each emotional state dictates needs that are motivated by the desire to feel secure, to feel safe, and to be stabilized. Inwardly, these individuals feel highly vulnerable and insecure. Typically, they relate to themselves from moment to moment. Each emotion (and the moods that they produce) defines their inner psychology on an ongoing basis. Inwardly, there is a fundamental desire to be taken care of, to be nurtured, by someone whom they can trust. There is a core desire for someone to help them feel stable, safe, and secure. The deep inner need for this is its own causal factor, generating the different emotional states in the first place.

The reason for this, typically, is that these individuals have missed a key step in their behavioral development as children. This step occurs around twenty months of age when the baby learns to internalize one or both parents in such a way that when the parent is not physically nearby or present, the baby still feels safe and secure. Missing this step becomes a causal factor leading to the displaced emotions of childhood manifesting in their adult life. These displaced emotions are essentially the emotions of a young child.

The root cause of this is that they bring forward from other lifetimes emotional imprints and pre-existing patterns that are defined by some cataclysmic emotional event in which their ability to feel inwardly secure has been severely compromised. Whatever the specific event was, it becomes a casual factor generating an inner abyss of emotional volatility and cross-currents of unpredictable emotional states. Even if they had parents who were loving, nurturing, and doing their very best to help them feel secure when they were a baby, it is never quite enough from the child's point of view. As adults, this same effect can occur even when they have loving and supporting people in their lives, for the same reasons. Even when the Venus in Cancer person is given the love, nurturing, and the stabilizing effect that they desire, it is never quite enough.

Venus in Cancer people have an inherent emotional expectation that is projected into their relationships in which others should somehow just know what they need without actually verbalizing what that need is. It is simply a deep, silent expectation. This is exactly what babies and small children do. They just naturally expect their needs to be identified and met by the parents. When this does not occur to the baby's satisfaction, they instinctively cry or scream in varying degrees of intensity. Similarly, the Venus in Cancer person, as an adult, silently expects their needs to be understood and met. When this does not occur, the unmet expectations produce emotional behaviors that can even shock the Venus in Cancer person themselves. These behaviors range from a deep, permeating silence in which the subconscious intent is to draw or pull someone into their emotional state in order for it to be identified and worked with, to extreme emotional displays that are driven or caused by displaced anger. The cause of this kind of extreme behavior, resembling a coiled spring that snaps under stress, is a build-up of emotional frustration. The emotional reaction is usually disproportionate to the event or circumstance that triggers it.

Because these people relate to themselves on an emotional basis, they naturally relate to others on an emotional basis. Because they are perpetually "hearing" or "listening" to their own inner emotional reality, they can naturally identify or "hear" another's emotional state, and the needs that any given emotional state generates, even when the other person is not verbalizing or actively projecting what that emotional state or reality is about. Venus in Cancer people have an inherent ability to emotionally empathize with other people, to silently tune in. When others are perceived to be in a state of emotional distress or need, the Venus in Cancer person naturally responds with very real emotional caring, wisdom, support, nurturing, and love. They will naturally encourage others to let out their emotions, and they will want to hold and embrace another who is in need. The very essence of their touch or holding is warm, consuming, and reassuring. This reflects their own need to be reassured through touch and holding. More than words, the Venus in Cancer person responds to touch and holding because this is exactly how babies and small children are reassured when they are upset for whatever reason. For Venus in Cancer people, trust is established through touch, and through a silent emotional resonance with another that operates beyond the spoken word. This is very important to understand because of the Venus in Cancer person's inherent fear of being too vulnerable. Even verbalizing what they need, or are feeling, can be too vulnerable a situation for these people. In fact, the typical verbal response of these people when asked how they are doing, especially when some deep emotional state or need is causing a deep inner withdrawal from their environment, is "I'm fine" even when they obviously are not. This kind of response is instinctual, and is a form of the survival instinct relative to their fear of vulnerability and their fundamental distrust of most people. Thus, for those that are close to them and with whom there is a trust, the very best way to encourage them to come out of their emotional shell is through touch combined with soft, soothing words.

Sexually, Venus in Cancer desires and needs very strong touch, holding and kissing in order to feel sexually secure and trusting. Whereas Venus in Aries can simply get on with it, the Venus in Cancer person needs to be "warmed up" first. Inherently, these people desire and need to connect and merge the emotional energies or bodies first which then allows for a deep, permeating, and slow sexual merging to occur. When this occurs, these people can feel very erotic and create erotic sexual environments that stimulate the emotional and sexual senses. But unless the Venus in Cancer person feels emotionally safe and secure, they will be sexually insecure. Some will be sexually immature, and can exhibit forms of sexual infantilism, such as wanting to be spanked, sexual pedophilia, a male preoccupation with breasts or nipples, a female preoccupation with the penis, impotence or frigidity, etc. When the Venus in Cancer person is in love and feels safe and secure, they can be very sexually giving and truly make their partners feel loved, safe, and secure.

For a positive evolution to proceed, the Venus in Cancer person must inwardly embrace its polarity: Capricorn. This means that they must learn how to minimize the projection of their external dependencies in order to feel emotionally secure, safe, and stable. They must learn that the security, safety, and stability that they are desiring exists within themselves. They must learn to become responsible for their own "emotional child." In order to do this, they must learn how to evolve their emotional consciousness in such a way as to be able to become aware of the specific causes or origins of any given emotional state that they find themselves in, versus just being caught up within it without knowing why. By doing so, they can develop emotional self-knowledge, which allows them to become emotionally responsible for themselves—to become emotional adults. They will empower themselves and minimize their projected needs, lose their fear of vulnerability, and thus learn how to relate with people in a much more straightforward and forthcoming way. In this way they will learn how to be in control of their emotions versus letting their emotions control them. They will attract others who encourage them to be responsible for themselves, and they will naturally encourage others to be responsible for themselves. Thereby, the "inner child" lives in a very positive and healthy way because it has now taken responsibility for its own actions.

Famous People with Venus in Cancer

Bjorn Borg
Fidel Castro
Dean Martin
Lord Louis Mountbatten
Calvin Coolidge

VENUS IN LEO

As a pre-existing pattern, individuals with Venus in Leo have a very deep and intense inner focus that archetypally desires absolute creative self-actualization. Just as the Sun gives and sustains life in our solar system, these people have an inner wellspring of creative potential that allows them to sustain themselves. This "inner sun" is ever radiating and inexhaustible. Inwardly, they "hear" the call for creative self-actualization, and they give themselves the right to actualize themselves in any way they see fit. In this sense, they are the center of their own created universe and naturally expect all else to revolve around and support their desires for self-exploration and actualization. Whereas Venus in Aries manifests a primitive form of narcissism because it is so unformed and instinctual, Venus in Leo manifests a conscious narcissism because it is fully aware of its own creative potential.

Venus in Leo people expect others to understand how wonderful and special they are, and to tell them so. There is a fundamental need for positive and supportive feedback of their efforts for creative actualization however those efforts manifest. When this feedback is not positive enough, or supportive enough, then the Venus in Leo person can inwardly feel unworthy and that the results of the efforts they are making are something less than what they had expected. Conversely, these people can shower others with very positive support and praise. This is very sincere and honest, yet is a reflection of their own inner expectation for others to do this for them. The only time that the Venus in Leo person does not favor another with such support and praise is when they interface with someone who is perceived to be a potential competitor in the same area that they are creatively actualizing themselves in. This can occur because, again, Venus in Leo people are the center of their own universe. Thus, someone who is perceived to be equal to or ahead of themselves changes their orientation to their own universe—they are not the "star" anymore.

Inwardly, Venus in Leo people relate to themselves as an unformed piece of clay that is waiting to be sculpted, a canvas waiting to be painted, an inner landscape desiring to be explored in all possible directions, or a universe waiting to be created. These people are literally "full of themselves." Within itself, Venus in Leo has no inner sense of limits whatsoever. Whatever they feel drawn to do they simply expect that they *can* do. The very deepest frustration occurs when they realize that there *are* limits to what they can accomplish or do. This evolutionarily necessary experience occurs in order to create a sense of humiliation of the ego. This must occur to counteract the Leo tendency to delusions of personal grandeur.

Within themselves, Venus in Leo people are quite optimistic, enthusiastic, and future orientated. They have a deep and positive feeling about themselves and life in general, and create many activities that lead to a sense of self-pleasuring and self-knowing. Generally, they simply feel good about themselves. They are deeply self-focused, and can focus on whatever is it is that they are trying to accomplish. The primary cause that creates a sense of brooding is when the Venus in Leo person feels inwardly blocked from being able to create, or when circumstances in their life are perceived to be thwarting or blocking their need for a necessary freedom or independence in order to creatively actualize. At worst, the Venus in Leo person can creatively actualize intense emotional tantrums and displays of a very melodramatic and negative nature.

In their external relatedness patterns, they have an inherent ability to make others feel really good about themselves, to "pump up" others, to provide positive motivation that encourages others to actualize whatever they are trying to accomplish, to make others feel "special," and to radiate a platonic kind of love that makes others feel embraced and regenerated just by being in their presence. This occurs because they themselves want to be heard and acknowledged by others. Thus, they have a great ability to hear where another is actually coming from, and to acknowledge this through validating and encouraging efforts at whatever it is that the person is focused on. Through positive feedback and support, they can help others focus on what they need in order to become more free and self-actualized. Conversely, when the Venus in Leo person is feeling inwardly blocked, or when they feel blocked by external circumstances, they can either totally withdraw from any kind of interaction with another, or become very spiteful and disdaining of another's efforts.

In their intimate relationships, the Venus in Leo person has a deep need to always keep the relationship in a kind of "love affair" situation. This is because the Venus in Leo person might as well die as be taken for granted. They need to be the sole focus of their partner's attention, and they desire to be considered special at all times. Their need to feel loved, and to be loved, is permeating desire that is never quite satisfied on an ongoing basis, though it can be satisfied on a momentary basis. As long as they feel that they are being loved and treated in the ways that they expect, they can also make their partners feel as if they are the very center of the universe. The Venus in Leo person must have creative independence that allows them to act on any desire that is based in self-actualization or discovery. Beyond the necessary independence, they also require a partner who encourages and supports their self-development. When this is extended by the partner, they will do exactly the same for them. The Venus in Leo individual is naturally a very powerful, self-directed, and self-motivated person who is strong willed and highly narcissistic. Thus, they will attract, and be attracted to, others who inwardly vibrate in the same way. The resulting relationship will be a highly self-indulgent one in which life can be lived to its fullest potential. The Venus in Leo person can be very generous. When they are in love, and feel loved, they can truly make another feel loved in ways that are quite unique.

When the Venus in Leo person feels that they are being taken for granted, or when their partner does not spend enough time with them, or when their partner feels that they are more important than the Venus in Leo person is, or when the partner is not monogamous, then the flip side of their Venus in Leo nature will manifest an intense emotional withdrawal that produces an inner vibration of disdain towards the partner. At this point they can become quite mean and cruel, and can completely belittle or humiliate the partner. They can manifest incredible emotional dramas of a melodramatic nature that are motivated by their need for attention, love, and recognition. They can create a life structure in which the other person is completely shut out. They can seek out love affairs with someone who will supply them with the love and attention that they need. And, of course, the Venus in Leo person can attract partners who manifest the very same behaviors when they feel that they are being taken for granted, etc. When this kind of degeneration occurs, the Venus in Leo person has become so self-absorbed that they simply couldn't care less about the feelings or needs of the partner, especially when the partner is perceived to be thwarting them in some way.

Sexually, Venus in Leo people have a natural love of the body and the sensuality that can manifest from it. Because of their strong narcissistic orientation, they can be intensely onanistic. It is as if they use their own sensuality and sexuality as a form of personal and symbolic self-actualization and metamorphosis. They view the body and sexuality as a kind of artwork in which they feel the inner freedom to create as they desire. At a body level, the Venus in Leo person emanates a vibration of strong sensuality, and a seductiveness that is natural yet consciously actualized. It is played with, so to speak. In relationship to another they can be intensely passionate and consuming in their sexual expression when they feel good with the partner, or, conversely, totally withhold their sexuality when they do not. At this point they will either satisfy themselves through different forms of autoerotic activities because of their strong sexual natures, or seek out "affairs" for the same purpose. Because of the principle of creative self-actualization, the Venus in Leo person is quite open to sexual adventures or experimentation of all kinds other than any form of sexual expression leading to a sense of humiliation or degradation. Venus in Leo desires monogamy, yet also enjoys sexual flirtations and innuendoes since this feeds their need to feel special, important, and singled out.

For evolution to proceed, the Venus in Leo person must inwardly embrace its polarity: Aquarius. Essentially, this means that they must learn to objectify themselves versus perpetually living in a subjective reality that does not allow them to be experienced as equal to everyone else. For these people to fully and completely actualize themselves in the creative ways that they inwardly feel, they must learn to acknowledge the larger group, community, and society that they are living within, in such a way as to understand what that larger group needs. Once they understand that, they will be able to integrate themselves in very creative and unique ways within the larger group. But until they understand this larger framework in which they operate they can feel totally frustrated, because no one seems to acknowledge what special gifts and capacities they do have. In relationship, they must learn to give without that giving being motivated by their own need to be given to. They must learn to validate and acknowledge another's reality and needs without being told how wonderful and special that they are first, or in return. And they must learn to receive or accept feedback from other people even when this feedback conflicts with their own inner evaluations of themselves. In essence, they must learn that they are part of a very large universe, not the center of it. When this occurs, the Venus in Leo person will be always self-confident in a relaxed kind of way, versus having their self-confidence, and the positive self-image that this implies, dependent on others telling them how special they are.

Famous People with Venus in Leo

    Jimmy Carter
    Mary Baker Eddy

Heinrich Himmler
Alfred Hitchock
Gustav Mahler

VENUS IN VIRGO

As a pre-existing pattern, the Venus in Virgo individual relates inwardly in very self-analytical and critical ways. In evolutionary terms, these individuals have been and are in a cycle wherein the desire and need has been one of personal self-improvement, and of an inner adjustment in how they have been inwardly and outwardly relating to themselves and others. The desire for personal improvement and adjustment reflects and implies that something has come before in which these people to not feel "right" or good about. Whatever this is, it implies guilt and the consequent need to atone for the guilt. Atonement caused by guilt correlates to a standard of judgment that, by its very nature, reinforces and causes the guilt itself. This standard of judgment is typically a belief system whose underpinnings are defined by a rigid set of rights and wrongs of a moralistic and religious nature, beliefs that essentially define the human being as something less than perfect when measured against a perfect God or world. The Venus in Virgo person uses this belief system to generate the desire and need for personal improvement and adjustment of how they have been inwardly and outwardly relating to themselves and other people.

Venus in Virgo individuals have usually had a series of prior lifetimes in which they have desired to deflate their excessively egocentric orientation to life, and lifetimes in which they have desired to remove all causes of personal delusions of grandeur. In addition, these individuals typically have desired, over a series of lifetimes, to align themselves with their *actual* inner reality as contrasted with any personal illusion or delusion of an egocentric nature that was previously considered to be real. Both desires generate an inner reality in which the Venus in Virgo person feels an excruciating inner aloneness, an inner emptiness, and an inner feeling of being very small. Whereas the Venus in Leo person feels inwardly to be godlike, the Venus in Virgo person feels like the proverbial grain of sand on an immense beach. Because of their need and desire to remove all forms of personal delusion and illusion, and the desire to deflate an excessive egocentric orientation to life, these individuals create an intensely self-critical and analytical consciousness of self that archetypally desires to humiliate itself at an egocentric level. Consequently, these individuals have a negative feeling about themselves that creates the sense of never being good enough or perfect enough. This sense or feeling is reinforced, again, by a standard of beliefs in which the individual compares (comparison is a Venus function) itself to something that is more perfect and better than itself. This comparison function is also applied to other people whom the Venus in Virgo person respects in such a way as to be used to belittle him or herself. Because of this, the Venus in Virgo person can be very endearing to other people because they reflect and exhibit a very real humility that naturally deflects any excessive personal acclaim. In many cases, these individuals cannot accept or receive any acclaim or positive feedback whatsoever.

Because these individuals carry a conscious or unconscious guilt and desire to atone for that guilt, they create a form of personal masochism in which they must crucify themselves in some way. The pathology of masochism thus creates the inner and outer reality of crisis that can have many forms and applications. Crisis always leads to analysis, and analysis caused by crisis leads to self-knowledge for those individuals. The forms of personal crucifixion leading to crisis can manifest in a diversity of ways.

It can manifest as a deep inner abuse of oneself that manifests externally as being attracted to abusive people and relationships. It can manifest as perpetually submerging their own legitimate needs to the needs of other people. This reflects an inner feeling of guilt and the consequent thought that they do not deserve to be given to or acknowledged for what they need. It can manifest as all forms of self-undermining activities that lead to a sense of personal defeat and humiliation. It can lead to all forms of personal escape as a way of avoiding confronting the deep inner abyss of aloneness that they feel. It can be seen in the workaholic syndrome, keeping oneself compulsively busy, keeping the mind engaged in all kinds of superficial nonsense, the unconscious creation of one crisis after another in order to keep the left brain engaged so that it can avoid peering into the inner emptiness, the manifestation of physical problems of all kinds, or excessive food intake (compensation for inner emptiness). A variation of this is the bulimic syndrome which reflects the true complexity of this archetype in its most difficult applications or manifestations. In essence, this condition reflects deep inner guilt and the need to atone for it—to expel it through the act of vomiting, relative to a negative self-image that feels empty and devoid of any inner meaning, which in turn causes the excessive intake of food in order to feel full. This is also a *de facto* sexual act, because food intake is a sensation-oriented act that displaces the sense of inner emptiness through the intake of the food which is then "released." The releasing effect thus mimics a sexual orgasm of an intense nature, which in turn reinforces the guilt linked with the sexual act in the first place—sexuality being something less than "pure." Thus, the natural sexual desire is suppressed either through guilt or because of a fear of being "contaminated" by another person. The sublimation of this natural function can lead to not only the food problem as a form of compensation, but to any one of the above behaviors. Conversely, Venus in Virgo people can also involve themselves in indiscriminate sexuality, or being compulsively sexual, as a way of filling up the inner void.

Venus in Virgo people are plagued by a deep sense of inner doubt which is caused not only by the desire to deflate their egos, but also by the excessive inner analysis that creates a diversity of competing thoughts and perspectives. In turn, this can lead to an inner paralysis of their ability to take action as necessary. When these individuals consider some new project, or some new direction, or some new strategy leading to self-improvement, they will make these new ways seem so big and complicated that it reinforces their sense of personal inadequacy. Thus, they can defeat themselves before they even start. The way out of this self-defeating dynamic is to realize that the path to perfection, self-improvement, or the actualization of their abilities occurs one step at a time.

In their relatedness to other people, the Venus in Virgo person is quite self-effacing, humble, and ever ready to help another. They are natural givers. Because they have a deep inner pain born of too much crisis, they can naturally relate to the pain or problems of other people. Accordingly, these folks can be extremely good at helping other people solve their problems. The advice that they generate is practical and sound, but unfortunately, they are not so good at taking or applying the advice they give to others towards themselves.

Because of the inherent masochism that defines the Venus in Virgo individual, they do not feel that they deserve to be helped, but rather to be hurt, abused, taken advantage of, manipulated, deceived, criticized, or invalidated. They attract others who are emotionally crippled in some way. This is actually an "outpicturing" of the fact they themselves are emotionally wounded and deeply troubled. All too often, because of these dynamics, the Venus in Virgo person attracts others in intimate relationships who are very self-oriented, and who expect to be served and helped in a very unequal way. These types of partners typically deny the nature of their own emotional reality, and project those realities on the Venus in Virgo person. Of course, these projections are usually very critical and negatively judgmental, and play right in to the Venus in Virgo person's inner dynamic of self-doubt, guilt, and atonement.

All too often these people sacrifice their own needs and purposes to their partners. They feel that this is the only way to maintain and sustain the relationship. Because of all of this, the Venus in Virgo person typically feels victimized by life in general, and other people specifically. Feeling victimized, they can create a consciousness in which they feel powerless to change the conditions of their life. Consequently, there is an ongoing dissatisfaction with their lives which manifests as either a silent, stoic, accepted suffering, or as an overt verbal manifestation that can wear on those in close proximity.

Sexually, the Venus in Virgo person is structured in such a way as to want to serve or please their partners. This is another form of personal sacrifice in which they experience vicarious sexual fulfillment through the sexual satisfaction of their partners. Unconsciously, the Venus in Virgo person can embody the archetype of the slave and master dynamic. Depending on other astrological considerations in the birth chart, the Venus in Virgo can either be the master who has learned a variety of sexual techniques and methods designed to induce intense stimulation in their "slave," or the slave who has no choice but to respond to the sexual will of the master. At worst, this can manifest as overt S&M-type sexual practices. Conversely, Venus in Virgo can also be asexual because of the deep, unconscious guilt association with the life of the senses and the body, and the fear of being "contaminated" in this way. The suppression of this natural function produces a sublimation manifesting in a nervous, uptight, anxiety-driven individual who is critical and judgmental to an extreme degree. As with Gemini, there is a strong mental orientation to the sexual act that produces an ongoing analysis of what is occurring when it is occurring that leads to self-knowledge. This mental, observational overlay to the sexual act produces its own frustration that can lead to being attracted to ever more intense forms of sexual stimulation as a way of getting out of their heads, and into their bodies. Venus in Virgo embodies the extremes, sexually speaking, from being asexual to absolute sexual immersion that has no limits whatsoever.

For evolution to proceed, the Venus in Virgo person must embrace their polarity: Pisces. This starts by understanding that the cause of the deep inner aloneness that they feel reflects an unresolved spiritual need. This individual must align inwardly with a spiritual system that promotes a direct inner connection to God. Once this inner connection is made, and practiced daily, the inner pit of aloneness will dissolve. This spiritual system must be defined through the principles of compassion and love, must be gentle and kind, and rooted in natural principles so that God is understood as an evolving force instead of inherently perfect. In this way, the Venus in Virgo person can change their inner standards of judgment, dissolve the build-up of guilt and the need to atone for it, and allow for a deep self-acceptance based in the goal to be a little bit better each day. Negative self-feelings will change into positive ones, which will then allow the Venus in Virgo person to attract differently. Now they will attract others who are also compassionate and forgiving by nature, who are accepting and supportive instead of critical and judgmental, who will encourage them to develop their abilities and capacities, and who bring them the message that they are lovely people who do not need to be their own worst enemies anymore. In this way, they will learn that there are only solutions to life instead of life being just one big problem.

Famous People with Venus in Virgo

Robert Jansky
Hank Williams
Amelia Earhart
Wolfgang Von Goethe
T. E. Lawrence

VENUS IN LIBRA

As a pre-existing pattern, individuals with Venus in Libra have learned to understand who they are as individuals through the initiation of all kinds of relationships with people who symbolize the diversity of life itself. Through the initiation of such relationships, the Venus in Libra person learns to evaluate who they are as individuals through comparison and contrast what which they are not: this person values this, that person values that, and so on. Thus, through relationships, these individuals learn about who they are as individuals through a counterpoint awareness that is defined by that which they are not.

One of the myths that many astrological authors and teachers support is that Libra, as an archetype, is inherently balanced. The reality is the Libra is *learning* balance. Archetypally, Libra is inherently defined through extremes—the opposite of balance. For those who have Venus in Libra this means that, by nature, they are cyclically driven between the extremes of too much social interaction, and the reactionary extreme of too much social isolation. The causal factor in this dynamic of extremes is based in the fact that Venus in Libra people are motivated to discover their sense of self through social interactions of all kinds. This typically leads to a situation or condition in which they become overwhelmed by the realities of those that they are socially interacting with. The Venus in Libra person thus cyclically becomes inwardly destabilized by losing the sense of self or inner centeredness. This causes the opposite dynamic to manifest—to cyclically isolate from all social interaction. This reaction occurs, obviously, in order for the individual to stabilize itself through such isolation. The individual then attempts to rebuild itself from within. This reactionary cycle is a reflection of the survival instinct that is embodied in the Taurus side of Venus. Remembering that an inconjunct naturally exists between Taurus and Libra, these two extreme cycles are triggered because of this natural inconjunction. When excessive social interaction occurs, then the inconjunct manifests as an inner crisis leading to the cycle of withdrawal from such interaction. When excessive withdrawal from social interaction causes an inner implosion then the inconjunct manifests as an inner crisis causing the cycle of necessary social interaction to occur.

The archetype of Libra reflects a psychological condition in which the Venus in Libra person feels that they can only value themselves to the extent that other people value them. It creates a condition in which their sense of inner worth and meaning is linked to how much other people value and give meaning to them. Because it can be so extremely important that others value and give meaning to them, the Venus in Libra person all too often will reflect and support the reality of those that are important to them even though that reality is not the actual reality of the Venus in Libra person. In this way, they lose touch with their own reality. Thus, they can seem to be many different kinds of people depending on who they are immediately interacting with. It is for this reason the Venus in Libra person has been so typically characterized in the astrological cookbooks as a chameleon.

This chameleon effect also occurs for another reason. The archetype of Libra correlates to the principle of relativity. As Einstein pointed out, the only absolute is relativity itself. The Venus in Libra person inherently understands this principle in such a way as to be able to relate to the diversity of values and beliefs, and to the lifestyles they create. They can therefore support others in their lifestyles no matter how different they are. This is why they can seem like a chameleon to others who are more fixed in their relatedness patterns to others—Venus in Taurus, for example.

It is precisely for this reason that the Venus in Libra person can cyclically lose the sense of self. They can understand the relativity of all things so deeply that it creates an inner confusion of what to value, what to believe, and who they actually are. Whatever the existing reality may be for the Venus in Libra person, they are forever aware of other possibilities as symbolized and reflected in the lives of other people. This awareness of relativity can induce a very active imagination in which they feel what it would be like to live in this or that way, to try to feel what it would be like to live like that person, etc. This inner dynamic thus contributes to the questioning of who they are in a total sense. Because the inner sense of self is defined in relation to other people under Venus in Libra, these individuals all too often attempt to discover and actualize their individuality through the values and beliefs of other people.

The Libra archetype also correlates to the dynamics and principles of balance, equality, fair play, and justice. Venus in Libra people exhibit these principles strongly in their social interactions. Compromise and negotiation are the hallmarks of their social natures. They can also exhibit strong anger when their sense of justice, fair play, and equality are violated. For them, the axiom "treat others as you yourself want to be treated" is tattooed on their souls.

In intimate relationships, the Venus in Libra person desires and strives toward role equity and interchangeability. They value the psychology wherein each person in the relationship is equal to the other in every sense. They are exceptional listeners with the ability to hear and understand objectively the reality of their partners. As a result, they naturally expect to be treated in the same way, with the same respect. They are natural givers to other people in general, and to their intimate partner specifically. This is because Venus in Libra people have a need to be needed. This is caused, again, by their sense of self-worth being linked to the value that others give to them. Thus, to give is to be needed. To be needed is to be valued. To be valued is to have meaning for another. To have meaning for another is to have meaning for oneself.

Consequently, they naturally expect others to give to them even though many have an intrinsic difficulty in asking for what they need. For many, this occurs because they do not know what they need specifically, and for others there is an inherent fear of upsetting the relationship if they do ask for what they need. In both cases, not asking for what they need becomes a causal factor that undermines their desire for role equality and equity within the relationship.

A typical cause of these people's inability to ask for what they need is traceable to their childhood. Libra is archetypally square to Cancer and Capricorn. Generally, this promotes a situation where the Venus in Libra person grew up in a family in which their needs were not honored or embraced by one or both parents. Instead, one or both parents was always telling the child what they needed, and what was expected of them based on their *own* needs. When the child attempted to assert its own needs, the parents would not listen, and then reinforced their expectations. This effectively undermined the actual identity and authority of the child. Consequently, the child was made to feel insecure relative to its actual needs and desires, with a resulting fear of being negatively judged by others. Additionally, the child learned that love and acceptance would only be extended when and if he or she would conform to the expectations and needs of one or both parents. As a result, many individuals with Venus in Libra have learned to be reflections of other people's values, beliefs, and lifestyles. Consequently, the vibrational nature of Venus within the individual attracts partners who expect the Venus in Libra person to be extensions of their own realities.

Sexually, the Venus in Libra person is a natural giver who can be extremely sensitive to the needs, feelings, and desires of their partner. They harmonize instinctively with the vibrational nature of their partner, and reflect the sexual reality of their partner as a result. This occurs because the Venus in Libra's sense of self-worth, value, and meaning are deeply conditioned by how much value and meaning another extends to them. Thus, to give sexually to their partners means to harmonize with and reflect the partner's sexual desires and needs. In addition, the Venus in Libra person has a fundamental desire for love and acceptance that manifests as mirroring the partner's sexual reality. Consequently, their own specific sexual desires become undeveloped or submerged. For some, this will lead into experimenting with different sexual lifestyles as suggested to them by the different partners that they are with, or through relating to different people who reflect different sexual lifestyles. Many attract partners who expect the Venus in Libra person to act out the sexual desires that define their reality, not the reality of the Venus in Libra person themselves. When this occurs, the Venus in Libra person will progressively create a build-up of anger because their fundamental need and desire for role equality, interchangeability, and equity becomes violated. Anger then becomes a motivational force that leads to and creates sexual aggression.

On the one hand, this can be a very positive psychological development for the Venus in Libra person because it symbolizes that he or she is learning to ask for and seek out what they desire and need. In an existing relationship, this can manifest finally as sexual role equality, as the Venus in Libra person begins to initiate the sexual dynamics that reflect his or her own desires. If the existing relationship does not allow this, then the Venus in Libra person may use this anger to seek out other partners who will fulfill their sexual desires. On the other hand, this sudden assertion of their needs can also create a situation in which the partner becomes angry, and that anger creates extreme sexual intensity as the partner tries to reassert sexual control. It can also create a situation where the partner withholds their sexual energy from the Venus in Libra person who is now asserting or asking for what they need.

The Venus in Libra person will manifest a natural sexual grace and beauty. As a result, many become the symbol or vehicle on which others project their sexual fantasies on. This creates a deep frustration and anger in the Venus in Libra person because they want to be loved and accepted for who they are, not just because they are the basis of someone's projected fantasies. They need a partner who will encourage them to fulfill their own sexual natures and needs. They need a partner who has the capacity to awaken them through sensitive touch, and who has the capacity to create sensual atmospheres that induce an erotic response. The Venus in Libra person, evolutionarily speaking, is also balancing their inner anima/animus, seeking the integration of the inner male and female into a state of inner balance. This requires, as a result, a need to give and receive, to assert their own needs and listen to the needs of the partner. Sexual role equality will then follow. For some, this will lead to same-sex attraction or bisexuality.

For evolution to proceed, the Venus in Libra person must embrace its polarity: Aries. This means that they must learn to inwardly listen to themselves instead of always listening to other people. By learning how to listen to themselves, they will then learn how to assert and communicate their own inner reality. By so doing they will then learn how to remain inwardly centered in all social and intimate situations. By learning how to stay centered within themselves in social and intimate situations, they will achieve a state of inner balance in which they can embrace, understand, and support the realities of other people without excessively compromising or undermining their own. By learning how to listen to themselves, they will learn how to trust their instincts, and by learning how to trust their instincts they will learn whom they can trust, and whom they cannot. In addition, they will learn when to be socially interactive, and when not to, thus achieving a state of balance. In this way, they will attract people who encourage them to discover and actualize themselves, others who are not afraid of their need for independent self-actualization within a relationship.

Famous People with Venus in Libra
Grace Kelly
Bo Derek
King Hussein
Christopher Colombus
Jawaharlal Nehru

VENUS IN SCORPIO

As a pre-existing pattern, individuals with Venus in Scorpio have learned to inwardly relate to the depth of their Soul and inner life, through an intense self-examination that has focused on the nature of their motivations, intentions, fears, and desires. These individuals are psychologically orientated within themselves, and, consequently, towards other people. Why, why, why? defines the inner essence of what these individuals inwardly hear, and defines the essence of how they relate to other people. Inwardly, the Venus in Scorpio individual is like a compressed coiled spring that cyclically expands and contracts in such a way that each expansion/contraction leads to ever-deeper levels of self-knowledge of an emotional and psychological nature. The inner compression that is motivated by the necessity of self-knowledge produces a vibrational intensity that radiates from the Soul. The auric atmosphere that surrounds the Venus in Scorpio person, as a result, is one of a penetrating intensity that is able to evaluate the essence of any situation or person that he or she interacts with.

The intensity of the auric atmosphere that radiates from the Venus in Scorpio person is quite interesting in that it is analogous to the eye of the eagle. The eye of the eagle is uniquely structured to have the ability to focus on the large picture while at the same time telescopically zooming in on its point of focus. In the same way, the Venus in Scorpio person inwardly relates to his or her inner landscape, and simultaneously relates to the outer environment and other people.

Inwardly, they are forever monitoring their interior environment, their ongoing state of beingness, in a general way. Within this state of beingness, the Venus in Scorpio person will then zoom in on any given emotion, feeling, sensation, thought, inspiration, dream, or desire in order understand the causal factor, the "why" of its origin. Understanding the causal factor in this way thus leads to self-knowledge or understanding. When this is occurring, the Venus in Scorpio person deeply internalizes in such a way as to shut off the external environment. For those who do not understand how the Venus in Scorpio person inwardly relates to him or herself, this can be quite disconcerting.

The intensity of the internalized focus radiates outwardly in such a way as to cause others to feel generally threatened without necessarily knowing why. The reason for this effect is that the vibrational magnetism that is radiating from the Venus in Scorpio individual magnetizes the Soul structures of others in such a way as to cause an instinctual response of insecurity. Most people are not accustomed to looking at themselves as deeply as the Venus in Scorpio person is. Thus, when others are in proximity to the auric atmosphere radiating from the Venus in Scorpio person, they are instinctively magnetized at a Soul level. This in turn causes their own survival instinct to be activated at an unconscious level because of the depth of the reaction that is created within them relative to the nature and structure of their own reality. It is as if contact with the Venus in Scorpio person causes them, for some unknown reason, to question who, why, and what they are. This effect is but a reflection of what is occurring within the Venus in Scorpio person at all times. The intensity of this effect on others is relative to how deeply compressed and withdrawn the Venus in Scorpio is within him or herself at any given moment. The inner intensity meter can range from one to ten!

Outwardly, the Venus in Scorpio person relates to the environment and others in the very same way. On the one hand, they deeply, quietly, and intensely survey and monitor the ongoing nature of their environment, and the people in it. This allows them to to remain in a state of stability and security. This ongoing monitoring is absolutely necessary for the Venus in Scorpio person because every one of them is born into this life, as a pre-existing pattern, with fundamental fears of betrayal, loss, and abandonment. Thus, their survival instinct is intensely geared and conditioned by these fears. Accordingly, the generalized monitoring of their environment is highly attuned to the potential of any person, condition, or circumstance that may cause these instinctual fears to manifest as reality. When they detect any potential threat to themselves or those that they love and care for, the Venus in Scorpio person's eagle eye will zoom in and focus on that perceived threat with the intensity of a laser beam.

With their survival instinct conditioned in this way, the Venus in Scorpio person instantly evaluates any person, condition, or event that may constitute a threat. The pre-existing survival instinct in these individuals is oriented to preparation for any possible life situation or condition. This dynamic of evaluation and preparation is, again, conditioned by their inherent fears of loss, betrayal, or abandonment, and determines how they will respond to any person or life situation. This is why the Venus in Scorpio person appears to be defensive and distant in their initial interactions with others.

An evolutionary intention that all Venus in Scorpio people have had over many lifetimes is one in which their Souls have desired to remove all sources of external dependence. This intention has manifested because of the Scorpionic tendency to overly identify with, and give too much meaning to, any person, condition, or situation that allows them to feel safe and secure. Anything or anyone meeting these requirements will typically be attached to for as long as possible. When this rigid and fixed attachment becomes a casual factor inhibiting further growth and evolution, then a removal of that which is preventing the necessary growth has and will occur.

On an inner basis, this process of enforced removal will also manifest when the Venus in Scorpio person has become too fixed and rigid in their inner relatedness patterns within themselves. In other words, they will periodically eliminate what they feel they inwardly need in order to maintain a sense of meaning in their lives when those lead to a fixity of how they are relating to themselves.

This enforced removal occurs in order to induce necessary growth. Rarely does the Venus in Scorpio person consciously realize when they have projected too much meaning or intensity into a person, life condition, or inner dynamic that symbolizes security and safety to them. Thus, when that which they have overly identified with is removed from their lives, the psychological experience is one of intense loss, betrayal, or abandonment. The typical reaction is rage and anger, because the temptation when this occurs is to feel victimized (Scorpio is part of the natural triad between Cancer and Pisces). As a pre-existing pattern, many people with Venus in Scorpio are born with such anger.

The real issue, again, is that whatever the Venus in Scorpio person has focused on or determined that it needs for a sense of meaning, stability, and security to exist in their life has and can be rigidly held on to for too long. Because one of the underlying dynamics or laws of life in time/space realities is evolution, there is an inherent limit to the function and value of any given dynamic, condition, or relationship. Evolution is a function of metamorphosing limitations. Thus, when the Venus in Scorpio person has overly identified with something to the point of limiting his or her necessary evolutionary requirements, a removal of that which is limiting the growth will occur with or without the cooperation of the individual.

In their intimate relationships, the Venus in Scorpio person will naturally desire to probe the depths of those that they love. They are, again, naturally psychological. Thus, they will relate to their intimate others in terms of how and why they are psychologically and emotionally structured. They desire to know what motivates others, and what that person's intentions are for wanting to be part of their lives. Paradoxically, the Venus in Scorpio person desires to be with someone who can help him or her understand the depth of their own Souls, their fears, their needs, their desires, and yet simultaneously fear allowing anyone to get too close to them in this way. This fear, of course, is inherent because of the subconscious memories of loss, abandonment, and betrayal that have preceded the current life. Thus, the Venus in Scorpio person will "test" those that want to be close to or intimate with them. It is as if they require potential partners to prove their love or intentions before they will allow themselves to become open or available.

The Venus in Scorpio person desires to attract another who will help them understand the depths of their Souls, and will often attract others who desire him or her to do the same for them. All too often, as a result, the Venus in Scorpio person will attract others who will feel and expect that he or she can help them emotionally and psychologically heal and repair themselves. This dynamic can be very attractive to the Venus in Scorpio person because it creates an illusory sense of safety in which the partner appears to intensely need them. This dependency makes the Venus in Scorpio person feel safe, relative to the intensity of the expressed need. As a result of this, they will find themselves in the role of an emotional and psychological healer, which allows them to feel safe, yet simultaneously allows them to conceal their own deepest wounds and fears. The Venus in Scorpio person can conceal their deepest fears and emotions in many ways because of their inherent fear of being vulnerable. This fear is, of course, a reflection of uncertainty regarding whom to trust, and trust issues in general. When this kind of dynamic is created, the Venus is Scorpio person not only undermines their own deepest desires and needs in a relationship, and the desire for another to understand the depths of their own wounds and needs, but it also creates the karmic danger of manipulating the other to keep them dependent. The potential manipulation can occur because of their ability to identify the deepest emotional wound in the other, and by identifying that wound present themselves as the only one who can help them heal it. Yet unconsciously the Venus in Scorpio person does not really want that wound to heal, because then the partner would not need them, and then the sense of security and safety in the relationship that the Venus in Scorpio person is dependent on would not exist.

When this is the operative dynamic in the Venus in Scorpio's intimate relationship, it is a reflection of the permeating insecurity that they are born with. Consequently, this dynamic generates many manipulative forms of control that can be as extremely overt as they are subtle. And much to the amazement and bewilderment of the Venus in Scorpio's sense of reality, they keep finding out that there is no security in this type of relationship. This occurs because the types of people that they attract will only sustain the relationship for the duration of the need that attracted them to these people in the first place. Thus, this dynamic only guarantees the experience of loss, abandonment, and the emotional interpretation of betrayal for the Venus in Scorpio individual. Rarely do they understand that it is their own emotional dynamics linked with the fear of loss that is the causal factor in this experience. And just as rarely do they understand that they themselves can be manipulated by these types of partners as the partners themselves desire to have their own needs met.

In essence, both partners will attempt to limit the growth of one another relative to the needs that they both have that brought them together in the first place. This becomes the casual factor in the psychological and emotional manipulations. And by trying to limit the dynamics in the relationship to only those that reflect the needs that brought them into the relationship, they will exhaust those dynamics to the point where no more growth can occur. When the resulting limit of no more growth occurs, then the causal factor is in place that leads to confrontations and the loss of the relationship, unless a desire manifests that allows for new dynamics and experiences to occur. Because of these dynamics, the Venus in Scorpio person can thus be extremely jealous, possessive, and controlling of their partner. They feel threatened by situations real or imagined that threaten their control, and the partners they attract can be of like mind.

Some individuals with Venus in Scorpio, especially those that have Venus retrograde, have skipped steps in evolutionary terms. The nature of those skipped steps is specific to emotional dynamics. The reasons for avoiding or denying the nature of their emotional dynamics can have many causes, and each birthchart that has this dynamic must be examined to understand the individual reasons. These individuals will create a life in which, through evolutionary necessity, they will be plunged into their emotional body and dynamics through intense emotional and sexual experiences. The nature of these experiences is typically based on deep violations of trust, emotional disillusionment, emotional betrayal, emotional abandonment, and, in some cases, sexual violations of one kind or another. They will typically attract people who are emotionally dishonest, manipulative, narcissistic, and who may be pathological liars.

The Venus in Scorpio person requires an intensity of emotional and psychological experiences in order to become aware of the depths of their own dynamics, motivations, intentions, desires, and needs. The need for intensity manifests as a deep emotional communion or discussion with the partner, as a deep and permeating sexual experience that ignites the sensation body, or as deep emotional confrontations or cataclysms that enforce the question *why* to manifest within their consciousness. Another form of intensity that can lead to the necessary awareness is one in which the Venus in Scorpio person is almost totally emotionally isolated, not allowing for anyone to penetrate their carefully constructed emotional flak jacket. This kind of withdrawal leads to an inner compression that will generate awareness at some point, usually when they become exhausted from such isolation.

Their need for intensity exists because intensity forces an awareness of that which is hidden or unconscious within them. When the Venus in Scorpio person feels that they need something for growth and self-discovery, they will focus on it intensely. They will attempt to totally absorb whatever they need in order to grow. Through absorption, an osmosis takes place in which they become that which they have identified with and formed a relationship to. In this way, they feel secure and actualize their own power because of their ability to penetrate to the essence of that whatever have identified with and formed a relationship to. Their challenge is to understand when to let go or to change their inner dynamics, life conditions, situations, or the emotional/psychological dynamics that are existing between themselves and their loved ones specifically, and others generally. When this understanding and the consequent behavior does not exist, then this becomes the casual factor in creating loss, confrontation, abandonment, or betrayal that is experienced in a variety of ways.

The intensity of these types of experiences will force, at some point, an inner awareness of why these kinds of experiences are happening. This awareness will lead to self-knowledge, and self-knowledge will hopefully lead to change. If not, then the dynamic of repetitive compulsion exists until the Venus in Scorpio person becomes exhausted through the experiences that the repetitive compulsion dictates. When they become exhausted in this way, the Venus in Scorpio person will then finally apply the knowledge learned relative to the question of why.

Sexually, the Venus in Scorpio person desires an intensity of physical and emotional sensation. There is a fundamental desire to merge and be absorbed into the entire essence of their partner, and thus themselves. The intensity of sexual energy, and its release, allows for a relaxing of the inner compression of their Soul. Generally speaking, they are deep, passionate lovers who need to be gently and intensely touched. They have a keen awareness of the power of touch, and can instinctively know just how vulnerable they can be in a sexual situation through the quality and nature of their partner's touch. The current status or overall nature of their own inner being will be reflected in their own touch. Touch is the one dynamic in which Venus in Scorpio people cannot hide or conceal themselves. When they feel safe enough to make love with their eyes open there is no greater level of sexual intensity that can manifest from an individual. They can be acutely aware of the various sensations going on in their partner's body and Soul, and harmonize with those sensations in order to deepen and intensify them. Their sexual energy is constant even though some may attempt to transmute it through various other focuses.

Venus in Scorpio people manifest a deep fascination with the mystery of sexual energy, for it symbolizes the mystery of life/death/rebirth. It represents a vehicle of self-discovery to be explored in every possible way. Some will have desires to explore what others call sexual taboos because of an inherent resistance to being limited to sexual social conventions. Some will have desires to use sexual energy as a way of transforming themselves and/or heal themselves and others. Thus, these types will be orientated to sexual rituals and methods whose specific intent is to heal and transform. Others can use sexual energy as a way of controlling their relationship. Still others can use this energy as a way of hurting, possessing, and dominating their partners. A variation of this is using sex magic to get back at other people whom they have felt wounded by in some way. All Venus in Scorpio people naturally desire commitment and monogamy from their partners in every way, including sexually. By nature, they are naturally monogamous and value the dynamic of commitment. Of course, other life or birth chart factors can alter this natural condition.

The Venus in Scorpio person inherently emanates an intense, if quiet, magnetism that can instinctively excites others sexually even if they are not attracted to the Venus in Scorpio person as a whole. The actual attraction is not specifically sexual even though it may feel that way. It is actually based on the inner intensity that manifests from the Venus in Scorpio person, and this vibrational intensity is unconsciously interpreted by others as something they need within themselves, even though what that specific need is can essentially be unconscious or undefined. Vibrational intensity in any form is always interpreted by people as the possibility of transformation even when that vibration creates a fear reaction. The nature of this vibration that emanates from the Venus in Scorpio person reflects their own Soul's intensity. Thus, this vibration naturally stimulates the Soul structures of others. And, for some, this will automatically stimulate the primary brain wherein lies our sexual instincts and desires. Generally, the Venus in Scorpio person is just being who they are, unaware of the intensity that is manifesting from them. At worst, however, some Venus in Scorpio people who observe others reacting to them in this way will begin to consciously manipulate their sexual energy in order to fulfill some sexual desire or need that is connected with power.

For evolution to proceed, the Venus in Scorpio person must embrace its polarity: Taurus. The essence of this lesson is to realize that every projected need they create is connected to some deep inner wound. The projection of the need is thus motivated by the desire for another to somehow repair this wound. Conversely, the intention in the Taurus polarity is to learn how to repair these wounds from within themselves. This will lead to a condition of self-empowerment, self-reliance, and self-sustainment that creates a deep and genuine state of inner security. Once this occurs, these individuals will relate to others in general, and their intimate partners specifically, in an entirely new way. Now they will encourage the independent actualization of their partner, and help motivate them to do this. Their partner will encourage them in exactly the same way. By changing their inner vibration in this way, they will attract differently. Thus, the dynamics of manipulation, control, betrayal, loss, and abandonment will disappear from their lives.

In addition, this lesson demands that they learn how to relate the nature of their emotional reality as it is without concealing it, altering it through misrepresentation, or representing it in oblique rather than direct ways. Until they learn how to do this, the Venus in Scorpio person will never have their greatest need and desire fulfilled—to have at least one other person in their life who totally understands who they are, how they are put together, and why they are put together this way. By learning how to do this they will simultaneously learn how to discriminate who should be in their life, and who should not be. By learning how to do this they will then learn how to identify the actual needs of their partner versus telling the partner what they need. And, of course, they can now attract another who reflects this very same psychological, emotional, and vibrational shift. The scorpion has now metamorphosed into the eagle via the Phoenix.

Famous People with Venus in Scorpio

Benjamin Creme
Nicholas Culpeper
Richard Dreyfus
President John Adams
Steven Spielberg

VENUS IN SAGITTARIUS

As a pre-existing pattern, the Venus in Sagittarius person has a deep need to discover and actualize their own personal truth. This need is conditioned by the nature of that which confers a sense of meaning and purpose in their lives. That which constitutes value and meaning in their lives will in turn condition their orientation to, and thereby determine, the nature of their beliefs. And the nature of their beliefs will constitute the nature of their personal truth. In other words, the Venus in Sagittarius person must have a guiding philosophy of life in order to have a core sense of meaning and purpose.

Within this pattern, these people are committed to their ongoing personal evolution and growth. The Sagittarius archetype is defined through the archetypes of fire, mutability, and yang. These archetypes in combination create an inner energy that is defined through perpetual expansion. As a result, the Venus in Sagittarius person is fundamentally restless, and is committed to the value of the personal freedom to pursue any experience they deem necessary in order to discover and actualize themselves. The need for freedom permeates these people, and they generally will not tolerate any condition or constraint that inhibits their independence or freedom. When such conditions or constraints exist, the Venus in Sagittarius person will progressively feel an inner alienation from those conditions or constraints, and the psychology or alienation becomes a causal factor or determinant in separating, at least inwardly, from those conditions or constraints.

Inwardly, the Venus in Sagittarius person feels and knows that they are connected to something that is much larger than themselves. In a phenomenological sense, it is as if they instinctively know that there is a manifested Creation, and that there must be a universal truth or inherent laws and principles that can explain the nature of the Creation that appears phenomenal. Thus, there is a simultaneous need to understand not only their personal truth, but how that personal truth is connected to the Ultimate Truth that is the basis of the manifested creation. Connecting their personal truth to belief systems of a philosophical or religious nature that correlate to Ultimate truth thus becomes the core value, meaning, and purpose for their lives. Inwardly resonating and relating to themselves in this way will condition how they relate to other people. This conditioning function serves as a vehicle that allows them to discriminate who they will relate to in general, and who their intimate others will be specifically. In addition, the need for personal freedom and self-discovery also serves to condition with whom they will relate to in every way: generally and intimately.

The Venus in Sagittarius person is firmly centered in the right brain. As a result, they relate to themselves in non-linear, image-based terms that are defined as ever increasing concentric circles that attempt to embrace the totality of life itself. This will reflect itself as a deep thirst for knowledge and experiences of a diverse nature that will in turn allow for the Venus in Sagittarius person to discover the underlying principles, archetypes, or dynamics that can explain the causal factors in what appears as diverse and contradictory. As a result, these people are highly intuitive, and have an inherent wisdom that is free from the constraints of linear, left-brain logic of a deductive nature. The inherent knowledge, wisdom, and intuitiveness of these people is a reflection of their capacity of inductive logic—the ability to grasp the whole first, which allows for the individual parts of that whole to reveal themselves in their own natural order.

Because their inner space is defined by ever-increasing concentric circles that attempt to embrace the whole of life, these individuals have an inner vibrancy that is buoyant, light, free, and enthusiastic. There is an innate capacity to see the famous light at the end of the tunnel, an ability to see the light within the dark. There is an inherent focus on solutions versus being caught up in problems, and there is a natural humor that embraces the vision of the absurd because of this. The Venus in Sagittarius person values the nature and function of humor as a vehicle that can lead to healing in a variety of ways, and in all kinds of conditions. They have the ability to laugh at themselves, and they have the ability to make others laugh at themselves, especially when others or themselves are taking themselves too seriously. They are very natural and spontaneous people, fun loving, and naturally project sincerity and honesty. The projection of sincerity and honesty is a reflection of their own desire for personal truth.

One of the inherent problems that the Venus in Sagittarius person has is a *generalization* of truth. They feel that their personal truth, or the truth reflected in their philosophical or religious belief system, is the truth for all. Belief systems of any kind determine how any of us interpret and give meaning to any kind of experience. The Venus in Sagittarius person typically hears and evaluates other people through the prism or filter of their own personal truths and beliefs. This can create a situation in their relationships with others where they always seem to be, or have to be, right. And when they are challenged or disagreed with, they all too often will attempt to convince and convert others to the validity of their particular point of view, much as a preacher in a pulpit attempts to convince others to the righteousness of his or her convictions. Accordingly, there are times in their relatedness patterns with others that the Venus in Sagittarius person can seem to be very insensitive, to the point of being extremely blunt. This can have the effect of hurting others' feelings even though this is not the conscious intention of these individuals.

This way of relating to others is a reflection of how they are inwardly relating to themselves. Again, the Venus in Sagittarius person's deepest sense of inner meaning and purpose are dependent on the nature of beliefs that allow for a personal connection to a larger whole—the Cosmos or God. The way this connection is understood or constructed becomes the basis of their truth at any moment in time, and constitutes their sense of meaning and purpose as a result. To have this challenged or questioned by anyone but themselves is to simultaneously create a loss of meaning and purpose. Thus, there is a deep need to defend those beliefs and convert others to them in order for the Venus in Sagittarius person to sustain their sense of values, purpose, and meaning. This is one of the forms that the survival instinct takes when Venus is in Sagittarius.

Another common problem that they have is one wherein they can exaggerate whatever their perceived problems are, exaggerate or embellish the retelling of an experience that they have had, or exaggerate the descriptions of others who may have violated them in some way. This can even manifest as the fabrication of total lies. At worst, the Venus in Sagittarius actually believes in their own lies to the extent that the lies become their actual truth, so to speak. The causal or operative dynamic that can cause this effect is based on the Sagittarian archetype of perpetually needing to expand in ever-increasing concentric circles. In effect, it is the principle of expansion that can cause exaggeration leading to outright lies. Within this causal factor is a little-known fact about the Venus in Sagittarius person—that within themselves they can feel deeply inadequate. The inner experience of inadequacy is caused by the natural linkage of Sagittarius to Virgo, Pisces, and Gemini—the natural mutable grand cross. The specific connection to inadequacy occurs through Virgo and Pisces, and the dynamic of exaggerations, embellishments, or total lies becomes magnified through Gemini. Sagittarius correlates to the dynamic of compensation in all its senses and manifestations. In this case, the Venus in Sagittarius person can compensate for their sense of personal inadequacy (which occurs through the Venus function of comparing oneself to others) by the creation of exaggerations, embellishments, or total lies. And because the Venus in Sagittarius person is innately sincere, natural, convincing, and has a gift for storytelling, it can be very difficult for others to know just when they are not telling the actual truth.

In their intimate relationships, the Venus in Sagittarius person is forever needing and trying to balance their need for independence within the context of their relationship. Because these people have an almost absolute need for perpetual growth within themselves, they need and desire an intimate other who is also committed to personal growth. This will then allow for the dynamics within the relationship to be defined by a mutual commitment to growth. In effect, these individuals need to be in a relationship in which there is an ongoing sense of adventure. The Venus in Sagittarius person will simply experience a deep alienation from their partner when the relationship has degenerated into a stale, static routine. They need a partner who can mirror and reflect their own reality of intellectual and philosophical pondering, a partner with whom they can interact in this way at an equal level. The Venus in Sagittarius person needs this kind of intellectual or philosophical stimulation, and to be periodically challenged by their partner through such types of discussions. When this occurs, they will have a tremendous amount of respect for their partner, and will sustain their enthusiasm for the relationship. When this does not occur, then they lose their respect for the partner and become progressively alienated.

Because of their fundamental restlessness, the Venus in Sagittarius person innately desires physical movement and travel. This restlessness, again, is a reflection of their need to explore the diversity of life in order to understand the underlying principles or dynamics that are the basis for the diversity in the first place. Thus, they require a partner who will allow them to travel alone without feeling threatened, or a partner who will travel with them so that the sense of discovery and adventure can be mutual. The best scenario, however, is one wherein their partners will allow them to travel alone sometimes, and to travel with them at other times.

By nature, the Venus in Sagittarius person needs levity, humor, lightness, and optimism to pervade their intimate relationship. If they are with a partner who is constantly too serious or withdrawn, this will also become a casual factor creating a state of alienation and withdrawal from such a partner. They will naturally encourage the independent actualization and needs of their partners, and will develop a deepening respect for their partners who independently actualize their own life purposes. They will not respect a partner who just wants to hang on to them without developing their own identity or life purpose, or a partner who attempts to restrict their need for necessary freedom and independence. In addition, the Venus in Sagittarius person is naturally spontaneous and extremely adaptable to life conditions and changes, and who values and needs this same quality in their partner. They are very natural people who couldn't care less about carefully constructed social personas—in fact, they have a disdain for such people. Honesty and truthfulness are extremely important to them, and they naturally desire a partner who is honest and truthful in every way. When they feel right about their partner and their relationship, the Venus in Sagittarius person can be very giving, attentive, passionate, and truly make the partner feel really loved. They will let the partner know just how much they are appreciated, and can naturally make their partner feel really good about themselves. Conversely, when they are feeling alienated and removed from the partner, they can be tactless in pointing out the deeper truths of a not-so-nice nature, with the effect of making the partner feel worthless and devastated.

Sexually, the Venus in Sagittarius person is quite ardent, giving, spontaneous, and natural. They can be quite playful, and are naturally open to sexual adventures of all kinds because of their need for a diversity of life experiences. This is important for them because, again, if their sexual life degenerates into a predictable routine, then the seed of restlessness will bloom into attractions to others who offer and reflect their need for adventure and growth. By nature, the Venus in Sagittarius person is not monogamous because of their need for unrestricted growth. It is not that they are incapable of being monogamous, but in order for this to occur they need a partner who is willing to sexually grow with them, one who is open to sexual spontaneity, who is sexually versatile, and who does not preclude any way of being sexual. The Venus in Sagittarius person requires the diversity of sexual experience as yet another way of knowing themselves totally.

For evolution to proceed the Venus in Sagittarius person must embrace its polarity: Gemini. In essence, this means that they must learn that their particular point of view, their truth, and their beliefs are relative, and not the only or absolute truth. Thus, when they are relating to others they must learn how to hear them in such a way as to be able to understand the actual reality as it exists for the other, versus interpreting what they are hearing through the filter of their own beliefs. In this way they will learn that "truth" is not only relative, but they will learn to let other people be "right" from the point of view of their own convictions and beliefs. As a result, they will learn how to be Socratic in their relatedness patterns with others versus indulging the inherent tendency to "convince and convert." The underlying pattern of inadequacy will then change. This, in turn, will negate the temptation to exaggerate, embellish, or lie. In addition, by learning how to listen to others in such a way as to embrace another's reality as it exists for them, they will learn how to communicate to others from the point of view of that person's reality versus always communicating from the point of view of their own reality. As a result, others will respond to them in an entirely different way because they will now have the feeling of being listened to and understood. Once this occurs, others will feel more equal to the Venus in Sagittarius person, versus being made to feel inferior because of the unevolved Sagittarian need to always be right. Once the feeling of equity is established in this way, others will be much more open to the beliefs, opinions, and points of view of the Venus in Sagittarius person. In this way, the natural teaching ability of these individuals can be received and applied. And the Venus in Sagittarius person will realize that others may just have something to teach him or her too!

Famous People with Venus in Sagittarius
>   Harry Chapin
>   Georges Gurdjieff
>   Rudyard Kipling
>   John Lily
>   Kahlil Gibran

VENUS IN CAPRICORN

As a pre-existing pattern, the Venus in Capricorn person has learned to be very cautious and controlled in how they express themselves and relate to other people. This external relatedness pattern is a reflection of how they have learned to inwardly relate to themselves: the Venus in Capricorn person has very deep feelings and needs that take time to surface into their conscious awareness. Even when they do surface these individuals require time to make sure, and feel secure, that what they are feeling, or are needing, is correct. Even then, they can be very slow to relate, share, or communicate these feelings and/or needs to others because of a pre-existing fear of rejection and/or false judgment. This pre-existing fear has occurred because these individuals have experienced rejection and/or wrong judgment all too often early in their life, from one or both of their biological parents.

The nature of Capricorn, as an archetype, correlates to the phenomena of time and space, and how time and space are structured or organized. It correlates to the phenomena of finitude or mortality, and to the nature of how collectives of people organize themselves into structured groups or societies with consensus-formed, manmade laws, regulations, norms, taboos, and customs. This in turn creates social expectations of how people should integrate and conduct themselves within the group or society (the expectation to conform) which, in turn, becomes the basis of social judgments. And when the expectation to conform to what the consensus expects does not occur, this becomes the basis of guilt.

In addition, Capricorn correlates to the structure and nature of consciousness in human form, to the nature of structure in any form, and to the use of form. It also points to the need to change the nature of structural form when that form has become counterproductive to necessary change—that is, when it has served its use and become crystallized. In psychological terms, Capricorn correlates to the function of conscious reflection which allows for a simultaneous awareness of the overall state of our beingness and what we need to change, inwardly and outwardly, in order to grow. Because of Capricorn's correlation to time and space, finitude, and mortality, it also correlates to psychological/emotional maturation, aging, defining the focus of our life via goals and ambitions, and the self-determination that this requires. Negatively speaking, this can produce the psychology of futility, pessimism, fatalism, and self-defeat.

The Venus in Capricorn person has typically been born into family structures in which the parental reality has been defined by the consensus of the society in which they live. Consequently, the parental reality has typically had a heavy undertone in which the child has been expected to conform to the parental value system. When the child deviated from these expectations to conform, he or she was made to feel guilty in covert or overt ways through the use of judgment. A related dynamic within the general pattern of expectation to conform to parental values is one wherein the parents have projected on the child a rigid code of conduct that the child is expected to adhere to even when the parents themselves do not. The cliché "Do as I say, not as I do" applies here. This creates the very real perception in the child of hypocrisy and double standards. Within this, the very way in which the parents related to themselves has typically been very rigid, controlled, emotionally distant, and perfunctory. There is a lack of spontaneity, and a lack of any real demonstrations of affection or love between them. Quite the contrary: the parents are generally very controlled in their emotional interrelatedness with one another. The nature of their relationship is commonly defined by predictable routine and order which each parent expects the other to adhere to and maintain. There is also a mutual fear of being too vulnerable with one another, and their sexual life is either blocked or distorted in some way. All of this has served to "imprint" the overall psychology and emotional reality of the Venus in Capricorn child.

As a result of this, the Venus in Capricorn individual learned as a child to deeply compress and protect their feelings. They learned that their needs could not be acknowledged, supported, or nurtured by their parents. As a result, they learned to either conceal or suppress their needs. This process of learning to control their emotional demonstrations is a reflection of the survival instinct. It is based on the situation in which the parents expected the Venus in Capricorn child to act almost like miniature adults, to shoulder many duties and respon-sibilities—in short, to control or suppress the normal behavior of the child. This undermines and stifles the child's true nature and activities.

Because there has been no real emotional support or nurturing rel-ative to their actual needs and desires, there is a deep wellspring of insecurity that is born out of this type of parental environment. Thus, the normal emotions and needs of the child have become buried deep into the subconscious of many individuals who have Venus in Capri-corn. These emotions and needs become psychologically displaced and surface later on in their adult life. This is important to understand because whatever any of us suppress, for whatever reasons, becomes distorted. Thus, the emotions and needs of these individuals have typ-ically become distorted as adults because of the psychological dis-placement caused when they were children.

One of the displaced emotions that can surface in a distorted way concerns the nature of authority. Because of the typically authoritari-an nature of the parental environment the Venus in Capricorn person has had their own inner sense of authority fractured, suppressed, or crushed. As an adult, this displaced emotion can manifest in a few dif-ferent ways depending on the overall nature of the person in question, as seen in the totality of their birth chart. For some, their underlying insecurity will manifest as a very timid, shy, reserved, and fearful way of relating to other people in general. In their intimate relationships, this type will typically attract controlling, dominating, willful, judg-mental, hypocritical, and authoritarian individuals who more or less expect the of Venus in Capricorn person to be vicarious extensions of their own reality and to be dependent on them. This type of Venus in Capricorn person would have had almost no sense of being emotionally nurtured as a child. Thus, this additional displaced emotion now manifests as wanting to be taken care of by this type of partner: to be dependent in order to feel safe and secure.

For others, this will manifest in an almost opposite way. These types have so thoroughly imprinted the nature of the authoritarian parental environment that they become very intense, authoritarian types who perpetually need to assert and project their own sense of authority in order to feel secure. The underlying insecurity that haunts all Venus in Capricorn individuals becomes compensated for in this way. As a result, these types are instinctively fearful of losing their authority, and will do almost anything to sustain it. To them, the end justifies the means. They will typically feel afraid of anyone else who has legitimate authority, and will generally challenge, or in some way attempt to undermine, the authority of such people in order to sustain their own. The means most commonly used are contrived and harsh negative judgments and pronouncements, and power plays in which they attempt to block or thwart the goals and ambitions of others. This type, even if they have no actual authority, will attempt to associate with others that do. Their sense of authority is thus created through vicarious association. In their general relatedness patterns with others they will appear stoic, controlled, project an authoritarian stance, and attempt to control others through the use of judgment in one way or another. An example of this point could be the person who was the co-author of a book, who continuously reminded the other author that it was important to keep their names in the public eye in one way or another—the implied judgment being that if they did not, then no one would give them any interest or attention. On an inner basis, this type is emotionally frozen and fearful of their vulnerability.

In their intimate relationships, these types attract one of two types of partners. One type will be just as oriented to outward success, appearances, and social ambition as they are. Their inner life will be just as emotionally frozen as well. They may relate well through the commonality of their external goals and ambitions, yet their inner emotional relatedness will be slim to none. The other type will be just the opposite: a very emotionally needy individual who is essentially looking for a *de facto* parent to be in relationship to. This type will be very dependent, and essentially attempt to live through the Venus in Capricorn's identity and reality. They will have no real life of their own, and subconsciously feel safe in being dominated and controlled. When this type of Venus in Capricorn attracts that kind of partner, it is really a reflection of their own subconscious desire to lose control, to be cared for, and to be nurtured more or less like a baby. Of course, they would never admit to this even though it is true. This subconscious desire reflects yet another form of the displaced emotions of childhood that were conditioned by living in the antithesis of a warm, caring, and supportive emotional environment.

Within all Venus in Capricorn individuals lies a very deep and reflective consciousness. To others, this can create the appearance of a withdrawn, quiet, reserved, conservative, and serious person. One of the potential causes for this reflective, inward-looking focus is the fact that many Venus in Capricorn people are born with an unresolved grief, or a grief that has been created in their early life which is also unresolved as adults. As a result of this, the Venus in Capricorn person can seem as if they are in a perpetual or cyclic state of mourning. Their hearts seem to be burdened and sad. There can be many causes of this condition. The typical causes are childhoods in which there was not real love, caring, or nurturing; adult relationships that were devoid of any real emotional interaction, love, or support; the witnessing and experiencing of political or religious upheavals in which many people were hurt or destroyed; and/or political or environmental conditions in which great plagues, famine, or physical destitution occurred. Another typical cause can be a situation where the Venus in Capricorn person was, or is, in a relationship lacking in any real inner relatedness with the partner and which, in turn, created an attraction to another who could or would give them what they needed. Yet, because the Venus in Capricorn person is inherently oriented to honoring their commitments based on their sense of obligation, duty, and being responsible, the attraction to another has been typically suppressed and not acted on. Thus, this creates a deep inner suffering leading to a state of grief or mourning. The results of whatever the causes have been have produced a more or less traumatized heart, and an emotional structure that lies deeply buried within these individuals. In the Anton Chekhov play *The Seagull* there was a character that was always dressed in black. A person asked her why she always dressed this way. Her answer was "because I am in mourning for my life!" This character symbolizes the heavy heart of Venus in Capricorn people until they are unlocked.

This is a rather sad state of affairs because, in reality, the Venus in Capricorn individual is a highly emotional person. Deep within themselves they are intrinsically warm, caring, nurturing, and sensual. Yet because they have learned to protect themselves due to the fear of being vulnerable and wrongly judged, and because their emotional body is essentially traumatized due to the above causes, it requires a very special kind of person to help them unlock their emotional nature. This kind of person must be very patient and gentle in encouraging the Venus in Capricorn person to access their feelings and needs. They must be the type of person who can help them understand the basis of what constitutes their own inner judgmental patterns, and to help them be free of those patterns. Within this, this type of person must have a deep understanding of the nature of societal and parental imprinting, and how it has caused the Venus in Capricorn person to conceal and suppress their natural emotional needs. They must be able to teach these individuals that it is necessary for them to learn how to relate, express, and communicate themselves freely and openly—to ask for what they need. This is essential, because all too often the Venus in Capricorn person silently expects that their partner should just know what they need without asking. In this way they recycle their sense of disappointment linked with childhood—the inner child's disappointment in its parents' unwillingness to give to it what it needed.

All of this must be done through positive reinforcement and non-judgment. Over time, this approach will help the Venus in Capricorn person hear differently. Instead of hearing and being over-sensitive to judgmental, critical, and authoritarian words which reflect the nature of their childhood imprinting, they will now hear words of acceptance, empowerment, and encouragement. They will hear that they are good and loving people who do not need to feel guilty for who they are. They will accept encouragement to define their own unique values, and to structure their life accordingly. They will begin to examine the nature of their conditioning patterns, and, in so doing, to be as free from those patterns as possible. Above all, the Venus in Capricorn person needs another who will hold and touch them so that the early lack of nurturing in their early environment can be healed as an adult. In fact, the key to unlocking the Venus in Capricorn person occurs through touch. Once they feel a sense of safety in this way, the Venus in Capricorn person will naturally begin to open up in a very slow and methodical way.

Once the Venus in Capricorn person is unlocked, their natural warmth, depth, and loving natures will be revealed. Instead of seeming forever reserved, serious, sad, fearful, and strangely old even when young, the opposite will occur—the inner child that resides deeply within will be set free. Now they will seem almost childlike in their emotional expressions, playful, and enthused instead of being morose and depressive. Instead of being controlled in their emotional relatedness with another, they will now be free to express their love and feelings as they occur. They will discover that their feelings and needs are deep, and they will learn that it is all right to have these deep feelings and needs. When this occurs, they will begin to radiate a deep and earthy sensuality that is magnetic and attractive to many people. Instead of walking with closed shoulders, head bowed, and protective clothing, they will now walk upright, head held high, dressing as they please. In their intimate relationships they will become very giving, supportive, loyal, warm and highly sexual.

Once the inner child is set free in this way the Venus in Capricorn person will begin life anew, no matter what age they are when this finally happens. At this point they will find themselves reflecting on the nature of their past. In this reflection they will develop a deep self-knowledge which will allow them redefine not only themselves, but the very nature of what we all call reality. In this way, they will redefine their sense of purpose relative to their role or function within society. And once this is done they will set themselves in motion to actualize this sense of purpose because of the inherent self-determination that they are born with.

Sexually speaking, the Venus in Capricorn person is naturally monogamous. They will naturally value the power of commitment. Conditioning patterns not withstanding, the Venus in Capricorn person is naturally a deeply sexual archetype. By nature, they need to be "warmed up" through holding, touching, and kissing before actual intercourse. They need the act of sexual intercourse to be long and sustained. The depth of the Venus in Capricorn person's feelings can be ignited through the length of the sexual act. Because of the inherent tendency to withhold or suppress their feelings, needs, and emotions, the Venus in Capricorn person also desires sexual intensity. The degree of intensity directly corresponds to the unlocking of their feelings, needs, and emotions. They require fidelity from their partners because of the pre-existing pattern that creates a fragile and negative self-image. If their partner sleeps with someone else, then this will only add to the feeling that there must be something wrong with them. They require sexual integrity, honesty, and respect. If a partner attempts to sexually subjugate them, or to degrade them for any reason, the Venus in Capricorn person will feel intensely contaminated, dirty, and guilty.

This will only add to, and deepen, their negative self-judgment. When the Venus in Capricorn person is unlocked they discover that their sexual nature and need is constant. There is not much of a need for sexual experimentation. Straight, hard sex is their main orientation. Many will have an attraction to the anal canal as a source of sexual stimulation because, symbolically speaking, the anal canal represents that which we suppress in ourselves. Thus, when this area is stimulated sexually the Venus in Capricorn person is actually unlocking that which has been suppressed within them. Many will also have an oral sexual orientation as well. This typically occurs because of a breakdown in the early bonding process between mother and child linked with nursing. This breakdown thus creates a form of emotional arrest or displacement that manifests in their adult lives as an oral sexual orientation. The sexual intensity that the Venus in Capricorn requires can also uncover one of the deepest fears that they have: the fear of losing control, yet desiring to do so. The Venus in Capricorn person thus affected must learn that this fear is actually linked with the fear of being too vulnerable. Consequently, the sensitive lover will encourage them to "lose control" because real freedom and growth for the Venus in Capricorn person lies in their accessing the core of their emotions: that which is most vulnerable.

For the Venus in Capricorn person who remains locked, their sexual nature can be frozen to the point of being frigid or impotent. A lesser form of this is when the sexual act is simply reduced to a sense of perfunctory duty and obligation: the "grin and bear it" approach for women, and the woman as simply a sexual object for the man. For many, this will simply translate into no sexual activity whatsoever. This condition or state of affairs occurs when there is an unconscious or conscious association of guilt linked with the natural sexual needs and desires of the body and Soul.

For evolution to proceed, Venus in Capricorn must embrace its polarity: Cancer. In the last several years, ever since Neptune and Uranus began their transit through the sign Capricorn relative to Pluto transiting Scorpio, there has been a tremendous focus in the world of psychology to uncover and heal the inner wounded child. The natural polarity to Capricorn is Cancer. Archetypally speaking, the two signs that most perfectly correlate to this focus are Capricorn and Cancer. Thus, the Venus in Capricorn person must embrace Cancer in the sense of reflecting deeply on the nature of his or her psychological imprinting created by the nature of the parental environment, and, through extension, by the nature of the society that the Venus in Capricorn person has been born into. In this reflection the intention must be focused on how this imprinting or conditioning has shaped and defined the Venus in Capricorn's self-image. In essence, the evolutionary intention reflected through Cancer is to totally re-create a new self-image that is free from the shackles, chains, and conformity reflected in the imprinting and conditioning of the parental and societal environment. In this way they will not only feel different about themselves, but they will learn to "hear" differently from within themselves. Now they will learn that what they are hearing about their needs, emotions, and feelings are messages that reflect their need to heal the negative self-image created in childhood.

In this reflection, the Venus in Capricorn person will discover that they have become "emotionally arrested" at some point in their early life. This means that their emotional development and maturation became blocked or stopped at some point when they were children. They are living the wounded child syndrome. Thus, to evolve, these people need to go backward in order to go forward (the Cardinal archetype). In order to create a new self-image, Venus in Capricorn people must take themselves back to the time in which this wounding or emotional arrest took place. Through reflection they will discover childhood memories that house the causal factors of their emotional arrest. By focusing on those memories, these individuals will determine how their self-image in general and their emotional dynamics specifically were shaped and defined. In essence, it is from this time forward that these individuals must learn to "decondition" themselves in order to re-create a new self-image.

Once this deconditioning begins the Venus in Capricorn person will allow the inner Cancer archetype to live and thrive. They will learn to allow their feelings, needs, and emotions to be unearthed and set free—to remove all guilt associations linked with the very essence of their beingness. They will learn to relate their emotions, feelings, and needs in a free and non-restricted way. They will lose their fear of rejection and false judgment. They will learn the security that they have been looking for lies deeply within themselves. They will discover self-empowerment in this way. They will learn who to trust, and who not to trust. Those that will accept them, and encourage them to be who they are, will become those that they trust. They will learn to create a new self-image that will allow them to integrate into society in a new way, based on values that are consistent with their intrinsic individuality. In this way, the inner child will heal and be set free to become an adult who is self-secure, healed, and unafraid to be who they are.

Famous People with Venus in Capricorn

John Bloefeld
Robert Bly
Terry Cole Whitaker
Neil Diamond
J. Edgar Hoover

VENUS IN AQUARIUS

As a pre-existing pattern, Venus in Aquarius individuals are and have been rebelling against, or liberating themselves from, common value systems and relationship forms as defined by the consensus of the society they live in. The causal factor that generates this rebellion is an emphasized feeling within the psychology of Venus in Aquarius people of being different—a sense of cultural alienation or estrangement. As a result of this archetype, these individuals learn about the nature of their individuality, the feeling of being different, through a process of elimination—an awareness of what they are not that precedes an ongoing awareness of who and what they are.

A perfect example on a collective level that illustrates this archetype was in the 1960s when Uranus was in Libra (naturally Venus ruled). At that time there was a massive rebellion among young people against the prevailing consensus social value system and the ways that society expected intimate or marriage-type relationships to be defined—namely, as role specific. The rebellion at a collective level created the slogan "free love" in which many of the young people began to experiment (Uranus) with different forms of relationship specifically, and a radical reformation of social, political, and economic values generally. This radical rebellion among the young people over time began to be integrated among the prevailing status quo of society in such a way that society itself began to change at a mainstream level.

Even though the archetypal intent of Venus in Aquarius is to rebel against the prevailing consensus of the existing society, there are three reactions to this intention as reflected in the people who have it in their birth chart. The first reaction is one wherein there is an absolute rebellion against everything that the consensus symbolizes. This reaction will correlate to individuals who feel totally disconnected not only from the existing society and their parents, but also a total disconnection from their prevailing peer group. As a result, these individuals will stand as a group of one if necessary rather than conform to any expectation from any source. The second reaction will correlate to individuals who are also rebelling against the prevailing consensus, yet will form relationships to other individuals within the existing peer group who also feel just as alienated as they do. In this way, they join forces with this group of people who now stand apart from the consensus as a group. This estranged group now has a collective impact on the prevailing society in such a way as to change it in one way or another. Beyond the example cited above, Uranus moving through Libra in the 1960s, the "punk rockers" of the 1980s illustrates this point. The third reaction is a paradoxical one (Uranus directly correlates with the dynamic of paradoxes). In this reaction, these individuals rebel against not only the prevailing consensus, but also against their own peer group. This rebellion takes the form of trying to resurrect value systems, and ways of being in relationship, that comes from some other time in the collective past. A current example of this phenomena, as of this writing now that Saturn has transited Aquarius, is the movement among some young people of rebellion against having sex with anyone until marriage.

The causal factor that generates the necessary rebellion or liberation from the prevailing consensus of social values and the expectations that these values create in general, and the ways of being in relationship specifically, is *detachment*. Archetypally speaking, the evolutionary intention within the sign Aquarius is to objectify, in a non-emotional way, the nature of reality at any level that one focuses on. In order to objectify anything, the ego within consciousness must separate itself from its own subjective reality. For this to happen, detachment becomes necessary. When consciousness is in a detached and objectified state from its own egocentric reality it is then able understand the overall nature and structure of any dynamic in its totality: how the nature and structure of any dynamic came to be the way it is, and what is necessary for it to grow or evolve. This archetypal function within consciousness is necessary. If it did not exist, growth would not be possible. A state of absolute crystallization would occur.

The three possible ways that the Venus in Aquarius individual can react to the archetypal intent of liberation or rebellion from the prevailing consensus of social values and expectations, and the ways of being in relationship, will determine specific value associations and the meaning they generate. The specific value associations will thus determine or create the vibrational magnetism of attraction (Venus) that correlates to the types of people that the Venus in Aquarius person attracts into their life. This is the principle of like attracting like which leads to social groups of people. For Venus in Aquarius to have a sense of meaning and purpose in their lives, it becomes necessary to form social relationships with people of like mind. The commonality of shared values that this creates sustains their own individual values. In many ways, then, the Venus in Aquarius person is dependent on the commonality of shared values within specific social groups of people to have any individual sense of purpose and meaning. To be able to inwardly relate to themselves as an individual, to have individual meaning, is to be part of a larger social group. It is from this larger social group of shared values, and the meaning that these values create, that the Venus in Aquarius person will choose whom to be in intimate relationships with.

The type of Venus in Aquarius person who is in absolute rebellion against the consensus, including their peer group, will not be able to relate (Venus) to any existing social grouping of people. They will only be able to relate to other people on an individual basis—other people who are as socially alienated and as iconoclastic as themselves. If they are able to relate to any kind of social group, it is to the extreme radical edge whose values are aimed at completely overthrowing the existing system, including the consensus of their immediate peer group. The vibration of rebellion is extremely intense in these people, and this vibration will permeate their entire way of being, how they dress, appear, think, and relate themselves to others. The intensity of this vibration will naturally create an insecure and defensive reaction in all other people who are not like themselves. This occurs because the vibration and values of rebellion naturally challenge the security of all others who are aligned with social groups of one kind or another, the security dynamic being linked with others of like mind. This reaction is analogous to a group of yuppies sitting around a cocktail party table becoming happily drunk and, from stage left, someone throws a tarantula onto the cocktail party table. This type of Venus in Aquarius person is the tarantula.

This type will typically appear arrogant, superior, righteous, angry, iconoclastic, and intellectual. They will express themselves through some kind of radical or revolutionary mental construction of one sort or another. They stand apart from all others and project, overtly or

186 Pluto: The Soul's Evolution through Relationships

covertly, critical atom bombs at anyone or anything that supports identifying with "the system" at any level, in any way. The very sense of meaning and value that they give to themselves is dependent on, and linked with, this almost absolute detachment from the social system. They can form friendships or alliances with other individuals who reflect this same psychological orientation to social reality. These friendships or alliances typically occur on a sporadic, moment-to-moment basis. And from this small amount of like-minded people they can choose or form intimate connections that may be just as sporadic and short-lived as their overall pattern linked with others at a friendship or alliance level.

Such a person is intimately attracted to those that are radically different. The sense or experience of passion is linked with intimacy being ignited because of the fact of being different, which ignites the natural curiosity of Venus in Aquarius. Because Aquarius as an archetype desires to know how whole systems are structured and put together, the curiosity function thus creates a Venus desire to know how the individual system of someone whom they are intimately attracted to is put together in such a way as to make them different. Inwardly resonating together in their individual differences born of rebellion thus stimulates this type of Venus in Aquarius passion for individual intimate relationships. Once the curiosity function has been satisfied, the passion may dissipate almost overnight. Thus, this type of Venus in Aquarius person typically goes through various intimate relationships that can only be sustained for small lengths of time. This type desires a fundamental freedom to explore and experiment with life as she or he sees fit. There is a rebellion against the idea of commitment in a relationship, which leads to a rebellion against the values associated with monogamy.

The second type of Venus in Aquarius people mentioned above is not quite so absolutist and isolated. They will relate to their immediate social peer group who are rebelling against the existing society, and the prevailing social values and ways of being in relationship that are expected by that society. A simple example of this dynamic, again, is the "punk rockers" of the late 1980s. From mainstream society's point of view, these individuals will appear to be social misfits—irresponsible, narcissistic, immature, and the causal factor in what used to be called the "generation gap." The group itself will be perceived by society as hurling the atom bombs of criticism, and the group will have the effect of creating insecurity within the consensus because of the challenge to the existing social values of the times.

Those within this group will perceive society at large as irrelevant and without meaning. Detaching from mainstream society, and the values that it promotes, thus creates a psychological perch on which this type of Venus in Aquarius person can also appear self-righteous, arrogant, superior, iconoclastic, rebellious, alienated, and angry. Yet this type needs and desires to be part of the immediacy of the peer group who, as a social grouping, is rebelling against mainstream society. Their sense of meaning and purpose is dependent on belonging to this type of social group. Each individual within the group can represent the group as an individual, yet that "individual" is a function and reflection of the group. What this means is that the individual who appears to be so different as perceived from the point of view of the consensus would not even exist unless there was a social grouping of these "individuals" in the first place. This is because their individual "rebellion" is dependent on other people who are also rebelling. If not for their supportive peer group, this type of Venus in Aquarius person would not have the inner courage to stand as a group of one if necessary (unlike the first type described above).

This is a very critical point to understand—that so many who identify in this way with their immediate peer group do not embody or reflect the archetype of rebellion or liberation in the sense that it actually defines their Souls as individuals. It can and does reflect their Souls on an immediate social grouping level relative to their peers. This type of social group at a peer level has occurred throughout time in all social systems, and is always embodied in the youth of the generation. And necessarily so, because this social grouping has the effect of changing, in some way, the existing consensus. In this sense, it is an evolutionary determinant that is part of the overall Creation from an intrinsic or natural point of view, operating from generation to generation. Because the majority of these individuals are not defined at an individual Soul level through the desire of individual liberation or rebellion from the consensus, this social group becomes assimilated or absorbed into the mainstream as they become older. The social causes or issues that were reflected in their youthful rebellion also become assimilated by the consensus. Inevitably, some change in the consensus occurs because of it. Thus, as this group becomes older, they begin to rebel against their own rebellion!. Another Uranian paradox. A modern example of this point is reflected in the "hippies" of the 1960s and early 1970s who became "yuppies" in the 1980s. Only a small few in this original group sustained the original rebellion reflected in the hippies as a whole.

This point is important to grasp for another reason, one that concerns the nature of the friendships that we form, and the values we define that create how we are in our intimate relationships. All of us go through the initial rebellion of youth in one way or another; rebelling against our parents' reality, and through extension the larger society in which we are born. Uranus changes signs every eight years. Each sign that Uranus is in correlates to what, why, and how each generation of youth rebels. For those who have Venus in Aquarius, this peer group bonding is especially emphasized, important, and necessary.

This is because they have an essential evolutionary lesson that concerns the nature of friendship, and the need to define their own sense of meaning and purpose. Through extension, this correlates to the need to define their own unique way of being in an intimate relationship. Thus, as this type of Venus in Aquarius becomes older, and begins to assimilate into the existing social system, they effectively rebel against they very rebellion that motivated them in youth as an extension of their immediate peer group. The friendships that were formed through the shared values of youth now become rebelled against unless those friends also begin to assimilate into the existing society. And the ones that do not rebel against the initial rebellion will rebel against those who do. The lesson of friendship is thus learned through what can be called *situational values.* If the values (and the meaning associated with those values) are relatively the same, then friendships are formed. Once they change, for whatever reasons, the existing friendships can be lost or broken in some way. The real issue here, and the lesson, becomes this: a true friend will always be a friend no matter what, and everyone else is an acquaintance.

By experiencing the disillusionment of broken or lost friendships, and by rebelling against the initial rebellion of youth defined through peer group association, this type of Venus in Aquarius person is learning to define their own unique value system, which is a function of their individual sense of meaning and purpose in life. They will learn to define their intimate relationship requirements, their essential needs, as a reflection of their overall sense of purpose and meaning in life. At best, this will create a relationship dynamic in which both individuals reflect an attitude of uniquely defining the relationship as an extension of each of their individualities.

The third type of Venus in Aquarius person mentioned above is also very much a rebel, in the sense of rebelling against not only their own peer group, but all people who live a contemporary lifestyle.

They identify with value systems associated with another time—the past. They will appear very conservative, traditional, and iconoclastic as a result of this, and will only form social or intimate relationships with those of like mind. This type is dependent on forming these small social alliances in order to have any individual sense of meaning, value or purpose.Thus, they will form a relatively small sub-strata within their own generation, and even smaller within the existing society. They will also advocate social causes or revolution linked with challenging the existing value system of society at large. They can seem or appear just as superior, arrogant, judgmental, and angry as the other two types of Venus in Aquarius people. The value system that they orientate to is generally very limited and rigid, and their attitude is typically one of a righteous authoritarian who has the self-created right to impose those values on all others.

In their intimate relationships, the Venus in Aquarius person is generally a good friend above all else. Most have the intrinsic ability to understand objectively the reality and individuality of their partner—to understand how and why their partner is the way that they are. As a result, they typically understand what their partner needs for their life to keep growing and evolving. And most can give their partner what they need in this sense. They are good listeners, and can reflect back to their partner exactly what they are hearing as the partner intends it. Thus, they can be exceptional at keeping the conversation moving forward in an ever-evolving way that leads to sudden insights and resolutions. They can also be very adept at posing questions, and leaving it at a question level in such a way that the one receiving the question creates a gestation within their own consciousness leading to the answer from within themselves.

By nature, the Venus in Aquarius person is not monogamous. As stated before, they need a basic freedom in order to manifest their cyclic or perpetual changes. There is an inherent rebellion against restriction in any form. Restrictions imply conditions. In love, the Venus in Aquarius person rebels against conditions that will restrict love and its expression. It can be just as easy for these people to find deep, sudden, and intense love with someone overnight as with someone for a lifetime. Thus their attraction function (Venus) can occur suddenly and unexpectedly. Again, they are attracted to that which stirs their curiosity, to that which appears different and unique. Others who vibrate in this way will stimulate the Venus in Aquarius individuals. This can create real problems in their relationships if they are not honest about this, and if their partner cannot live in this way. The Venus in Aquarius person needs freedom to engage and create many different kinds of social networks with different kinds of people.

Because of this, the Venus in Aquarius person needs a partner who is very secure within themselves. They require a partner who is willing to challenge the existing consensus of what life means in general, and how to be in relationships specifically. They need a partner who is willing to cyclically change the dynamics in the relationship, or to change as necessary. They require a partner who is intellectually sophisticated, and who can match or keep up with their own thinking process. This thinking process is typically eclectic in some way, and fast-moving. It can be very difficult for the Venus in Aquarius person to truly love or respect another if they do not intellectually respect them. There simply is a fundamental need to experiment with different values and ways of looking at life because, again, the Venus in Aquarius person learns about who they essentially are by becoming aware of what they are not. And they need a partner who can experiment with them in this way.

The Venus in Aquarius person has a deep, inner detachment from within themselves. This detachment primarily manifests on a feeling or emotional level. The evolutionary intention in this is to objectify their feelings, needs, and emotions in order to be aware of their causes. This leads to self-knowledge. In evolutionary terms, this symbol will always occur as a reaction to lifetimes in which the individual was lost to their emotions, feelings, and needs. This inner detachment can create the appearance within these people of not being totally integrated. This is an appearance only. For Aquarius, integration occurs through the vehicle of detachment. For those in intimate relationship to the Venus in Aquarius person, this detachment can be very frustrating when they do not understand its function or intention. In the middle of the deepest emotional crisis or turmoil the Venus in Aquarius person seems aloof and unmoved, somehow calm in the middle of the storm. Or when the partner now is pouring out his or her emotional guts to the Venus in Aquarius person they are met with nothing but cool, calm, detached, and objective feedback. Yet this is the function of Venus in Aquarius.

Of course, other chart factors can condition this. For instance, the Venus in Aquarius person can also have Mars conjunct Neptune in Libra in the Eighth House, which would create the opposite effect. In such a case, an absolute emotional/psychological empathy would result, mirroring the other person's emotional state. But the function of Venus in Aquarius is to learn how to objectify through detachment, so after the immediacy of the moment of this way of relating had passed, the Venus in Aquarius function would instinctively attempt to objectify what all the emotional/psychological dynamics were about, and the reasons for them.

The Venus in Aquarius person can also be very erratic and unpredictable in their life directions, the realities that their ever-shifting needs create, in their feeling and emotional states, and in their extreme cycles of communicating/not communicating. They can be just as unpredictable in their reactions to people, with sudden and unexpected behaviors that reflect these reactions. In these situations, the words that come from their mouths may be quite unexpected and upsetting. Again, this kind of unpredictability can be very difficult for others to understand, let alone tolerate and accept. Because of this, the Venus in Aquarius person is very quick on their feet, and can adapt to changing life conditions or social situations quite adeptly.

Sexually speaking, the Venus in Aquarius person will reflect the sexual values that are reflected in their immediate peer group—a group, again, that is rebelling against the existing sexual values of the consensus society that they are born into. Simply stated, if the existing consensus advocates free sex or non-monogamy, then this group as youth will rebel against this and promote monogamy. Conversely, if the existing consensus advocates monogamy, then this group as youth will rebel against this, and promote non-monogamy. The causal factor is simply the evolutionary determinant to rebel in order to effect necessary change within the existing consensus.

On the other hand, the Venus in Aquarius person is inherently defined by the need to experiment. Thus, many will engage in sexual experiments in order to discover who they naturally are through the process of elimination. Others will continue to sexually experiment simply because they find this exciting, based on the fact that what they are doing is "different." A few will experiment with sexual ways of being that can be quite bizarre if bizarre is understood from the point of view of what is considered as "normal." An example of this was a client of mine who claimed that she was having sexual intercourse with a disembodied spirit who was a prior life lover. For others, Venus in Aquarius can promote an asexual response to the sexual impulse that exists in all human beings. This is the type who is totally living in a mental reality devoid of, or detached from, their emotional dynamics. Physical or sexual living is considered by these types as somehow degenerative to their overall sense of purpose and meaning.

Most of these individuals have an observational awareness during the sexual act. It is as if they are watching themselves and their partners during the sexual act. This observational quality linked with detachment can create a deep knowledge of how sexual energy can be used, directed, or manipulated. On the one hand this can produce very adept sexual lovers who are extremely aware of everything that is going on in their partner. They know how to harmonize themselves with the feelings and sensations that are occurring within their partner. In this way they know how to keep those feelings and sensations moving ever-forward, which can lead to incredibly deep sexual responses. Some who have this capacity can actually help another become more sexually alive, free, and open. And a few who realize that they have this capacity will then use it as a form of power to create a dependency in their partner. A few of my clients who were oriented in this way could actually take another who was sexually frozen and turn them into sex machines, so to speak. On the other hand, this can create a deep frustration because the Venus in Aquarius can never really seem to fully engage in the sexual act. They are always observing. This frustration can then lead them into experimenting with different and more intense ways of being sexual so that a total engagement can take place. Yet, because of the very nature of Aquarius, this will never really happen even in the midst of the most intense sexual situation.

The sexual rhythm, the sexual need cycle of Venus in Aquarius people also is unpredictable. Within the archetype this runs the full range from no sex at all, to infrequent need, to moderate need, to average need, to total, constant need. The only time it is predictable is when certain types with Venus in Aquarius need it all the time! As stated before, the Venus in Aquarius person is inherently non-monogamous. This applies sexually as well. Sure, anyone can learn to be monogamous, including this type. For this type to be monogamous, though, they must have a partner that perfectly reflects their own sexual desires, and the reality that these desires create. And then be prepared for those desires to change! A simple curiosity with someone who appears different or unique can stimulate their sexual desire. This can be difficult for an existing partner because most of use want to be the sole focus of our lover's attention.

For evolution to proceed, the Venus in Aquarius person must embrace its opposite: Leo. The essence of this evolutionary lesson is for Venus in Aquarius people to learn how to separate themselves from the immediacy of their peer group in order to actualize their own unique and specific value systems. They need values, and the meaning that these values reflect, that are consistent with their own individuality. The intention within this is to creatively actualize their own unique sense of individual purpose within the larger social group, their generation, and, through extension, within society as a whole.

In order to do this, the Venus in Aquarius person must learn to use their intrinsic capacity for detachment to stand apart from their immediate peer group. By detaching in this way they can then intellectually objectify why the immediacy of their peer group is defined through the types of value associations that it is—namely, the evolutionary need to rebel against the preceding generation and the existing consensus. Within this detachment they can realize that any peer group automatically creates a psychological pressure to conform to its values, and the ways of being that those values dictate. Understanding this, the Venus in Aquarius person can then learn to objectify him or herself in such a way to question whether or not the values advocated through the peer group are truly consistent with its own individual reality. If they are not, then the challenge for the Venus in Aquarius person is to separate from this peer group in order to discover, through separation, just exactly what their own specific individuality is. In this way they will formulate their value systems, and creatively actualize a life that is consistent with those values. And, in this way, they will become more perfectly aligned and centered within their own individual reality.

Famous People with Venus in Aquarius

Charles E. O. Carter
Sepharial
Paul Cezanne
Frederick Chopin
Marlene Dietrich

VENUS IN PISCES

As a pre-existing pattern, the Venus in Pisces person has been learning to embrace, on an archetypal level, a transcendent value system in order to create a sense of ultimate meaning in their life. The evolutionary process leading to this need has been a series of lifetimes in which the individual has experienced a tremendous amount of personal and social disillusionment. This has created a sense of total meaninglessness associated with temporal values. Many individuals with Venus in Pisces have not consciously conceptualized or realized the archetypal intent, which is to embrace a transcendent, spiritual value system. This is important to understand because until they do, they will not have a clear and solid sense of who they are, and the experience of disillusionment will continue to occur.

For these individuals, the inner world is more or less like a giant movie in which a diversity of images, plots, scenarios, and possible realities swirl around in different combinations. Within this inner world the Venus in Pisces person instinctively imagines him or herself in these different roles, like an actor who assumes the identity of a specific character. By imagining and "trying on" these different images and identities, like different parts in a movie, the Venus in Pisces person tries to relate to the ones that *feel* most like him or herself. An additional cause that creates this need is rooted in a deep inner feeling of impurity, and the guilt that this implies. The guilt ignites an instinctual reaction of denial at an unconscious level. Thus, the individual will have a nebulous negative feeling about him or herself. These feelings are then compensated for through the Piscean imagination—by creating false identities linked with the movie-like nature of their inner world. This creates the psychological dynamic of "illusion as reality."

These inner dynamics are very problematic because the Venus in Pisces person knows at a core level that these different images and identities are not who they really are. Nevertheless, they will try to make them real, to convince themselves that they are real, by acting them out through external manifestation, just like an actor in a play or movie. They will manifest the appropriate clothes, hair styles, home environment, types of possessions, and other factors that are symbolic of whatever the imagined identity is. Many individuals with Venus in Pisces actually succeed in convincing themselves that the artifact they have created is real. By externally manifesting the persona and the circumstances that reflect the inner imagination, it now seems tangible. They can point their finger to it and convince themselves and others because it obviously appears to exist.

A variation of this dynamic correlates to Venus in Pisces individuals who feel so inferior and weak, so without any personal power, so victimized by life itself, that they allow themselves to become vicarious extensions of someone else's reality. These people relate to themselves through the value systems, and the meaning that those values denote, of someone else. The Taurus side of Venus requires a personal effort to actualize and realize one's inherent values and resources of oneself. Venus in Pisces people can find it very difficult to make such an effort because they have no clear sense of themselves or of their inherent values and resources. Thus, the reverse of necessary effort occurs—laziness and a lack of any personal effort to define values that are consistent with who they intrinsically are. The old cliché "go with the flow" becomes the guiding motivation of these types of such people, and they go with the flow of someone else's reality because it can be easy to do. They do not have to take personal responsibility for themselves because they are essentially allowing themselves to be taken care of by someone else who is defining their reality for them.

In both cases, the Venus in Pisces person feels that they are either being punished for some undefined reason, or that they need to punish themselves for being something less than "pure." Punishment implies guilt with the consequent need to atone for the guilt, or to be angry because of the guilt. Some with Venus in Pisces will totally embody the atonement/guilt dynamic leading to the pathology of masochism. Some will totally embody the anger/guilt dynamic leading to the pathology of sadism. And some will embody both dynamics leading to the simultaneous pathology of sadomasochism. Such people will flip-flop between guilt and anger depending on whether the nature of the immediate circumstances is passive or aggressive.

The causal factor of these pathologies is rooted in the fact that the Venus in Pisces person has had at least one prior lifetime in which there has been a deep immersion into the religious conditioning of Judaic or Christian philosophies. As a result, there has been an acceptance within their consciousness that life on Earth requires suffering as a requirement to enter the "Kingdom of God." They have accepted that God is perfect, and everything else in the Creation is less than perfect. They have accepted the doctrine of original sin that presupposes that the Soul separated itself from God. They have accepted the doctrine that flesh and spirit are mutually antagonistic unless limited to the procreational act. They have accepted that one must submit to God's will, that God is an anthropological male who is superior to women, and that, through extension, men are superior to women.

The acceptance of these doctrines at some prior point in time has come to constitute an inner standard of judgment, which becomes the causal factor in a psychological pathology of sadism or masochism that is acted out in various ways and degrees of intensity. Some who have

Venus in Pisces will continue to accept such religious doctrines because, again, they lack a clear image of who they actually are, and therefore cannot define a truly personal set of beliefs. Since the archetypal intent of Venus in Pisces is to embrace a transcendent value system, it thus becomes easy to "adopt" values and a belief system of a religious nature. This is yet another role to act out, in which they create a persona that reflects the essence of the religious doctrine in some way. The person in this role becomes very moralistic, constricted, and harshly judgmental of everyone else who is not in conformity to these doctrines. This orientation will ultimately lead to a state of absolute disillusionment and a state of inner emptiness, because these types of doctrines do not reflect the inherent truth of God.

For others who have Venus in Pisces, the opposite reaction to these doctrines will be manifested. These individuals will have rejected and rebelled against the doctrines at some point, and in this rebellion, triggered by anger over the nature of the doctrines, they would assume identities of an almost absolutely hedonistic way of living. Under this dynamic, the life of the Venus in Pisces person seems to be almost totally devoid of anything of a spiritual nature. The flesh and senses become glorified in one way or another, and/or values associated with materialism replace the values of spirituality. Some who react in this way may reflect a perfunctory acknowledgment of spirituality without actually living a life that is defined by spiritual or transcendent principles. This reaction will also lead to a state of disillusionment because of the ultimate emptiness that hedonistic and materialistic living eventually lead to.

Most people with Venus in Pisces create a synthesis or composite of these two extremes. On the one hand, they experience a vague feeling or acknowledgment of spiritual values that go more or less unmanifested. On the other hand, they create and attempt to manifest images of themselves that are based on the worldly values of the society they are born into. This dynamic can create the psychology in which these types feel that nothing is real, and the more real they try to make something the less real it becomes—even when there is "evidence" to support that reality. This reaction will also lead to progressive disillusionment, because the ultimate sense of meaning that the Venus in Pisces archetype requires cannot be found in this way.

The causal factor in the psychological experience of disillusionment in all of these reactions to the Venus in Pisces archetype is rooted in one simple truth: Until there is a conscious actualization of transcendent values and belief structures that reflect the ultimate meaning of life—the Natural and Inherent Truths of the Creation that exist of themselves—the experience of disillusionment will continue. When realized and acted on, these values will constitute the core meaning for the Venus in Pisces person's inner and outer reality, and of how they inwardly and outwardly relate to themselves and others. Life will still seem like a movie, but this movie will be the movie of God, not the movies that are created by a disillusioned ego who attempts to find the meaning for its life in worldly forms that contain no essence.

The realization of God's movie will start with the realization that the idea of perfection is an illusion, since the only perfection possible is based on a Creation that remains unmanifested and unformed. It is only when that which is unformed and unmanifested has been manifested into the totality of all forms through a projected act of Creation by God that the idea of perfection occurs within consciousness. Once this is realized, manmade laws and man-made religions will give way to Natural law, allowing for an understanding that what we call God in simultaneously perfect and imperfect. The interaction of perfection and imperfection reflects the interaction of the unmanifested and the manifested. This simple truth is the causal factor in involution and evolution. In this way compassion, love, acceptance, and forgiveness of our imperfections will replace critical, harsh, and abusive judgments issued from manmade religious doctrines that attempt to artificially subjugate and control the natural spirit in the human being.

For those Venus in Pisces individuals who have committed themselves to spiritual values, and the lifestyle that those values correlate to, illusion considered as reality will relatively not exist. It will only continue to exist until an understanding of the Natural Laws that are inherent to the Manifested Creation are understood. For these people, the journey to that understanding is already under way. It is just a matter of time. Where they are in that journey will directly correlate to how they relate to themselves inwardly, and thus how they relate to others. This will run the full range from rabid fundamentalists who see their religion as the only true religion to the truly enlightened Soul who realizes that God has created many paths to the same goal. To arrive at this state of awareness, it is necessary at key points in the spiritual journey to achieve the dissolution of any "religious" or "spiritual" thought forms that do not allow for that realization and/or awareness. A perfect example of this point is found in the life of Edgar Cayce (who had Venus in Pisces). As a young man, he more or less reflected rigid Christian beliefs that included no doctrine of reincarnation—life was just once around. Yet in his Piscean trances and dreams he became aware of the existence of many of his own past lifetimes, as well as the prior lifetimes of many others, many of which could actually be documented in various ways. Thus, his trances and dreams had an effect of dissolving his belief and value structures, as defined in rigid Christian doctrine. Accordingly, he evolved further down the transcendental road leading to awareness and realization of the Ultimate Truth of Natural Laws that predate the human species.

Because of the transcendent impulse reflected in the Venus in Pisces archetype, all these individuals will be inherently idealistic. They will have ideals for themselves, and they will have ideals for how everything should be. The problem here is not the dynamic of ideals. The problem is with the expectations that are simultaneously linked with those ideals. Disillusionment occurs to many of the Venus in Pisces people because the expectations linked with the ideals are unrealized, defective, or not actualized in some way. Ideals also imply judgment when the perfection of the ideal is not realized. In essence, the Venus in Pisces person commonly has value systems, and the meaning associated with those values, that are rooted in all kinds of "should bes." This dynamic becomes the basis of all kinds in inner and outer judgments that these individuals pronounce on themselves and other people. All too often, these individuals subject themselves to various degrees of frustration and defeatism. They also cause frustrations for the people who are subjected to their unrealistic expectations. The lesson to be realized by the Venus in Pisces person is that the value is in the effort, and not necessarily in the outcome. They also need to realize that most people are doing the best that they can based on what they have to work with. Here again, compassion must replace unnecessary judgment.

All Venus in Pisces people are ultra-sensitive. They feel life in excruciating and exquisite ways. They are naturally emotionally empathetic to everyone and everything. Their psychic structures feel, and unconsciously osmose, the immediate and overall realities around them. As a result, they unconsciously duplicate the realities of those immediate to them, and the realities reflected in the collective consciousness. This, of course, can overwhelm the Venus in Pisces person who is not rooted in spiritual reality. It becomes its own causal factor in feeling confused, disoriented, feeling afraid for no reason, the inner sense of "losing it" or going crazy, or sudden uprisings of inexplicable emotional states. These effects are based in the transcendental intention of Venus in Pisces. It demands a progressive dissolving of anything that prevents direct connection to, and realization of, the Ultimate Truth. Since most individuals who have Venus in Pisces do not understand this dynamic, this situation causes the survival instinct intrinsic to Venus to manifest as a desire to almost totally shut down and withdraw from the external circumstances of their lives. This occurs cyclically, and helps them to restabilize themselves.

In their intimate relationships, the Venus in Pisces person is a naturally giving individual. They will always try to support their partner in whatever ways are required. They are good listeners who can identify with whatever the partner is saying. As a result, the partner feels as if they have been heard. They are highly sensitive and vulnerable people who reflect a natural kind of innocence and naiveté. They are in love with the idea of love, and, as a result, are highly romantic. Their romantic, dreamy nature lends itself to a high degree of imagination or fantasy that can become very creative. This creativity can manifest as creative problem solving, poetical abilities linked with metaphor and allegory, food preparation, colorful and decorative homes, musical ability, writing, a natural psychic capacity that just "tunes in" without knowing how or why, the way that they dress, etc.

Conversely, the intimate relationships that they form rarely if ever correlate to the "ideal" partner that they consciously and unconsciously desire. As a result, many will "settle for less" because it is the best that they think they can do. This dynamic becomes a causal factor in cycles of depression and meaninglessness, generating all kinds of escapist scenarios. At worst, this causes the Venus in Pisces person to become involved in all kinds of addictive and compulsive behavior. These activities can include indulgence in drugs and alcohol,constant and compulsive reading of books, excessive movie-going, compulsive clothes buying, eating disorders of one sort or another, compulsive sex, or the development of all kinds of phobias or various mental disorders. As an example, I had a client with Venus in Pisces who was married to a Protestant minister. She appeared to believe in the life of what a Protestant ministers wife "should be," yet secretly advertized herself as a "call girl" who would make house calls, so to speak.

For a relationship to be really positive and healthy, the Venus in Pisces person needs a partner who realizes that they are much, much more than what their constructed persona suggests, even if this is a spiritual persona. It is all too easy for the Venus in Pisces person to hide behind this carefully constructed persona because of the fear of being vulnerable, and because of their fear that no one who saw who they "really were" would want to love them. Yet for the Venus in Pisces person to attract such a partner, they must first accept who they are without unnecessary and artificial judgments that emanate from man-made moralities of a religious nature. Once this occurs, they can attract a partner who will embrace their totality and love them for who they are. Once the Venus in Pisces person realizes that they are being loved for who they are, they will let down their instinctual walls of self-protection. Their persona will collapse, and their hypersensitive natures can be freely expressed. The natural innocence that they embody will manifest in a childlike way. They will learn to receive and accept the love that they so desperately need. They will be loved for who they really are versus being related to, and only understood, through the persona that they create. In this way the shackles of a self-created frustration based in the feeling that no one knows who they are, or what they need, will be removed.

Sexually speaking, the Venus in Pisces person can run the gamut from sex only as a procreational act to a sex life in which they act out sexual scenes created in their imaginations. They can range from an absolute fear of feeling anything that their body creates via the senses to absolute immersion into the senses. Most Venus in Pisces people have a natural shyness about their bodies, at least when they are naked. By nature they are sexual givers who enjoy giving pleasure to their partners. As a result, they also must learn how to receive. Archetypally speaking, the Venus in Pisces person requires a very gentle approach to love-making. Touch, foreplay, romantic atmospheres, some wine or a few tokes of marijuana, music and candles set the stage for the Venus in Pisces person to become totally engaged. Sexual role playing and sexual fantasies of one kind or another become natural and psychologically healthy activities for the Venus in Pisces person when they have a feeling that their partner is honest, sincere, and without ulterior agendas or motives. Archetypally, the sexual act is "sacred" to the Venus in Pisces person—it is pure and clean in its natural state. For some, this will translate into employing sexual/spiritual doctrines and methods that have the intention of uniting with the divinity of their partner, and the ultimate divinity together.

For evolution to proceed, the Venus in Pisces person must embrace its opposite: Virgo. This means to create a highly introspective focus of self-analysis that will allow them to objectively discriminate between reality and illusion. In so doing they will be able to discern the actual condition and state of their inner beingness as it is. The intention in this polarity is to align the individual with their actual reality versus the illusions, delusions, and images that the Venus in Pisces individual creates and considers to be real because they exist in actual form. This is a very difficult intention to consciously grasp and work with, because it inevitably leads to great psychological pain. Disillusionment is one of the most difficult of all human experiences, and will always lead to anger in one way or another. Yet anger, which is an instinctual emotion, can be used in a positive way to motivate these individuals to always put the light of conscious awareness into their inner world so that images born of illusion no longer define their reality. In order to do this, it is necessary for the Venus in Pisces person to align themselves with some spiritual system that involves meditation in one form or another. Physical practices such as yoga, the "spiritual running" approach advocated by Sri Chinmoy, Tai Chi and so on are also excellent ways to accomplish this intention. Dream journaling, writing diaries, conversations with trusted friends who are natural psychologists that can help them understand their emotional/psychological make-up, and a well-grounded type of work are all beneficial to actualizing this intention.

Famous People with Venus in Pisces

Edgar Cayce
Sonny Bono
Joan Grant
Manly Palmer Hall
Carl Payne Tobey

Now that we have completed our examination of the general themes that Venus correlates to in terms of our inner and outer relatedness patterns, and how these patterns attract the reflection of our own inner reality, I would like to say again that these are general themes that are not conditioned by any other factor, astrologically speaking. Every archetype in the birthchart, a planet in a sign for example, is conditioned by other planetary archetypes. These conditioning factors include aspects from other planets, the specific houses that the planet in question is in, and so on. It is imperative that the astrologer be able to integrate, synthesize, and interpolate all the conditioning factors in the birth chart to be truly competent and of positive service to another individual. With that said, I would now like to briefly address the human experience of changing needs within our relationships.

THE TRANSITS OF VENUS

Life within the manifested Creation is not static. It is forever changing through the process of involution leading to evolution. All of us know that we are in a perpetual state of becoming. Thus, our needs reflected in our desires also change. Specific to relationship dynamics, our changing desires, and the needs they create, can be measured in a variety of ways. One of the most basic and simple ways is the transit of Venus through our birthchart. The Venus cycle is generally from nine to fourteen months, depending on whether it goes retrograde during the cycle or not. Again, Venus moves into apparent retrograde only every 548 days. When Venus does go retrograde, it will be transiting somewhere in the birthchart. This is a very significant time for all individuals on Earth because it will correlate to a time frame in which we must reexamine and reflect on the overall nature of our reality. The intention in this is to become aware of what we no longer need in our lives—the dynamics or circumstances that are now counterproductive to our need to grow and move forward. At the same time, it creates an awareness of what we *do* need in order to move forward. Thus, new value associations will gestate into our conscious awareness that will require action when Venus goes direct. Focusing this archetype into our relationships creates the awareness of what the existing dynamics are that are no longer needed or necessary. Consequently, it creates the awareness of new needs that will allow the relationship to grow, from an individual point of view.

This is important to grasp, because unless you share the same Ascendant with the corresponding signs on all the house cusps with your partner, the Venus retrograde will be in different houses for the two of you. Thus, each individual within the relationship will be reflecting on different dynamics leading to a different awareness of what they feel is necessary for the relationship to move forward. For the relationship to evolve in a balanced, equal way, it is important that each partner embrace what the other is feeling and relating concerning these issues. This will create a win/win situation. The specific issues or dynamics that need to be reflected on and changed, as well as what the new needs are, of course, are symbolized in the actual sign and house in which Venus is retrograde. Even though it may be in a different house, Venus will be in the same sign. Being in the same sign creates the basis of a mutual, common, shared focus that allows for a positive, clear dialogue. Through this commonality, the individual variations relative to the specific houses can hopefully be understood and consciously worked with.

When Venus goes retrograde through transit, it can correlate to a time in which we re-experience old issues or dynamics that we may have felt that we have already worked through or left behind. It can also be a time in which unresolved karmic issues that exist between us and our partner suddenly reappear, or when karma brings old friends or lovers back into our life. If we meet someone for the first time during a Venus retrograde cycle, someone who has some direct impact on our life in some way, or we have this effect for someone else that we have just met for the first time, then this correlates to a past-life connection in which something has not been finished, completed, or resolved—for better or worse. Accordingly, the Venus retrograde cycle is an excellent time to complete karmic business.

Generally speaking, the transit of Venus is relatively gentle. It rarely portends major upheaval in our life, or in our relationships. It is also a very simple dynamic to observe and work with. Simply observing its movements through the houses and signs will correlate to the immediacy of our inner and outer needs on an ongoing basis. It can correlate to our immediate focus within our life and in our relationships. If, for example, the Venus is in Gemini moving through my Eighth House, this can correlate to a time in which I become inwardly aware of some old emotional or psychological wound that is "triggered" by some circumstance that my partner creates. The challenge would be to acknowledge the wound versus the Eighth House temptation to conceal it. If I conceal it it would progressively smolder within me, which could lead to some intense confrontation with my partner at some other point. My behavior at that point would be disproportionate to whatever the circumstance was that finally blew off the manhole cover of my concealment. This could then lead to an ugly scene that was not necessary. Conversely, if I communicated (Gemini) to my partner that she had triggered some old emotional wound right then and there, then this would become the basis of a shared dialogue in which we could deeply examine the nature of the wound, and what to do about it.

On the other hand, there are times during the cycle of the Venus transit that can correlate to stressful developments or circumstances in our relationships. These moments can occur when the transit of Venus is in a First Quarter square to its natal position, in opposition to its natal position, or in a Last Quarter square to its natal position. Difficulties will arise if there is some pre-existing condition within the relationship that has not been addressed or acknowledged. In this case, these aspects will bring it to a head, so to speak. The actual conditions can be determined through considering the archetype of the natal position of Venus by house, sign, and aspect, and where the current transit of Venus is occurring by house and sign.

Other astrological methods that can also reveal very dynamic information about the ongoing evolution of our Venus archetype involve the Venus Return chart, other planets aspecting Venus through transits and progressions, and the progression of Venus itself. Venus in the yearly Solar Return chart also sheds light on this evolution.

VENUS IN THE COMPOSITE CHART

Lastly, Venus in the composite chart is important to examine. Again, the composite chart reflects two people in a relationship who have made mutual agreements to be together for many reasons. These reasons are reflected in the overall nature of the composite chart. The understanding of this chart starts, again, with the bottom line consideration of the natal Pluto, its polarity point, the South and North Nodes, and the location of their planetary rulers. Once this is understood, a correct analysis of all the other symbols can occur. Venus will correlate to the shared values, and the meaning that those values create, in the relationship. It will correlate to how the couple relates to themselves as a couple, and how they interrelate within the relationship. It will correlate to how they are able to hear what each other is saying, and how each of them "mirrors" the other. It will correlate to how they are able to give and receive love from one another, and what the capacity is for necessary change and evolution within the relationship. Let us examine an example chart (Chart #13) and create a brief analysis of it in order to understand these principles.

Briefly, this composite chart reflects two people who are Caucasian, were raised by middle-class parents with middle-class values, were exposed to the conditioning of the Christian religion from a societal or cultural point of view, and were subjected to intense psychological abuse by their parents, with one of them being severely sexually abused. Evolutionarily speaking, both were in the spiritual state or condition. And, as individuals, both had skipped evolutionary steps. The nature of those skipped steps concerned emotional and sexual dynamics. Rather than dealing with those issues, both had avoided them by attempting to embrace spiritual philosophies and values, and the lifestyles that reflected those philosophies and values.

Our first analysis starts by understanding the following factors: Pluto is in Leo in the Tenth House, and its polarity point is in Aquarius in

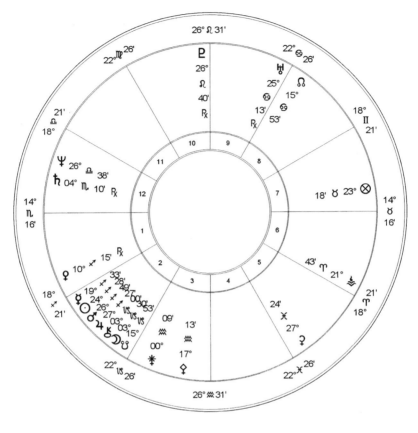

Chart #13

the Fourth House. The South Node is in Capricorn in the Second House with its planetary ruler, Saturn, in Scorpio in the Twelfth House forming a sextile to the Capricorn Moon, which is also in the Second House. The North Node is in Cancer in the Eighth House, its planetary ruler being that same Capricorn Moon. With the planetary rulers of the South and North Nodes being linked through the sextile, it can be clearly seen that in order to move toward their evolutionary future they must unlock and reexperience the past first—to recover the skipped steps. This evolutionary requirement is also demonstrated by the fact that the Nodes are in a Cardinal archetype, and Pluto itself is in a natural Cardinal house, as is its polarity point. For evolution to proceed through the Cardinal archetype, there is a need to go backward in order to go forward.

This couple reported to me that they both felt that they had shared many past lifetimes together, that they had a feeling of knowing each other "forever," and that they had specific past-life memories and images of being linked through the same families of origin in various ways. By examining the nature of astrological symbols linked with Pluto and the Nodal Axis, these feelings and memories would appear to be not only accurate, but obvious.

When these two people first came together in this life they did indeed spend a great deal of time talking about and discussing what had occurred to them as children. They discussed the emotional and psychological impact that each of their parents had on them. In this way they both realized that, as children, they were made to feel guilty and that there was something "wrong" with them. Each had a very negative self-image because of this. Both had learned to inwardly isolate themselves from the impact of their parents, and in this isolation developed a very active fantasy life through which they could escape. All of this is reflected in the composite chart in various ways. Pluto is in the Tenth House, the South Node is in Capricorn in the Second House, and Capricorn's planetary ruler (Saturn) is in Scorpio in the Twelfth House, forming a trine to the Second House Capricorn Moon.

As adults, both had experienced psychologically and sexually abusive partners. Through their discussions, they began to realize the linkage between what occurred to them as children and the types of partners they attracted as adults. The fundamental evolutionary intention of the relationship, as seen in the composite chart, is to allow them to liberate themselves from the impact of the past in order to create a positive new self-image. This is reflected in the Fourth House polarity of Pluto being in Aquarius, the North Node being in Cancer in the Eighth House relative to its planetary ruler (the Moon) conjunct Chiron in Capricorn in the Second House, and Jupiter, Mars, and the Sun being in Sagittarius. With the Moon also sextile Saturn in Scorpio in the Twelfth House, this couple would change from feeling victimized and defeated because of the past to accepting the responsibility for manifesting what they both needed to experience from an evolutionary and karmic point of view. In this way they would empower themselves, through the relationship, to become totally self-determined to break free from the impact of the past.

To accomplish this aim, they involved themselves in deep emotional and psychological discussion in which they reflected together on the negative influence of their childhood conditioning. Progressively, they embraced belief systems that involved Natural Law (Sagittarius) and that were experiential. This is reflected in the dominant Sagittarian archetype in this chart, and because Uranus in Cancer in the Ninth House is conjunct the North Node in Cancer in the Eighth House. The Eighth House requires proof, and thus experience. Venus is also in Sagittarius, inconjunct the North Node, and sesquiquadrate to Uranus (the planetary ruler of the Fourth House) in the Ninth House. Thus, their shared values (Venus) are connected to Natural Law (Sagittarius).

This couple began to unlock their past, and move towards their future, by making a commitment to a shamanistic philosophy. This involved ancient and sacred sexual methods (Venus inconjunct the North Node, the planetary ruler of the South Node occupying Scorpio in the Twelfth House) that allowed for the necessary emotional and sexual healing. It also allowed them to liberate from the current cultural sexual conditioning. This philosophy allowed for them to experience Nature as a conscious living whole in which they could transcend the limitations of time and space, and allow Nature to be their spiritual "teacher." These shared values thus created the sense of meaning and purpose for their relationship, and as individuals.

With Venus in Sagittarius in the First House, they related to each other in totally honest ways; without lies, deceptions, or distortions. Each considered the other to be the most important and special person, and they treated each other accordingly. Each promoted individual development and actualization for the other. They both learned to "hear" beyond spoken words when they communicated with one another (Venus in Sagittarius conjunct Mercury in Sagittarius). As a result, they developed a high degree of intuitive awareness of one another, and of each other's emotional, psychological, sexual, and spiritual needs. They simply had a "good feeling" about being with one another, and of what each needed. Because they deeply valued each other and the relationship, they were able to freely give and receive love from one another: Venus in Sagittarius is Jupiter ruled, which creates the "good feeling" that allows for the free giving and receiving of love. And with Venus in a Mutable archetype within the First House, their capacity to adapt to necessary change is guaranteed by their mutual commitment to grow and evolve beyond the past.

It is interesting to note that when this couple first met one another in this life, they each had very significant progression of Venus occurring. One had progressed Venus conjunct the South Node and Sun in Sagittarius. This progressed Venus was also forming a trine to natal

Pluto, and was sextile to natal Neptune. The other had progressed Venus conjunct natal Jupiter, which was also receiving a conjunction from the progressed Sun. At the same time, one had the transit of Pluto forming its last conjunction to their natal Venus, and the other had the transit of Pluto forming its last separating semi-square to their natal Venus. The transit of Venus itself was in Aries within both of their Fifth Houses. In combination with these other factors, this created a "love at first sight" and an immediate recognition of one another based on their past-life connections.

Chapter Eight

The Phasal Relationship of Mars and Pluto

All of us are aware that we are in a continuous state of *becoming* throughout life. This awareness is reflected through the archetype of Mars. As stated in *Pluto: The Evolutionary Journey of the Soul,* the planet Mars directly correlates to how we identify and instinctively act upon the desires that emanate from our Souls. This is why Mars has been considered as a lower octave of Pluto. In essence, Mars correlates to the subjective consciousness at an egocentric level that allows us to be aware of the types of desires that we have. There are two important archetypes to consider within the relationship between Mars and Pluto. One is the specific phasal relationship between Mars and Pluto, and the other is the specific house and sign that Mars is in.

Let us remember that from 0° to 360° is a complete cycle. This cycle reflects an evolutionary progression from beginning to end. There are eight primary phases within this cycle, each primary phase measuring 45°. Thus, from 0° to 45° correlates to the New phase. From 45° to 90° correlates to the Crescent phase. From 90° to 135° correlates to the First Quarter phase. From 135° to 180° correlates to the Gibbous phase. From 180° to 225° correlates to the Full phase. From 225° to 270° correlates to the Disseminating phase. From 270° to 315° correlates to the Last Quarter phase. From 315° to 360° correlates to the Balsamic phase.

To measure the phasal relationship between Mars and Pluto, simply use Pluto as a starting point, and in a counter-clockwise direction measure the amount of degrees of separation between it and Mars. This will correlate to the phase that exists between Mars and Pluto. This point is very important because the phasal relationship between Mars and Pluto will specifically correlate to how long the core evolutionary and karmic intentions reflected in the natal position of Pluto, its polarity point, and the South and North Nodes with their respective planetary rulers, has been under way.

In general, it takes eight lifetimes to work out or through the specific evolutionary and karmic intentions reflected in the main karmic/evolutionary axis within the birth chart. Thus, since there are eight primary phases, the phasal relationship between Mars and Pluto correlates to how many lives have preceded the current one that we are living relative to those intentions. These are *primary* lives—lifetimes in which the core evolutionary and karmic intentions are being directly worked on. There are also what I call *subsidiary* lives that occur after a primary life, in which those intentions are worked on indirectly in various ways. Thus, if the Mars/Pluto phase is First Quarter, for example, this would correlate to an individual who had two previous primary lifetimes working on the main karmic/evolutionary axis exhibited within his or her birthchart, the current life being either the third primary life, or a subsidiary life in which this was occurring.

A primary life can be determined when Mars is in one of the following major aspects to Pluto: conjunction, semi-square, square, trine, sesquiquadrate, inconjunct, or opposition. These aspects symbolize evolutionary gates or stations that correlate to the ongoing evolutionary progression of the Soul at every level of its totality. It is also important to understand that any of the aspects that we consider can only have its archetypal meaning understood in the context of the primary phase it exists within.

THE EIGHT PRIMARY PHASES AND THEIR ASPECTS

As necessary background for this chapter and the next, it will be useful to succinctly discuss the archetypal design of each primary phase, and the aspects that exist within these phases.

The New Phase. The New phase correlates to a brand-new evolutionary intention reflected in the Soul's desire to initiate a new way of being. This phase is instinctual and yang. It correlates with the need to initiate a diversity of experiences, to take action in order to begin the actualization of the new intention. The consequences of and reactions to the actions taken create the beginning of knowledge of what

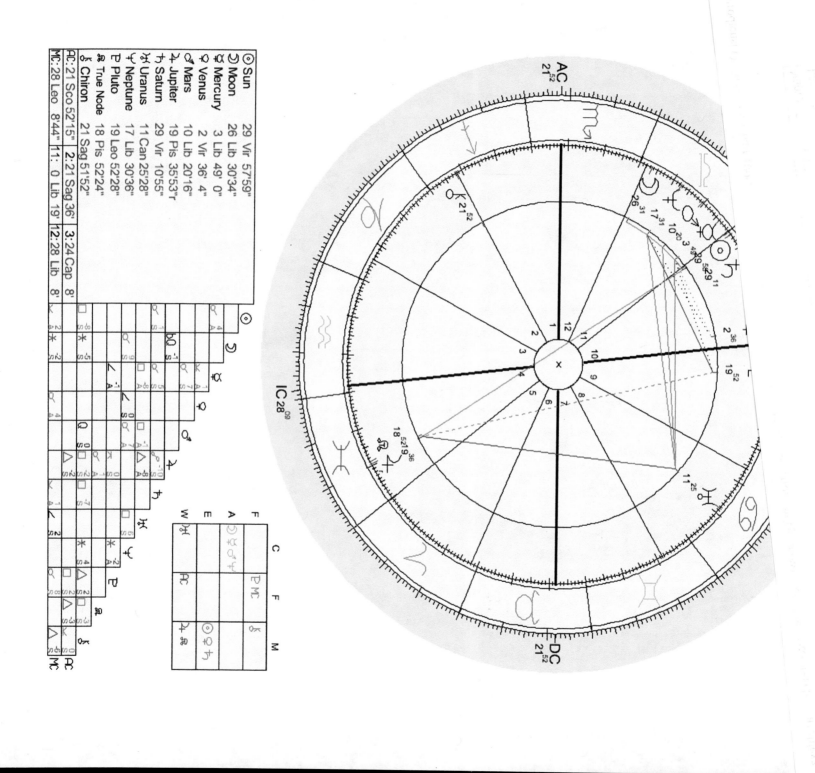

☉ Sun	29	Vir 57'59"
☽ Moon	26	Lib 30'34"
☿ Mercury	3	Lib 49' 0"
♀ Venus	2	Vir 36' 4"
♂ Mars	10	Lib 20'16"
♃ Jupiter	19	Pis 35'53"r
♄ Saturn	29	Vir 10'55"
♅ Uranus	11	Can 25'28"
♆ Neptune	17	Lib 30'36"
♇ Pluto	19	Leo 52'28"
☊ True Node	18	Pis 52'24"
⚷ Chiron	21	Sag 51'52"
AC: 21 Sco 52'15"	11:	2:21 Sag 36'
MC: 28 Leo 8'44"	12:	0 Lib 19'

	C	F	M
F		♇ MC	⚷
A	♀ ☿ ♆		
E			☉ ♀ ♄
W	♅	AC	♃ ☊

the new evolutionary intentions and requirements are. There is a desire to break free from the past cycle in this phase so that the experiences necessary to an awareness of what the new intention is about can occur. The fear of being absorbed by the past, or the previous cycle that precedes the New phase (the Balsamic phase) generates the desire for absolute freedom in order for independent actualization of this new evolutionary cycle.

Within the New phase, there are four aspects that correlate to specific phases of development, as follows:

- 0° (Conjunction) The planets unite in function so that a new evolutionary purpose and cycle can begin in an instinctual way. The new cycle or purpose will be projected spontaneously, without any egocentric awareness. It is pure, unchecked expression or action. Random experiences will be initiated in order to begin the process of self-discovery in this new evolutionary phase.

- 30° (Semi-sextile) The emergence or formation of a conscious and egocentric identification with the new evolutionary purpose or cycle. Random action narrows as the individual begins to sense specific directions or experiences that will allow realization or discovery of what the new evolutionary purpose or cycle is about.

- 40° (Novile) The conscious and egocentric awareness and identification of the new evolutionary purpose begins a gestation process wherein subjective growth toward the development or actualization of the new purpose begins by giving it personal or individual meaning. In other words, the individual becomes aware of moving in new directions, and that these new directions are highly personal in nature. The sense of self-discovery is heightened and the narrowing of random experiences continues.

- 45° (Semi-square) This is a transitional evolutionary gate or aspect that moves the evolutionary intention from the New to the Crescent phase. Whereas the New phase required all kinds of external activity, the Crescent phase requires a consolidation and internalization of experience. When the semi-square aspect is still applying within the New phase by orb, it creates a conflict between desiring yet more experiences, and the desire to slow down, consolidate, and internalize in order to create a structure in which the new discoveries can be integrated.

The Crescent Phase. This is a yin phase wherein the evolutionary archetype is internalized, established, and oriented to creating personal or individual forms and structures that will allow for the new evolutionary intention to take root. This requires a personal effort, because the temptation or fear of sliding back into past patterns can also occur in this phase.

Within the Crescent phase, there are five aspects that correlate to specific phases of development, as follows:

- 45° (Semi-square) As the evolutionary intention evolves from the New to Crescent phase, it begins to intensify. The Soul now struggles to establish and make real the purpose in an individual way. This intensity is due to the fact that the Soul is attempting to pull away from all past conditions that may bind it to an old order, pattern, or way of being.

- 51° (Septile) The Soul now associates the new evolutionary purpose or cycle with some form of personal or special destiny. Experiences and actions are initiated in order to realize or discover what this special purpose or destiny is. The action taken can be sporadic and confused, or clear and consistent, depending on the planets that are in this phase and aspect. Pluto/Uranus, for example, could produce sporadic action versus Sun/Pluto which could produce clear and consistent action. There is also a "fatedness" to this aspect in the sense that the Soul will create contacts with key people or circumstances at critical moments that have the "fated" intention of keeping the person aligned with the evolutionary intention of this phase.

- 60° (Sextile) The process of consciously understanding the new evolutionary cycle and purpose occurs through contrast and comparison. The Soul must isolate itself from the impact of the external environment in order to realize and discover from within itself that which is uniquely new and individualistic. Action is now internalized as the Soul affects self contemplation in contrast to focusing on the overall nature of external reality. The Soul can now understand the issues pertaining to the past, individually and collectively, and, in so doing, understand what experiences, methods, or skills to use to foster the development of the new evolutionary purpose in an individual way.

- 72° (Quintile) The Mars/Pluto quintile indicates the process of creative transformation through the internal individualization of the new evolutionary purpose. The meaning of the emerging evolutionary purpose becomes highly individualistic and specific. This new purpose is nearly ready for externalized action, although there is still something of a struggle because of the pull of the past.

- 90° (Square) This aspect creates a high degree of internalized compression within the Crescent Phase, and reflects a key evolutionary progression from the Crescent to First Quarter phase. The internalized compression within this phase induces an inner awareness of what the new individual structure or forms are that have become progressively refined through the preceding phases and aspects. These individual forms or structures reflect the initial evolutionary intention in the New phase. The First Quarter Phase will require the external actualization and integration of these new forms into the Soul's circumstantial reality. This aspect also intensifies an unconscious fear of failure in which the Soul feels that it does not know how to establish these new structures or forms into the existing society. This in turn creates a fear or temptation to slide back into old patterns or structures. As a result of this, the square aspect within the Crescent phase creates an inner push/pull in which the Soul cyclically withdraws and remains apart from social interaction, and then asserts itself into social interaction in an effort to test and establish these new patterns, forms or structures.

The First Quarter Phase. Dane Rudhyar called this phase a "crisis in action." This is quite true because this key evolutionary gate correlates to the need to establish and make real the new evolutionary patterns reflected in the original impulse in the New phase. The fear of failure and of sliding back into old patterns is now very intense. These fears create a crisis in which the Soul will attempt to try on many hats, so to speak, in an effort to discover just what hat most perfectly reflects the new patterns. These different hats reflect different directions and different ways of being that are highly individualistic. "Which hat is it?" becomes the essence of the crisis.

Within the First Quarter phase, there are four aspects that correlate to specific phases of development, as follows:

- 90° (First Quarter square) The individual meaning of the new evolutionary purpose now must be given a new form to operate through in order to be fully actualized or established within the individual. The specific nature of the form is relative to the specific nature of the planets that are aspected in this way. For example, if Mercury is square Pluto the new form would involve a new system of intellectual organization and the resulting opinions. The new form would evolve by analysis of the intrinsic weaknesses or deficiencies in prevailing intellectual systems or bodies of knowledge. This analysis would produce the new intellectual insights. If the planet was Venus, then new forms of relationship or new ways of being in relationship would have to occur. Creative tension is produced through the process of moving forward with this new form versus the compulsive temptation to slide back into old patterns of behavior. This creative tension also manifests itself because the Soul may not yet know how to actualize or establish the new form. The resulting tension or confrontation is usually seen as the individual against him or herself, against society, or against all that constitutes the past. From an evolutionary standpoint, this new form or mode must be actualized or established before the individual can move on.

- 102° (Biseptile) Following the square the new form required at that evolutionary junction in once again identified as a special destiny of a highly individualized nature. This aspect produces a remembrance of whatever was identified at the septile aspect. Now the desire is to exteriorize this evolutionary cycle or intention, to create a personal reality that reflects this new purpose. As a result, the element of "fate" occurs in such a way that the Soul will create the necessary circumstances that will manifest at key points in the individual's life that "point the way" to that special destiny and personal reality.

- 120° (Trine) The individual is now full of him or herself, so to speak. The desire and intent of the new evolutionary purpose demands creative actualization. This aspect also produces the potential for conscious awareness of the entire process—the whole scope of past conditions that have led to this moment. The individual can now create a personal reality that clearly reflects the new evolutionary purpose that began at the New phase conjunction. The individual can easily understand what must be done in order to create this reality, and can easily integrate this within him or herself as well as establishing it as a personal lifestyle within the existing social reality.

• 135° (Sesquiquadrate) This is a very powerful aspect that reflects an evolutionary transition between the First Quarter phase and the Gibbous phase. The intention in this aspect is one wherein the egocentric structure within the personality that the Soul has created must experience a humiliation. This occurs as a reaction to the willful assertion of the ego that has been living for only itself as it has sought to discover and actualize the new evolutionary intention, patterns, forms, and structures. Now the evolutionary process is one in which the ego must progressively align itself with the needs of the overall social environment. This occurs through experiencing resistance and blockage from the social environment. The ego is forced to analyze and reflect on why this resistance is occurring. Via this new understanding, the ego now learns to adjust its strong sense of individualized purpose and the forms, patterns, and structures that reflect that purpose to the common needs of the social environment.

The Gibbous Phase. The Gibbous phase reflects another evolutionary transition wherein the Soul now intends to humble itself in order to begin the process of social integration of the original evolutionary intention reflected at the New phase conjunction. The Soul is preparing to integrate into social reality as an equal among other people. Until now, the Soul has inflated itself through an egocentric self-development of the original purpose. The inflated balloon of the ego must now be popped.

Within the Gibbous phase, there are five aspects that correlate to specific phases of development, as follows:

• 135° (Sesquiquadrate) This represents a continuation of the process begun while this aspect occurred in the First Quarter phase. The challenge of this aspect can continue to produce negative results, because the individual may refuse to adapt and adjust his or her newly won and realized intent. If so, then the individual is thrown back on the past and experiences confusion as to how to establish the personal reality and purpose within the external environment until the necessary adjustments are made.

• 144° (Biquintile) If the sesquiquadrate aspect was experienced negatively, this aspect will serve to realign the individual with the original evolutionary purpose by relating it to the individualizing process that took place at the quintile aspect. An analysis must now take place as to how to link the evolutionary purpose to the needs of others and the environment. This analysis must be done so that the new purpose can serve the needs of the whole. It is through service that the individual gives a deeper meaning to the nature of his or her evolutionary purpose.

- 150° (Inconjunct) This aspect brings either clarification or confusion regarding the individual's self-concept as it is identified in the original evolutionary intent. The individual is aware that there is something "special" to do in relation to the evolutionary intent, yet does not know how to link this purpose through service to the whole, or to others. This aspect produces some form of crisis in order to induce analysis of what needs to be adjusted within the ego in order to establish the Soul's reality or purpose within the framework of the social environment. Humility must replace self-inflated or willful expression.

- 154° (Triseptile) This aspect promotes clarification of the individual's self-concept and evolutionary purpose as it relates to the needs of others, the environment, or the whole. The necessary self-analysis that promoted a purging of self-inflated delusions of grandeur during the inconjunct aspect now evolves into an essential humility that allows the individual to prepare to integrate his or her purpose within the context of the social environment.

- 180° (Opposition) When this aspect occurs within the Gibbous phase, it correlates to a state of preparation for the evolutionary intent's manifestation within the Full phase—the need to integrate into social reality as an equal. Accordingly, the ego experiences the full force of other people's will, desires, and reality in such a way as to enforce awareness that the drives of others are just as strong as its own.. This awareness occurs through the experience of being "opposed" by the beliefs, values, attitudes, and needs of other people. This opposition can create anger and fear within the ego, creating a temptation to oppose that which is opposing itself. This reaction takes the form of cyclically withdrawing altogether from social interaction, and willful assertion of the ego within social interaction. Such attacks and retreats will continue to manifest until the soul is able to integrate into the social sphere as an equal.

The Full Phase. This phase can be quite problematic, because the Soul is equally divided between the opposing forces of wanting to be completely free and independent, and the need to actualize or fulfill itself through relationships of all kinds. This inner opposition typically creates cycles in which the individual fluctuates between the extremes of complete social immersion, and cycles of complete social withdrawal. In either case, the nature of the extremes produces its own problems. On the one hand, complete social immersion leads to a cumulative state in which the individual feels overwhelmed by the impact of so many people who represent all kinds of values and lifestyles. This has the effect of making the individual feel that they have lost their own essence, so to speak. This then sets in motion the next extreme, in which the individual tries to totally isolate from this overwhelming impact. This creates an equally unbalanced situation in which the individual "implodes" inwardly. Isolated from the perspectives of social contact and context, the individual loses all perspective about him or herself. Feeling over-isolated and confused, the individual now rushes back into social immersion. Back and forth, back and forth. The key, of course, is to learn how to balance these two competing desires. This will lead to the actualization of the real purpose of this archetype, which is the progressive socialization of consciousness. In this context, the individuals learn what the social system needs from them, and how to socially integrate their individual purpose. To learn balance is to learn how to pay attention to their instinctual nature. When the instinct occurs to withdraw from social interaction, then the challenge is to simply honor this. When the instinct occurs to become socially involved, then the challenge is to simply honor this. In this way, balance is achieved

Within the Full phase, there are five aspects that correlate to specific phases of development, as follows:

- 180° (Opposition) At this evolutionary bridge and juncture, the individual meaning given to the original evolutionary intent must now be given social meaning. It must be related to and shared with others. This aspect produces the necessity to give the original evolutionary purpose a socialized context or framework to operate through so that the individual can continue the ongoing evolutionary development initiated at the New phase conjunction. In order to do so, the individual must enter into social relationships revealing that he or she is an equal among others. The individual must learn to listen to others through relationships in order to evaluate his or her own individuality, and must learn how to relate or apply the evolutionary purpose in a way that is needed by others.

Nevertheless, the opposition often produces a potential confrontation of will and clashing desires, because the individual may feel that their personal power or sense of personal identity is being absorbed and lost through the necessity to interact with others. They may have a sense of losing control of their personal destiny, and the power to shape that destiny from a strictly egocentric point of view. The individual may choose to resist the necessity of developing an expanded social awareness, and of being pulled out of self-oriented narcissistic world, by attempting to dominate others through strength of will—to shove their personal purpose down the throats of others in order to feel powerful and secure.

Until the person succeeds in linking his or her individual purpose to a social need, and becomes an equal social being, he or she will remain at this evolutionary gate. The force of the opposition is contained in the ideas, values, beliefs, and needs of others as contrasted with the individual's own needs, ideas, beliefs, etc. The opposing force is also reflected in the dual desires of the Soul, which translates into personal will confronting higher will in this context. The desire to return to the Source manifests as the need to move onward, and the desire to maintain separateness manifests itself as the need to remain where one already is for security reasons.

- 206° (Triseptile) The original purpose and individual meaning was given social meaning at the opposition. Now it is ready to cooperate with a social or collective need in a realized state.

- 210° (Inconjunct) The new social evolutionary purpose or intent serves to clarify the individual's concept or awareness of personal and social limitations—of what he or she can and cannot do, and of what is required of the individual by others in order that the social purpose may be expressed. If these limits are transgressed, then intense emotional confrontations will occur in order to reinforce this lesson in awareness. The waxing inconjunct induced personal humility. The waning inconjunct will induce social humility and purification.

- 216° (Biquintile) The socialized evolutionary purpose is now further refined through the individual's awareness of his or her special capacities, abilities, or capabilities as contrasted or evaluated against the capabilities, abilities, or capacities of others.

- 235° (Sesquiquadrate) When this aspect occurs within the Full phase, it is preparatory to entering the archetypal intent of the Disseminating phase. Accordingly, the egocentric consciousness of the Soul is forced again to expand itself to now understand the nature of the existing social customs, rules, regulations, laws, and traditions that define the current society that the Soul is born into. This is necessary in order to integrate the socialized evolutionary intention that has preceded this aspect. For example, an individual who had Pluto aspected to Mercury in this way could feel that the role of a psychologist would be the best form and structure through which to integrate their individualized evolutionary purpose in a social way. This aspect would then create the awareness of what society dictated in order to be an authorized psychologist—going to school, securing credentials, etc.

The Disseminating Phase. The Disseminating phase reflects the ongoing socialization of the evolutionary intention reflected in the original New phase conjunction. Now it becomes absolutely necessary for the Soul to learn everything that there is to learn about the nature of the existing society that it is born into. The consensus reality of the society will have already established rules, customs, traditions, laws and rules that allow that society to live together as an organized unit. The additional evolutionary requirement is to integrate the purpose of the original intention within the society in such a way as to fulfill the Soul's social obligations.

Within the Disseminating phase, there are three aspects that correlate to specific phases of development, as follows:

- 235° (Sesquiquadrate) A new crisis now occurs, because the individual must learn everything there is to learn about culture and societal traditions, customs, norms, rules, laws, regulations, and taboos before the socialized evolutionary purpose can be established with the society. The crisis occurs because the individual is ready to disseminate the purpose, to apply and establish it, but must learn how to establish it on society's terms.

- 240° (Trine) This aspect correlates to the evolutionary process of expansion and refinement of the abstract and social consciousness. The individual now has the power and ability to understand how the society works, and on that basis will know how to institute and establish his or her own individualized social purpose within it. The individual can now shape and disseminate the

purpose because others (society) will not feel threatened or unnecessarily challenged by the individual.

- 270° (Square) When the square occurs within the Disseminating
  phase, it is preparing the Soul for another key evolutionary development, which will be reflected in the Last Quarter phase. Accordingly, it creates a crisis in the consciousness of the Soul that
  has become socialized through absorption into society's beliefs,
  customs, values, moralities, etc. This crisis is based on the evolutionary need to move away from those conditions in order to expand the consciousness yet again toward the universal and the
  timeless. At this juncture, the Soul cannot conceive of the new
  thought forms that reflect this need for expansion. It only knows
  that the existing thought forms reflected in consensus opinion are
  too limited and no longer relevant to its need. Therefore, this aspect creates a rebellion against the consensus.

The Last Quarter Phase. Dane Rudhyar called this phase a "crisis in
consciousness." It is a major crisis involving the individual's belief systems—of knowing what to believe. Belief systems reflect the human
need to create philosophies, including religious philosophies, that explain the nature of our phenomenal existence. Any group of people
will have a consensus belief or philosophical system that explains the
nature of phenomenal existence. In this phase, the Soul must rebel
against such consensus belief systems in order to expand its consciousness and embrace the universal truths—those not limited by any
belief system. Thus, this phase correlates to a "shedding of skins" in
which the Soul progressively begins to decondition itself from the impact of consensus opinion. In a larger sense, this phase correlates to
the beginning of the process in which the Soul desires to bring to culmination and completion anything that is not finished or resolved
from the cycle of development that has preceded this phase.

Within the Disseminating phase, there are five aspects that correlate to specific phases of development, as follows:

- 270° (Square) The Soul, having learned all there was to learn
  about society and culture, and having become a socialized being
  in that context, now experiences a process of repolarization of the
  consciousness. This crisis in consciousness revolves around the
  tension between the Soul's evolutionary accomplishments of the
  past and the Soul's evolutionary drive toward the future. The intent is to begin a preliminary building of new foundations of

awareness and knowledge that embrace the universal, the time-less, and the absolute. The old patterns, beliefs, cultural truths, and societal values will no longer serve as the map through which the individual creates social and personal meaning. What to believe, what to think, and how to relate become pressing issues as the individual begins the journey of deconditioning him or herself.

- 288° (Quintile) The evolutionary intent here is to transform consciousness in relation to individual and social identity. The individual must learn to relate inwardly in an entirely different way, because he or she is more than an egocentric or socialized person. This reorientation process is leading the individual into visions and awareness of his or her universal or timeless Self, and the relationship to the Ultimate Other. The individual must now learn to see him or herself in relation to the cosmos. There is increasing knowledge or realization of the individual's cosmic role in relation to the functions or duties performed in this life.

- 300° (Sextile) The new creative identity of the individual in relation to the cosmic whole is now given a productive purpose and understanding. In light of this, the individual can fulfill their universal and social role in this life. The transition between the past and the future can either be easily made or easily resisted at this evolutionary juncture.

- 308° (Septile) Individual action is taken with respect to the perceived universal and social purpose, and by relating this purpose or role to some special destiny. The potential for misapplication or misidentification of this role and purpose still exists, though: specifically, the potential for delusion. However, at key times this aspect will produce circumstances or situations to set the individual straight if he or she is in error or confusion. If there is uncertainty about the role or purpose, circumstances or situations will arise to teach or remind the person of that purpose.

- 315° (Semi-square) When this aspect occurs within the Last Quarter phase, it correlates to the evolutionary preparation for the Balsamic phase. Accordingly, there is a high degree of internalized stress that revolves around the need to withdraw from all social interaction in order for the new seeds in awareness to occur that reflect an understanding of the universal and the timeless. Also highlighted is the need for the individual to fulfill existing obligations and duties.

The Balsamic Phase. This phase correlates to the evolutionary need to bring to completion the entire cycle begun at the New phase conjunction so that a brand-new evolutionary cycle of development can begin. All unfinished or incomplete business, patterns, stages of development, etc. will be recreated so that the necessary culmination can take place. In addition, the consciousness of the Soul now begins the process of culminating the mutation within it that started at the Last Quarter phase. Thus, the consciousness now becomes highly internalized and self-contemplative as it reflects on and considers the nature of Universal Reality, and how the individualized consciousness is a reflection of that reality.

Within the Balsamic phase, there are five aspects that correlate to specific phases of development, as follows:

- 315° (Semi-square) A new evolutionary crisis emerges as the individual begins to accelerate the mutation between all that constitutes the personal and cultural past and the future—the unknown, the unconditioned, the timeless, and the absolute. This crisis is also based on a conflict or collision of desires and needs. On the one hand, the person wants to withdraw in order to internalize the consciousness so that he or she can become aware of the new seeds or impulses relative to a new evolutionary cycle of development. There is a need for self-contemplation and experimentation with new forms, thoughts, and experiences that reflect these new seeds or impulses. These experiments may create real conflict and confusion, causing the individual to attempt to recover the past. In this case, eventual disintegration will occur. Such an individual needs to form new kinds of social relationships with others on the same evolutionary path. On the one hand, the individual is required to fulfill his or her social duties and obligations. On the other hand, the individual wants to withdraw in order to experiment with new ways of being in every way. This produces a conflict. The key is to do both, and to follow these contrasting rhythms as best as possible when they occur.

- 320° (Novile) The seeds of the new evolutionary cycle begin an active gestation process. Like light bulbs turned on in a dark room, the Soul becomes aware of new thoughts, perceptions, and revelations as to the nature of the new evolutionary cycle and purpose to come. Peering over the precipice, the individual is ready to jump. Negatively, the individual can become confused and may attempt to retreat into the past as these revelatory thoughts now threaten his or her existing reality and security. This cycle is based on the cumulative effect of actions in this and other lives. Frustration may result from an awareness of the need to complete the karmic and evolutionary intent of this life.

- 330° (Semi-sextile) The new evolutionary cycle begins to become clear in the form of complete conceptions and ideas which the individual may attempt to establish in this life. In other words, the individual may attempt to formulate him or herself around timeless values and beliefs in the time and space-bound context of his or her culture. Such a person will be considered strange and different by others who do not understand or comprehend what he or she is attempting to do or establish. He or she is thus challenged to to remain committed to and centered on their timeless vision. The whole evolutionary cycle begun way back at the original conjunction in the New phase is now rapidly dissolving. Some individuals will experience this as a sense of meaninglessness and emptiness, and will manifest a diffuse or undefined personal identity or purpose in relation to the planets in this condition. The key is to let go of the past and to allow new patterns, ideas and impulses to enter the consciousness of their own accord. Approached in this way, these new thoughts, ideas, and impulses become the light that illuminates the path to the individuals' future.

- 360° (Conjunction) An evolutionary cycle has been completed. From the point of the waning semi-square (315°) through the conjunction, the transition of focus from egocentric consciousness to universal consciousness was initiated. Any two planets found in this condition within the birthchart (from semi-square through the conjunction) has completed, or is completing, an entire evolutionary cycle. The individual will never again experience those planetary functions in the way that they were previously experienced. A totally new evolutionary cycle is about to begin. Planets forming this type of conjunction become the potential vehicles through which the universal, the timeless, or the Source can be consciously experienced or sensed. Conversely, they can serve as the vehicles through which the individual experiences confusion, disassociation, alienation, disillusionment, and discontentment in order to learn about the nature of illusion, in the sense of making some delusion or illusion the ultimate meaning that they desire and need. In essence, the experience of disillusionment teaches that ultimate meaning cannot be found through any external condition or person.

The Soul, Pluto, actualizes the main karmic/evolutionary dynamic in the birthchart through the phasal relationship between Mars and Pluto in the ways described above. Once these ways are understood, the next step is to link them with the specific houses and signs that Mars and Pluto occupy. Remember that the actual house and sign of Mars, and the aspects that it is making to other planets will correlate to how the desires that emanate from Pluto manifest consciously through Mars. As a result, Mars correlates to our conscious desire nature—the types of desires that we are consciously aware of and instinctively act on. These desires will also include our sexual desire nature, and the types or kinds of sexual experiences that the Soul desires that reflect its evolutionary and karmic requirements. These same dynamics and principles apply to composite charts, and describe how a couple instinctively acts on the main karmic/evolutionary axis through Mars. In synastry charts, the placement of one's Mars in the other's birthchart will correlate to how each individual's conscious desire nature impacts on the other. Relative to sexual desires, the mutual Mars placement in each other's birthchart will correlate to the relative compatibility of these desires, as well as describing the possibility of sexual karma that may exist between two people.

Chapter Nine

The Nature and Function of Mars

At this point, it may be useful to succinctly describe how the desire nature of Pluto is consciously acted out through Mars. This will be done by describing how Mars manifests in a birth chart, as defined by its occupation of each sign. Again, these will be general, archetypal themes that do not reflect the cultural conditioning, socio/religious imprinting, or the evolutionary condition or state.

MARS IN ARIES

This will correlate to a Soul that desires to break free from all kinds of past patterns, and to begin the evolution of all kinds of new patterns. These new patterns will specifically evolve through the house that Mars is in, the house that the sign Aries is in, the planets that Mars aspects, and the houses that these planets are in. Mars in Aries correlates with an instinctual resistance to anyone or anything that restricts, or attempts to restrict, the necessary freedom to explore whatever experiences the Soul deems necessary in order to accomplish its evolutionary intention. Mars in Aries will reflect a necessarily self-centered, narcissistic orientation to life. There is a strong sense of having something special to do or accomplish. These individuals can serve as examples for others to break new ground because they have an innate courage to do so themselves. The will is strong, as is the need to establish their own authority. Anger will occur when these individuals feel judged or controlled by external authority.

Sexually, Mars in Aries requires independence. The sexual desire nature is defined by a need for many kinds of sexual experiences with many types of people. Sexually willful and assertive, these individuals can also be quite sexually narcissistic. Their sexual nature is strong, constant, and intense. The Soul is strongly integrated into the body, and the physical/sexual body becomes a primary focus within consciousness. They become powerfully stimulated and amazed at the intensity of sensation within the body that is produced through sexual stimulation. They form quick and instinctual sexual attractions to others. The specific types of desires within this archetype are determined by the house that Mars is in, the house that the sign Aries is in, the planets that Mars aspects, and the houses that these planets are in.

As their lives evolve, these individuals need to learn the Libran polarity. This involves learning that other people's needs and desires are equally as important as their own, learning how to treat others as equal to themselves, and learning how to freely give versus instinctively expecting to always be given to. Sexually, these individuals must learn how to listen to their partners' needs and desires in order to harmonize with them.

Famous People with Mars in Aries

Tycho Brahe
Clint Eastwood
Herb Elliot
Xavier Holander
Elisabeth Kubler-Ross

MARS IN TAURUS

Mars in Taurus reflects a desire nature that seeks to become self-sustaining and self-reliant. This placement will correlate to a Soul that desires to discover, actualize, and establish its own value system and the meaning of a life reflected in those values. As a result, there is an instinctual resistance to accepting or adopting the value systems of anyone else, including the value system of the existing society that the Soul is born into. Mars in Taurus correlates to a deeply internalized focus that generates a defiant stance of separateness and independence from the overall circumstantial conditions of society. Remaining instinctively separate from those conditions allows the Mars in Taurus person to become aware of the types of desires they need to act upon that will allow for an actualization of the values that most perfectly reflect the meaning of the current life. Great rewards will come through sustained efforts focused on the goals and objectives that will lead the Soul forward in its evolutionary requirements. The house that Mars in Taurus is in, the house that the sign Taurus is on, the aspects that Mars makes to other planets, and the houses that those planets are in will correlate to the specific focus in subjective consciousness in which the Soul actualizes the individual sense of meaning for its life, and the value system that reflects that meaning. Self reliance will be learned through these dynamics.

Sexually, Mars in Taurus reflects a desire nature that seeks to use sexual energy as a vehicle for the metamorphosis of emotional and psychological limitations. In order to accomplish this, the Soul will create sexually confrontational situations in which the emotional and psychological reality, and the needs that reflect this reality, surface into awareness. At worst, this can manifest as sexual violence in one form or another. Relative to the desire to become self-reliant, Mars in Taurus can manifest as strong masturbatory tendencies. As a result, the sexual nature is strong and constant.

The Mars in Taurus soul is strongly grounded in the body, manifesting a strong physical and sexual magnetism that is instinctive. This magnetism creates a vibration of attraction that creates the necessary sexual experiences through which the Soul learns about the nature of sexual energy, and the proper or improper use of it. On the one hand, the sexual nature can be quite primitive in the sense that Mars in Taurus can focus on sex for its own sake—a desire for intense physical stimulation only, as if the Soul is somehow separate from the body and emotions. On the other hand, the intensity of sexual experience that the Mars in Taurus creates instinctively unlocks the depths of the emotions that lead to the Soul. Therefore, a progressive dissatisfaction will occur when sexual energy is limited to just physical intensity. This dissatisfaction reflects the Mars in Taurus core desire for a total connection to their Soul and the Soul of the sexual partner. By experiencing the limitation of just physical sex, the Mars in Taurus person evolves into sexual desires that seek total absorption with the sexual partner, and thus absorption to the Soul within.

Until this is realized, the dynamics of sex as power, control, manipulation, and being attracted to others as sexual objects, or others being attracted to the Mars in Taurus person as a sexual object, will occur. When this occurs, the dynamics of sexual addiction, sexual slavery, sexual infidelity, and relationships that are created for sexual reasons only will occur. The real lesson begins when Mars in Taurus transmutes profane sex to sacred sex. They must transform themselves from the prostitute or gigolo to the pure state achieved when the Soul and body are united through sacred sexual practices. The specific types of desires that reflect this archetype are determined by the house that Mars is in, the house that the sign Taurus is on, the aspects Mars is making to other planets, and the houses that they are in.

As their lives evolve, these individuals must eventually embrace the Scorpio polarity. In essence, this means to create a desire to focus on the nature of their motivations, desires, intentions, and overall psychological dynamics. They need to move from "this is just the way I am," to "this is why I am this way". This polarity demands that such individuals allow themselves to grow, from the limitations that the instinct of self-isolation imposes to a reality that allows acceptance of reality as relative. Thus, they see that other peoples' values, beliefs, ways of being, etc. are just as important and valid as their own.

Famous People with Mars in Taurus

Augustus Caesar
Adolf Eichmann
Robert DeNiro
Catherine the Great
Shirley MacLaine

MARS IN GEMINI

Mars in Gemini reflects a desire structure that is energized through the motivation of independent thinking, and the desire to question every accepted opinion established by any authority. As a result, the mental temperament is argumentative and combative. Mars in Gemini desires to create its own mental constructions about the nature of things, to expand its level of awareness and consciousness through the expansion of its mental horizons. This will occur through the formation and reformulation of mental constructions or ideas that become ever larger and more expansive. The desire to continually expand and know more means Mars in Gemini will even challenge its own ideas at key points in the evolutionary journey. The desire nature is very restless and curious, and can pursue many different directions simultaneously. The weakness in this is not following through or completing anything (two pages in a book are read without completing the book, etc.) since what was curious or interesting yesterday may be boring today!

Sexually, Mars in Gemini manifests a mental desire to explore and understand the diversity of all possible sexual orientations and behaviors. To say that Mars in Gemini is sexually curious would be an understatement. Many will study the sexual traditions of many other cultures in the desire to obtain as much sexual knowledge as possible. On a physical level, Mars in Gemini can find it very difficult to disengage its mind from the sexual act. There is an inner voyeur that is forever observing the physical act of sex. This observation creates a mental amazement regarding sexual activities. This can be frustrating to the individual, as well as to the partner. This frustration can lead to the use of sexual methods that lead to physical intensity as a way of bypassing the mental orientation inherent within Mars in Gemini. There can be strong desires to experiment with sexual toys or devices as a way of achieving sexual stimulation. There can also be a desire to challenge the limitation of gender roles, or the manifestation of bisexual or homosexual desires. At best, Mars in Gemini creates sexual versatility and adaptability to the desires of both partners. In and of itself, Mars in Gemini will not preclude any possible sexual scenario.

Mars in Gemini can also reflect karmic or evolutionary conditions that manifest as sexual issues between one's siblings or parents. When this occurs, the sexual development of the Mars in Gemini person will be arrested. This will lead to a form of sexual infantilism, where the individual will be sexually immature as an adult. The genital region, as a result, can be "frozen" because the nerves (Gemini) have become restricted. In females this can manifest as a dry and tight vagina, while in men this can manifest as impotence. Premature ejaculation can also occur, because the mental possibility of sex over-stimulates these nerves.

As their lives evolve these individuals must embrace the Sagittarian polarity. In essence, this means the desire to actualize one guiding philosophical system of thought that serves as a foundation to which the various mental constructions can be consistently related. This creates a consistency of perspective and a consistency of thought. It allows for a consistency of interpretation of the phenomenal reality that we participate in. It is also important that this polarity be embraced so that such individuals learn to access their own unique "truth," versus the "truths" that are all too often projected on them by other people. Sexually, it means to distinguish between natural sexual laws and expressions, and the sexual "fads" of the day— to move from "try anything once" to "this is consistent with who I am and what I need."

Famous People with Mars in Gemini

Sean Connery
John Denver
Barbra Streisand
Queen Margarethe of Denmark
Teresa of Avila

MARS IN CANCER

Mars in Cancer will correlate with a Soul that desires to create a safe, secure personal reality in order for its evolutionary intentions to be actualized. The primary structure or form that Mars in Cancer will instinctively orient to in order for this security to be realized is that of family, home, and trusted friends. By extension, this drive reflects the core evolutionary intention of the Mars in Cancer archetype—to move from seeking its security needs through external forms or structures to realizing that the security it requires lies within itself. In order for this evolution to take place, the Mars in Cancer person will typically be born into a family situation in which the parents do not meet these projected security needs in some way.

This can manifest in various scenarios, such as emotional conflict between the parents in which the child learns that something can go wrong at any moment, having parents who divorce, experiencing disruptions within the family structure on an ongoing basis, having one or both parents who are emotionally domineering and demanding towards the child, or having one or both parents that emotionally or sexually abuse or violate the child in some way. When the projected and expected emotional security needs of the child are not met, the psychological and emotional consequences will lead to displaced anger, and to a total breakdown of trust. Sexual abuse or violation in childhood will lead to a deep sexual anger and distorted sexual desires as the child moves into puberty and adulthood. In combination, these displaced emotional and/or sexual dynamics will be "acted out" on other people. One of the worst forms of this "acting out" of displaced emotions can manifest as pathological jealousy. Another example is reflected in the Mars in Cancer person becoming "emotionally frozen," stemming from the fear of being emotionally vulnerable.

The house that Mars is in, the house that the sign Cancer is in, the house and sign that the Moon is in, the sign of the Fourth House and the location of its planetary ruler, and the aspects that these planets form to other planets and the houses that those planets are in, serve as the primary ways through which the Mars in Cancer person learns how to become inwardly secure. It is through these dynamics that the displaced emotions of childhood are "triggered". As such, they serve to progressively make the Mars in Cancer person aware of the causal factors that ignite their emotional states or relations. In this way, emotional self-knowledge takes place over time—a key intention of Mars in Cancer. The phasal relationship between Mars and Pluto will show how this is accomplished.

Sexually speaking, the Mars in Cancer person will be born with fundamental fears of insecurity linked with the act of birth itself. The anxiety of separation from the womb of the mother is symbolized by not only the birth moment, but also by the cutting of the umbilical cord. As a result of the separation anxiety experienced at birth, the Mars in Cancer person will exhibit a deep fear of sexual vulnerability which mirrors the fear of emotional vulnerability relative to trust. The emotional and psychological compensation for these fears is to create situations in which the Mars in Cancer person attempts to totally control their emotional and sexual life. As a result, Mars in Cancer can be very sexually and emotionally possessive, domineering, and irrationally jealous. Hypocritically, they can demand that their partner be absolutely faithful while at the same time giving themselves the right to have sex with someone else. Their sexual energy and needs are directly linked with their existing emotional dynamics. Because the emotional dynamics can be so complex in the Mars in Cancer person, the nature of their sexual dynamics can be just as complex.

The root issue, again, is linked with the original anxiety of separation from the womb at birth, and, through extension, with the various causal factors of emotional problems from childhood. As a result, men who have Mars in Cancer can have a preoccupation with the breasts of women, and a strong oral orientation to the woman's vagina. Women can have a strong oral orientation to the mouth of the man, and to the male sexual organ. This orientation reflects the child's need to bond with the mother at birth through breast feeding, and the security that this creates in the child. In essence, it also reflects the Mars in Cancer person's desire for the original security of the womb.

For some who have Mars in Cancer, various forms of sexual violence or dominance can manifest because of their unresolved anger. In women this can manifest as psychologically, emotionally, and sexually "castrating" the man in some way, and in men it can manifest as sexual power over women. Such men use women as sexual objects in order to build up an otherwise weak male self-image. Some will remain sexually arrested or immature, which will also cause various forms of sexual dysfunction. Sexual distortions can be focused on children or on people who are very much younger or older. Some children who have Mars in Cancer, and who have been sexually abused by a parent, will desire or attempt to have sex with other children, or with a sibling.

Once the Mars in Cancer person realizes the evolutionary intention of inner security, their emotional and sexual orientation to life will change. Instead of being controlling, domineering, and possessive they will become supportive, nurturing, and display an incredible emotional empathy that can truly heal the emotions of others. They will reflect a deep emotional wisdom that is offered in non-manipulative ways. They will be self-empowered, and seek to empower others. Sexually, they will be secure from within themselves, and will no longer fear being sexually or emotionally vulnerable. They will encourage and support the emotional and sexual vulnerability of others. They will desire to emotionally and sexually unite with another so that the sexual experience becomes a source of emotional and psychic renewal. When this occurs, the Mars in Cancer person has realized the evolutionary intention of their Soul.

As their lives evolve, these individuals must embrace the Capricorn polarity. Essentially, this will mean learning how to accept responsibility in their own actions, to become totally self-determined, to become emotionally and sexually mature, and to access the causative factors for their various emotional states, along with the sexual desires that manifest from them.

Famous People with Mars in Cancer

O. J. Simpson
Willie Brandt
Diane Keaton
Maria Montessori
Taylor Caldwell

MARS IN LEO

This will correlate to a Soul who desires to take charge of and be in total control of its life and destiny. With Mars in Leo, the Soul desires to creatively actualize its evolutionary/karmic intentions and requirements to the fullest possible extent. As a result, the dynamic of creative independence will be emphasized relative to a personal will structure that instinctively resists any circumstance or person that attempts to restrict any experience or direction that the Mars in Leo person desires to act upon. In essence, Mars in Leo desires to be the master of its own life. Mars in Leo will reflect a Soul that appears to be self-inflated and self-important, expects to be acknowledged for how special it is, and instinctively acts in such a way as to appear to be the very center of the universe. Mars in Leo will reflect a Soul that is highly focused, intense, creative, rigid, passionate, dignified, inspiring, narcissistic, and selfish. In evolutionary terms, there will be reasons for the Soul to have Mars in the sign of Leo. For example, it is not uncommon for such a Soul to have had a series of recent lifetimes in which there was not sense of personal power, and to have experienced life in a way that was beyond their personal control. As a result, the Soul desires to counteract this experience through manifesting and creating a life in which a necessary Soul strengthening can occur. Looked at in this way, it can be understood as a necessary development for the Soul. The astrologer must positively reinforce this intention to the client, because typically such a client would have repeatedly heard from many people that they are too selfish, etc.

The house that Mars in Leo is in, the aspects that it is making to other planets and the houses that those planets are in, the house that the sign Aries is on, the house that the sign Leo is on, and the location of the Sun (the planetary ruler of Leo) will all correlate to how and where the archetype of creative actualization of the Soul's karmic and evolutionary intentions will specifically occur.

Sexually speaking, Mars in Leo will manifest desires of creative self-discovery that will not tolerate restrictions from any external source. The only source of restriction will occur from within itself—any sexual behavior or expression that creates a loss of personal dignity or esteem will be resisted with great force. Mars in Leo will manifest an intense, deep, passionate, assertive, and narcissistic orientation to the sexual experience. There is a high degree of focus on self-pleasure. In men, this can correlate to the "Adonis complex," where they expect to be sexually worshipped. In women, this manifests as the "Cleopatra complex," where they also expect to be sexually worshipped. In both men and women there will be a strong focus on using their own bodies as temples of creative self-discovery through autoerotic practices. In men, there is a glorification of the phallus as a symbol of metamorphic power. In women, there is a glorification of the vagina as a temple of birth and regeneration. Many will be highly creative in designing masturbatory practices that allow for a deep intensity of psychological, emotional, and physical sensation, the intensity of which serves to renew and release the Soul simultaneously.

In their sexual relationships, the Mars in Leo person is focused on experiencing their own intense stimulation through their partner. The partner serves as a vehicle through which this stimulation occurs. Through increasing the degree of stimulation and sensation in this way, the Mars in Leo person thus stimulates the partner because of the of the inner intensity of their own sensations. The specific nature of the types of sexual desires that the Mars in Leo desires to creatively actualize can be determined by the actual house that Mars is in, the aspects that it is making to other planets, and the houses that those planets are in. The phasal relationship of Mars and Pluto will correlate with how this is done.

As their lives evolve, these individuals must learn to embrace the Aquarian polarity. In essence, this means learning how to validate themselves from within themselves without constantly demanding praise and recognition, but also how to best actualize their creativity and need for recognition within the context of what society needs from them. Such people have an evolutionary need to validate and acknowledge the purposes and creativity of others as being equal to their own. They must ultimately understand that the source of creativity does not originate from their own egos or Souls, and that they must help others actualize their own creative purpose. Sexually, it means to learn how to objectify and embrace the sexual desires and needs of their partner—to listen and learn how to satisfy their partner's needs and not just their own.

Famous People with Mars in Leo

Ram Dass
Jim Jones
Paul McCartney
Getrude Zelle (Mata Hari)
James Dean

MARS IN VIRGO

Mars in Virgo will correlate to a Soul that desires to create essential crises as a vehicle through which to actualize its core evolutionary and karmic intentions. In addition, the Soul desires to humiliate and purify itself, and to create experiences of disillusionment in order to understand the nature of its actual reality—and the reality of anyone or anything else. This is essential, because the Soul within the last few lifetimes has been less than honest in terms of its motivations, intentions, desires, and agendas or circumstances that those desires have created. As a result, the Mars in Virgo person will necessarily emphasize the archetype of personal discrimination in the sense of coming to terms with the actual reality of its desire nature—in other words, to stop creating "hyperrationalizations" that mask the nature of its desires.

The archetype and pathology of sadomasochistic psychology is reflected by the Soul who manifests Mars in Virgo. Depending on the specific conditions, the Mars in Virgo person will either create masochistic or sadistic conditions for itself at specific moments in time. The conditions of masochism reflect the cyclic need for crisis associated with powerlessness and humiliation, and the conditions of sadism reflect the cyclic need for crisis associated with the misuse of power and domination. The crisis that both conditions symbolize enforces the need to analyze the reasons for the nature of the crisis. Analysis, over time, leads to awareness of those reasons. Progressively, the awareness of the various reasons for crisis will equal a self-knowledge grounded in personal discrimination and honesty. The Mars in Virgo individual will have achieved the penetration and removal of personal illusions, delusions, and lies that mask the nature of their actual reality.

In addition, Mars in Virgo reflects a Soul who desires to penetrate and understand the nature of its core feeling of utter aloneness and emptiness. This desire is progressively actualized as the Mars in Virgo person realizes that their attempts to escape from this inner aloneness, and an inner restlessness that keeps them doing one thing after another, does not work. In the last analysis, the Soul who manifests Mars in Virgo will realize that the essence of this inner aloneness and emptiness is created by the evolutionary need to embrace a spiritual or religious reality that is practiced on a regular basis—to connect the personal will with a higher Will. However, they must be careful—the nature of this spiritual or religious reality must be based in natural principles or laws that reflect the inherent equity and interrelatedness of the manifested Creation. Once this connection is made, the pathology of sadomasochism will be eliminated, personal honesty and integrity will be realized, and the inner emptiness will now be full of the living universe as an experience from within. The house that Mars is in, the aspects that it is making to other planets, the houses that those planets are in, the house that the sign Virgo is in, and the location of its planetary ruler (Mercury) will all correlate to the types of crises that are created in order for the necessary realizations to occur. The phasal relationship between Mars and Pluto will correlate to how this is done.

Sexually speaking, Mars in Virgo will express itself through the pathology of sadomasochism. The range of expression can be from an absolute denial of anything sexual, to a total absorption into sexuality as a primary focus in life—sexual addition. These forms can range from overt masochistic practices, to overt sadistic practices, with all combinations therein. A common application of the masochistic archetype in women and men is to focus on sexual methods and techniques that serve to stimulate and please the partner to the exclusion of themselves—a form of masochistic self-sacrifice. The pleasure that is experienced by the Mars in Virgo person is the vicarious pleasure that is experienced through the partner. A common application of the sadistic archetype in women and men occurs through "sexual games" in which the partner is physically restrained in some way.

Because Mars in Virgo creates a personal energy system that is focused upon what it lacks, a deep inner energy of emptiness, the temptation is to fill up this emptiness with something of an external nature. Linked with sexual dynamics, this can lead to sexual addiction, or the "always keeping busy" syndrome as a way of diffusing such energy—this becomes a *de facto* sexual act. This dynamic can also exist when the Mars in Virgo Soul experiences an almost absolute lack of sexual life with another person. Even "normal" sex can be experienced as lacking from the Mars in Virgo point of view. As a result, the Mars in Virgo person will typically create sexual imagery that excites their mind and Soul. Instinctively, they will then desire to make real the inner imagery relative to sexual situations with a partner(s) and/or to visit sexual environments in which such imagery is acted out; this can include sexual magazines. During sexual intercourse, the Mars in Virgo person is then "making love" to the imagery because of the excitation this produces, instead "making love" to actual person that they are having intercourse with. When this occurs, this is actually a form of sexual sadism because it is a way of humiliating the partner. To the extent that such a partner conforms to these types of sexual desires, the Mars in Virgo person can be quite satisfied. When the partner does not or will not conform to these types of the desires, this becomes a potential ignition point of physical, psychological, or sexual abuse by the Mars in Virgo person—an anger fueled by frustration dictating such behavior. And because of the inner sense of lack or emptiness, the Mars in Virgo person can compensate through manifesting an extreme sexual/physical intensity that attempts to consume and overwhelm the partner; a form of sadistic dominance. Conversely, the Mars in Virgo person can desire to be consumed through physical/sexual intensity on a repetitive, compulsive basis as a way of feeling full in order to replace the sense in inner emptiness; a form or masochistic surrender.

As life evolves, these individuals must learn to embrace the Pisces polarity. Essentially, this means to expand their consciousness from the immediate or specific circumstance or dynamic to the "whole picture" through which they can understand the basis or cause of what is immediate. In so doing, these individuals can stop the perpetual cycle of experiencing one crisis after another as a way of being. Within this, it is essential that they also focus on the nature of the belief systems that have had the effect of making them feel guilty, with the consequent need to either atone for this guilt, or be angry because of it. Focusing on such belief systems will then allow them to make a necessary and critical adjustment from patriarchal beliefs that promote this guilt/atonement or anger dynamic to beliefs than emanate from natural laws that promote compassion and self-acceptance. In turn, this will dissolve the cause of deep inner stress and anxiety, because the individual will realize that the Ultimate Source of Creation is Itself imperfect. Thus, the inner feeling of inadequacy will also be dissolved, as well as the deep inner sense of anger that can be projected on others as criticism and a willful undercutting of others' abilities, capacities, and potentials.

Sexually, this will allow for these individuals to accept their sexual natures and desires as they are. No longer will there be any guilt association with those desires, thus removing the causal factor in any form or manifestation of sadomasochistic sexual practices. They will now learn that it is just fine to have their own sexual needs fulfilled versus always trying to please the partner first and experiencing fulfillment through their satisfaction. By removing patriarchal beliefs, men will no longer feel sexually inadequate relative to gender assignments manifesting from the patriarchy (performance expectations). Women will no longer feel that sexually that they must submit or surrender to a man's will (masochistic expectations.). As a result, both men and women will feel the freedom to just be who they naturally are.

Famous People with Mars in Virgo

Greg Allman
John Dean
Raquel Welch
Julia Child
Amelia Earhart

MARS IN LIBRA

Mars in Libra will correlate to a soul who desires to actualize its karmic and evolutionary intentions through the initiation of relationships with a diversity of types who represent different values, beliefs, and ideas. In this way, the Soul is able to expand its consciousness through the importation of new ways of understanding the nature of reality. In evolutionary terms, the Soul is desiring to learn new ways of being in relationships with other people, to challenge the culturally established and sanctioned forms of relationship dynamics, to learn how to balance its needs for independence with its needs to be in relationship, to learn how to give and receive in equal ways, to learn how to understand the nature of its projections onto people (and vice versa), to learn to create new understandings of itself through the information and perspectives of others, and to learn about the karmic law of sexuality that binds and bonds people over many lifetimes.

As a result of these desires, the Mars in Libra person will be instinctively attracted to many different kinds of people throughout life. Many of these attractions will lead into short-term relationships in which much conversation and discussion will take place in an exchange of ideas, information, and so on. Relative to the nature of Mars, many of these connections will have a sexual undertone that may or may not be acted on. The instinctual tendency is to act on this sexual feeling, however. Mars in Libra, in and of itself, desires to have the necessary freedom to be able to act on its instinctual attractions to others, including the possibility of sexualizing some of these attractions. It is through involvement with others in various ways that the Mars in Libra person is able to understand the specific nature of their individual reality. Through a free-flowing exchange of ideas, values, and information, they are able to make a determination of their own specific values, beliefs, and reality. This evaluation is accomplished through comparison and contrast to the realities of others. Through such exposure to diversity, they learn about the relativity of truth, and the various lifestyles that reflect each individual's personal truth—that there is no one right way that fits all.

As such, Mars in Libra reflects a Soul that is able to accept and support the individual reality of many different kinds of people. Mars in Libra Souls reflect a unique quality to objectively listen to others in such a way as to "hear" what they are saying without the filter of their own subjective reality. Accordingly, the Mars in Libra Soul is very attractive to other people because they feel heard, accepted, and empowered by a Soul that desires to give them what they need. Through the act of giving, Mars in Libra learns that it will receive what it also needs. In this way, its evolutionary and karmic intentions become realized.

Sexually speaking, Mars in Libra reflects a Soul that desires to inwardly unite the inner male and female through sexual role equality. Within this, there is a keen instinctual nature that is able to harmonize with the sexual energy of the partner. This instinctual harmonization reflects the Mars in Libra desire to give. In this way, a mutual harmonization takes place wherein the partner gives back, producing a mutually deep and permeating sexual response. Mars in Libra contains a unique gift to unlock and set free the sexual energy in a partner who has been "locked up." Typically, Mars in Libra is very sexually refined with a keen sense of touch and sexual grace.

The Mars in Libra Soul is also learning about sexual karma. This is reflected in the desire to initiate a diversity of relationships with many types of people, stimulating Mars in Libra's desire to continually expand its conscious horizons. Many of these connections, again, will have sexual overtones. Because Libra is a Cardinal archetype, many of these connections can be initiated on a relatively brief basis without any real follow-through or completion. Once the sexual fluids are exchanged through any form of sexual contact, a mutual exchange of karma occurs. As a result, a karmic link is established. The key for Mars in Libra is to complete each connection it has with another, even if such a connection is the famous "one night stand." They must enter each connection with conscious awareness and intention that is mutually understood instead of a "love them and leave them" attitude. When the Mars in Libra person becomes attracted to someone, but is already in an existing relationship, it is karmically necessary to be honest with the existing partner and not to enter into such a connection without honestly communicating and informing the partner about such a connection. When this does not occur, additional karma is created with that partner.

As their life evolves, the Mars in Libra person must embrace their polarity: Aries. The Mars in Libra person is often so instinctively aware of other people's needs that they lose sight of their own desires and needs. Instinctively, many other people project their needs, agendas, and expectations onto the Mars in Libra person, who eventually becomes overwhelmed, confused, and no longer in touch with their own needs and desires. At this point, a wellspring of anger suddenly surfaces, and can be projected on anyone—even people who are not the cause of the anger. Thus, Mars in Libra must learn to honor its own instincts as they occur. Whether their instinct triggers a need to be absolutely alone, or to interrelate with others, they need to do so immediately and without guilt or apology. Honoring their instinctual nature (Aries) in this way creates a state of ongoing balance, versus extremes.

Sexually, this means for them to honor their own needs, not just the needs of the partner. Mars in Libra can become so involved in the sexual needs and responses of a partner that they lose touch with their own needs and desires. Sexual equality means for them to attract partners who are just as sensitive to them. Equally aware, both become more than satisfied.

Famous People with Mars in Libra

Lenny Bruce
Johnny Carson
John Lennon
Dory Previn
Therese De Lisieux

MARS IN SCORPIO

This placement will correlate to a Soul that desires to penetrate and understand the mystery of itself. Mars in Scorpio will produce an extremely intense energy system that is inverted from within itself. The inversion of this energy is used by the Soul to consciously focus on the nature of its desires, the nature of its motivations and intentions that are reflected in those desires, and the psychology that those desires, motivations, and intentions produce. The Soul's intention is to understand the nature of its emotional dynamics and the fears that emanate from those emotional dynamics, to understand the nature of its anger and rage, to understand the nature of personal power and the proper and improper use of such power, to understand the right use of will at an egocentric and Soul level, to understand how the misuse of will is linked to manipulating others in order for the Mars in Scorpio person's desires to be met, to understand the nature of its personal limitations relative to what is and is not possible, the reasons and role of inner and outer confrontation, and to understand the nature of sexual energy and the right use of such energy. Within this, Mars in Scorpio reflects a Soul that desires to do a tremendous amount of personal work on itself in the sense of evolving beyond and metamorphosing the nature of all its fixed patterns of behavior and compulsions of all kinds. In this way, the Soul actualizes its karmic and evolutionary intentions.

Sexually speaking, Mars in Scorpio desires to use the intensity of its sexual energy as a vehicle to unite its ego with its Soul, as well as uniting itself with the ego and Soul of another. The intention is to merge in both ways so that the limitations of the ego are metamorphosed through merging with the Soul, and, through extension, to the Divine. Mars in Scorpio will use sexual energy as a vehicle of emotional and psychic renewal, and as an outlet of the build-up of deep, intense, and compressed emotional energy. Karmically, Mars in Scorpio desires to learn the value of emotional/sexual commitment versus following every compulsive attraction. Within this, Mars in Scorpio desires to learn about its sexual compulsions, its attraction to sexual taboos, the nature of sexual possession and the jealousy that follows, the nature of its projected sexual fears linked with a partner's potential infidelities, and the nature of its sexual desires that are linked with the archetype of the Dark Eros.

In evolutionary terms, Mars in Scorpio must learn, and desires to learn, that karma is directly osmosed and exchanged through sexual union with others. Sexual discrimination becomes a key lesson as a result. In addition, it must learn the difference between sexual intensity used as domination, possession, and as a potential vehicle to work out its built-up anger and rage—sex as power—versus the need to use such intensity as a vehicle to unite the Soul and Divinity from within itself, and with another.

As their life evolves, Mars in Scorpio individuals must embrace their polarity: Taurus. The Mars in Scorpio emotional and sexual addictions, and fears linked with loss, betrayal, and abandonment that can create a fundamental fear of real intimacy can be overcome and evolved beyond by embracing the Taurus lessons of self-fulfillment, self-reliance, and self-sustainment. In so doing, an evolution in attitude and inner orientation has been accomplished that produces a state of self-empowerment. These individuals have learned to use themselves as their own vehicle of metamorphic change.

Famous People with Mars in Scorpio

Larry Flynt
Ellen Burstyn
Jimi Hendrix
Alice Cooper
Arthur Bremer

MARS IN SAGITTARIUS

Mars in Sagittarius correlates to a Soul who desires to actualize its evolutionary and karmic intentions through a progressive expansion of its mental and philosophical horizons. The lure of the distant horizon forever calls to the Mars in Sagittarius Soul. Following this call will take such a Soul into a series of adventures throughout life. Each adventure reflects a key learning experience in which the underlying principles of life are progressively understood and the Soul understands its place in the scheme of things. In this way, such a Soul will understand the nature of its evolutionary and karmic intentions and experiences. The nature of these adventures are simultaneously inward as well as outward.

Such a Soul's personal energy system is boundless and restless, and this energy is focused on the intuitive rather than deductive or empirical rationalisms. Mars in Sagittarius reflects a Soul who desires to understand the linkage between the physical and non-physical worlds, and the truth or principles reflected in this linkage. This dynamic is reflected in the desire for personal truth, and personal honesty. As such, Mars in Sagittarius reflects a consciousness that is driven to expose all its personal lies, exaggerations, indiscretions, or half-truths. Accordingly, there is a desire to help others understand their own truth, to expose their own lies, and to teach others about the larger dimensions of life itself.

Typically, the Mars in Sagittarius Soul has had a series of recent lifetimes in which life was very intense or cataclysmic in a variety of ways. As a result, they desire to learn about the lighter side of life—that life can be fun and light. As such, laughter and humor, learning to laugh at oneself, and teaching others to laugh at themselves, reflect themselves in the Mars in Sagittarius individual.

Sexually speaking, Mars in Sagittarius reflects a Soul who desires, and is defined by, the freedom to explore any kind of sexual experience that there is an instinctual attraction to. The motivation within this is reflected in the desire for personal and impersonal knowledge. The desire for freedom creates a sexual psychology that is essentially free from sexual inhibitions of a moralistic nature. Within this, the Mars in Sagittarius Soul intuitively understands that sexuality is a natural part of life—that it is an inherent principle within Nature. As such, there is a desire for sexual adventures of all kinds, and a desire for partners who are just as free to explore sexuality in this way. Sexuality in all its various expressions becomes a vehicle in which these Souls understand the larger connections to life itself. As such, many of these Souls are natural sexual teachers in the sense of helping others understand the deeper issues within themselves that are linked with their specific sexual behavioral patterns. Within this, there is a desire for sexual honesty, and a desire to expose sexual dishonesty within itself and/or the partner. As a result, it is not uncommon for the Mars in Sagittarius Soul to attract partners who are not honest about their sexual history.

Mars in Sagittarius also desires to know how the partner is feeling, or has felt, relative to sexual experience through conversations and discussions that follow the sexual act. This will also include discussions with the partner about the individual sexual histories. This desire again reflects the need to connect the sexual experience to the larger elements of life. In this way, deeper personal truths are revealed to the partner as well as the Mars in Sagittarius Soul itself. Many who have Mars in Sagittarius can be natural sexual healers.

Mars in Sagittarius reflects a strong and constant sexual nature. They bring the spirit of adventure to the sexual experience, and are instinctively passionate and intense. The passion that fuels their intensity is the passion of spirit focused within the physical body, and the desire to consciously experience the descent of spirit within the physical body. Instinctively, the Mars in Sagittarius understands the right use of sexual energy as a vehicle for personal renewal and as a positive outlet that allows other areas of life to be maintained in their proper perspective. Generally speaking, the Mars in Sagittarius Soul must learn to sexually slow down, as their sexual instinct can become overly stimulated. This creates a high degree of arousal and stimulation that can lead to quick and intense physical orgasms. In women, this leads to a multi-orgasmic energy system, and in men it can create premature ejaculation, causing frustration for the partner.

As their life evolves, it becomes necessary for the Mars in Sagittarius Soul to embrace its polarity: Gemini. In essence, this means for them to realize that whatever they have come to understand about the nature of "truth" is not the only truth. If effect, it means that there are many roads that lead to the same goal, and that the temptation to argue with others who do not reflect their specific version of the truth is based is a security dynamic that causes them to feel insecure when their truth is questioned in some way. The need is to understand that if someone else does not agree with them, this does not mean that whatever their understanding of truth is wrong—it is only relative. Once this understanding takes place, the instinct to rip apart another's argument based on a disagreement of ideas will no longer occur. This is a real challenge, because for most Mars in Sagittarius people, their intuitive capacities are extremely developed—they just know what they know without empirically knowing how or why they know it. This produces real frustration for them because others do not seem to operate in this way; what seems so obvious to them is obtuse to others. Thus, a real frustration can manifest at others' "slowness" relative to philosophical intellectual understandings. Beyond the obvious lesson in patience, this requires learning the Gemini lesson of learning the language structures that most other people use. Learning these language structures thus allows them to communicate their own knowledge, ideas, or thoughts through the language structure that most others use. As a result, others will more easily understand these individuals. In turn, the causes of frustration can be minimized.

Famous People with Mars in Sagittarius

Warren Beatty
Agatha Christie
Judy Garland
Prince Charles
Joan Baez

MARS IN CAPRICORN

Mars in Capricorn will correlate to a soul that desires to penetrate and set free all causes of personal inhibitions, constraints, restraints, and repressions. As such, this placement reflects a Soul who desires to unlock the cell door of their inner prison so that the light of personal freedom can shine, a freedom that is not limited by moralistic or religious conditions that create an uneasy guilt that attempts to control the instinctual impulses that emanate from the Soul. Typically, Mars in Capricorn reflects a Soul who has had a series of recent lifetimes in which there has been an intense exposure to authoritarian control of man-made religions, and the moralistic societies that these religions create, and to the authoritarianism of parents who have been emotionally and/or sexually repressed. In combination, both forms of constraint upon these Souls have produced a deep, permeating anger that has been repressed. In combination, both forms of constraint have produced repression of the natural sexual instincts, and the instincts to just be who they are naturally. In combination, both forms of constraint have also caused the emotional reality of the Mars in Capricorn Soul to become "locked behind closed doors"—emotional denial and stoicism. Within this, the Mars in Capricorn Soul has experienced the double standards or hypocrisy of such authoritarian control and righteousness; that what occurs "behind the closed doors" is in opposition or contradiction to the nature of the religious or moralistic codes of conduct taught by the society, religion or the parents. The duality of double standards conditions such Souls to lead a "double life." They learn to present an external behavior and social persona that is at odds with the nature of their personal life, or what is occurring behind the "closed door" of their intimate and personal life. This "double life" reflects the Mars in Capricorn fear of external judgment and persecution. This also correlates to the fear of personal judgment. The fear of personal judgment is an extension of the heavy exposure to external conditioning of a highly moralistic/religious nature. Thus, to act upon the natural impulses or instincts emanating from the Soul will typically be in contradiction to the nature of such conditioning. To act upon these instincts will then give rise to the question "What does this mean about me?" As a result, this fear creates the psychology of concealment—to conceal their personal truth from others, and even to themselves because of the question "What does this mean about me?" All of this creates psychological repression. This in turn creates psychological distortions of all kinds, especially emotional and sexual distortion. Again, the intention of the Soul with Mars in Capricorn is to penetrate to the nature of such repressions and distortions, and to totally break free from any source that attempts to control, constrain, or repress any desire leading to the actualization of their individuality that is defined on their own terms. In this way, Mars in Capricorn will actualize its karmic and evolutionary intentions.

Sexually speaking, Mars in Capricorn reflects a Soul who desires to break free from all sexual inhibitions and sexual constraints. The repression of natural sexual desires over many lifetimes has created a deep sexual/emotional anger. The anger linked with repression has also created deep distortions of the sexual/emotional desires and needs. Because of the desire to unlock these distortions, and the closed doors that repress their natural sexual/emotional desires and needs, the Mars in Capricorn Soul will be highly sexed in this life. The first lesson for such Souls is to accept themselves as sexual beings. When this occurs, the psychology of concealment will be purged, and the fear of inner and outer judgment will cease to exist.

As a result of the current life intention, the Mars in Capricorn Soul typically attracts partners who are also quite emotionally and sexually fractured, repressed, or crippled in some way. These types of partners, of course, mirror the Mars in Capricorn Soul itself. Because of the intention and instinct to break free, to learn to accept themselves as emotional and sexual beings, the Mars in Capricorn person can attract partners who mirror their own sexual/emotional distortion. The manifestations of this can range from sexual violence, which can include being forced to have sex, to various forms of sexual domination and control, to sexual humiliation in which the Mars in Capricorn ends up feeling cheap or dirty in some way because of the nature of the sexual event or dynamics, to being attracted to certain kinds of environments—disco clubs, for example—in which sexual possibilities exist; the pretense of the disco club serving as the rationale that masks the actual intent.

All too often, the Mars in Capricorn must rely on some intoxicant (wine, for example) to unlock and relax its instinctual inhibitions. Once unlocked in this way, the normal "boundaries of propriety" are dissolved. Now disarmed, the sexual energy reflected in the Dark Eros of distortions caused by previous repression is unleashed. Unleashed, Mars in Capricorn individuals learn and discover that they are intensely sexual beings who have a deep and unresolved emotional need to be nurtured and healed. Sexuality becomes a vehicle through which these emotional needs are accessed. Through the intensity of the sexual exchange, an intensity based on duration and/or sexual frequency, the emotions come to the surface. Once the intensity is released through the act of physical orgasms, the harbor of emotional safety and need is found in each others' arms; at least for a while. Above all else, the Mars in Capricorn person desires to be emotionally healed and can truly bring the gift of emotional well-beingness to another. They can bring the gift of making their partners feel worthy, and important. They can help their partners define their own life goals and objectives, and help their partners actualize such goals through the psychology of self-determination. When personal integrity and honesty permeate the relationship dynamic, the Mars in Capricorn Soul desires to sustain the relationship

over the long haul—for life. As the Mars in Capricorn Soul grows older, their life force and their sexual energy become stronger. This occurs
as the "doors of the inner prison" are progressively unlocked.

As their life evolves, the Mars in Capricorn Soul must embrace its
opposite: Cancer. The essence of this requires that these Souls completely change the nature of their inner self-image, and thereby the
egocentric structure of their consciousness. For this to occur, it is imperative for them to reflect on all the causes that have lead to a cumulative state of guilt, and the negative self-image that this produces.
By so doing, these individuals will be able to see the causes of their
emotional restriction and deep fear of vulnerability that has been
compensated for through the creation of a stoic persona. This persona
has been used to control their deep inner emotional essence which
fears false judgment, or persecution. As a result, the deep inner fear
of losing control manifests as a desire to control everything in order
to feel secure, and to have a sense of authoritarian power. Yet deep
within these people is a desire to lose control, and to be nurtured and
taken care of by someone or something. The Cancer polarity demands that they learn how to safely access these desires and needs,
not only to be a whole person, but to evolve. Thus, the issue of safety that will allow this growth to occur becomes paramount. It becomes essential that these individuals only allow people that they
trust fully into their lives and personal environments. In this way, they
will slowly but surely learn how to accomplish these lessons and actualize these needs.

Sexually, the Cancer polarity will allow these individuals to access
their greatest sexual need—to lose total control of themselves. Safe
and sustained sexual intercourse of an increasingly intense nature will
be the means to accomplish this.

Famous People with Mars in Capricorn
Marlene Dietrich
Lily Tomlin
Uri Geller
Albert Einstein
David Bowie

MARS IN AQUARIUS
Mars in Aquarius will correlate to a Soul that desires to actualize its
overall life purposes on its own terms. In order for this to occur, the

Soul will create a personality that is energized (Mars) to detach from the immediacy of circumstantial life. This detachment is all-inclusive relative to the Soul's family of birth, its peer group, and the society into which it is born. Through detachment, the Soul is then able to objectively survey the nature of the values and beliefs that define the current structures of consensus reality. In this way, the Soul will aggressively rebel against any external pressure to conform to the expectations of parents, peer group, or society.

Early in life, the Soul will manifest this dynamic through an awareness of what it is *not*. Progressively, as the Mars in Aquarius Soul matures, the awareness of what it is not will transform into awareness of what it *is* as a unique individual—accomplishing self-definition through the values and beliefs that are unique to and reflective of its specific individuality. Mars in Aquarius will gradually create an entire lifestyle reflective of its instinctual feeling of uniqueness.

Mars in Aquarius reflects a Soul that desires progressive transformation leading to an ever-increasing realization and definition of its individuality. As such, the Mars in Aquarius Soul will be characteristically unpredictable. The instinct to transform and grow is so intense with Mars in Aquarius that it will even appear to rebel even against itself: to cyclically or continually change the very conditions that it has just created for itself. Mars in Aquarius reflects an instinct to experiment with different ways of being. It sees life as an experiment. As a result, the Mars in Aquarius Soul will also desire to create an essential courage in other people to break free from the status quo. For some, this will trigger feelings of discomfort and create an instinctual defensiveness For others, this will trigger an uneasy excitement because of possibilities that the Mars in Aquarius Soul stimulates within them. Such Souls are energized to radically transform the present life conditions of themselves, others, and society to reflect "the future" that they instinctively understand and sense, even when most others do not. It is in these ways that the Mars in Aquarius Soul actualizes it core evolutionary and karmic intentions.

Sexually speaking, Mars in Aquarius reflects a Soul that desires to experiment with all possible ways of being sexual. This includes the possibility of detaching from the sexual instinct itself—to be asexual or celibate. The instinct to rebel from current cultural social customs or morals leads such Souls into considering different ways of being sexual that many others would judge as kinky, weird, or bizarre. These "sexual deviations" can include group sex, group marriage, "open" marriage arrangements in which one or both partners are allowed to have sex with other partners, observational sex of a vicarious nature reflected in sex magazines, clubs, or theaters, experimenting with all kinds of sexual devices, restraint of the physical body that is then intensely stimulated in a variety of ways, many different forms of autoeroticism, and/or embracing spiritual sexual methods that allow for a transformation of sexual energy from the primal to the sacred.

Because of the core detachment of Mars in Aquarius, the sexual act is similar to a scientific experiment in which an observation is made of the specific effect of various methods of sexual stimulation on the subject. This detached observation (cause and effect) produces psychological/sexual knowledge for the Mars in Aquarius Soul. This detachment can also cause frustration for such Souls, because it does not allow for full engagement with the physical body. The mental dynamic in consciousness is always energized and observing. This frustration can cause a psychological anger to occur, in which the Mars in Aquarius person desires to fully engage their body in such a way that their mind becomes obliterated. This desire then leads into discovering ways to be sexual that are so physically intense or all-consuming that the mind can no longer observe the body. The unique gift that the Mars in Aquarius Soul has is to simulate and encourage the desire for sexual creativity in their partners, to stimulate desires buried within the unconscious of their partners. As a result, the Mars in Aquarius Soul desires partners that manifest the courage to be different in all kinds of ways, including the courage to sexually experiment.

As its life evolves, the Mars in Aquarius Soul must embrace its opposite: Leo. This means to fully creatively actualize that which is unique and different in them, and to encourage this same development in others without feeling threatened by the unique abilities that others may have. It also means to learn the difference between constructive rebellion and rebellion that is counterproductive or exists only for its own sake. For some, this will mean to learn how to stand as a group of one if necessary, and for others it will mean to learn how to independently actualize without the security of peer group approval. For all, it means that God has given them some unique ability, capacity, or gift that has the potential effect to be able to move various areas of life forward depending on the nature of their evolutionary condition (the four natural evolutionary conditions). Actualizing this unique ability will create some relative degree of acclaim or recognition from society or their peer group (Leo). This is a necessary evolutionary development and lesson, because all too often these souls have had at least one recent prior life in which they felt invalidated for who they were. To receive recognition or acclaim for their unique abilities becomes a positive and necessary counterpoint to that experience.

Famous People with Mars in Aquarius

> Lauren Bacall
> Mae West
> Leonardo DaVinci
> Nicolaus Copernicus
> Bobby Fischer

MARS IN PISCES

Mars in Pisces will correlate to a Soul that desires to penetrate and energize all of the desires that have been held in an unconscious state over many recent lifetimes. In evolutionary terms, Mars in Pisces reflects a Soul that desires to bring to culmination an entire cycle of evolutionary development so that a brand-new cycle can begin. In order for this to occur, the Soul must now act on all the remaining desires that have been held at an unconscious level and thus not acted on. For this to occur, for the desires to manifest within the subjective conscious awareness of the personality that the Soul creates, Mars in Pisces will energize the pineal gland within the brain. This gland secretes a hormone called melatonin. Melatonin does many things within the brain, including the inducement of images that emanate from imagination and fantasy. The nature of these images are ever-changing and shifting. As a result, the Mars in Pisces Soul creates an energy system in which there is a desire to act on these images; with each image, or combination of images, reflecting imagined "realities" that the Soul conceives for itself. Within itself, these imagined realities are quite "real". To others, these imagined realities can seem quite unrealistic, even though to the Mars in Pisces Soul they are real—they are real to the extent that the Mars in Pisces *believes* in them. To the extent that they are believed in, the Mars in Pisces Soul will attempt to make others believe in them also. Even though such Souls can believe in these imagined realities, others will feel that this kind of belief is naive, innocent, and unrealistic. The Mars in Pisces Soul can seem "ungrounded", as if they are not quite "all here", to others as a result.

Mars in Pisces operates beyond or above the "normal" time/space continuum through which most people are defined. As a result, the imagination of Mars in Pisces Souls is not limited by the awareness of pragmatic realities, circumstances, or probabilities that circumscribe most other people.This is a very interesting dynamic. On the one hand, Mars in Pisces has the inherent power to manifest and make real the desires within the unconscious that appear as initial imagination—the power of belief can make probable that which would be improbable for others. On the other hand, many of these imagined realities will not manifest into concrete reality no matter how strong the belief. When this occurs, the Soul is teaching itself three things—first, that to simply imagine this or that is acting it out anyway, the desire reflecting that which is imagined has culminated; secondly, that the egocentric will is not enough to make something happen, but that there is a need to align personal will with higher will; and thirdly, to also understand the nature of its desires that are reflected in the Soul's need to "escape" from normal reality; escapism as a psychological act of compensation relative to a "reality" that the Soul feels an essential alienation from. When this is the operational dynamic, the Soul with Mars in Pisces will then become susceptible to all kinds of addictions—sexual addictions or drug addictions, for example. When this occurs, the Mars in Pisces Soul must learn to examine the nature of its addictions with the intention of stopping all addictive behaviors.

Because so many of the desires that manifest through the Mars in Pisces Soul emanate from the unconscious, there is a fundamental breakdown within the conscious self—the inability to see or understand the connection between what circumstances are being created by the Souls, and the unconscious desires that are responsible for this creation. As a result, many of these Souls can feel victimized by life, and by others. When this occurs, Mars in Pisces generates an anger based in victimization. This anger, caused by the false sense of being victimized, then manifests as wanting to cause hurt, pain, or humiliation in other people whom the Soul has felt victimized by—to go from being persecuted to becoming the persecutor. This cycle of being victimized, then victimizing, will continue until the Soul finally is able to consciously understand and accept the direct linkage between the nature of its own desires, and the realities that these desires create.

Within this, the Mars in Pisces Soul reflects desires to become pure. The real question here is this: What constitutes purity? Purity implies perfection. The question becomes: What is perfection? These are real concerns and issues to the Mars in Pisces Soul. They haunt their unconscious with religions that advocate strict moral codes of conduct, these codes of conduct repressing or restricting all behaviors associated with natural law or principles. To the extent that conformity relative to these moralistic codes of conduct occurred, the sense of purity and perfection would result. To the extent that deviant behavior relative to these same codes of conduct occurred, guilt would result. All Mars in Pisces Souls have deviated from these artificial codes of conduct. As a result, all Mars in Pisces Souls have a deep, permeating guilt within their unconscious. There are two psychological consequences to this guilt—anger because of it, or the need to atone for this. Anger motivated by guilt will produce various forms of sadistic pathology. Atonement motivated by guilt will produce various forms of masochistic pathology. The Mars in Pisces Soul can thus reflect both pathologies depending on the nature of its existing psychological state at any moment in time. In classical psychology, these types of souls are classified as passive/aggressive individuals. In classical religion, these types are classified as the saints and the sinners. The real question, again, that the Mars in Pisces Soul needs to ask itself it this: What constitutes purity and perfection? At some point, these Souls will realize that the answer is based on the purity of their intentions, motivations, and desires that are openly and honestly embraced from within, and honestly and openly conveyed to other people. Within this, these Souls will realize that purity and perfection will be properly understood when an inner alignment is made with the inherent principles of Nature, natural law, versus an alignment with manmade laws and the religions that produce artificial ideas about purity and perfection. When this occurs, the unconscious sense of guilt that permeates the Soul structure will dissolve.

Sexually speaking, the Mars in Pisces Soul desires to experience a descent of spirit into flesh; to experience the power of the divine or God through the energy of sexuality. For some, this will lead to thoughts/desires to transmute gross sexual/physical expression into harnessing and focusing the sexual energy through various forms of spiritual practice. For others, this will lead to the employment of specific sacred sexual practices that are aimed at using the sexual energy to transfigure consciousness itself. For still others, this will lead to a necessary acting out of all the residual sexual desires of lifetimes that have not been acted on—that which initially appears as sexual fantasies within the interior of their consciousness. Through the necessary acting out of these desires, a process of elimination occurs that then allows for the core sexual desire to experience the descent of spirit into flesh relative to sacred sexual practices. The nature of these fantasies can be anything, depending on the specific nature of each individual. For still others, this can manifest as a cyclic immersion into many forms of gross or primary sexuality, and cycles of enforced celibacy reflecting the guilt associated with the cycle of gross immersion. For still others, this can manifest as a total immersion into acting out all kinds of sexual fantasies of a primary nature throughout life— an unconscious rejection of the desire to evolve into sacred sexuality. When this is the operational dynamic, the Mars in Pisces Soul will desire to be consumed, or to consume another, during the sexual act. And for still others, this will manifest as a conscious rejection of divinity outright—an unconscious anger at God. These types will typically desire perverse forms of sexuality defined by masochism or sadism. When that is the operational dynamic, sex as punishment becomes the primary orientation. Additionally, some Souls who have Mars in Pisces will have irrational sexual fears, or fears that have been caused by actual sexual events. When this is the case, the evolutionary intention is to examine the nature of these fears, and to heal these fears as a result. Specific sexual methods must be employed for this to occur. An example of such a method would be learning non-sexual touch. Through non-sexual touch, the Soul can learn psycho/emotional safety and trust. Once learned, sexual healing can follow.

The core intention with Mars in Pisces is to understand the difference between profane and sacred sexuality. Because of this, the Mars in Pisces Soul, especially in men relative to the times that we are living in, desire that their partner(s) be "pure": Angel Mary types who reflect the innocent qualities of the "virgin archetype." Yet, because of their own inner struggles over many lifetimes defined by the cycles of guilt/atonement, and guilt/anger, that have manifested as cycles of celibacy and immersion into many forms of primary sexuality, they attract partners who vibrate in exactly in the same way. Thus, they are initially attracted to people who appear innocent, sensitive, and "pure." Then, when they discover that these types of partners have had a sexual history that is very much like their own, they feel disillusioned and angry. This disillusionment and anger is projected on the partner in a variety of ways, which can include a total withholding of their emotional/sexual self. It can include verbal abuse in the form of projected judgments of a moralistic nature. It can include unconsciously wanting to hurt such a partner through intense sexual practices of a dominating nature; to overwhelm and make the partner helpless through intense sexual stimulation. It can include becoming sexual with other people thus creating humility—to humiliate—to the partner. And it can include becoming sexually or physically violent to the partner. Again, the key is for such Souls to realize the connection between what emanates from their own Souls, and the circumstantial realities that are created as a reflection of those emanations—desires. Once the Mars in Pisces person makes the conscious connection to their own inner duality, that what they are attracting is but a reflection of their own inner self, then compassion, nurturing, forgiveness, and a real healing of these wounds will occur—for both people. Once the transference is made between manmade religions to natural law, an acceptance of that which is natural will occur. Once this occurs, a healing and dissolving of the guilt leading to anger and atonement will also take place. When this takes place, the Soul with Mars in Pisces has realized its karmic and evolutionary intentions in this way.

As life evolves, the Mars in Pisces Soul must embrace its opposite: Virgo. In essence, this means to create a consciousness that is able to intellectually discriminate and understand the connection between the desires that emanate from within themselves, and the circumstantial realities that these desires create. Once this is accomplished, the feeling of being victimized by life will dissolve. They will then learn to take responsibility for their own actions, and stop blaming everyone else for the very conditions that they have created for themselves. By creating a consciousness that is able to mentally analyze and discriminate, these Souls will then be able to discover the origin of anything that manifests from within themselves—fears of all kinds, the nature and cause of all their desires and the reasons for those desires, the causes of their anger, and so on. This type of mental overlay is essential because it promotes analysis, and analysis will promote self-knowledge. This self-knowledge can then be applied in such a way as to not only change themselves where necessary, but also to understand what to do in order to heal whatever specific wounds they have.

Famous People with Mars in Pisces

Bob Dylan
Hermann Hesse
Christine Jorgensen
Dorothy Hamill
Shirley Temple

A NOTE ON MARS RETROGRADE

Archetypally, Mars retrograde at birth is very interesting to consider. The reason for this is that Mars correlates to the instinctual desire to take action on the desires emanating from the Soul—to be self-actualizing. To take action means one's energy moves out from the center, or the Soul. Mars, of itself, does not like restrictions of any kind. It desires total freedom to do whatever it desires to do. But Mars retrograde causes the instinctual energy to take action on the desires emanating from the soul to become inverted—to return to the center. This effectively places a restraint on the energy of Mars, constricting its normal outward flow. So the question becomes this: Why has a Soul reached an evolutionary and karmic situation wherein it is necessary to have Mars retrograde?

The answer is that such a soul intends to create a consciousness in which any action taken on its desires is a considered action versus an impulsive action. This will typically apply to a Soul who has had some previous lifetimes in which it had been wildly impulsive, compulsive, and too egocentrically willful. Such an orientation has typically produced many problems and confrontations with others generally, and intimate others specifically. Major confrontations with external authorities is also a common result. Thus, the Soul must counteract these behavioral patterns through creating a consciousness, that will pause and consider prior to taking action. Accordingly, the ego must learn to listen inwardly to that which is stronger than itself—the Soul, and, through extension, God. In this way, the "taming" of the ego occurs, and the actions taken are aligned with the Soul's overall intentions.

On a sexual level, the inverted energy of Mars "heats up" the inner energy field of the individual. The actual evolutionary state of any given person will correlate to how this inner heating up is responded to. For those in the consensus right up through the second stage of the spiritual state, this will manifest as a frequent desire and need to release sexual energy in order to "cool down" the inner energy. This need for frequent release is not dependent on others—Mars retrograde can take care of its own business, so to speak. In evolutionary and karmic terms, the intention of Mars retrograde at a sexual level is to make the person aware of the nature of its sexual desires, and the reasons for those desires.

A NOTE ON THE TRANSIT OF MARS

The transit of Mars correlates to the leading edge of what the Soul is currently desiring to focus on. Through Mars, we are always in a continuous state of becoming—a state of evolution. To continuously become means we are forever moving toward the future. To move toward the future implies a current moment, and a past. Thus, the transit of Mars correlates to the leading edge of our ongoing evolution, yet to move forward enforces the awareness of where we currently are, and have been. In this way, we must confront whatever the existing circumstances are in our life, as well as the dynamics within us, that in any way thwart, block, or stifle this necessary movement toward the future. A Mars transit through Cancer in the Eighth House, for example, would correlate to a time frame in which the Soul would necessarily have to confront the nature of its emotional fears, wounds, psychological dynamics that are preventing growth at an emotional level. Strongly involved with these are trust issues and sexual issues. Issues of personal power and will would also be alive and afoot. When in an intimate relationship, the Soul would have to confront why it was in the relationship, why the other was in the relationship, and the overall purpose for it. The intention in this transit is for emotional renewal and growth, which is now linked with emotional self-knowledge. To accomplish the intention, the indicated dynamics would have to be confronted and consciously worked with. Inner and outer emotional/psychological confrontations would also need to occur.

The transit of Mars can also directly correlate to our sexual cycles of activity and behavior. Here again, the principle of evolution is in operation. Nothing is static in our universe. Our sexual desires, and the reality they create, also evolve. The transit of Mars through the houses and signs directly correlates to what our current sexual desires and needs are, and the reasons for them. For example, Mars transiting through the Third House in Aquarius would possibly manifest as a need to create some sexual newness or experimentation. As a result, such a person would find themselves thinking about these matters, and communicating their thoughts to the partner if they are in a relationship. If the partner was open to this, then this current sexual dynamic could be satisfied. If the partner was resistant, the person may feel tempted to rebel against this resistance by seeking out a temporary partner of like mind. The existing partner may find this out, which would then lead to massive arguments and confrontations. This would serve as a clearinghouse for the pent-up frustrations that they each had with the other. This situation could be used positively to change all kinds of dynamics in the relationship, not just the sexual ones.

The Mars transit has a two-year cycle relative to returning to its natal position. Thus, every two years the Soul renews itself with respect to the natal signature that exists between Mars and Pluto. Because each house and sign correlates to archetypes that have a spectrum of dynamics within them, every two years the natal intention of Pluto is renewed through the Mars return, yet is actualizing different dimensions within the total archetypal spectrum of any given sign or house. In this way, evolution occurs.

Chapter Ten

The Phasal Relationship of Mars and Venus

From an evolutionary point of view, the phasal relationship between Mars and Venus will correlate to how the Soul is oriented to actualizing the relationship dynamics for itself, and how its needs for necessary freedom in order to actualize its overall evolutionary and karmic intentions interrelate. In addition, the phasal relationship between Mars and Venus will correlate to how new or old these archetypal dynamics are—how many primary lifetimes have occurred in which the Soul has been working toward the fulfillment of its evolutionary and karmic intentions relative to the formation of intimate relationships with other people. In composite charts, the phasal relationship between Mars and Venus will correlate to the archetypal way in which the couple actualizes the relationship, and correlates to how many primary lifetimes have preceded the current life in which the relationship dynamics reflected in the phasal relationship of Mars and Venus have occurred.

THE MARS AND VENUS PHASES

Since we have discussed the phases, and the aspects within the phases, if you allow yourself to intuitively reflect on the archetypal natures of Mars and Venus combined with the phases, you will be amazed at the degree of intuitive insight and realization about how Mars and Venus work together in the individual and composite chart. The next step is to allow yourself to consider the actual houses and signs that Mars and Venus are in. This will supply a tremendous level of information and insight. At this point, I would like to briefly list the Mars/Venus phases. These descriptions are the general themes within the archetypes of the phases. When Mars and Venus are in a specific aspect, i.e. a Gibbous Phase inconjunct, then refer to the archetypal definitions described earlier. This will supply necessary detail to help understand what stage the Mars/Venus linkage is at relative to the overall phase that exists between the two. Following this, I will describe an actual case history detailing the Mars/Venus phase, the house and sign of Mars and Venus, and how to integrate this.

The New Phase (0°–45°) A brand-new cycle of evolutionary development is beginning relative to relationship dynamics. An entire cycle has culminated, and the Soul now reflects an instinctual desire to learn how to be in relationships in a new way. This new way is not consciously known by the Soul at this point. As a result, the Soul desires and requires the freedom to initiate all kinds of new ways of being in relationships with people. This is more or less like walking into a department store and trying on various coats in order to see which one fits, and which ones do not. The soul is employing a process of elimination through trial and error. As a result, the Soul will be instinctively attracted to many different kinds of people, all of which symbolize different values, desires, and ways of being. The impulse and instinct in this phase is to initiate connections to these different types of people, to form some kind of relationship, so that an experiential knowledge can take place over time. This allows for an accumulation of information and knowledge to take place that will progressively allow the Soul to understand the actual needs and desires that reflect its new evolutionary intentions relative to relationships.

In composite charts, this same archetype is operative when the Mars/Venus Phase is new. The couple is setting themselves in motion to discover new ways of being in relationship to one another. Again, the process of trial and error will be in operation as the couple instinctively acts on new value associations, and the meaning that those values imply, that will allow the couple to relate to the fact of their relationship in new ways. The couple must allow for all kinds of new directions to take place within the relationship, and to resist the temptation to define the relationship according to cultural standards. Both people within the relationship must encourage and allow one another an essential freedom to independently explore new ways of thinking, acting, and being so that what is learned in this way can then be brought back to the relationship. In this way, each partner will contribute to the process of the new ways of being in and establishing their relationship.

The Crescent Phase (45°–90°) Following the New phase, the evolutionary need and desire of the Soul is to begin to establish in concrete and real terms what it has realized during the New phase. This will require great effort, as the new evolutionary cycle begun during the New phase is still very young. The temptation to borrow, adopt, or mimic the ways of being in relationship, and the values that those ways symbolize that culture or society sanctions is strong. In order to withstand and resist this temptation, the Soul must look deep within itself and remain in touch with the emerging value associations that will define its orientation to the new relationship archetype. The key is for the Soul to manifest the courage to stand apart from society so that the internal awareness of what these new value associations are can be sustained. This is a phase of inner empowerment for the Soul as it forms a new way of relating to itself, and thus to other people. The Soul will learn to say "This is who I am, this is what I value, this is what I need as a reflection of those values, and I only want to interrelate with others who can support this."

In composite charts, this same archetype is operative as the couple desires to create necessary isolation from all others who expect the couple to be like everyone else. The couple will have subconscious memories of the prior phase in the sense that there has been much testing and experimenting with new ways of establishing their relationship. There may possibly be subconscious memories of separation because of this trial-and-error technique. As a result, the couple will desire to withstand social forces and pressures to conform to the culturally conditioned ways of being in relationship, and will desire to deeply internalize the relationship—to become a closed unit, so to speak. Within this, each person must empower one another to establish their own individual evolutionary and karmic intentions and requirements. The temptation is to deeply internalize together that they become clone-like extensions of one another. This temptation must be resisted because it will lead to an inertia that will stop the relationship from growing and evolving.

First Quarter Phase (90°–135°) Following the Crescent phase, the Soul has had two previous primary lifetimes to become progressively aware of the nature of the new value associations that correlate with the evolutionary intention of establishing the relationship dynamic in new ways. The new ways of being in relationship with others reflects the new ways in which the Soul has been learning to relate to itself, and the sense of meaning that the Soul has for itself. In the First Quarter phase, the Soul has evolved into a fundamental courage to stand apart from everyone else, and willfully asserts its individual values to all others who do not share in such values. The crisis inherent to this phase correlates to the Soul's fear of forming relationships with others in general, and intimate relationships specifically. The Soul feels that if such relationships are formed, then their hard-won sense of individuality will become reabsorbed or lost into and because of the relationship. This fear will lead the Soul to "keep one hand waving free" within the context of any kind of relationship. In this way, the Soul attempts to guarantee its individuality by always having the back door open, so to speak. This can create real relationship conflicts for such a Soul, especially in an intimate relationship, because the Soul cyclically appears to totally engage, then totally disengage. The challenge in this phase is for the Soul to realize that the individuality that has been established will not be lost, that this fear is a fear only, and to align with other individuals who have the same courage to project their own individuality in the face of the consensus. Similarly, they need to choose an intimate other who is evolutionarily evolving in the same way.

In composite charts, this phase will correlate to a couple who have subconscious memories of isolating themselves from the impact of others specifically, and society generally, in order to deeply internalize and establish their own unique values as a couple, and the sense of meaning for a life that those values correlate to. In the current life, it becomes evolutionarily necessary for each of them to establish their own independent lives within the context of the relationship. In this context, each will learn to actualize their own individuality relative to the karmic and evolutionary intentions that each has, yet this individual actualization will reflect what they have learned together as a couple. This phase requires an expansion of what has already been learned. This expansion will take place through the relationship as the couple interacts, and it will take place through independent discovery as each partner pursues individual areas of interest. Contraction and expansion of the relationship is the evolutionary result. Crisis will result in the relationship if one or both partners attempt to overwhelm each other through trying to control what this necessary expansion is about. The challenge is for each partner to encourage and support individual expansion for one another. In this way, each will contribute equally as the relationship interacts from within itself. At best, this couple will serve as examples and empowering allies for other couples or individuals who seek to break free from the shackles of cultural conditioning.

The Gibbous Phase (135°–180°) Following the First Quarter phase, the Soul has had three previous primary lifetimes to become progressively aware of the new evolutionary intention reflected in its inner and outer relationship dynamics, and the values reflected in this new pattern. Emerging out of the First Quarter phase, the Soul must now learn to inwardly and outwardly adjust how it has been relating to itself and others. The nature of these adjustments reflects the Soul's intention of preparing itself to relate to others on an equal basis. In the First Quarter phase, the Soul has necessarily evolved through a deep and self-centered orientation to itself as part of a necessary focus on self-development. In the Gibbous phase, the Soul has entered an evolutionary stage of development in which, on an inner basis, it will become very self-critical. In this stage, the Soul inwardly analyzes all of its shortcomings, inadequacies, imperfections, indiscretions, and lacks with the intention of deflating itself. In essence, there is an inner need to humiliate itself. Outwardly, the Soul creates relationship dynamics in which others will also relate to the Soul in very critical ways. The crisis of this phase is one wherein the Soul can interpret these critical messages from others as persecution. If it feels victimized, the Soul will become quite angry and hypercritical of others. Inwardly, the Soul will begin to doubt its own self-worth. When this is the operational dynamic, the intimate relationships that are formed will never be good enough. Both partners will be critical of one another, and neither will ever feel completely right in the relationship. Doubt about the relationship will be cyclic or constant. The challenge is for the Soul to realize that it intends to humble and deflate itself in this phase of development. Understood in this way, the Soul can then adjust how it is interpreting the critical messages of others. It can see that these messages must be gracefully received because these "external" messages are really reflections of the messages or thoughts from within itself. Accepting the messages in this way will allow the Soul to adjust how it is integrating itself with the world—how it is relating to others in general and intimate others specifically. Instead of willful self-assertion, the Soul must learn to relate and give to others from the point of view of self-sacrifice. In this way, the Soul will evolve from superiority through inferiority which will then allow for equality as it moves into the Full phase.

In composite charts, this phase will reflect a couple who is now learning how to adjust the ways in which they have conducted the relationship, how they have been relating to themselves as individuals because of the relationship, and how they have been relating to one another through the relationship. For this intention to occur, the couple will create necessary crises within the relationship that will enforce a necessary analysis as to why the crises are occurring. Positively, the nature of the crises will promote necessary discussion that will allow each of them to become aware of what the necessary adjustments are within the relationship. These necessary adjustments will then allow the relationship to continue to grow and evolve. Negatively, the nature of the crises will create a situation wherein one or both partners feel that they are never good enough for one another, that one or both are always having to sacrifice themselves, their purposes, and their needs to the other, and to a deep feeling of doubt about whether this is the right relationship or not. The key in this phase is for both partners to learn how to serve one another unconditionally. In so doing, the needs and desires of both will be perfectly met.

The Full Phase (180°–225°) Following the Gibbous phase, the Soul has now learned to adjust its ways of inwardly relating to itself and others. Mars and Venus are now archetypally in opposition. Thus, there is a dynamic state of stress within the Soul. It must now struggle to learn how to balance its own needs and desires within the context of other people's needs and desires. The Soul is learning how to be an equal among other people. It is learning how to listen to others in such a way as to actually hear what they are saying, to objectively understand the meaning reflected in others values, and to confirm the needs that emanate from those values. The Soul is learning how to give to others, and learning that by giving it will receive exactly what it needs from others without asking. The Soul is learning how to integrate its specific needs, desires, and the meaning for its life reflected in its own value system into social reality. Within intimate relationships, the Soul is learning how to balance its desires and needs for independence within the need and desire for relationship. For a state of balance to occur, the Soul must learn how to honor the instinctual impulses that reflect the need to be alone with the need for intimate and/or social interaction, and to honor these instincts as they occur. The Soul is learning how to give to an intimate partner exactly what they need according to the partner themselves, as opposed to what the Soul thinks that they need. This requires true listening which will allow for an objective awareness of the other's reality. When this lesson is learned, the Soul will have a partner who does exactly the same for them.

In composite charts, this phase will reflect a couple who is in a critical stage of development together. The stages of evolutionary development symbolized in the phases that have preceded the Full phase now come to a head. Whatever dynamics or issues that have occurred between them prior to this life that have not been resolved will now manifest. These issues and dynamics will become magnified at this stage of development, and become the potential basis of polarization within the relationship. In a polarized state, the couple may feel the temptation to separate and go their own ways. Or they may simply live in a polarized state, and lead more or less independent lives. The reason for this, when it occurs, is reflected in the Gibbous phase which preceded this current phase. In that phase, one or both partners may have felt that they sacrificed too much of their personal desires and needs to the other. If so, this becomes a psychological cause of resentment and anger. In the Full phase, both partners will feel the need to assert their own realities and needs. They will want to have these needs satisfied, not sacrificed. Thus, the potential for polarization occurs wherein neither partner will defer to the other. In that case, there is a real danger in that each partner will project on the other irrational assertions that have little resemblance to the reality of this life. The challenge and need here is for each person to realize that at this stage of evolutionary development each has a need to develop and actualize their own desires and needs that are consistent with their individual evolutionary and karmic requirements. This will require that each learn to truly listen to one another, and to continue to give to one another accordingly. In this way, each will feel supported and accepted, and, as a result, each will have their own needs met.

The Disseminating Phase (270°–315°) Following the Full phase, the Soul has now learned to understand the nature of the overall social system. As a result, the Soul is now able to actualize and integrate its specific value system, the needs these values reflect, and the overall sense of meaning for its life that these values symbolize, into the social and societal sphere. The specific desires that the Soul has for what it wants to accomplish with its life can now be more or less easily actualized and integrated within the society. The social sphere or society is receptive to what the Soul wants to do and accomplish. Social interactions are not difficult during this stage of evolutionary development. Intimately, the Soul knows what it desires and values from another, and will attract others who also know what they desire and need. As a result, the Soul at this evolutionary stage of development will find it relatively easy to attract and secure the type of person that it desires, and to be in a relationship in which the core dynamics reflecting its desires and needs are fulfilled.

In composite charts, this phase will reflect a couple who has come a long way together relative to the previous phases of evolutionary development. As a result, each will have a clear vision of one another, a good understanding, and an equally clear vision of their own desires and needs as symbolized in their own evolutionary and karmic intentions. Accordingly, there will be relative ease in actualizing and integrating not only their own lives into the existing social structure, but also relative ease in understanding, embracing, and encouraging each other for what each desires to accomplish in life. Within the relationship each will find it easy to listen to one another, to understand what is being said by one another, and to be there for one another. The dynamic of giving and receiving will be more or less balanced. The roles within the relationship are clearly understood and accepted.

The Last Quarter Phase (270°–315°) Following the Disseminating phase, the Soul has now entered into a stage of evolutionary development wherein a crisis of values, and the meaning of life that those values symbolize, begins to occur. The Soul will now begin to desire to expand its level of awareness in order to relate to itself in a more universal sense—to leave behind the evolutionary limitation of relating to itself as a socially defined entity. As a result, the Soul will desire to look beyond the immediacy of its current culture or society. It will want to embrace ideas and philosophies from other cultures that offer different perspectives on the nature and meaning of life. In this way, the Soul will begin to inwardly relate to itself in ever-larger ways. Consequently, it will progressively value and need other people who feel within themselves that they are also standing outside of the current society, yet are still operating within it. Attracting such people of like mind becomes essential for the Soul, because this provides the necessary support that will allow the Soul to progressively move forward.

The crisis within this phase is reflected in the Soul's desire and need to continue operating within the existing society while it inwardly allows itself to question what constitutes the meaning of life. These types of questions will progressively produce an alienation from the existing society, which can ignite a temptation to withdraw from society. The challenge is for the Soul to remain integrated within society while at the same time allowing this inner expansion to take place. The Soul in this phase of evolutionary development requires an intimate other who is also in the same phase. When this does not occur, the dynamics within the relationship will be contentious because of the conflict of values that will exist between the two people. This will produce a progressive alienation within the relationship, as there will no real basis of relating to one another in a meaningful way .

In composite charts, this phase will reflect a couple who has come a long way together over many lifetimes. Each person within the relationship will desire to understand the deeper reasons for the relationship and the deeper reasons for their individual lives. In evolutionary terms, the couple faces the challenge to progressively disengage from the nature of the current cultural conditioning that defines the reasons and meaning for relationship, and the value associations that define the roles within relationships. This challenge will require the couple to embrace together new ways of thinking that reflect a much larger way of understanding life. They need to simply be open to all kinds of possibilities.

This challenge can create an uneasy sense of insecurity within the relationship. This is because the couple has just emerged from the Disseminating Phase, where it was relatively easy to integrate their relationship within the conditioning of the existing society—thus the security linked with "normalcy." To move away from this conditioning can result in a sense of insecurity. Paradoxically, real security will be realized when each partner accepts the challenge of this evolutionary phase and encourages the other to explore any direction that will expand their level of consciousness. The resulting awareness of relativity is what this expansion symbolizes. If either partner attempts to restrict the necessity of such growth because of insecurity fears, then the relationship will suffer. This will lead to stress and conflict in their interrelatedness because the evolutionary impulse is to move forward. If this occurs, then one or both partners can become attracted to other people who are themselves desiring to stand back from the existing society, and who desire to expand their own consciousness by embracing all kinds of different and new ways of thinking. Potentially, this can lead to a break in the relationship wherein each person ends up going their own way. When this occurs, it becomes the causal factor of karmic incompletion that leaves key dynamics unresolved.

The Balsamic Phase. This phase will reflect a Soul at the culmination of an entire evolutionary cycle. It reflects how the Soul has defined its own values, ways of relating to itself and other people, and its sense of life's meaning. As a result, there will be a core detachment and alienation from the existing society, which will offer nothing to the Soul that is relevant or meaningful to its desire and need to embrace ultimate or transcendental principles. This alienation from societal norms and precepts will drive the Soul deep within itself. A Soul in this evolutionary phase of development will be highly reflective and essentially introverted. Deep inner ponderings and wonderings about the transcendental meaning of life will take place, along with a desire and need to form relationships with the spiritual principles of life. For many, this will manifest as forming relationships with spiritual teachers or gurus. These types of relationships will be simultaneously impersonal and personal. Other Souls in this phase may project the transcendental meanings that they seek on other people. Such Souls are setting themselves up to experience massive disillusionment, because these projections do not allow them to understand the nature of the other person's actual reality.

The true intention within this evolutionary stage of development is to form a relationship with transcendent or spiritual principles. This "ultimate relationship" that the Soul desires is between itself and the Source of All, and will only be found within. The Soul requires an external partner who is defined in the same way. Generally speaking, an individual who has a balsamic Mars/Venus phase can only really feel right with another in an intimate relationship who also has their Mars/Venus in a Balsamic phase. This will allow for an unconditional love to exist within the relationship in which both partners support and encourage the inner development of each. Until the Soul realizes and acts on the intention in this evolutionary phase, it can follow, and become confused by, any illusion or delusion considered as the ultimate meaning that it is seeking.

Because this phase correlates to an evolutionary culmination, the Soul must embrace the inner meaning of timeless values that allow the Soul to actually experience its own immortality or timeless existence. Accordingly, there is a need to expand the frontiers of consciousness to allow for a living inner relationship with the Divine to occur. In this way the seeds of the new cycle to come will emerge into consciousness. Within this, it is necessary for the Soul to be actively reflective on the nature of the entire past cycle that has lead to this point.

Through such reflection, a deep self-knowledge will take place that al-lows the Soul to culminate the cycle now coming to closure, and pre-pare it to move forward into the next cycle of evolutionary develop-ment. Because of this intention, the Soul will attract all kinds of people, intimate and otherwise, who have all been part of, or linked to, the Soul's prior lifetimes in some way. These people will be individuals with whom the Soul has "unfinished business." It is necessary for the Soul to culminate and bring to completion any such issues now, so that they do not impede a free flow into the upcoming new cycle.

In composite charts, this phase will reflect a couple who has trav-eled a long way together over many lifetimes. The intention is to complete and bring to culmination all the dynamics that have defined their relationship over many lifetimes. They must now address all that is unresolved and unfinished. For many couples, this can be over-whelming and confusing, since the nature of whatever is unresolved or unfinished can come from other lifetimes. Thus, it can be difficult for the couple to know why or where any specific dynamic or issue is "coming from," because most are not consciously aware of the source. And because there can be so many "loose ends" of this type, the cou-ple may feel overwhelmed by these dynamics and issues.

When this occurs, it is essential that the couple create a "time out" to try to understand and resolve these dynamics and issues. Doing so will let the relationship settle into the natural quietness that defines the real essence of their relationship. Each partner can then reflect sepa-rately on the nature of what is occurring. This reflection will generate an inner awareness within each person as to the nature of what is oc-curring. In this way, each will provide an essential knowledge or wis-dom to the other that will allow for an agreeable resolution.

The couple must embrace transcendental or ultimate values to-gether that will allow the relationship to be inwardly defined and re-lated to in this way. Each partner must allow and encourage the oth-er to develop and actualize their own spiritual desires. In this way, an unconditional love will permeate their relationship, and will allow each of them to actualize an inner relationship with the Ultimate Oth-er. As a result, they will experience the divinity within one another. This can or will include sexual practices that also allow for a transfer-ence from primary to sacred sexuality.

Evolutionarily speaking, this couple is either now culminating their relationship, or else culminating an entire cycle of being together in specific ways that will lead to a brand-new cycle of development together. In the first case, this will mean that these two Souls will no longer have any karmic or evolutionary need to be together—their work is finished. In the second case, this will mean that these two Souls still have an evolutionary and karmic reason to continue to be together, yet to do so requires a total culmination and resolution of all that has come before.

ONE COUPLE'S EVOLUTION

Now that the general archetypal themes of the Mars/Venus phase has been discussed, it may be useful to study a case history in order to detail these dynamics. To do this we will focus on a couple. We will start by examining the relevant dynamics in each of their natal charts, and then view them as a couple through the lens of the composite chart.

Chart #14 is the natal horoscope of a man who was born in Germany. His evolutionary state was the second stage of the individuated condition—a state of anger and alienation resulting from his inability to integrate into consensus-based society. He was not exposed to any heavy religious conditioning by the parents, but he was exposed to the nature of the Protestant religion within the context of German culture. He was raised by middle-class parents who were in the consensus state, evolutionarily speaking.

Again, for an accurate analysis of any birthchart to occur, the relevant conditions of any individual's birth must be understood. These conditions include the evolutionary condition or state, the nature of the society or culture's conditioning imprints on the person's identity and reality, the nature of the parental reality that serves as the initial imprinting, and the family's economic conditions along with the value associations that such conditions produce. In this case history, we will focus on the overall conditions symbolized through the interrelation of his Mars and Venus.

Mars is in Libra conjunct the South Node in the Eighth House. The North Node is in Aries (ruled by Mars) in the Second House. Mars is also conjunct the asteroid Juno (New phase), trine Mercury which is in the Twelfth House (First Quarter phase), trine Jupiter which is in the First House (First Quarter phase), semi-square Pluto which is retrograde in the Seventh House (Crescent phase), and square Uranus in Cancer which is retrograde in the Fifth House (Last Quarter phase). Uranus is forming a T-square to the Nodal Axis and Mars. Venus is in the First House in Aquarius sesquiquadrate to Mars (First Quarter phase).

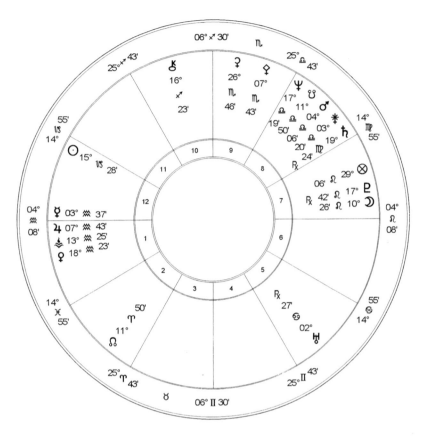

Chart #14

Any horoscope in which Mars is conjunct the South Node indicates that the person will be born with unresolved anger. In this chart, Mars is not only conjunct the South Node, but is the planetary ruler of the North Node. Thus, the current evolutionary intention is to re-create certain prior-life conditions which will serve as a causal factor in triggering this unresolved anger so that it can hopefully be resolved. For this man, the initial trigger would be his biological mother. This can be seen through his Mars squaring Uranus retrograde in Cancer, with Uranus squaring the Nodal Axis. In addition, Venus is sesquiquadrate Uranus, and Mercury, the planetary ruler of the Fourth House, is inconjunct Uranus. With Uranus being retrograde, indicating the need to repeat or relive unresolved prior-life dynamics, it is clear that this woman has been his mother before.

It should be clear that this man is intensely emotional—simply examine the nature of his Eighth House. He has had deep emotional expectations over many lifetimes (Mars conjunct the South Node in Libra) of needing to be emotionally understood, accepted, and nurtured for who he inherently was and is. With retrograde Uranus in Cancer squaring Mars and the Nodal Axis, these emotional expectations would have been unfulfilled by his mother in both past and present. The mother has rebelled and essentially rejected him over many lifetimes. She has attempted to impose her own values and expectations on him—values and resulting expectations based on consensus reality. It can be seen that her rejection of him is an extension of her rebellion against the biological father, with whom she was essentially in a polarized state and going through the motions of being in relationship. Because his Soul has evolved to the second stage of the individuated state, these values and expectations of the mother would have the effect of making him feel unwanted and unaccepted. As a result, his own expectations relative to the mother would go unfulfilled yet again. Thus, his Soul has re-created the necessary conditions to trigger the unresolved anger he brought into this life.

In addition, the mother would be quite powerful and domineering, as seen through his Moon in Leo conjuncting Pluto in the Seventh House. The effect that this would have on him would be to not only trigger his anger, but also to make him feel victimized by the mother (Uranus inconjuncting the Twelfth House Mercury). So as a child, the original imprint was to feel unloved and unaccepted by the mother. This has triggered the unresolved prior-life dynamics of anger and feeling victimized by the mother. As the displaced emotions of his childhood moved into the sphere of adult relationships, he found himself feeling victimized and angry toward women in general.

Within this pattern, it should also be clear that there has been sexual violations to him relative to the mother. These violations, over many lifetimes, would run the range from overt sexual abuse to sexual and psychological innuendo. Thus, his anger also includes sexual anger linked with the mother, and, through extension relative to the displaced emotions of childhood (retrograde Uranus in Cancer) to all women. All of this in combination, over many lifetimes, creates a Soul who has fundamental fears of abandonment, betrayal, and violations of trust. With Uranus squaring the Nodal Axis, an ongoing evolutionary intention is to liberate from these patterns. To do so, the Soul must necessarily re-create the appropriate conditions.

It should be understood that this man has had, and continues to have, an evolutionary intention wherein he is trying to learn how to validate his own self-worth. This can be seen by the North Node in the Second House relative to Venus (the planetary ruler of his South Node) being in Aquarius in the First House. Uranus in Cancer in the Fifth House, squaring the Nodal Axis and Mars, also reflects his need to liberate from external expectations of this kind. Yet, coming into this life, he will necessarily have to repeat prior-life conditions and dynamics before this lesson can be learned.

With the Mars/Venus phase being First Quarter with a sesquiquadrate aspect at 134°, he is at a key evolutionary transition point between the First Quarter and Gibbous phases. Remembering that the dynamics we are identifying have been in place prior to the current life, this key transition can only occur by repeating those dynamics first. The essence of this transition can only occur through the creation of an emotional, psychological, and sexual crisis (Mars/Venus in a sesquiquadrate aspect). The essence of this necessary crisis will be linked with relationship dynamics that involve the core issues. These include the general emotional expectations linked with other people (Venus in Aquarius), expectations linked with women in general (Uranus in Cancer squaring Mars in Libra, Venus in Aquarius sesquiquadrate mars in Libra, Venus in Aquarius being the planetary ruler of the South Node in Libra, Venus in Aquarius in opposition to Pluto and the Moon in the Seventh House, and Venus sesquiquadrate Uranus), and expectations of intimate female partners specifically (Venus opposing the Moon and Pluto in the Seventh House, and, again, the planetary ruler of the South Node in Libra occupying the Eighth House).

The essence of the crisis which will allow the key transition to take place involves the necessity of repeating prior life conditions in this life in order for evolution to proceed. The essence of this karma is reflected in his unresolved anger toward his mother, and, through extension, to all women via displaced emotions of childhood that were not met. This anger is also linked to other people in general, involving idealized expectations of how he should be treated by others, and how others should treat others through overall social interactions. This is clearly seen through Venus in Aquarius trine Neptune in Libra, and reiterated by Neptune conjunct the South Node, which in turn is linked back to Venus through its rulership of Libra.

Karmically speaking, this man has psychologically, sexually, and emotionally compensated for his anger by attracting women into his past lifetimes, and in this life, that were and are just as wounded and emotionally, sexually, and psychologically damaged as himself. Because of this own fear of vulnerability, betrayal, abandonment, and loss, he would typically present himself as someone who could help them heal these types of wounds. The Eighth House patterns correlate to a person who would have unique psychological gifts, insights, and understandings based on his own emotional and sexual turmoil over many lifetimes. By presenting himself in this way, an act of compensation, he would attract to himself women who appeared to be more needy than himself. Thus, he creates a relationship dynamic in which he presents himself as being able to help or heal these types of women. Relative to Venus in Aquarius in the First House, he would have the unique ability to objectively understand the individual psychology, needs, and desires of such women. He would have the ability to make such women feel "special." Through the Eighth House Mars he would have the ability to "empower' such women in a variety of ways. This would be done through initially entering into a friendship with these women (Venus in Aquarius in the First House). He would engage them in discussions of various kinds, the intention (Eighth House) of such discussions being to "play back" whatever it was that they wanted to discuss (Venus in Aquarius, Mars in Libra, Uranus square the Nodal Axis). Through such discussions, the women would feel listened to, accepted, and understood, and would then feel secure and emotionally embraced by him. This would then lead into a deepening of the connection, from friendship to intimacy.

Through intimacy, he would then present himself as someone who could also help them heal their sexual wounds. With Mars in Libra in the Eighth House square Uranus in Cancer in the Fifth House, trine Mercury in the Aquarius in the Twelfth House, trine Jupiter in Aquarius in the First House, semi-square Pluto in the Seventh House, and conjunct the asteroid Juno in Libra in the Eighth House, he would have had many lifetimes learning sexual methods and rituals. His sexual energy would be intense because it is fueled by the inner compression of his own desire to merge with another (the Eighth House linked with the archetype of Libra). And because of the unresolved emotional dynamics with his mother, his sexual intensity is based on igniting and bringing these emotions to the surface.

He would have a unique ability to help women unlock their emotions through sexuality, due to his ability to harmonize with their emotional/sexual energy. With Mars in Libra in the Eighth House relative to Venus in Aquarius, this would initially occur through touching and kissing. By learning how a woman responded to his touch, he would gain the necessary feedback (Uranus in the Fifth House square the Nodal Axis and Mars, which are sesquiquadrate to Venus) to understand how their emotional/sexual energy and system worked. This would allow for a progressive deepening of their emotional/sexual response (Mars in the Eighth House). This deepening would also occur because of the linkage of Mars to the Twelfth House Mercury. From other lifetimes he would have developed a knowledge of how the nervous system is linked with sexual energy and its stimulation. Mercury correlates to the hands. Thus, he would be very adept at using his hands in very sensitive ways (Twelfth House) to stimulate the body and genital area in order to excite (Aquarius) the sexual energy. Mars linked with Jupiter will usually correlate to a man who has a larger than normal penis. Thus, when the moment came for him to penetrate a woman with his penis, the act of penetration itself would further intensify the sexual energy because of the degree of stimulation that the woman would feel by having to make herself "more open" in order to accommodate him. This also correlates to becoming more psychologically and emotionally open—to become vulnerable.

In this way, he would finally feel emotionally safe within himself. Feeling safe would then allow him to engage his own emotions, and the inner compression of his emotions would manifest through the sexual exchange. As a result, his sexual energy would be very intense and overwhelm not only himself, but also the women. And part of this emotional/sexual intensity would be fueled and motivated by the original anger linked with his mother. Thus, there is a duality of sexual motivations and intentions—sex as power in the sense of reducing the women to an absolute state of vulnerability based on his sexual ability to create overwhelming sensation leading to "orgasms of the Soul" on a sustained basis, and sex as psychological, emotional, and sexual empowerment and healing.

The specific karma that comes from this is based on his own fears of abandonment, betrayal, fears of loss, and violations of trust. Because of these fears he will have a fear of commitment to anyone in this life, as indicated by the grouping of Mars, South Node, Saturn, Juno, and Neptune all in the Eighth House. These fears are compounded by his North Node in Aries, by Venus, the planetary ruler of his South Node being in the First House in Aquarius and in opposition to the Seventh House Pluto and Moon, and Uranus square the

Nodal Axis, Mars, and also sesquiquadrate to Venus. These archetypes correlate to an emotional paradox linked with relationship. On one side of the paradox is his desire for total freedom, and on the other side of the paradox is his desire for total relationship. Relative to his fears, this will correlate to a fear of entrapment in any one relationship—the Eighth House pattern in this context. Thus, over many lifetimes, he has attracted women in the ways that we have been discussing. Many of these women have become dependent on him because of his abilities and capacities (Pluto and the Moon in the Seventh House). And he has desired to make them dependent on him in these ways because this makes him feel worthwhile, important, powerful, and validated: the very things he expected from his mother. Yet, because he has felt essentially abandoned by his mother, he will work out his residual and displaced anger by abandoning the women who become dependent on him. This will be done primarily through having relations with many different women at the same time, even having "extra" women in his life while having a primary partner.

His current karmic situation is specific not only to being born through a woman who has been his mother in past lifetimes, but also to reattracting and repeating relationships with the many women with whom he has been involved. The evolutionary and karmic intention is to hopefully bring all of this to a culmination point in this life (the planetary ruler of the North Node being conjunct the South Node), and also to liberate from these patterns in this lifetime (Uranus square the Nodal Axis, Mars, and sesquiquadrate Venus).

An additional intention is to learn how to commit to one partner in this life (Pluto conjunct the Moon in the Seventh House, Mars conjunct the South Node in the Eighth House). The key transition reflected in the Mars/Venus phase will thus demand experiential crisis so that this can be accomplished. The nature of the relationship crisis demonstrated in this phase/aspect will lead to necessary analysis—the nature of the crisis in the first place. Analysis will subsequently produce self-knowledge Thus, many of these women will produce psychological and emotional confrontations. Mars and the South Node in Libra in the Eighth House, Pluto and the Moon in Leo in the Seventh House, and Uranus in Cancer in the Fifth House indicate feedback from others. Such messages from others are actually the symbolic messages and thoughts emanating from this own Soul because of the evolutionary intention to bring this pattern to culmination in this life. The challenge with Jupiter (Jupiter correlates with how we interpret phenomena), in opposition to his Pluto and Moon, trine his South Node and Mars, and inconjunct to his Uranus, is to learn how to interpret these messages gracefully and correctly. Instead of relying on the old life pattern of defensiveness (Mars/South Node in the Eighth House), he must learn to receive and interpret these messages as objective truths (Jupiter in Aquarius) about himself. He can then integrate and assimilate these messages in such a way as to effectively change these repeating dynamics of many life-times. Once this occurs, he will finally attract a partner who will already be self-empowered and self-reliant. She will desire to be with him sim-ply because she wants to be with him, and not because of need or com-pulsion. She will be as psychologically, emotionally, and sexually deep as he is. And because of the Mars/Venus phase, she will reflect a strong self-developed individuality which will help him learn to give and re-ceive in equal ways—that to give is to receive.

Let us now turn to the woman in this case study of a relationship in evolution. Chart #15 is the natal chart of this woman, who was also born in Germany. Her evolutionary condition is in the beginning of the third stage of the spiritual state. She was born to parents who were very firmly in the second stage of the consensus state. Their econom-ic conditions were of the lower middle class. She was not exposed to heavy religious conditioning by the parents, yet as a child she took herself to the Church of her own volition, indicating the connection to "spirit" in this evolutionary state.

In her birth chart, Mars and Venus are in Capricorn in the Second House, and are in the Balsamic phase. They both form trines to the Tenth House Pluto/Uranus conjunction in Virgo. Venus is forming a waning quintile to the Twelfth House Moon in Libra. Because Venus and Mars are conjunct, I would also include Mars in this aspect. Both are forming Crescent phase septiles to Neptune, which is conjunct the Ascendant in Scorpio. Mars and Venus are both conjunct the Capricorn Sun in the Second House. They are also forming a Last Quarter sextile to Chiron in Pisces in the Fourth House, a Last Quarter square to Juno in Aries in the Fifth House, a Disseminating trine to Ceres in Taurus in the Seventh House, and Venus is in a Full phase sesquiquadrate to Ves-ta in Taurus in the Seventh House, whereas Mars is in a Disseminating sesquiquadrate to Vesta.

In essence, this is a woman who was born to parents who had no ability to understand who their child was. This situation occurred be-cause of the evolutionary differences between her and her parents. She was consequently not nurtured or loved in meaningful ways. Her

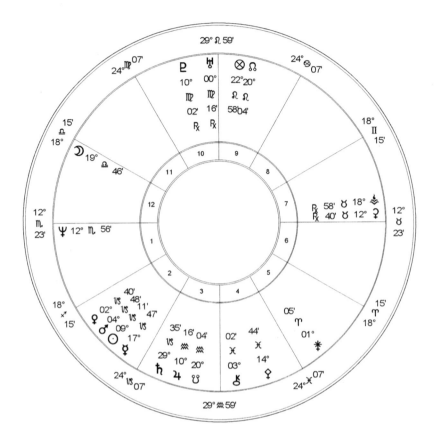

Chart #15

parents expected her to be a miniature adult, and she was given many duties that would normally be the parents' responsibility. With Neptune on the Ascendant and the Moon in the Twelfth House, she compensated for this through the world of inner fantasy and imagination. As she grew into puberty, she progressively withdrew into the inner sanctum of her room. By this time, her parents were polarized and having affairs with other people.

The Balsamic Mars/Venus phase symbolizes an entire cycle of relationship dynamics that are coming to culmination and completion in this lifetime. Relative to her evolutionary condition, she had spent many previous lifetimes dedicated to spiritual development. This development began in the Matriarchal traditions long ago: her South Node of the Moon in Aquarius conjunct Jupiter is also conjunct the South Node of Neptune in Aquarius. Thus, her original spiritual root comes from the Matriarchal times (the original Matriarchy was established during the last Aquarian Age). As the matriarchy gave way to the patriarchy, her spiritual development was adjusted to fit the new paradigm. Whereas matriarchal spirituality included the senses and sexuality, the patriarchy advocated their suppression. Thus, she came to accept and integrate the patriarchal suppression of the senses and sexuality into her spiritual quest (Mars/Venus in Capricorn in the Second House, and trine to the Tenth House Pluto/Uranus conjunction in Virgo).

Yet it should be clear that Mars and Venus in the Second House relative to the connection to Pluto and Juno correlates to an intensely sensual and sexual individual. This is also seen through Ceres and Vesta being in the Seventh House in Taurus. With Vesta in opposition to Neptune in Scorpio, this would correlate with a Soul who had learned and practiced some very profound ancient sacred sexual practices of a metamorphic and healing nature in some quite distant prior lifetimes. This is actually a core dynamic within her, and constitutes one of the essences of her intended healing in this life. This is based on the fact that in more earlier and distant prior lifetimes she actualized herself through the role of the "sacred prostitute." Archetypally, this role was played out in certain cultures in such a way that the sacred prostitute was considered to be highly spiritually advanced. As such, she was used by such cultures to heal and advance the development of other people, who were designated by priests and priestesses, through the act of sexual intercourse. The healing and advancement would occur through the exchange and mutual osmosis of sexual fluids. The sexual fluids contain the genetic nature of our evolutionary and karmic development. The sacred prostitute was able to absorb and dissolve the karmic and evolutionary conditions of those that she had intercourse with, and those that had intercourse with her absorbed the spiritual energy of her Soul. This then allowed for their advancement. This archetypal signature in her horoscope can be seen through several factors. Vesta is in Taurus in the Seventh House, which is trine the Tenth House Pluto, inconjunct the Twelfth House Moon in Libra, and sextile Pallas in Pisces in the Fourth House. Both Pallas and Vesta are forming inconjunctions to the Twelfth House Libra Moon, and thus a Finger of God or Yod is focused on the Moon. Vesta is trine to Mercury in Capricorn, which is the planetary ruler of her Eighth house Gemini cusp. Vesta is also sesquiquadrate to Mars and Venus in Capricorn in the Second House, and in opposition to Neptune in Scorpio conjunct her Ascendant.

Over time, the role of the sacred prostitute changed. Those that were considered "sacred vessels" in this way were now forced to be celibate. For those who violated this enforced celibacy, the punishment was to be buried alive. This doctrine of enforced celibacy created her original guilt relative to her natural being, and also created the original suppression of that which was natural to her. Thus, as she evolved through time relative to the transference of the matriarchy to the patriarchy, she became progressively conditioned to suppress her senses and sexuality. Thus, with Mars and Venus being in Capricorn relative to the Tenth House Pluto and Uranus, she created a deep inner guilt associated with her natural sexual and sensual nature. With Neptune in Scorpio square the Nodal Axis (skipped steps), and connected through Mars and Venus through the Crescent phase septiles, it has become necessary to end the suppression of that which she inherently is, and, in so doing, to recover the skipped steps. This must also be done in order to culminate the Mars/Venus Balsamic phase. Relative to her displaced emotions caused by the nurturing and love that she needed but did not receive as a child, she was attracted to older men as she became ready for relationships in this life. When she was sixteen she decided to have her first relationship experience.

She became attracted to a man fifteen years older than herself. This man was just as insensitive as her father. Just as the father attempted to dominate her (Pluto in the Tenth House), so too did this man. Even though she told him she was a virgin, he simply did his thing in a very forceful and hurtful way. Later he forced her to perform fellatio through threats—a *de facto* rape. Vesta in the Seventh House connected through the sesquiquadrates to Mars and Venus, and Juno in Aries making a square to these planets, correlate with sexual violence of this type. Since Vesta is also square the Nodal Axis, and in opposition to Neptune (which effectively creates a Fixed Grand Cross), the skipped steps of intimate relationships, and the need to repeat key relationships with certain types is clear. The nature of her imprinting in this life, linked with this first experience, effectively created deep fear and anger toward men. She became emotionally and sexually frozen as a result of this. Nevertheless, because of the evolutionary intention to recover skipped steps in order to culminate an entire relationship cycle, she soon became involved with another older man in which the same dynamics occurred. And then again with another man, resulting in the same thing again.

When she was seventeen, she met the man described previously (Chart #14). Their connection started through discussions of all kinds of topics in which he simply presented himself as a friend, with no sexual pressure whatsoever. He recognized through his natural psychological skills that she was a very wounded and emotionally needy person. He recognized that she was very fearful and angry. He also recognized, relative to his evolutionary state, that she was compensating for her deep inner feeling of being so different than most around her by trying to be like all the other "normal" people in German culture. Thus, he recognized that she was not in harmony with herself (the Yod involving the Twelfth House Moon in Libra inconjunct both the Seventh House Vesta in Taurus and the Fourth House Pallas in Pisces). This lack of harmony with her essential nature has created her inner crisis. Yet because this Moon is quintile to Mars and Venus, and Neptune is septile to them (fated circumstances that occur to keep the Soul aligned with its destiny), she attracted this man in order to be realigned with her inner being. By putting no sexual pressure on her, he allowed her to feel safe. In this way, she began to trust him.

We will now take a look into the nature of the relationship between these two people by analyzing their composite chart (Chart #16). Again, a composite chart symbolizes the "entity" of the relationship, and is created by calculating the planetary and house cusp midpoints of the couple. With their composite Pluto in the Eighth House, it should be clear that they have had very deep Soul connections prior to this life. Moon in Virgo square the Nodal Axis indicates that there has also been a crisis within the relationship that essentially revolved around emotional dishonesty. With Pluto forming an inconjunction to Venus, Mercury, and Chiron in Capricorn in the First House, the nature of this crisis would involve being involved with other people while trying to sustain the relationship, and not being honest with one another about these types of connections. This would have led to the skipped steps through one or the other terminating the relationship for these reasons. In this lifetime, they have come together again to resolve these issues. With the South Node in Sagittarius in the Twelfth House, these two would have a deep sensitivity toward one another, and the capacity to forgive. It is this capacity to forgive that allows the skipped steps to be recovered.

In the current life, the man was eleven years older than the woman. Thus, he had a great deal more life experience when they met. Becoming aware of all of her inner dynamics through their early

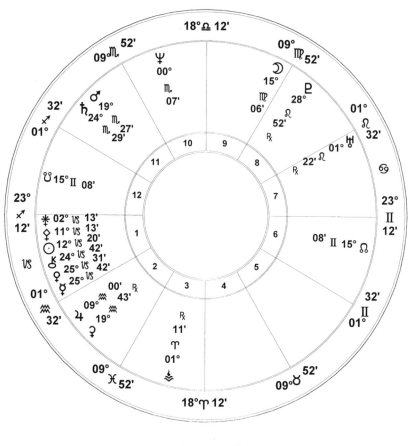

Chart #16

discussions and his inherent empathy only stimulated his desire to help her regain harmony with her inner being. With Jupiter (the ruler of the composite South Node) in Aquarius in the Second House, they already had lifetimes together in which they rebelled against "the system." The value structure of the relationship was defined by this rebellion. This dynamic is restated through the First House Venus in Capricorn (the First is an Aries house), Mars and Saturn being in Scorpio in the Eleventh House, Mars in a Crescent phase square to Pluto, and Saturn in a First Quarter square to Pluto. This is a couple deeply involved in challenging the authority of the system—its values and what constitutes proper conduct. With Venus inconjunct Pluto, they found their power through such a rebellious attitude. This aspect, occurring in the Gibbous phase, also demonstrates that each of them had learned to give to and serve one another, and that their own needs were met by so doing.

In this life, because he was older, these natural recognitions in him about her situation served to motivate him to help her return to a state of inner harmony—to realign with her inner being. As this progressed, she became more and more attracted to him. Finally, this led to sexual intimacy. Because of his unique psychological and sexual skills, he had the ability to "open" her, and she experienced the depth of her own Soul through the intensity of their emotional/psychological and sexual relationship. By helping her to unlock in this way, he served to help her validate who she actually was. This connection had already been established in a past life, as seen in Jupiter (the ruler of the South Node) being in Aquarius in the Second House, Pluto occupying the Eighth House, and Mars and Saturn being in Scorpio in the Eleventh House. Because her own Mars and Venus are trine Uranus, he helped liberate her from the psychological act of compensation which manifested as trying to appear like everyone else. By unlocking the depths of her sensuality and sexuality, he helped her recover those skipped steps.

She in turn helped him learn to become committed to just one person without having affairs with others. The Virgo Moon squaring the Nodal Axis had the effect of causing guilt linked to such patterns in the past and the resulting desire for atonement. As their relationship unfolded, they both had intentions to make it permanent. He knew that he could accomplish his own life intention in this respect. Yet because of her emotional displacement and neediness due to her difficult childhood, she had the tendency to become too dependent on anyone who would offer such security (Vesta and Ceres in Taurus in the Seventh House).Relative to her Mars, Venus, Sun, and Mercury all being in her Second House, and with Taurus on the Seventh House, which is the ruler of Venus, her Soul's intention is to learn a fundamental self-reliance.

This happy story now has an unhappy ending. Four months after they came together, the man died. Again, the karmic dynamic of the Moon in Virgo in the Ninth House square the Nodal Axis creates a crisis leading to the termination of the relationship, leaving the relationship incomplete. With the Virgo Moon squaring the Nodes, the relationship remains incomplete, yet they will pick it up in another life where they left off—the stated intention is to be monogamous to each other. In addition, it can be argued that he unconsciously sacrificed his life in order for her to learn the essential lesson in self-reliance that her

Soul is desiring—an ultimate act of unconditional love (his South Node conjunct Neptune and Mars in the Eighth House). This event forced her back into herself in a state of enforced self-reliance. Yet she had been awakened and validated. With Mars, Venus, Sun and Mercury in the Second House, it should be clear that one of her major life lessons is self-reliance. This lesson is restated through Vesta and Ceres being in Taurus in the Seventh House.

Even when she was young, she had an extremely close relationship with her brother. They were enmeshed in many ways. When she was eleven years old, he died of leukemia. The shock of this contributed to her inner withdrawal from the family, and forced her to begin learning self-reliance early in her life. This pattern continued into her adult life with the loss of this man who helped her remember her essential nature. His death threw her back into herself again. After this, any time she became too needy or dependent on any subsequent partner some circumstance would occur that would force her back on herself yet again—events such as a trusted partner having sex with someone else. Within this lesson. she is also learning discrimination in terms of who to involve herself with sexually and intimately (Pluto conjunct Uranus in Virgo trine Mars and Venus in Capricorn). This lesson is a reflection of the distant echo of the lifetimes spent as a sacred prostitute. When the Soul intends to learn something, it will learn it through creating and re-creating the necessary circumstances until the lesson is learned!

Chapter Eleven

The Composite Chart
and Pluto

In this chapter, we will be discussing Pluto and the composite chart. The key idea to remember is that the house and sign position of the composite chart Pluto correlates to what the evolutionary intention and the mutual desires of two people were *prior to this life*. As a result, the house and sign position of the composite Pluto will describe not only the recent core dynamics, but also where the relationship was left off, and consequently the point at which the couple picks up and starts their relationship again. The polarity point, by house and sign, that falls 180° from the composite Pluto will correlate to what the current evolutionary intentions or reasons are for the relationship. It defines the ongoing evolutionary development and progression of the relationship.

I will only focus on the natal position of composite Pluto and its polarity point in this chapter. But again, we mustn't make judgments based on isolated factors. For a total analysis and understanding of these intentions to occur, we must also study the South and North Nodes of the Moon by house and sign, and the location of the planetary rulers of these nodes by house and sign. Further details are supplied by analyzing the aspects that these planets and nodes make to other planets, and the houses and signs that these planets are in. Again, the phasal relationship between Mars and Pluto will correlate to how the couple will actualize their current-life evolutionary intentions and achieve the evolutionary transition between the past and the future. The house and sign placement of composite Mars will correlate to the combined subjective will of the couple that manifests as instinctual desires to accomplish the evolutionary intentions reflected in composite Pluto. The aspects that Mars is making to other planets, and the houses and signs that these planets are in, will correlate to additional archetypal dynamics that manifest as subjective desires and will in order to accomplish the purposes of the relationship.

I will identify the core archetypal themes of the composite chart Pluto through the houses and signs, and the relationship's current evolutionary intention as demonstrated in Pluto's polarity point. I will also show how these core themes manifest relative to the consensus, individuated, and spiritual evolutionary states. For most readers studying their own lives, composite Pluto will be in Cancer, Leo, or Virgo. Younger readers will have composite Pluto in Libra, and a very few in Scorpio. Thus composite Pluto is limited to a few signs, but it can be in any house of the composite chart. So the focus of this chapter is on the themes of composite Pluto's house position, as paired with a sign in the natural zodiac.

COMPOSITE PLUTO IN THE FIRST HOUSE OR ARIES

This placement reflects a couple's mutual desire to begin a brand-new cycle of evolutionary development together. It will correlate either to a couple who has come together for the first time in the very recent past, including coming together for the very first time in this life, or to a couple who has been together for a long time, has reached the culmination of an entire evolutionary cycle of development together, and are beginning (or have just begun) a new cycle of development. Because of this evolutionary intention to begin something new, which typifies the Soul's desire to be in a perpetual state of discovery, both partners will be relatively "headstrong" in terms of trying to shape, define, or control what these new directions can or should be. This can lead into Plutonian "power trips" in which each person tries to overpower the other. Each partner will have individual desires that reflect their own need to develop and actualize their independent realities. The potential danger here is one wherein one or both partners attempt to dominate or control the other and the direction of the relationship itself. This can lead to a polarized state wherein each partner ends up living life quite independently. The core challenge, reflected in this new cycle of development together, is to acknowledge the existing limitations (Pluto) of their individual and relationship dynamics, and to move forward together in order to evolve beyond those limitations.

The specific nature of these new directions can be determined by the house and sign of the North Node, the location of its planetary ruler by house, sign, and aspect to other planets; and the signs and houses that these aspected planets occupy. The South Node, the location of its planetary ruler by house and sign, and its aspects to other planets will correlate to what has culminated. In the case of a couple that is coming together for the first time, the South Node will correlate to how their pasts (as symbolized in their own natal South Nodes) have been shared in order to generate a commonality of understanding. The new directions that they intend to actualize through the relationship will be determined by the composite North Node and the location of its planetary ruler by house, sign, and aspects to other planets, and the nature of the houses and signs that those planets occupy.

Composite Pluto in the First House or Aries can also correlate to a couple who has come together in the ways described above, and have not been able to sustain the relationship. This can be a couple who has had some relatively brief, yet intense, encounters reflecting the above intentions. When this is the situation, it will reflect two people whose desires for independent self-discovery or actualization are so strong that, despite the instinctual intensity of their mutual attraction to one another, they can not come together in a shared relationship. In many of these cases, the initial basis of being attracted to one another will reflect a strong and intense sexual attraction. After the initial blaze of sexual fulfillment, they then begin to realize that the sexual dynamic is not enough to sustain a fully committed relationship.

In the Consensus state, composite Pluto in the first House or Aries will correlate to a couple with mutual desires to be "upwardly mobile" within their society. This focus has or will lead them into creating mutual and independent strategies and goals that correlate with gaining power within the system or society. The nature of this power usually means social position and/or money. This focus can become the basis of power struggles within the relationship as each has their own ideas of how to accomplish and actualize this desire. This can also cause a polarization within the relationship wherein each is so motivated and defined by this desire that it precludes any meaningful emotional and psychological interrelatedness with each other. Sex will then typically be used as the only way to connect with one another. In some cases even the sexual dynamic becomes non-existent because of a the emotional and psychological frustration with one another based on the limitation of focusing only on the desire of gaining power within the society.

In the Individuated state, composite Pluto in the First House or Aries will correlate to a couple who has a mutual desire to discover what the possibilities for life can be. The nature of these possibilities are separate from the normal conditioning of what life is, and how it should be lived, according to society. Accordingly, there will be a deep instinctual desire to explore all kinds of new directions together, which can create a strong sense of being on a special adventure with one another. Together they will combine their Soul energies to challenge the status quo of life. This can also create an unsettling effect within the relationship, as it is never really allowed to settle into a structure for too long, because the structure is cyclically or perpetually metamorphosing itself. Both individuals will be strong-willed and headstrong. Each will have their own instinctual feelings, thoughts, ideas, and desires of what these new directions and possibilities can be for the relationship, and for themselves. This can lead to power struggles within the relationship, and to the possibility of polarization because each person may fear being "swallowed up" by the other. If so, this will lead to resentment and a build-up of anger toward one another. Each will begin to project onto one another their beliefs about the other's intentions, motivations, and desires.

The sexual dynamics of this couple will be intense and will reflect the desire to explore new ways to be sexual. Sex as power can also occur when the relationship has degenerated into polarization based on anger towards one another. This can also include with withholding sex from one another or seeking other sexual partners. These dynamics can become the causal factor in separation, and a relationship that is not resolved in karmic or evolutionary terms.

In the Spiritual state, Pluto in the First House or Aries will correlate to a couple who has a mutual desire to independently actualize spiritual reality in their own ways. There will be a Plutonian resistance to following the spiritual ways or systems of anyone else. They will design ways to spiritually actualize the relationship that reflect the individuality of their relationship. These ways will perpetually or cyclically evolve through the metamorphosing nature of Pluto. The process of discovery linked with a new cycle of development demands an openness to allowing these new ways to be explored. Power struggles can occur when one person claims to be more spiritually evolved than the other and attempts to control their spiritual development and direction, and that of the relationship itself. When this occurs, it can lead to a polarized state wherein each person isolates themselves from the other through the nature of their individual spiritual practices. Sexuality can also be a cause of conflict because of the spiritual patriarchal presumption that sexuality undermines spiritual progress or development. A couple in this condition must challenge this presumption in order to resolve this potential conflict. Human beings didn't create the law of sexuality; God did. Thus, to confront the limitation in this presumption means to learn that sexual energy can be used to overcome the limitations of the ego that only identifies with itself, and to access God or divinity through the employment of sacred sexual practices. The challenge is to allow the relationship to spiritually evolve in new ways that operate independently of anyone else, and to allow each other to spiritually evolve in ways that are consistent with their own unique natures.

POLARITY POINT IN THE SEVENTH HOUSE OR LIBRA

Because Pluto in the First House or Aries reflects a couple who is beginning a new cycle of evolutionary development that has begun within the most recent of past lifetimes or is just now beginning for the very first time, it is essential that the couple learn how to listen to one another. Each person must strive to actually hear and understand the other's reality as it exists for them, not to listen and interpret what the other is saying through the subjective filter of their own reality, which then becomes the basis of subjective projections and misunderstandings. Because this is a new evolutionary development, this intention can effectively be actualized in a very basic way. In the beginning of the relationship, this can translate into each person asking the other, "Is this what you mean?" The intention in this polarity point is to create a relationship whose core is defined through absolute equality, role interchangeabilty, and giving to the other instead of always taking. For this to occur, each must learn to listen to the other so that the new directions for the relationship can be created together in equal ways. When this is done, the potential power struggles stemming from individual will are metamorphosed, and the individual will of each changes into a relationship will of both. The couple is now harmonized and working together in order to actualize the intentions and nature of the new cycle of development.

When this is done, an allowance will occur wherein each person will encourage the individual ways, desires, and needs of the other that reflects their own evolutionary requirements to be actualized, instead of feeling threatened by this, which is the causal factor in becoming polarized or creating power struggles with one another. As a result, the couple will now feel that they are working together as an equal and harmonized unit, versus the feeling of working against each other. The couple will have a deep appreciation of one another for the strength of their individual power and overall identity. A deepening of the relationship will evolve that allows for a actualization of all its possible dimensions. The awareness of these fuller dimensions will constitute the ongoing initiation of various possibilities reflected in a variety of life directions, discoveries, and adventures which will lead into a succession of future lifetimes together. These primary evolutionary themes reflected in this polarity point of Pluto will pertain to all the evolutionary states.

COMPOSITE PLUTO IN THE SECOND HOUSE OR TAURUS

The archetypal dynamics that correlate to a couple with composite Pluto in the Second House or Taurus reflects a mutual desire to investigate, question, and define a value system that will create the sense of meaning for their relationship. This desire is also motivated by the couple's need and desire for a core sense of stability within the relationship. In evolutionary terms, a couple with Pluto here will have had some previous lifetimes in which there have been separations from one another for various reasons, and lifetimes in which there has been a lack of basic material sustenance, which affected the very survival of the relationship.

Consequently, the most recent prior lifetimes together have been focused on compensating for these conditions. The desire to stabilize the relationship has focused on defining a value system that would create a real sense of permanency and solidity—to establish that which can not be taken away. Thus, there has been a mutual desire to minimize external dependencies so that the survival of the relationship is guaranteed. Within this, because of the subconscious memories of separation from one another, a couple with Pluto in the Second House or Taurus has compensated for these memories by desiring to possess one another. This has created a situation wherein each partner has projected their need for physical, emotional, and psychological stability on the other. Each person has consequently made the other mean too much. Often, the couple has desired to isolate itself from any potential intrusion or threat from the overall environment.

The survival instinct is extremely intense in such a couple. As a result, they will be highly attuned to conditions or situations that symbolize any potential threat to their relationship and overall life conditions. The desire to protect the relationship, and one another, is very intense. The couple will thus appear highly defensive in their dealings with others. They will be highly selective, and deliberately slow, in terms of letting other people into their carefully protected life.

A component in the survival instinct within all forms of life manifests as the procreational instinct. As a result, a couple with Pluto in Taurus or the Second House will have a very intense and permeating sexual desire for one another which is rooted in the instinct to survive together. They will value sexuality and give it a high degree of meaning within the relationship. Typically, the vehicle of sexuality is used to provide the thread of stability and continuity within their relationship. Sex keeps them grounded and rooted so that no matter what else may be occurring within the relationship and the outside world, their sense of stability is maintained. The sexual relationship that results is typically very intense and permeating, and each partner can be very sexually possessive of the other. Fears of infidelity, and projections based on such fear, will typically haunt the relationship. This reflects the subconscious memories of other lifetimes in which separations have taken place for various reasons.

Potential problems that such a couple could have been recently confronting in the most recent prior lifetimes together, because of the dynamics that have preceded these most recent lifetimes, can include dynamics in which one or the other, or both, has attempted to limit value definitions that correlate to the meaning for the relationship, and life itself. When this occurs between the two people, this can correlate to power struggles wherein one or the other can feel that they are being controlled, manipulated, and limited from exploring other values and meanings that reflect their own need to evolve and grow. When this occurs within the relationship as a unit, a mutual desire to limit the exploration of other values, and the meaning associated with other value systems, an evolutionary condition is produced in which the couple has overly identified with very limited values because of their desire for stability and continuity. The whole sense of meaning for the relationship, and, through extension, life itself, it thus deeply limited to those narrow values. This limitation will thus block necessary growth in evolutionary terms. Over time, this limitation will induce the very effect that the relationship most fears—a loss of meaning for the relationship which will then lead into psychological, emotional, and physical isolation from one another. This will occur because the very nature of the limited values, and the meaning associated with such values, will no longer have any value or meaning. They will have reached a limit—Pluto—in which the need to be defined by those values becomes exhausted. These enforced limitations can also extend into the sexual dynamics, and the value associations linked with sexuality. Pluto in Taurus or the Second House is inherently fixed. Thus, the couple can become stuck or rooted in their ways of being sexual with one another. This can cause "sexual burnout," because the need to evolve the sexual dynamics becomes blocked. When this occurs, the couple may become sexually isolated from one another. The sense of sexual value and meaning that they once held for one another also becomes exhausted. This can become intensely frustrating for such a couple, because both will remain highly sexed as individuals. Isolation from one another through sexual exhaustion or burnout will then typically lead into a situation wherein each is then reduced and limited to compulsive masturbatory activity.

In the Consensus state, composite Pluto in Taurus or the Second House will correlate to a couple with mutual desires that define a value system, and the sense of meaning for the relationship and life itself, exclusively focused on material concerns. As a result, this couple will have an intense focus on material wealth. The desire to amass material possessions will correlate to the sense of stability and continuity that they feel they need. Focusing on how to actualize this desire will constitute the nature of their interpersonal relatedness. It will permeate the nature of their discussions and the ways in which they relate to one another. This desire will limit the nature of their interrelatedness to an intense focus on material acquisitions, ways of achieving this, and ways of maintaining it. The fear that they may lose what they already have will also produce a hoarding effect. An extreme form of such miserliness can manifest as being very wealthy, yet appearing to be very poor in terms of the clothes that are worn, the house that they live in, etc. They will buy the cheapest even when they can afford the best. Even when this is not the case, there will be a typical secretiveness regarding material resources. For others, this dynamic can manifest as "flaunting" their material status, and, within this the possibility of living beyond their material means.

Pluto here can also be an indicator of difficult karma associated with material stability. If the means used to acquire material stability have been manipulative or dishonest in recent prior lifetimes, this couple has or will experience karmic consequences manifesting as a loss of material possessions in some way, or of being relatively blocked from acquiring them in the first place.

Sexually, this will normally be a couple who is limited to the missionary position, in which the sexual act is more or less reduced to just releasing the build-up of energy. This may be intense, yet it is obviously limited. This couple will reflect the sexual values and customs of the society that they are born into, and no more. Some in this condition will transmute the sexual energy through the compulsive focus of material acquisition. Sex as power, control, and domination can also be a subconscious motivation within one or both.

In the Individuated state, this placement will correlate to a couple who has had mutual desires to rebel against the pre-existing values associations, and the meaning that those values connote for the sense of purpose for life itself, of the society that they have been born into. The very nature and purpose of what it means to be in relationship as defined by society will be questioned and rebelled against. This will reflect a couple who desires to define their relationship specifically, and life generally. Accordingly, they will desire to isolate the relationship from the undue and intrusive impact of society generally, and all others who do not reflect or symbolize their own values and ways of living specifically.

This couple will be intensely exclusionary and introverted. The basis for necessary growth and evolution is limited to that which occurs within the relationship. Again, this reflects the fears that result from subconscious memories of separation from one another in other lifetimes, and the need to possess one another as a compensation for these fears. As a result, they have learned that the dynamics of the relationship itself serve as the basis for their necessary growth and metamorphosis. Consequently, inertia can occur wherein they compulsively rely on ways of interrelating that have served and worked well in the past, and resist embracing the necessity of evolving beyond those ways. This can lead to a state of stagnation which can promote or cause alienation and isolation from one another. The couple in this condition creates necessary cycles of confrontation. The intention within this confrontation is to metamorphose the limitations that are reflected in their self-enclosed unit. Within this limitation, however, there will be a high degree of value placed on individual self-discovery and actualization, and an orientation to creative work. Within this evolutionary condition there is an acknowledgment of the necessity of making money, of the desire and need to be physically secure, yet it is not the primary focus. They will do what is necessary to keep the relationship stable in this way, and no more. The danger, again, is for one or both to try to control, limit, or manipulate the individual expansion of values associated with self-discovery of an individuated nature.

When this occurs, power struggles will result as one or the other asserts their own will to do what they feel they need to do.

Sexually, this is a couple who has rebelled against the socially accepted ways of being sexual, and the sexual value associations of society in general. Accordingly, there is a mutual desire to penetrate to the deeper levels or meaning of sexual energy, and to explore its use. There will be a high degree of mutual sexual magnetism and attraction that will manifest as investigating and exploring the deepest ways of being sexual together. This mutual desire and bond will not preclude any way of being sexual together as long as each feels that the other's intentions are real, sincere, and legitimate. Sex is used as a vehicle for keeping the relationship stable and secure, as a means to emotional renewal, and as a way of penetrating the Soul of one another. A mutual desire to be possessed by one another can result from this, because the sense of being possessed equals the feeling of being secure, safe and stable. Sexual compulsion and addiction to one another becomes a potential danger as a result. Using one another as sexual objects relative to each other's specific sexual desires and needs can also occur, although this is not a problem as long as each is honest with the other in terms of where they are "coming from." When such honesty does not occur, then negative sexual karma will be created between them.

For a couple in the Spiritual state, Pluto in the Second House or Taurus will correlate to a desire to embrace spiritual values as a way of creating the sense of meaning and purpose for their relationship, and for life in general. This placement will reflect a couple who has confronted the limitations and emptiness of material values and the types of lives that those values create long before the current life. There will be an essential disdain for such values, even though they will understand the necessity for many people to embrace them. In this evolutionary condition, the couple has already learned to be unconditional in their love for one another, and they have learned to support one another's need to deeply withdraw from the world. Each will be highly internalized, and this internalization will produce a couple who is essentially quiet with one another a great deal of the time, and who have learned to interrelate with one another through such silence. There is a high degree of non-verbal communication wherein each is highly attuned to the vibrational energy of the other.

They have learned that ultimate survival is linked with much larger forces—God—than with any other factor. As a result, this type of couple can live anywhere in the world, in any kind of condition, and still be isolated from it. They do not allow the impact of the environment to disturb the deep center of their spiritual reality, because of a fundamental detachment from the environment reflected in this evolutionary condition. They have learned that the Ultimate Source will supply what they need in order to survive on the material plane, and will have an abiding trust in this fact even though this belief can appear irrational to others.

The essential problem, even in this state of evolution, is one wherein this couple is still too self-enclosed. This reflects a subconscious fear of losing one another, and a fear of letting others get too close to the relationship in such a way that the inner tranquility and peacefulness could be disturbed. Additionally, some in this condition can attempt to limit, control, or manipulate the spiritual growth or direction of one another. At worst, one will claim to be the only valid spiritual teacher for the other. When these conditions exist, the one who is being controlled in this way will progressively withdraw from the relationship. Another condition that can exist is one wherein the couple itself has focused exclusively on one system of spiritual values as being the only way to spiritually evolve. This will produce a spiritual limitation in evolutionary terms. Thus, a necessary spiritual stagnation will occur at some point in which no further spiritual growth can occur. When this occurs, a mutual isolation from one another will follow so that the inner compression produced through such isolation induces new desires, awareness, or thoughts about how to embrace something new so that spiritual growth can proceed.

Sexually, this will reflect a couple that has evolved into embracing sacred sexual values, and the implementation of sacred sexual practices that allow for a mutual penetration of each other's Souls. In this way, they penetrate the inner Divinity of each, and thus access the Ultimate Divinity together. They have learned that the roles of giving and receiving are the same, sexually and otherwise. Sexual compulsion and addiction will have been replaced by a keen attunement with the natural sexual rhythms that exist between them. They will follow these natural rhythms even though the rhythms themselves may be inconsistent. When they fail to mutually correlate, neither one will create a sexual pressure dynamic toward the other. They will simply take care of this need by themselves as necessary. In a very few cases, this evolutionary condition will reflect a couple who have naturally evolved to a state of celibacy together.

POLARITY POINT IN THE EIGHTH HOUSE OR SCORPIO

This polarity point reflects the evolutionary need to confront the nature of any existing limitation that is preventing necessary growth to occur. The nature of such limitations will be found relative to the nature of the value associations that the couple has, and how those values determine not only how they are relating to themselves in the relationship, but how they are relating to the world, and the meaning that they ascribe to life itself. Thus, this polarity point will produce a metamorphosis of value associations and ways of relating through crises that occur at critical junctures. Typically, intense situations or conditions will occur in order to enforce this intent. Sometimes this will require a separation if one partner is so fearful that they attempt to totally control and manipulate the life of the other. Of course, this replays the person's fear of losing the partner all over again. When this occurs, the intensity of the emotional shock will force the affected person to examine why this has happened. Through self-examination of a psychological nature, they will hopefully realize the answer. This polarity point demands, in evolutionary terms, that each person become fully self-empowered, and fundamentally self-sufficient.

In addition, this polarity point requires that the couple open up the relationship. They must learn how to share themselves with other people, and with the world. The specific ways to open up the relationship can be determined in each case by locating the house and sign of the North Node, the location of its planetary ruler by house/sign, and the aspects that it is making to other planets. By learning to open up and share themselves in this way, they will allow the relationship to grow and evolve, and will allow for the intensity of the relationship caused by the deep introversion within it to decrease—to take a breath of fresh air. In this way, the deep fears linked with separation or loss that manifest as a variety of emotional states can be examined and worked with. This is critical, because as long as the couple attempts to remain in an isolated state, these fears and the consequent emotional states that they can produce can become distorted through the compression of isolation. Opening up the relationship according to the placement of the North Node and its planetary ruler will allow for a conscious awareness and appraisal of these fears and the consequent emotional dynamics. In this way, the couple can now face head-on the different issues that these dynamics produce, and hopefully create psychological and emotional strategies to safely deal with them. This will accomplish the demonstrated evolutionary intention, because new value associations will be produced which, in turn, will allow them to relate differently together. In essence, they will no longer need to possess one another, and, as a result, they will be free to simply be together because they want to be. These primary archetypal themes reflected in Pluto's polarity point will apply to all of the natural evolutionary states or conditions.

PLUTO IN THE THIRD HOUSE OR GEMINI

Composite Pluto in the Third House or Gemini correlates to a couple who has had a mutual desire to expand their relationship, to move it forward through rapid growth, and to confront any limitation or blockage that prevents this growth from occurring. Pluto has a direct correlation to the nature of our personal psychology, our deepest emotional dynamics, the nature of our desires, motivations, intentions, and that which constitutes our deepest need for security, consistency, and personal power. Composite Pluto in the Third House or Gemini will thus reflect a couple who has desired to expand their relationship through an intense examination of one another's psychology, motivations, intentions, desires, and emotional needs. This has occurred in the most recent of prior lives together as a reaction to lifetimes before wherein they had reached a limit, and were relating to each other in ways that were no longer conducive to growth. For the relationship to be sustained, there has been a mutual agreement to expand the relationship dynamics through embracing new ways of thinking about life in general, and new ways of understanding the relationship specifically.

There is a dual track that the couple follows to fulfill this intention. On the one hand, there are deep and intense discussions that are directly motivated by the desire to explore and penetrate to the core of each other's emotional psychology—to learn how each is "put together," so to speak. These types of discussion reflect a mental detachment through which each can examine the nature of the other's desires, motivations, needs, etc., and the reasons for these things. A deep and permeating knowledge of each other is progressively gained in this way. On the other hand, this type of discussing ignites the intention to grow and expand on the nature of these pre-existing dynamics, individually and within the relationship, through a mental openness to examining these dynamics through the consideration of different ideas that originate from many different sources and new perspectives.

These two themes interact. Communicating different and new ideas has the resulting effect of igniting the underlying and preexisting emotional/psychological dynamics in each other, and discussing those preexisting dynamics has the effect of stimulating new ways of thinking about those dynamics.

At key points in such discussions, each person will trigger dynamics in the other that reflect where each is most invested in maintaining pre-existing ideas, opinions, or beliefs that serve to justify or rationalize some pre-existing psychological/emotional dynamics—dynamics that are heavily invested in because they constitute personal security, power, and ways of being that are familiar. These dynamics, and the behavioral patterns that they dictate, are the very dynamics that brought the relationship to a standstill in previous lifetimes. It is exactly at these key points that the intention to grow and expand both individually and as a couple is meant to take place. The danger that exists when these core dynamics are triggered is for one or both to feel fundamentally insecure, threatened, and disoriented—to experience a loss of power because these core dynamics are being challenged. The specific danger is one wherein one attempts to manipulate the mental constructions of the other in order to defend and maintain whatever the threatened core dynamics and associated behavioral patterns are. This is done through a Plutonian focusing that can penetrate to the weakest link in whatever the new ideas are that reflect necessary change, or a new perspective reflecting a new way of thinking about that core dynamic. Penetrating to the weak link thus allows for an unraveling of the entire thought structure symbolized in the new idea or perspective. Collapsing the new ideas in this way allows for maintenance of the existing dynamic. Karmically speaking, this can create a situation wherein one or the other, or both, has attempted to control and manipulate the thoughts of the other in order to have some desire or need met which is not being honestly communicated. Pluto in the Third House or Gemini symbolizes the power of persuasion. If the power of persuasion is used to mask a darker agenda that is not being honestly communicated, then negative karma will be produced. If this "brain washing" took place in a prior life, then the partner who was on the receiving end will feel a deep resistance and repulsion toward the other on contact in the current life.

Because of the mutual intention to grow and expand the relationship through igniting the key dynamics that prevented growth in other lifetimes, many topics or subjects of discussion will occur. The couple will reflect a deep curiosity and restlessness to explore all kinds of new ways of thinking symbolized in these various subjects. "What

about this, or what about that, maybe it could be this way or that way"
will be underpinnings in such discussions. The evolutionary condition
of the couple will influence the types of subjects discussed, yet there
will be an openness in all evolutionary conditions to expanding the relationship through new ideas and ways of thinking. Because Pluto is
the origin in all human beings of the natural law of sexuality, sexual
energy, and the desires that emanate from this energy, discussions of
sexuality will pervade all the evolutionary conditions of couples with
composite Pluto in the Third House or Gemini. Generally, there will
be a curiosity and openness to new ways of being sexual, and sexual
energy will be excited between the two people relative to the degree
of mental stimulation that each can feel through the other.

Pluto in the Third House or Gemini can also correlate, in some cases, to a situation wherein the two people have been related before
through being siblings. And in some of these cases the normal sexual
boundaries that exist between siblings have been transgressed, and
there has been sexual contact. For some, this sexual contact has been
consensual. In this case, a deep, permeating sexual relationship has resulted; the nature of this sexual contact being secret from other family members. For others, the sexual contact was not consensual—one
sibling forced the other to be sexual. This situation will reflect an older sibling who has manipulated the mind and emotions of a younger
sibling in order to create a situation of being sexual with them. In some
of these cases, the parents have found out, which then led into a
forced separation between the siblings. In the case where the siblings
mutually consented and had a deep, positive connection to one another in all kinds of ways, including sexually, this forced separation
has created a deep and unresolved pain that will exist between the two
on contact in the next life in which they come together. And they will
come together, because of this unresolved pain and the desire to re-
connect. This reconnecting could occur in the current life (a potential
meaning of the Third House or Gemini composite Pluto), or would
have occurred within the most recent of prior lifetimes.

In the Consensus state, this placement will correlate to a couple
who has had mutual desires to expand their relationship dynamics
through creating all kinds of new experiences that allow for new information and perspectives to occur. The nature of these new experiences in this state can range from going out into all kinds of social
situations such as dancing, movie going, partying, camping, partici-
pating in various sporting activities, to reading various types of books

together that reflect the nature of the human drama. Relative to the consensus state, this will also include the "pop psychology" books that have proliferated in modern times. The importing of new ideas that these types of activities induce constitutes the basis of discussion in which a mutual exchange of ideas takes place that will hopefully allow for a commonality of agreement to occur that serves the intention of opening up the relationship to new experiences and ways of understanding one another.

This can be a particularly challenging situation because, relative to the Consensus state, many culturally held beliefs that are so typically assumed to be "the way it is" will necessarily be confronted through the importation of ideas and information that challenge these assumptions. Within this, the discussions and conversations that are generated as a result of exposing the relationship to so much cultural relativity through the different social interactions that they involve themselves in, and the differences in people that reflect different ways of being, can "trigger" the inner dynamics in each that must be confronted and changed—that which they have been most invested in which has been the previous basis of stifling the growth of the relationship. These triggers can then become the basis of confrontations with one another, arguments, and the potential of "brainwashing" one another through trying to manipulate the thoughts of each—finding the weak link in any given mental construction symbolizing new thinking and perspectives, and collapsing the entire mental construction in order to defend and maintain an existing dynamic that one or the other is afraid to change. If this occurs on a sustained basis, one of two things will happen. Either this will eventually lead to a separation or termination of the relationship, or one or the other, or both, will mentally acquiesce or defer to whatever new thoughts are creating the confrontation, yet inwardly not change whatsoever.

Sexually, this will reflect a couple who is open to investigating new ideas about sexuality because of the need to evolve their relationship in this way as well. Typically, this will manifest through exposing themselves to whatever the current culture is orientated to in a sexual sense. In cultures like ours, this will manifest as all the sexual ideas promoted through magazines like *Playboy, Playgirl, Penthouse,* the *"Joy of Sex"* type sexual manuals, and sometimes pornographic films. Much of this type of material involves "sexual imagery" such as sexual positions, different places to have sex, and sexual clothes. Importing this type of information thus becomes the basis of discussions in which, again, there is an intention to reach a commonality of agreement that allows these types of sexual experiences to take place. The essence of this dynamic is mental stimulation that leads into the physical act. As such, it can be difficult for either partner to feel totally engaged in their bodies because of the overlay of mentality that has been created through importing sexual information and ideas of this kind.

In the Individuated state, this placement will correlate to a couple who has had a mutual desire to confront the existing limitations in their relationship through exposing themselves to an absolute diversity of life experiences. Coming together in relationship will create a "combined soul" that is in an almost perpetual state of restlessness. Their combined energies create an intense restlessness within the relationship that serves to stimulate all kinds of desires that will manifest into a mutual exploration of any area of life that offers new and stimulating information. Investigating a variety of written material that correlates to the "leading edge" of society (in our times this will be the "New Age" type of material), viewing avant-garde movies, engaging in all kinds of social gatherings in which these types of thoughts or information are discussed, traveling in and outside the country of origin in order to understand the relativity of belief and value systems, partying with like-minded people, and physical activities of all kinds will reflect this restlessness.

Exposing themselves to this kind of diversity accomplishes the intention of expanding the dynamics in the relationship. In an individuated state, the couple will be very open to experimenting with many different ways of defining their reality, both individually and within the relationship itself. There is a potential danger in this, however, because a couple in this evolutionary state will have the temptation to adopt ideas and ways of being that emanate from the avant-garde element of society. The issue here is adopting ideas from this element that are not consistent with who they inherently are, or what they actually need. Their search for leading-edge thought can lead them to adopt new ideas, perspectives, and ways of being that work for others but are not right for them.

The reason for this temptation in the individuated state is that this couple has not yet formed from within itself what the new dynamics are, and the ways of being that these new dynamics would create. As a result, there is a temptation to adopt or borrow, to try on, the "consensus" ideas that emanate from the avant-garde edge of society—the "New Agers" of our times, for example. When this occurs, the couple will feel like they have expanded the relationship, and each other, for a time because they are "with it." The wear the right clothes, know the newest and most "hip" words, are defined as being part of the leading edge. Yet, at some point, this will all crash down around them as their individual and combined Soul attempts to realign itself with what is right for them as individuals. What they are truly seeking are new ideas, perspectives, and dynamics that reflect who they are, not what is "correct" from the point of view of the avant-garde element within the consensus society. This issue can be a source of intense disagreement and confrontation between them at various points. Sometimes both will be realigned in this way at the same time, at other times one will feel the need to realign and the other won't. When one does and the other does not, then confrontations and disagreements will occur. This dynamic becomes the vehicle through which the possibility of manipulating and trying to control the thoughts of one another exists.

Sexually, this will correlate to a couple who will intensely investigate sexual ideas, and ways of being sexual, from all over the Earth. Importing information in this way thus stimulates deep conversations about which sexual practices to explore, and which not to. Again, the danger in this evolutionary condition is to adopt ways of being sexual that are not consistent or right for them. As an example, the late 1960s sexual revolution created a heavy orientation to all kinds of new ways of being sexual, including the "open marriage" idea. Many people tried this at the time because it was on the he "leading edge" of society. Yet many who tried this only ended up psychologically and emotionally damaged or destroyed because it was not consistent with their inherent natures. Similarly, a couple in this condition must be very careful in not involving themselves in ways of being sexual that are not right for them. Again, the intensity of sexual mental stimulation through such discussions will lead into the actual sexual act. Sexual imagery plays a large part in this, and produces sexual intensity when the imagery is acted out with one another. Because of the duality of Gemini or the Third House, a couple in this evolutionary condition will also desire to play both sexual roles. At times the man will be either dominant or passive, and at other times the woman will be either dominant or passive. One or both of the partners in this condition will have bisexual desires. When this is the case, these desires must be honestly expressed, and allowed to be acted on. The consequence of not doing so will be sexual secrets, and emotional and psychological dishonesty.

In the Spiritual state, this placement will correlate to a couple that mutually desires to investigate the relativity of spiritual laws, traditions, and practices. This intention has manifested in the most recent of prior lifetimes as a reaction to lifetimes that preceded them—lifetimes in which their spiritual development became blocked or stifled because of a fixed rigidity that was focused within a spiritual system that only allowed them to progress to a certain point. As a result, the couple has desired to confront these limitations and move beyond them through embracing a variety of spiritual practices. In this way, they have been learning that there is no one right way that applies to everyone.

An inherent danger in this condition arises when one or both partners have been avoiding difficult emotional dynamics through escaping into the spiritual dimensions. When this is the case, these unresolved emotional dynamics and issues (Pluto) have been or will become the causal factor in generating not only blockage to real spiritual progress, but also create spiritual "power problems" within the relationship. The nature of these problems is revealed by the unresolved and underlying emotional dynamics. As a result, one or both partners will or can attempt to dictate how to be "spiritual." They will determine the right practice, the time duration of such practice, pick apart the spiritual effort of the other, or present themselves as being more spiritually evolved than the other. In time, this has led or will lead to emotional, psychological, and spiritual isolation from each other wherein the spiritual practices are used as a shield to buffer these types of assaults. The challenge that such a couple faces is to embrace new ways of being spiritual. Specifically, they should orient to a new system or way that emanates from matriarchal spiritual traditions. The reason for this is that the essence of these types of traditions totally involves the emotional and physical bodies as a starting point for the expansion of consciousness.

Another danger that can exist for couples in this evolutionary condition is one wherein they over-expand in their desire to collect so much information about different spiritual practices and traditions. At this point, they become somewhat like a library that is full of all kinds of information. When this occurs, it can become psychologically and spiritually difficult for the couple to decide what new system to commit to that best serves their purposes. Trying this method, and that method, ad infinitum will only produce spiritual fragmentation and a lack of cohesion. When consciousness expands it must have a "base line" to refer the expansion to. Without such a base line, the expanding consciousness can become "spiritually insane." It now hears "voices" from unknown origins that direct the consciousness to do this or that, or supplies "messages" that contain a variety of "teachings" that are irrational by their very nature. Thus, it is imperative for a couple in this evolutionary condition who has Pluto in the composite Third House or Gemini to have a baseline—a specific practice and tradition that is consistently adhered to.

It is also necessary for a couple in this condition to have a commonality reflected in a shared spiritual tradition. This is vital, for it creates a common base line that the couple can refer to consistently. Thus, no matter what issues, problems, or dynamics come up between them, there will be a mutual way to understand and interpret what is occurring. In this way, their solutions will be reflected in the commonality of their shared practices and traditions. When this is not the case, when each person has their own specific practices and traditions that have too much variance from the other, then a common understanding of whatever problems occur does not happen. This will create polarization between them, and serve as the basis of "spiritual power problems" as they battle over who is right and who is wrong. This is interesting when it occurs, because each partner will expound to others in general about the relativity and validity of different spiritual systems, but in their interpersonal dynamics this understanding is rarely extended. For those with a partner who subscribes to a different spiritual system, it is critical to not attempt to change what the other is doing. The challenge then becomes developing a commonality of language in which each totally understands what the other means as understood from within the framework of each other's spiritual language. When this occurs, the couple can live together in great peace, respecting that which constitutes individual differences, which will then allow their Souls to mentally merge. When this occurs, they will realize that there really were not any differences in the first place!

Sexually, a couple in this condition will typically attempt to transcend the sexual impulse through routing the sexual energy in the body into the mental dimension of consciousness in order to expand it—to have mental orgasms of realization! This typically occurs because of the patriarchal spiritual teaching that sexual activity undermines spiritual progress. Since only two percent of the entire world population has evolved into a natural state of celibacy, this enforced "transcendence" can only cause spiritual, emotional, physical, and psychological problems and distortions. Transcendence means suppression for most in this situation, and that which is suppressed becomes distorted. Unless one or both are naturally evolved into a state of celibacy, it is essential that they embrace sacred sexual practices that emanate from either matriarchal or shamanistic spiritual traditions. The intention in these practices is to use sexual energy to expand the consciousness. Typically, the sexual energy in the body for such couples is not constant—it comes and goes at irregular intervals. When it is present, it becomes necessary to acknowledge it as such, and to employ these practices at that time.

POLARITY POINT IN THE NINTH HOUSE OR SAGITTARIUS

The evolutionary intention symbolized in this polarity point is for the couple to understand what really constitutes their "personal truth." This is very critical relative to the couple's ongoing expansion of their relationship dynamics and personal dynamics. The essential orientation of the composite Pluto in the Third House or Gemini is to expand the relationship dynamics through opening up to all kinds of new possibilities that have been stimulated through the importation of information and ideas through social interactions, books, movies, classes, travel, etc. This type of information is of a left-brain nature. With the polarity point in the Ninth House or Sagittarius, it becomes necessary for the couple to shift their focus together to the right brain—the intuitive dynamic within consciousness. This transference allows a deeper level of awareness to occur with respect to all the different possibilities of how to expand the relationship. Thus, instead of operating on a trial-and-error basis, or by experiment, it now becomes necessary to link these different ideas and possibilities with the intuition, which will serve as the "signal" that "informs" the couple about which possibilities to act on, and which not to. The intuitive element in our consciousness simply knows what it knows without necessarily knowing why it knows what it knows. Thus, these signals will not be long, drawn-out intellectual constructions. The signal will simply register itself within the consciousness as a "knowingness"—the idea simply feels right or wrong. To allow this shift in consciousness to occur will allow the couple to be in consistent alignment with their combined "truth" with respect to what to act on, and what not to. The couple will learn the difference between response and reaction—a response is a considered action, whereas a reaction is an action taken without real consideration. Astrologically speaking, the polarity point of Pluto by house/sign, the location of the North Node by house/sign, the location of the North Node's planetary ruler by house/sign and aspects to other planets, and the houses/signs that these planets are in, will correlate to the ways to naturally expand "personal truth" for each relationship.

In addition, this polarity point must be invoked in situations where, in the context of discussion about new ways to grow and evolve, one or both partners has key dynamics "triggered" that promote resistance to the possibility that is being discussed.In turn, this resistance can create the dynamic where one attempts to control or manipulate the thoughts of the other in order to sustain the existing dynamic. The key when this occurs is to stop this type of interpersonal communication, and to take a "time out." In this context, it is then essential that the one who is having a defensive reaction learn how to allow the intuition to provide realizations that provide an awareness as to what the underlying resistance is about. Intuition is not an analytical process. The way to access the intuition in this way is to simply pose a question (i.e., what is this resistance about), and then to allow the intuition to provide the answer of its own volition. The answer will simply surface into awareness at the appropriate time by and of itself. If both partners can manifest the courage and honesty to do this, it will lead to maximum growth for each individual, and maximum growth for the relationship that is now aligned with the "truth" of their relationship. The archetypal themes reflected in this polarity point will apply to all the evolutionary conditions.

PLUTO IN THE FOURTH HOUSE OR CANCER

Composite Pluto in the Fourth House or Cancer will correlate to a couple who has had a mutual desire to create a tightly structured reality through which to feel safe and secure. These types of desires are a reaction to prior lifetimes in which various kinds of circumstances or interpersonal dynamics have occurred which caused great emotional upheavals. This would include separation from one another, either through forces that were beyond their control, or because of problems between them that lead to the necessity of separation, even though neither one really wanted to separate. The specific causes leading to separation can be determined in each case by examining the conditions symbolized by the house and sign of the composite Pluto, stressful aspects that it may be making to other planets and the houses and signs of those planets, the location of the South Node by house and sign, and the placement of its planetary ruler by house and sign. Examine closely the stressful aspects that the South Node is making to other planets, and the stressful aspects that its planetary ruler is making to other planets.

Whatever the conditions may be, a couple with a composite Pluto in the Fourth House or Cancer will be deeply insecure because of the separations in prior lifetimes. There can be an intense fear of being threatened by external forces, or of suddenly being left by the partner. This fear, and the reaction to it, has been a causal factor in creating different situations within the relationship, and reactions to the external environment. Within the most recent of past lifetimes, the reaction to those separations has been to secure the relationship. For example, within the relationship one may have attempted to emotionally control and manipulate the other. The forms of such control and manipulation can range from creating emotional and psychological conditions wherein one is made to feel absolutely dependent on the other, to creating conditions of psychological and emotional terror and fear wherein one or the other is afraid to leave, to creating a mutual situation wherein each compulsively focuses on the existing emotional wounds of the other in such a way as to create a de facto parental dynamic, to a situation in which each alternates between the roles of helper and helped. This effectively maintains not only mutual dependency, but also the wounds which neither one really wants to heal. Either partner could also use emotional withdrawal as a way of inducing insecurity in the other in order to emotionally manipulate them into meeting their needs.

The reaction to the external environment, relative to this underlying insecurity, has been to close off the relationship as much as possible from the impact of anyone, or anything, that could pose any potential threat. In combination, these reactions within the relationship and to the external environment have produced a situation of intense psychological and emotional proximity to one another. The intensity of proximity has created a high degree of emotional compression within the relationship. This emotional compression has produced cycles of silent internalization together, and cycles of emotional interaction that can range from total togetherness to total emotional explosions of a confrontational nature. Excessive proximity has created psychological and emotional distortions, and a lack of "breathing room." As a result, each can harbor anger relative to the feeling of being restricted in their personal development. Each can blame the other without ever realizing that both have had a simultaneous need to keep the relationship close and proximate, but also to step outside the relationship in order to engage in independent activity. These dual desires or needs have created an emotional paradox within the relationship. Without realizing that this paradox originates from within, each partner blames the other for their own feelings of being contained and restricted.

The inherent danger with composite Pluto in the Fourth House or Cancer is one wherein the couple keeps re-creating conditions that are echoes, remnants, and reflections of other lifetimes in which the separations took place. The fear of separation can be so strong, and the issues in past lifetimes so unresolved, that the couple keeps unconsciously projecting those conditions into the current life. In this way, forever living in the past, they effectively keep re-creating the very conditions that produced the fears of loss in the first place. Thus, the relationship cannot ever feel secure and safe. Even during the cycles in which the relationship does feel close, safe, and secure, the unconscious fear that this condition may end creates conditions that lead to intense insecurity. This syndrome represents the ever-shifting rug under the feet of the relationship, so to speak.

Amazingly enough, these ever-shifting emotional cycles are intentional from an evolutionary point of view. The evolutionary intention symbolized by Pluto in the composite Fourth House or Cancer is for the couple to penetrate together to the very causes of their different emotional dynamics and states, both as a couple and as individuals. This correlates to their desire for self-knowledge at an emotional level and for the knowledge of the emotional basis of their fears for the relationship. The key is to create a conscious intention to focus on the causes for the different emotional states or dynamics, and not to become simply become engulfed and lost in those emotions. The additional challenge contained in composite Pluto in the Fourth House or Cancer has been for each of them to create conditions of developing a state of inner security with each other as individuals. This intention can be very hard to consciously understand, because most people on Earth generally project their security needs outside of themselves, forming dependencies of all kinds. Yet until such a couple grasps and understands this intention, the projection on one another to get their security needs met will persist in the ways that we have been discussing.

The intention to penetrate to the causes of the different emotional states that manifest individually and within the relationship can cause either or both to take the role of a psychological interrogator. The person in this role will attempt to penetrate and demand explanations for whatever the other has or has not done—"Why did you do this, why did you do that, what was the reason for this or that, what were your motives or intentions for this or that," and so on. This can create a situation wherein the interrogated partner feels like they are being emotionally and psychologically raped. What motivates this type of behavior is the fear of emotional dishonesty, the fear of trust, and the need to be the "one and only" to the other—the most important person ever in the other's life.

Pluto in the composite Fourth House or Cancer can also correlate to a couple who, in evolutionary terms, has just recently switched gender roles. Previously, the man had been the woman and the woman had been the man. This can create its own unique set of emotional and psychological dynamics. Since the woman had been the man, and the man had been the woman, each of them will have memories to this effect at a subconscious level. As a result, both of them can psychologically and emotionally operate within those old gender roles. The man will be essentially operating through the female emotional psychology, and the woman through the male emotional psychology. When this is the observed situation, the evolutionary reason is to evolve the relationship forward, since they had reached an evolutionary limit to further growth in the old roles. In addition, it will correlate to the evolutionary need in each of them as individuals, and through the relationship dynamics, to begin the process of consciously integrating the inner female and male into a state of equal balance and actualization. Negatively, this switching can produce all kinds of emotional and psychological power plays involving who is going to control who, and/or who is going to be the "boss" within the relationship. It can also create a profound confusion with respect to the roles of giving and receiving.

In the Consensus state, this placement will correlate to a couple that has desired to secure the relationship through the creation of home and family in the most recent of prior lifetimes. The intention to do so will occur on contact with one another as a reaction to their subconscious memories of separation that preceded the most recent lifetimes together. All too often, such a couple experiences a high degree of interference from one or both sets of parents, who issue one judgment after another toward the relationship, and toward each individual person. Such parents are also highly insecure, and the compensation for this insecurity is to try and control the two people and their relationship through the use of negative and critical judgments. The unconscious motivation in this has been to try and drive a wedge between the two so as to maintain a primary orientation to the parents. By allowing this wedge to occur, each partner would have become progressively isolated from the other on an emotional and psychological basis. Over time, this isolation would become the causal factor generating separation.

Thus, the most recent reaction to this has been to secure the relationship through the creation of home and family, so that the symbolic nature of home and family equaled permanency, consistency, and continuity. Yet each will have subconscious memories of not being understood by the other because of projections that each made on the other that were extensions of the judgments of the parents. These memories can create an unconscious fear of the same thing happening again, which, in turn, can lead to the effect of emotionally hiding from one another even though they feel intensely drawn and attracted. When this occurs, they will then relate emotionally to each through their own children, instead of directly interfacing with one another. The displaced anger from other lifetimes can then be triggered relative to how the children should or should not be raised, or other parental disagreements which are used as a vehicle to work out the unresolved emotions with one another. Some in this condition will resist having children together because of the nature of their own childhoods.

For a couple in the Consensus state, the roles within the relationship will be more or less fixed because of the nature of current cultural conditioning. The man will be the man, and the woman will be the the woman, as defined by the prevailing social norms. This creates additional isolation, because they are not allowed to go beyond the boundaries of the roles. These sexually stereotyped roles can also be used to hide behind. It is essential that this type of couple learn how to create situations wherein they can relate to each other openly on a one-to-one basis, and in so doing relate a pure expression of the emotional dynamics that each needs to openly discuss with one another. They must learn how to confess to one another their deepest fears, feelings, needs, desires, and the causes of their anger toward one another without fearing more negative judgment. This results in emotional and psychological self-knowledge of each other, and thus creates the awareness of the dynamics within their relationship as a result. In the last analysis, this is the actual intention for the relationship, and the reason they came together in the first place.

Sexually, this placement will correlate to a couple who has been, and will be, quite conventional in their sexual relationship, allowing the nature of their sexual relations to be defined by the society that they are in. This can also be a situation wherein they stop being sexual with one another at a certain point within the relationship—usually when the last child has been born. This is a reaction to emotional isolation, if each feels that their emotional and psychological needs are not being fulfilled through the other. In the worst of cases, this can correlate to one or the other (usually the man) using sex as a form of acting out rage and anger. Thus, sexual power is used to humiliate, subjugate, or actually hurt the partner.

In the Individuated state, this placement will correlate to a couple who has had an intense desire to merge on an emotional and psychological level, as a reaction to the subconscious memories of separation in other lifetimes. The desire to merge in this way is a reaction to the fears of separation, and will lead into an almost total need to "hang on" to one another at all times. The intensity of proximity that this produces induces incredibly intense emotional dynamics to occur between them in which each can feel as if they are being swallowed up by one another. Confrontations occur at key and regular intervals as a result, and in time produce an intense degree of personal knowledge. Both will have a keen interest in psychological knowledge of a humanistic (as opposed to clinical or behavioral) nature. As a result, there is a deep temptation to psychoanalyze each other to tears. All too often, the nature of this analysis reflects the projections of their own unresolved emotional dynamics as individuals. They will project judgments about each other's intentions, motivations, desires, and agendas. Back and forth the projections fly until each individual begins to own and take responsibility for their own reality. Because of being in the individuated state, the nature of which is to rebel against external authority in order to individualize from the consensus, the causes of separation in other lifetimes is typically based on the rebellion that occurred when one attempted to overly control or manipulate the individual development and needs of the other. This creates the subconscious memory or feeling in which each will feel that they have been abandoned by the other. The problem was never one at a Soul level, because the Souls loved each other dearly, and want to be together. The problem was the inability to accept individual differences at a personality level, since those differences were perceived as threatening to the relationship. This was the basis of the need to control or manipulate, judge, or put down the individual needs of each. These memories only fuel and intensify the mutual projections, as well as fueling the need to merge as a safeguard against another separation.

In this evolutionary condition, each will have to be born into families in which neither one was understood or nurtured by their parents. As a result, each will have feelings of being rejected or disdained by their parents in some way. These displaced emotions of childhood become "acted out" via yet more projections onto the partner. In the individuated state, there will still be a strong need to "nest"—to create a home and family. Yet, because of the individuated state, they will desire to raise their children in exactly the opposite way that they themselves were raised. They will be totally emotionally present and available to their children, and encourage the actualization of the individuality that is inherent to each. In this way, they will subconsciously heal their own childhoods by raising their children in the ways that they wanted to be raised. This is a good thing, and will actually have a maturing effect in their own emotional and psychological interactions over time. The couple will rebel against traditional roles of gender assignment, and will more or less attempt to raise their children equally through role interchangeability. They will be fiercely protective of not only their children, but of the relationship itself. Not too many others will actually know what is taking place within the inner sanctum of their relationship.

Sexually, this placement can correlate to a couple who uses sex as a form of emotional control, and as a way of expressing unresolved anger. On the other hand, there is such a strong desire to merge emotionally and psychologically that the sexual union that does occur will be very intense—the sexual energy will be intensified through and because of the emotional energy. Many will have the subconscious desire to be in the other person, so to speak, as is they can never be close enough. This desire reflects the need in each to "return to the womb"— the source of maximum security and safety. There will be a rebellion against the sexual conventions of the current culture, and a desire and need to experiment with different ways of being sexual. For many, there will be a deep fascination and/or attraction to anal sex and oral sex. There is also a deep need to be held and touched, and to sleep together in ways that the bodies are always entwined in some way. Massage, including sexual massage, are strong needs in each because both will have needs for sexual healing in some way. Coming together sexually serves as a vehicle for emotional and Soul renewal. Some will use sexuality as a way of healing the emotional rifts and difficulties that occur.

In the Spiritual state, this placement will typically correlate to a couple that has unresolved emotional dynamics as individuals, and together. For any of us to move toward spiritual life and reality, we must undergo a progressive surfacing of all the impurities within us. Thus, in this condition such a couple will necessarily have a surfacing of all the unresolved emotions. This can create real turmoil for each of them, and for their relationship. This turmoil is caused by cycles in which their life together, and as individuals, seems very calm, peaceful, harmonious, and spiritualized. Then comes the cycle in which the unresolved emotions surface in varying degrees of intensity. These emotions are caused by deep insecurities in each of them, and between them. In evolutionary terms, they are in the process of progressively disengaging from all external dependencies, including their mutual dependency on one another. This can create fear in each at various points because of the emotional fear that "they don't need me anymore." The cyclic surfacing of these emotions can overwhelm and pollute the emotional, psychological, and spiritual atmosphere of good feelings between the two. The surfacing and projection of these emotional fears and insecurities will be quite childlike in essence. The challenge and the key for such a couple is to interpret correctly why this is occurring, and to realize that this is a natural consequence in spiritual development. Maintaining this perspective will allow them to not take that which is projected too personally. Responding in this way will allow for a progressive working through and resolution of these unresolved emotions. The worst that could happen is for one or the other or both to feel that these emotional projections are undermining their spiritual growth. This will lead to polarization, and possible separation. This can occur when one or the other fails to understand that these emotions must surface as a consequence of spiritual development. In essence, these emotions surface because there is a transference between the external home and the inner home of God.

The highest level of this stage of evolution will reflect a couple that has desired to create security together through a common commitment to the "inner home"—a commitment to God. As a result, the very structure through which they actualize and establish their relationship will be a total structure of reality that is defined by their mutual commitment to God and spiritual living. They have learned as a reaction to memories of separation that the only real security, that which cannot be taken away, is that which is found within. As such, they have learned to trust God as the ultimate parent, a parent who is ever loving and providing for what they need. Trusting this, the intensity based in the fear of separation has now almost totally dissolved. Inwardly, their desire to be together is beyond question. Yet if this does come about, they know that it is only a physical separation, not a separation of their Soul or spirit.

In evolutionary terms, this placement will correlate to a couple who has been together a long time, and has experienced a tremendous amount of life experience together—they have been through a lot. As a result, they will have a deep degree of emotional wisdom together, and as individuals. They will have a deep degree of "knowingness" of one another, and because of this they will exhibit an unconditional acceptance and love of one another. They will be simultaneously male and female together, the relationship evolving into a natural state of androgyny. Even when residual emotions linked with insecurity or fear do surface (which they can even in this state), they will have a way of gently letting such emotions move through one another while at the same time sustaining the spiritual and emotional awareness and understanding which allows for resolution of whatever the specific emotion is.

Spiritually, they will both be attracted to emotional forms of spirituality that are experiential and provable. In this condition, there will still be a need to isolate the relationship from the undue impact of the external environment. This, again, is a reaction to the separations that have occurred in other lifetimes. Thus, even though they manifest the understanding that God is in control of their lives, and that they can not really be separated anyway, the desire to be together in flesh and blood leads to this desire to isolate the relationship as much as possible anyway. Some will have families, and some will not. For those that do, they will raise their children in a spiritual atmosphere, yet allow for the independent development of each child according to the individual needs and realities of each. The love will be constant and unconditional no matter what occurs in their children's life.

Sexually, some such couples will desire to make love to each other's Souls and, through extension, to God. Others will have no need to have sex at all, or quite irregularly. The primary orientation will be to touching and holding, and allowing the sexual act to be very gentle, yet deep. Eye contact will be constant and sustained.

POLARITY POINT IN THE TENTH HOUSE OR CAPRICORN

The archetypal themes that correlate to the evolutionary intention symbolized in Pluto's polarity point of the Tenth House or Capricorn are linked with the need for the couple to emotionally mature together, and as individuals. Within this intention, the evolutionary need is for each of them to accept responsibility for their own actions, and to learn how to be responsible to one another—to own their emotional dynamics versus compulsively projecting onto one another. Within this, there is a need for each of them to become emotionally secure from within themselves, and on their own terms.

Additionally, it is vital that they only allow other people, including parents, into their lives who are supportive and accepting. In the case of parents who cannot or will not be, then this requires a total cutting off of that relationship. In time, the parents, in most cases, will become responsible for their own actions, which will then allow for significant change in how they are interacting with the couple. In this way, they will learn to open the doors of their relationship, instead of keeping the doors shut because of a fear that others will interfere with and threaten the relationship.

For those in the highest spiritual condition, the only real adjustment necessary is to open up the relationship to other people whom the couple can directly benefit relative to their emotional, psychological, and spiritual wisdom. For those who are evolving toward that condition, it is vital to sustain an absolute determination to remain rooted in their spiritual life even as the impurities reflected in various emotions surface. It is essential that they realize that the impurities reflected in various emotions will and must surface. It is essential that they realize that the relative lack of emotional caring and nurturing in their life was intended by their own Soul, so that the realization of what constitutes real nurturing that is everlasting could occur through connection to the Divine Source of nurturing and sustenance—God. Within these realizations, each partner can own their own state of being versus indulging the temptation to project onto the other the reasons for their deep insecurities.

PLUTO IN THE FIFTH HOUSE OR LEO

The deepest and most active archetype with Pluto in the composite Fifth House or Leo is one of creative self-actualization of the purposes and reasons for the relationship. This placement will correlate to a couple who has had a mutual desire to focus on the reasons and purposes that have brought them together, and to actualize those reasons and purposes as fully as possible. The purposes and reasons for the relationship can be determined through the polarity point of Pluto and the aspects that it is making to other planets, the placement of the North and South Nodes by house and sign, the placement of the planetary rulers by house and sign placement, and the aspects that these planets are making to other planets within the composite chart. This is true in all composite charts, but a couple with the composite Pluto

in Leo or the Fifth House will have combined desires to specifically focus on these purposes and reasons in order to consciously actualize
them in the fullest possible way.

Through this focus, the couple creates a deep sense of the power
of purpose. Within the overall purpose for the relationship, each partner will also have strong desires and needs for individual creative actualization of their own purposes. Thus, each partner will also be very
strong-willed and inwardly directed to actualize their own life purposes within the context of the relationship. Because of this, each partner will help the other in varying degrees to focus on what those purposes are, and to provide positive motivation in the actualization of
those purposes. As each is able to actualize those purposes, the relationship gains ever-deeper degrees of power and purpose. This dual
focus of individual creative self-actualization and the creative actualization of the purposes and reasons for the relationship creates a deep
sense of "specialness" within the relationship.

This is quite interesting in evolutionary terms, because it commonly reflects two people who have felt deeply insecure and powerless in relatively recent prior lifetimes. In the most recent of prior lifetimes, each has had the desire and need to discover and actualize
personal power through creative self-actualization of their individual
purposes as a reaction to those other lives. Through the formation of
a relationship, each has helped the other to self-actualize, which, in
turn, has empowered the relationship to focus on and actualize its purpose. In other words, through the creation of the relationship each has
found it easier to actualize their own individual purposes and reasons
for being. The relationship has thus generated not only the sense of
personal power, but also inner security.

Because each has had an evolutionary need to counteract the lifetimes of feeling powerless and insecure, each will have a desire and
need for the other to provide support for each of their efforts relative
to self-development. Encouragement and positive feedback will create
and re-create the need and desire for security and personal power.
This desire and need can be quite compulsive because of the depth of
insecurity that exists in each of them. The depth of the compulsion can
be such that it can create real power struggles in the relationship regarding who is more important, whose needs are more intense, and,
as a result, whose will is going to dominate. Just as the Sun is the center of our solar system, composite Pluto in Leo or the Fifth House can
create a situation in which each partner feels that they are the center

of the relationship. And just as all the planets revolve around the Sun, each partner can feel that the relationship revolves around them—that the relationship is only there to support their own specific purposes and overall life needs. When this is the operative dynamic, confrontations will occur in order to create the realization that each is as special as the other, and that each partner's needs for self-empowerment, self-actualization, and validation are equally important and valuable.

When such equanimity does not occur, one or the other may seek out other people to become involved with in order to have these core needs met. In recent prior lifetimes, many such couples have experienced the emotional shock resulting from such liaisons. When this has been the case, or becomes the case in this life, this type of emotional and psychological shock is intended to break up a self-centered egocentric complex. Even though this is the intention of such a situation, the typical reaction on an egocentric level is to feel crushed and "deflated"—the air is removed from the egocentric balloon of self-importance. Instead of realizing the reason for this turn of events—that the partner also has a desire and need to feel just as important and special as the other, that their needs and desires are just as real and important as the others—the one who has been "cheated" on in this way will typically become enraged because they are suddenly not as important or special as they thought. Unless they are prepared to look deeply into the reason for this situation, and make the necessary adjustments, the typical reaction is to become vindictive. Accordingly, they now seek out another person for themselves in order to regain their sense of personal power, and/or they could become emotionally, psychologically, or physically violent in order to humiliate, hurt, and redominate the other person.

Because of these types of dynamics, many couples with Pluto in the composite Fifth House or Leo have karmically unresolved issues with one another, and relationships that have not been completed. A common unresolved issue, and the karma that can be produced from such an issue, concerns children. Because many such couples have separated from one another in recent lifetimes, a power struggle over who would keep the children has also occurred. Rarely are the children's desires taken into account in such a struggle. The problem here is one wherein each partner feels that the children are extensions of themselves. This is why so many couples who have Pluto in the Fifth House or Leo have children together in the current life who have been part of their lives in other lifetimes—there is an unresolved karma with them too, as well as the dynamic of relationships that have not been completed. This is also why, in our times, so many men and women find themselves becoming stepparents to someone else's biological child. The karmic need to recover incomplete relationships with children they had in other lifetimes is being fulfilled in this way. Accordingly, stepchildren who are not specifically biologically linked to them will still feel like their own children anyway.

With composite Pluto in the Fifth House or Leo, the relationship can reflect a form of narcissism wherein the couple is essentially living for itself alone and excluding anything or anyone that does not support the purposes for the relationship. On the one hand, this is quite necessary because of the evolutionary intention and need to re-empower one another through the relationship. On the other hand, it can be quite limiting in the sense that each of us has limits—none of us reflects the totality of the universe. Thus, this exclusive focus will limit not only the growth of the relationship, but also the individual growth of each partner.

In the Consensus state, this placement will symbolize a couple who has a strong sense of purpose for being together as reflected in the overall signature in their composite chart. The overall purpose and reasons for the relationship will be actualized within the framework of the existing societies that they have recently been in, and are in now. At best, they will serve to support the development of one another's sense of personal purpose for their individual lives. Thus, they create a commonality of shared purpose wherein they can interrelate and interact in meaningful ways. This will almost always include the common purpose of raising children together in which they focus together on what is best for the children's individual development and needs. At worst, it will produce a situation of mutual polarization wherein each is subconsciously competing with one another to prove who is more powerful, special, worthy, and important. This wedge of polarization creates a situation wherein each feels that they are not being recognized or appreciated for who they are. These needs will then be met elsewhere or with others in a variety of ways, which only adds to the polarization. This can become a causal factor leading to "affairs," or seeking out other circumstances in which their need for recognition and validation can occur.

Each will be quite highly sexed, and there will be a high degree of sexual magnetism between them. The sexual conventions of society will be adhered to, yet there will be an element of creativity within the actualization of those conventions. Sexual union becomes a common ground on which each can meet and give to the other the power of their own Souls, and to feel and actualize the power within each partner. It is necessary that each is made to feel special to the other in this way, and sexual fidelity is an important part of this. When other factors in the relationship create a wedge of polarization, the temptation to "flirt" with and become involved with another can occur. Withholding sex as an act of psychological and emotional control reflects the need to be acknowledged, and can also result when such acknowledgment does not occur in other ways. It can also occur when one partner wants to do something sexually creative and the other does not. This creates resentment in the one who wants to do something sexually creative. This will then manifest as either withholding sex, seeking out another who will fulfill the desire, or both.

In the Individuated state, this placement will correlate to a couple who has desired to creatively actualize the purposes and reasons for their relationship in any way that they deem necessary. They desire to be in total control of their relationship and individual destiny. They will be fundamentally resistant to anyone or anything telling them how to go about actualizing themselves or their relationship. They will have a high degree of purpose for being together, and a high degree of purpose for their individual lives. The archetype of creativity will be highly emphasized within their relationship as it applies to actualizing the specific purposes and reason for it, as symbolized in the totality of their composite chart. Each can be highly supportive and giving to the other as long as each feels this is reciprocal. Under such conditions, the level of love and commitment to each other is very intense. Each helps the other discover and actualize their own power and purpose in very creative and unique ways. There can also be a high degree of self-pleasuring within the relationship, with each encompassing all kinds of activities that correlate with pleasure. The shared purpose of raising children can be strong, and both will focus on the individual and creative needs of their children.

At worst, one will attempt to control and manipulate the development of the other as a way of appearing more important, evolved, and special within the relationship. Over time, this will produce the seeds of rebellion in the one who is being controlled, and seeking out another who will supply the unresolved need for independence is a typical outcome. When this is the dynamic, the controlling partner can also feel displaced and threatened by the children. This is because they feel that the children have usurped their position as "center of the universe" in the attentions of their partner. This in turn can create real power problems in raising the children in particular, and within their relationship in general.

They will feel a high degree of sexual magnetism toward one another. The energy exchanged in their sexual union will be intense and permeating. The sexual dynamics will be creatively actualized in ways that seem natural to them, though often outside "the norm"—a rebellion against the sexual conventions of the existing society ignites the desire for sexual creativity. Metamorphosis of emotional, psychological, and egocentric limitations can occur through such a sexual union. Emotional and psychological renewal of themselves and the relationship takes place in this way. Sex as pure pleasure can occur. Sexual fidelity is a lesson they are learning together, and each will experience external "temptations" as a result. It is essential that sexual fidelity be sustained, because each has a need to be the most special and important person to the other. When this is transgressed, it can be extremely difficult to repair the wound produced.

In the Spiritual state, this placement will correlate to a couple who desires to understand together the nature of the Creation, and their cosmic role within the Creation. They will desire to understand the spiritual purposes and reasons for their relationship. Those purposes and reasons are determined by the overall signature in the composite chart. As individuals, they will both understand that they have a specific role and purpose to fulfill. Each will encourage the other through consistent encouragement and positive motivation to develop those roles and purposes. They will desire to understand together the long evolutionary trail and story of the many lifetimes that have brought them together. Their Souls will be highly magnetized together, and there will be a mutual desire to merge their Souls—not in the sense of extinguishing each other, but in the sense osmosing each other's power and strengths so that each individual becomes stronger, more self-actualized, and empowered through creating a combined will. In this state, personal will and personal creativity are linked with Divine Will and Divine creativity. Thus, the merging of will is motivated by the desire to access Divine Will together. They will mutually desire to be in attunement with this Higher Will, and, in this way, come to understand the spiritual basis, reasons, and purposes for the relationship. As a result of these mutual desires, they will both be able to focus on the necessity of examining the nature of all their unresolved emotional and psychological wounds. They will understand that for spiritual progress to take place, they will have to examine and heal those wounds. They will be able to sustain their perspective on the reason for, and nature of, those wounds, instead of becoming lost and consumed in them. Each will desire and attempt to heal the wounds of the other, and to create a form of emotional communion wherein the nature of the words and feedback have the effect of rebuilding each other into a positive state.

Sexually, this condition will correlate to a couple who desires to embrace sacred sexual methods that are not only used to heal emotional and sexual wounds, but are also employed to access the inner Divinity—and, through extension, the ultimate Divinity. A focus on those intentions produces deep pleasure for each at a Soul, emotional, and body level. The sexual magnetism that they feel toward one another is based on the magnetism they feel toward each other's Soul. Each will be deep givers in this way, and through giving they discover that their own need to be given to is met. The deep, profound sexual energy that is exchanged produces Soul renewal for each, and a vitality in their overall life force. The sexual/Soul energy is constant and is used for these purposes, just as meditation and other spiritual methods or practices are used to facilitate the ongoing spiritualization of their consciousness.

POLARITY POINT IN THE ELEVENTH HOUSE OR AQUARIUS

The archetypal themes reflected in this polarity point involve the necessity of understanding the larger social and planetary context that the relationship exists within. This means that the couple must resist having a narcissistic orientation to the relationship, only focusing on the specific purposes and reasons for its existence. It must strive to develop a larger awareness of the overall social context and conditions that the relationship exists within. As a result, this will change the orientation of the relationship from using the resources of the existing society as a means to actualize the overall purposes of the relationship to a state wherein the couple attempts to contribute to the needs of the existing society in some way.

Within this intention is the need to allow each other to develop and actualize their own specific individual needs, purposes, and desires as each deems necessary, and to allow for an involvement in any experience or activity that takes place outside of the relationship. This in turn requires the development of a totally objective awareness of one another that is free from subjective assertions of what each may feel that the other needs to do, and from attempts to control the other, which is motivated by a fear that they will no longer be the center of the other's universe. To develop this objective awareness requires discussion and emotional communion wherein each can present what they desire to do, and why, in calm and objective ways. The key is to do this in a way that disarms the other's fear of not being important enough, or special enough to the other. In this way, they will learn to become friends within the intensity of their Soul connection. This is especially important for those couples who find that one of the partners compulsively needs to present him or herself as more important, more special, and attempts to have the whole relationship support and revolve around that delusion.

In the spiritual condition, the only real requirement is to give back to others specifically, and the overall conditions of the planet generally, whatever constitutes the essence of their spiritual purpose as individuals, and the spiritual purpose for the relationship. This will require a specific structure and form to manifest through. Many such couples in our times have desires to start various "centers" to this end. A "center" is a consolidation of energy that is magnetized because of the consolidation. Thus, in our times these centers are proliferating all over the planet because so many couples in this condition have Pluto in Leo as individuals, and thus in their composite charts. This is a good sign because of the progressive movement towards or into the Aquarian age. Such centers are necessary, for they offer new ways of being that demand a liberation (Aquarius) from all the pre-existing conditioning patterns of the prevailing Piscean Age. Thus, they operate as "seed centers" in which new ideas are gestating that reflect the need to embrace new ways of being, and new paradigms allowing for a total redefinition of what is considered to be "reality." Couples in this condition have the evolutionary challenge to assist this process by offering themselves to those who would benefit in some way.

PLUTO IN THE SIXTH HOUSE OR VIRGO

Pluto in the composite Sixth House or Virgo is one of the most problematic and complex positions for Pluto to be in. As with Pluto in Leo, Cancer, and Libra, there are millions of people on the planet today who are in relationship with this signature. Essentially, it symbolizes a variety of archetypes reflected in the mutual desires of the Souls that come together in an intimate relationship with this symbol. These mutual desires span the range from having mutual desires for self-improvement to helping each other heal a variety of cumulative wounds. Pluto here emphasizes egocentric self-sacrifice to the other and the relationship. It also correlates to the difficult crisis situations in other lifetimes. Pluto in Virgo or the Sixth House can also correlate to a situation wherein one or the other has created massive crisis of a psychological and emotional nature to the other. When this is the case, when one or the other has created massive emotional or psychological wounds, this symbolizes the archetype of a sadomasochistic pathology. This is the most dark dimension of the composite Pluto in Virgo or the Sixth House. This dimension reflects a situation wherein one of the partners has a fundamental guilt/anger dynamic that permeates their unconscious, and the other has a guilt/atonement dynamic that permeates their unconscious. The intention of the sadistic one is to attract a partner to psychologically, emotionally, physically, and sexually abuse, humiliate, torment, and hurt. The intention in the masochistic one is to create a relationship in which they experience these dynamics, which always leads to a sense of disillusionment. Combined, they have had a mutual desire to act out their parts or roles, even though such a desire is not conscious.

For the couple who has Pluto in Virgo of the Sixth House, all of these archetypes can be active in various ways, and in different degrees of emphasis. The archetype of self-improvement reflects a couple who has had the desire to improve their overall lot in life within the most recent lifetimes. As a result of this desire, such a couple will be dedicated to doing everything possible to increase their material resources so that an easier life can occur. However, actualizing this desire has typically produced situations wherein one or both are continuously busy and involved in work and career. They become so focused on this desire that the interpersonal dynamics within the relationship suffer, since there is not enough time or energy left to focus on the relationship itself. This creates the sense of sacrificing their own emotional and psychological need for personal improvement. This kind of sacrifice thus creates its own kind of crisis, wherein each feels their emotional and psychological needs are not being met.

Other couples with composite Pluto in Virgo will have this same desire, but it will manifest in an altogether different way. These couples will emphasize self-improvement from an inner point of view. They will focus on analyzing and overcoming all kinds of self-defeating dynamics that have resulted in many crises, both in their relationship and as individuals, in many recent lifetimes. The emphasis of these couples is to "clean-up their act" so that they can live a life that is productive, efficient, and without crisis.

The archetype of desiring to help each other heal cumulative wounds reflects a couple who, as individuals, have both felt victimized by life—in other words, two people who have been acting out the pathology of masochism. Being fellow masochists, they deeply empathize with the wounds that each carries. An active dynamic in the pathology of masochism is self-sacrifice. Thus, each will equally attempt to give to the other what is needed in order for healing to take place. The problem in this situation is based on the compulsive need to create and re-create crisis out of thin air. This is because masochists have a core of inner guilt with a resulting need to atone for the perceived causes. This inner guilt creates a very deep negative self-image or feeling. The desire to atone for this guilt results in the psychology of self-punishment and the cycle of one crisis after another. Both partners do this, and both will alternate roles. The intention to heal is great, but it requires a desire that is honest and sincere. Until this is the case, these types of couples will eventually wear each other out.

The archetype in which one partner sacrifices his or her needs and desires to the other without the other reciprocating reflects a couple in which the sacrificing one has intensely hurt or wounded the other in some way in another lifetime that has preceded the most recent of prior lifetimes together. This couple has had a mutual desire to right a wrong together because of this. A promise to do so, and the acceptance of that promise, has been made. The problem here is that neither one will consciously remember what the original dynamics were that originally created this situation in another lifetime. As a result, the psychological dynamics are very difficult. The one who is doing all the sacrificing does not like it, yet deep inside knows that he or she can not change it—unconsciously knowing the promise was made at some point. Over time, they become very bitter, and can become quite sarcastic. The one who is receiving the benefit of the other's efforts enjoys it to no end, and can become quite dictatorial or bossy toward the sacrificing one—never letting the sacrificing one off the hook, so to speak, because of the injury that originally took place.

The archetype of helping each other through life crises reflects two people who have made a pact or pledge to one another at some point in their prior-life development and contact with one another. These are typically two Souls who have had a high degree of Soul empathy. In many of these cases, the nature of the prior-life connections has been personal, but has rarely been intimate. This is the nature of what occurs when two Souls have made such a promise or pact to "be there" for the other when necessary. On the other hand, many such people have tried to make their connection intimate because of the nature of the type of crises that they create. When people come together to deal with a crisis or cataclysmic situation, there is generally no time for wasted words or superficiality. People tend to get to know each other rather quickly. Thus, these types of couples have come together through crisis because of the mutual intention to do so. Some have tried to make the bridge to intimacy because the intensity of the crises has gotten them to know each other deeply. Rarely does this bridge to intimacy work out, because this was not the specific intention or reason for the connection in the first place.

The darkest dimension of this archetype is symbolized in the sado-masochistic pathology. A masochist will always attract a sadist, and a sadist will always attract a masochist. The most common way we know of this archetype in modern times is the "battered wife syndrome". The active archetypes are guilt/anger and guilt/atonement. The degree of intensity in the manifestation of this archetype is relative to the degree of guilt which creates a proportionate degree of anger or atonement. The one who is manifesting the pathology of sadism will always appear to the masochistic one in the beginning of their connection as a "silver-tongue devil." They initially appear as quite kind, sensitive, attentive, and somehow know all the right words to use in such a way as to "hook" the masochist: the masochist believes in them based on the nature of the words and how they are presented. They will appear to be wounded or needy in some way. Since the masochist responds to those who have been victimized by life, or those who express "sincere' desires to improve or change themselves in some way, the sadist knows how to "set the bait." At some point after the commitment has been made to the relationship, the sadist will progressively reveal their actual psychological and emotional agenda—to manipulate, control, dominate, hurt, torment, humiliate, criticize, and abuse the masochist in varying degrees of intensity. Initially, the masochist will create a state of denial that this is occurring, especially since the sadist can experience cycles of remorse in which they profusely apologize, and promise to "never to do that again." The masochist believes in the "potential" of what could be, and this focus not only blinds them to what is actually occurring, but creates a state of denial to the actual reality of what it occurring. It leads to the famous "second chance" over and over again. In the last analysis, the masochist will experience such a degree of disillusionment that reality is finally grasped—through intense and excruciating pain. The crisis of disillusionment enforces intense analysis as to what has and is occurring. Analysis of this type produces very painful self-knowledge. Only in this way can the masochist change. A sadist can only change when they ware willing to accept this fact in themselves though all too often when they are confronted with the reality of themselves it is met by denial. Denying their pathology, they then project onto the one who is confronting them in this way the very dynamics that define their pathology—the sadist now feels persecuted and attacked, and then persecutes or attacks the one who is perceived to be doing the persecution. Many couples who have Pluto in Virgo in the Sixth House manifest these dynamics together in varying degrees of intensity and emphasis.

For a couple in the Consensus state, all or some of the various dimensions of the overall archetypes described above can exist. Whatever the operative dynamics are within the relationship are operating primarily in an unconscious way. A real sense of crisis will occur at various points within the relationship that demands adjustment relative to the nature of the crisis. The function and nature of crisis is to bring into conscious awareness what has been primarily working at an unconscious level within the relationship. Bringing the operative dynamics into a consciously aware state thus induces analysis of those dynamics. Through conscious awareness and analysis, the couple can make the necessary adjustments, which allows for improvement and change within the relationship. This can only occur when there is a conscious desire to do so, which presumes that each is a condition or situation of acknowledging the operative dynamics in the first place. If one or the other, or both, is in a state of denial regarding these dynamics then nothing can change, and the crisis will continue until such an acknowledgment takes place.

For a couple in the Individuated state, all or some of the various dimensions of the overall archetypes described above can exist as well. The primary difference is that there is an awareness of whatever the dynamics are, and a progressive desire to liberate or change those dynamics. The primary key is for each of them to accept responsibility for their own actions and choices, and to not blame one another. Again, the dynamics of crisis generates the necessary analysis which, in turn, promotes understanding as to why those dynamics exist. Once this understanding occurs, it leads to the relevant ideas of how to adjust and change those dynamics.

In the Spiritual state, this placement will primarily correlate to a couple with the mutual desire for purification relative to deep feelings of guilt, and being "impure." The consequent need to atone for this guilt has manifested as an orientation to spiritual practices of an austere or ascetic nature, wherein all dynamics linked with the flesh have been denied and suppressed. Sacrificing the life of the senses on the spiritual altar of denial and suppression has typically caused a build-up of emotional and psychological frustration and resentment toward one another that is rarely consciously expressed towards one another. These displaced resentments then manifest as one partner being critical of the other's spiritual progress or practices. When this occurs, it is a variation of the sadomasochistic pathology. This creates its own kind of crisis, the purpose of which is to make the couple adjust the nature of their spiritual orientation and practices. This requires a reorientation to emotional forms of spirituality that allow the couple to access their built-up and unresolved emotions. Accessing the emotions in this way allows for their expression and consequent healing. This will facilitate a reorientation to sacred sexual practices, which allows the couple to spiritually progress to the next stage at some point in their future evolution together—a state of natural celibacy.

At the most evolved level in this state, couples will manifest a mutual desire to be of service to the larger community around them in some way. Each will live in absolute service and dedication to one another, and will exhibit an unconditional love for one another as an extension of their love of God. They will understand that each and all are manifestations of that One Spirit that we call God. They will manifest a very real and sincere humility, and their consciousness will not be identified with the individual ego, or with the "ego" of the relationship. In this condition, they will reflect a state of natural celibacy.

Sexually, the consensus and individuated conditions will manifest differently depending on what the archetypal dynamics are that define the relationship. This can run the range from perfunctory sex, no sex, sexual imagery created through fantasy or exposure to images emanating from sexual magazines or movies which one or both partners desires the other to fulfill through acting out the imagery during sexual activities, to one or the other sacrificing their own specific sexual desires/needs to the other relative to wanting to "please" that other, to sexual dominance or possession that will reflect itself through sexual intensity, to overt forms of sadomasochistic sexual practices. For those in the Spiritual State, the sexual dynamic can commonly be suppressed, whereas the actual need for most in this condition is to embrace sacred sexual practices such as Tantra.

POLARITY POINT IN THE TWELFTH HOUSE OR PISCES

The primary archetypal intention symbolized by this polarity point is to evolve the relationship to a state wherein the compulsion to create crisis is dissolved. The couple needs to learn how to live together without crisis, to evolve into a state of relative peace, and to just live life. This polarity point requires that each person learn to accept responsibility for their own actions and overall reality, and to stop blaming the other. It requires that they learn how to take a "time out" for the relationship in which they can focus on one another in order to reach resolutions. It requires a sincere desire to work together toward a healing a resolution of whatever the specific dynamics are that maintain a sense of perpetual or cyclic crisis. It requires stopping the pathology of masochism and sadism between them in whatever way that it has manifested. This initially requires a mutual acknowledgment of the situation which, in turn, will lead them into the necessary therapeutic strategies that will unlock and dissolve the inner dynamics and causes for these pathologies. Above all else stands the need for each of them to forgive the other for whatever has occurred in this or other lifetimes, and thus resolve the resulting resentment, anger, or sense of being victimized by the other.

PLUTO IN THE SEVENTH HOUSE OR LIBRA

Pluto in the composite Seventh House or Libra correlates to a couple who has a mutual desire within the most recent of prior lifetimes to learn how to be in a relationship in which the principle of equality is actualized in every aspect of their relationship. This will include role equality and interchangeability, and equal levels of giving and receiving. Within these intentions, they have had a mutual desire to learn the nature of the projection of their inner needs onto each other, to learn the nature of their expectations of a real and unrealistic nature, to learn when to give and not to give, and to learn about the nature of emotional dependencies which can lead to psychological enmeshment. These lessons have occurred within the most recent of prior lifetimes together as a reaction to earlier lifetimes in which the relationship between the couple was severely out of balance in the ways described above. Since then, they have been working very hard on counteracting the extremity of imbalance. With composite Pluto in the Seventh House or Libra, there is an ongoing need and desire to actualize the archetype of equality and balance.

This will be more pronounced in some couples than in others. Some couples will still be in a situation wherein one partner attempts to dominate the relationship through a test of wills. This type will be highly insecure and, as a result, will attempt to overpower the partner through strength of will in order to feel secure. In essence, this type of partner must manipulate and control the other in order to feel secure, and will expect that the relationship is meant to serve his or her needs. When these needs are not met in the ways that are deemed appropriate and necessary, such a partner will project all kinds of subjective judgments, conclusions, and motivational intentions onto the other person. The other person, in turn, may do exactly the same thing. This then leads to compulsive ongoing power struggles linked with a test of wills over who will prevail. In other cases the partner of such a person, acting out of fear, may simply recoil and psychologically withdraw, while trying to fulfill the demands of the dictatorial partner as best they can. When these are the dynamics that define the relationship, it obviously means that they have not evolved very far toward the actualization of the intentions reflected in this archetype. Sustained work toward these intentions must continue to occur. Such couples are amazingly dependent on one another even though they continue to fight and struggle. They reflect a psychological enmeshment even when they seem totally polarized, though it may not be apparent to the observer. This is the classic psychological paradox and dilemma of the "can't live with you, can't live without you" syndrome. This binding force exists because each of them has promised the other at some point in their evolutionary journey to work toward the archetypal intentions of equality and balance symbolized by Pluto in the composite Seventh House or Libra.

In other cases, the couple will exhibit the opposite dynamics. This will be a couple in which each partner has been trying to learn that each one's needs and desires are no more or less important than the other's. In order to develop this awareness, they have learned to listen to one another in such a way as to actually hear what the other is saying as it is meant and intended, versus hearing the other through the subjective filter of their own reality. Such a couple has desired to truly work on their relationship—to go the extra mile. As a result, this couple will be very strong together, and they will simply know without question or doubt that they are "meant" to be together. Through this evolved ability to listen to one another, they have learned about the nature of one another's desires and needs as individuals. Thus, they have been learning about the nature of one another's expectations, and the reasons for those expectations. Because learning to give to one another is a primary focus within the relationship, they have come to rely and depend on one another. Through giving, they have learned that their own individual needs are met. When both give, mutual fulfillment becomes the natural consequence. Because of all of these recent developments in their evolutionary journey together, they have become co-dependent. In varying degrees of intensity, this co-dependency has produced psychological enmeshment.

For a couple in the Consensus state, the degree of evolution toward the archetypal intent of Pluto in the composite Seventh House or Libra will determine the reality that actually exists for the couple. In the case of a couple with one very dominant and one very submissive partner, the dominant partner will create "emotional scenes" out of thin air. This partner, in reality, does not desire to sustain the relationship dynamics in this way even though it will appear so from a behavioral point of view. The reason for creating the confrontations and emotional scenes is that such a partner is trying to elicit a confrontational response from the docile partner who has become afraid to do anything except scurry around fulfilling unending demands. In effect, the dominant partner desires to be confronted and challenged so the intentions reflected in this evolutionary condition can be realized. Usually, such a relationship appears to be quite "normal" to the outside world. No one would suspect the power dynamics that are actually occurring within the home.

A couple in which both partners are equally confronting one another through a mutual assertion of will and are equally projecting their judgments concerning one another's motives and intentions has moved further along in the development of the archetypal intentions reflected in Pluto in the composite Seventh House or Libra. They will be leading a normal life as defined by the consensus society. The dynamic of love/hate will be intense. At key points in time, everyone in their immediate neighborhood will know exactly what is going on within their home—the intensity of the pitched battles and confrontational arguments will be heard by all. The mutual "triggering" of one another is instrumental in their mutual desire to move more completely toward the full actualization of their intentions.

A couple who has finally arrived at the full actualization of the intentions symbolized with Pluto in the composite Seventh House or Libra will also appear to be quite normal, according to the consensus. Yet what will set them apart, even within that framework, is that their relationship will be balanced in every way. They will appear as more or less "one person," even though there are two physical bodies to look at. Their wills have become harmonized, and they are working together toward life goals and objectives that are the same. A vibration of love will permeate their togetherness.

Sexually, the couple with very dominant and one very docile partner will manifest the dynamic of sex as power. The dominant partner will be invested in creating an intense response from the docile partner in order to validate an insecure ego. The only "equality" that the dominant partner is interested in is producing an equally intense orgasm in the partner. For the couple who equally confronts one another in a test of wills, the sexual dynamics are based in power also. Both will reflect a sexual assertiveness, and need to be in sexual control. This can produce a sexual "wrestling match," so to speak, to see who will end up on top. Using sex as a form of emotional control or renewal can also occur—withholding sex, or using sex as a way to "repair" the relationship. The couple who has actualized the real intention in this archetype will relate in total equality. Their sexual dynamics will be based on mutual love, caring, and giving. Role equality and reciprocity will be the hallmark of their sexual union. A harmonization of sexual energy can create a sexual oneness between them.

In the Individuated state, this placement will correlate to a couple that has had a mutual desire to rebel against the traditional roles of gender assignments within relationship as defined by consensus society. There is an active desire to merge the inner female and male within each of them—to arrive at a state of inner gender balance as individuals, and thus within the relationship. Confrontations have occurred and will continue to occur with respect to their individual differences. This happens because each has been psychologically enmeshed in a state of excessive proximity and dependency during the last few lifetimes together, and that which is perceived to be "too different" ignites a fear of loss or separation.

There is an abiding love for one another at a Soul level, yet the personal differences can create states of psychological and emotional withdrawal or polarization. This can occur when one or the other feels that their needs are not being met. Conditional giving can result. Alternating between cycles of deep love and happiness when the mutually projected needs of each are met, and cycles of polarization when they are not, will produce deep psychological discussions with one another. Self-knowledge is gained through such discussions regarding the nature of one another's expectations. Focusing on the nature of expectations allows each to become aware of the inner needs that are the basis of these expectations. Sometimes these discussions will be very productive, and sometimes they can degenerate into who is right, and who is wrong. The tendency to project judgments on another's intentions, motivations, and emotional agendas creates this effect.

Over time, this couple will learn to listen to the other in objective ways. As this occurs, each will finally feel like they are being understood. This evolution will take place in the Individuated condition because both partners desire to understand their individual lives, and thus the relationship, in a deeper and larger context than that of their existing society (as would be the case with a couple in the Consensus state). This larger context will be of a cosmological, metaphysical, or purely psychological nature. This larger context thus allows for a very different perspective relative to the nature of their interpersonal dynamics, and a deeper understanding of the dynamics and issues that exist between them.

Sexually, a couple in the Individuated state will desire role equality, wherein each can act out the male and female principles interchangeably. There will be a mutual desire to explore ways of being sexual that are independent of the existing social conventions. Creating sexual atmospheres in which their specific sexual desires can be acted out is a strong need. Both will be orientated to sexually giving to the other, resulting in a harmonization of sexual energy that then promotes a unity of sexual rhythm and response. Sex can also be used to heal hurt feelings produced through arguments and confrontations.

In the Spiritual state, this placement will correlate to a couple that has had a mutual desire to develop and actualize their spiritual desires and needs through the archetype of relationship. There are two primary ways to actualize from a patriarchal point of view—the path of the monastic, and the path of the householder. Evolving in the latter way, this couple has learned to rely on each other for spiritual support, nourishment, and perspectives as they have tried to balance their inner relationship with God, and the relationship they have with one another.

"What does God want from me, what do you need from me, and what do I need from myself?" have been the three primary dynamics that each of them have been trying to understand, and to keep in a state of balance. In the earlier stages of this evolutionary state, this can be quite a struggle. The challenge and lesson in this condition is to understand that the balance point is ever-shifting, and not consistent or predictable. Thus, they need to orient to the immediacy of what is needed—my partner or child needs me right now, I need to put more energy towards God right now, or I need to put more energy into other needs that I have right now. Responding in this way thus allows for continual balance.

The couple in this condition desires to know the karmic or spiritual reasons for their relationship, and together they will embrace a spiritual value system that correlates to their sense of life's meaning. Their spiritual value system will create the basis of how they relate to themselves and the relationship. The principle of giving to one another specifically, and to others generally, will be highly emphasized and developed between them. A harmonization of will reflected in their spiritual merging of Souls will create a sense of being "twins." They have an awareness of one another at all times because their vibrational natures are highly attuned to one another. They hear each other even when no words are being spoken. There is a natural deference to one another. Equality of role and gender has been attained. Each is equally important or non-important as the other. At the highest level in this condition, the couple will serve as examples to others of what a true spiritual marriage is: just as the ancient Indian god and goddess Ram and Sita did.

Sexually, there will be a total harmonization of ego, will, and Soul that allows a merging of these energies to take place. Merging their energy in this way will allow for the inner Divinity in each to be experienced. Slow, gentle, and progressively deep sexual movements will take place. Sustained eye contact will occur. The sensual enjoyment of God is experienced through one another. Touching, holding, and massage is very important and necessary.

POLARITY POINT IN THE FIRST HOUSE OR ARIES

The evolutionary purpose of this placement is for the couple to continue to work toward a state of absolute equality wherein each partner's individual reality, desires, and needs are met in a state of perfect balance. Until this is realized, it will be necessary for such a couple to learn how to break free from their co-dependency. For this to occur, it is essential that each learn to create a life and reality for themselves that is independent of the relationship, yet exists within it. Each partner must encourage this development in each, and learn to not feel threatened when it occurs. If it cannot occur, if one or both partners thwarts or blocks this necessary development, necessary separations or termination of the relationship will or may be necessary. The paradox here is that the more each partner feels free to act on what each needs for their own individual development, the more each will desire to maintain the relationship.

For most in the Spiritual state, it is essential that they learn how to become progressively independent from one another for their spiritual growth to proceed. They need to learn how to sustain their spiritual progress from within themselves relative to the inner relationship with God. At the highest level in this condition this will have already occurred and, as a result, will presage the fact that this will be the last time that they will be in an intimate relationship together, since they have reached a point of absolute culmination with respect to their evolutionary journey together spanning many, many lifetimes.

PLUTO IN THE EIGHTH HOUSE OR SCORPIO

In my counseling practice, which has spanned over twenty years, and over fifteen thousand clients, roughly forty percent of all the intimate relationships that I have worked with have had composite Pluto in the Eighth House. I feel that this is the most difficult position for composite Pluto, because the couple who has it is dealing with issues and dynamics together at the actual Soul level, not the personality or ego level. Such a couple has an incredibly intense magnetic attraction toward one another, somewhat like the moth being attracted to the proverbial flame. Within the intensity of the attraction, most couples also have a fear or repulsion that is experienced in a primarily subconscious way. This fear or repulsion is typically overridden by the attraction. It is not given too much attention, nor is it acted on in most cases in the beginning of the relationship. There are many reasons for this simultaneous attraction and repulsion, just as there are many reasons why, in most cases, the couple responds to the magnetic attraction leading toward their relationship instead of responding to the subconscious fear or repulsion which would prevent the relationship from occurring. Let us examine this deeply.

The Eighth House, Scorpio, and Pluto correlate to the nature of our unconscious desire nature, and the reasons for those desires in evolutionary, karmic, and psychological terms. The nature of desires determines the nature of our motivations, intentions, and the psychology of our consciousness. In combination, these dynamics create a necessary limitation within our consciousness of what is possible to actualize relative to the totality of life, and what is not. Thus, we are limited to the specific life focus determined by the nature of our desires as we progress from life to life.

Since Pluto, Scorpio, and the Eighth House also correlate to the natural law of evolution, the desire to grow beyond limitations, we are all attracted to people, circumstances, and symbols of power that represent something that we are not. This type of attraction serves to make us aware of the nature of our limitations. Thus, the nature of such attractions is reflected in our desire to grow, evolve, and metamorphose beyond our limitations. To do so, we must become aware of the causes for those limitations. This awareness occurs through forming relationships to that which symbolizes what we feel we need in order to grow. This is the common motivation within most people that causes the attraction to occur to this person as opposed to that person. By forming a relationship to that which we are not, an natural Plutonian osmosis occurs in which we become that which we have formed a relationship to, causing evolution and growth to occur. The fundamental problem in this archetypal dynamic is that most of us are not consciously aware of why we do what we do. The sources of our desires, motivations, and intentions are primarily unconscious. This is why so many such attractions become compulsive. It is also why the karma of using and being used by others can occur between people. This, in turn, creates violations of trust, betrayal, abandonment, and loss. This is why sexual karma can be produced: the deepest instinct in people, reflected in our need to secure that which we feel we need, is to sexualize it; thus, using sex as a vehicle to possess what we desire.

Couples who have composite Pluto in the Eighth House or Scorpio have had a mutual desire to possess and become what each symbolizes to the other. Each one has reflected capacities, qualities, abilities, and resources that the other has desired to develop. This mutual desire has caused them to penetrate to the depth of each other's Soul. This desire induces the wish to merge the Souls together, and by merging to become one Soul—a Soul larger, more powerful, and freer from limitations than the individual Souls alone.

The mutual desire to merge has created its own unique problems over many lifetimes. One of the deepest problems is linked with fear emanating from their individual egos. The ego structure within the personality or subjective consciousness that the Soul creates in each life becomes intoxicated with its own life. The ego becomes used to feeling separate from anything that it is not—separate, and thus individual. Therefore, the desire to merge at a Soul level creates the fear in each partner that they are being pulled into a dark inner abyss through one another—that the sense of individuality at an ego level will be extinguished. This in turn has created a simultaneous attraction and repulsion—attraction at the Soul level because of the unconscious desire to merge the Souls, and repulsion at an ego level because of the fear of losing distinct individual identity.

This fundamental archetype within the composite Eighth House Pluto has created and caused its own karma between the two people. The intention to merge the Souls has created a condition within their combined consciousness wherein they have necessarily desired to penetrate to the very depths of one another—each other's Soul. Penetrating to the depths of one another has caused a condition wherein everything that one another is must become exposed to the light of day: psychological dynamics and complexes, emotional dynamics and the reasons for those dynamics, the causes of insecurity, the nature of one another's motivation and intentions as symbolized and created by their desire nature, and so on. As this occurs, the egocentric structures within each of them has become afraid at regular intervals throughout their evolutionary journey with one another. The nature of this fear is based in the elimination of individual identity, and the fear of becoming too exposed; most of us are more comfortable just being what we are without the intensity and scrutiny of honest psychoanalytic self-examination of a perpetual nature. For Souls to merge, they must necessarily confront and eliminate all existing impurities. Thus, the intense desire to penetrate to the depths of each other's Souls in order to merge requires the ongoing mutual exposure of one another's inner dynamics so that the impurities in each can surface. It is exactly this ongoing desire to penetrate to the depths of one another that induces the fear at an egocentric level—the fear of exposure, and the fear of losing egocentric identity. As a result, couples who have the composite Eighth House Pluto have typically experienced separation or termination of their relationship for these reasons. Karma is created when one or the other leaves the relationship when one or the other does not desire this to occur: violation of trust is the specific cause for the karma in this situation. When one or the other, or both, has had the experience of having their trust violated, this in turn will create the feeling of being used or manipulated relative to "getting" something that one or the other, or both, wanted from each other. Thus, the karma of being manipulated and used by one another is a common dynamic and karma that exists with a couple who has composite Pluto in the Eighth House or Scorpio.

Because of the desires to merge the Souls, every other dynamic within their total beingness together will become intensified, individually and together. Couples who have composite Pluto in the Eighth House or Scorpio are the most intense of relationships as a result. The desire to merge necessarily produces a deep, permeating psychological way of relating to one another. Each will have a desire to understand the psychological dynamics of one another—the nature of each other's psychological and emotional needs, their sexual desires and needs and for what reasons, to focus on all existing emotional, sexual, or psychological wounds with the intention of identifying the causes of such wounds, to heal those wounds, and a desire to penetrate to the depths of one another through the intensity of their sexuality. The intensity of the sexual energy together will also have the effect of causing all that is unresolved between them from this and other lifetimes to surface, as well as that which is unresolved within each individual to also surface.

These archetypal manifestations occur for another reason, too. Because it is very common for a couple who has a composite Eighth House Pluto to have experienced separations from one another wherein one or both has felt betrayed in some way, each will have a need to "test" the other; to make sure about where the other is "coming from". Each will have a unconscious desire or need to make the other "prove" their love, motives, or intentions for wanting to be together with one another. Thus, the probing and penetrating of each other's inner being becomes the result of this desire and need to "make sure." Because each partner will be inherently insecure from within themselves, and because there will be an unconscious insecurity linked with one another based on previous-life separations, the all too common reaction to these insecurities is for the couple to be together to much—excessive proximity wherein proximity equals security because each always has an eye on the other.

Excessive proximity can become its own cause of emotional, psychological, and sexual distortions of all kinds. It can become a causal factor in loss of perspective on the relationship, and one another as individuals, and can add to the fear of becoming possessed or swallowed up by one another and the relationship—enmeshment in the worst form. This, in turn, can become a causal factor in which one or the other, or both, suddenly asserts an egocentric will manifesting as either total or partial withdrawal from the other within the context of being proximate, or seeking out external activities or environments in which the other is not included; or both. Commonly, these external activities or environments, and the experiences therein, are secretive in nature. This has and can occur for three reasons. Either one or the other is unconsciously trying to undermine or sabotage the relationship relative to the fear of being swallowed up by it, or one or the other is trying to assert his or her egocentric will to do whatever they please without restraint or restriction, or one or the other is being motivated by a vindictive desire to "get back" or even with the other for some wound that has been created by the other. Thus, a common karma that couples have with composite Pluto in the Eighth House or Scorpio is a karma of secrets—a karma a secrets thus causes a karma of dishonesty.

Because each can feel that the other has been dishonest, and because each will have feelings of being used, manipulated, betrayed, and abandoned by the other for all the above reasons, a couple with composite Pluto in the Eighth House or Scorpio commonly has deep unresolved anger or rage at one another. This combined with a deep attraction or love creates a love/hate dynamic, or the attraction/repulsion dynamics. Relative to unresolved anger or rage, the desire to hurt one another can be quite strong. It will operate primarily at an unconscious level in the beginning of their connection, but can become more conscious as time goes on. This typically manifests as the thought to "get even" in some way. It can also manifest as desiring to dominate or control by force of will. This can then create a power struggle in the relationship, centered on issues such as whose will dominates, whose needs are most important, who will the relationship revolve around. This can manifest as each attempting to dominate the other's will in very active and intense ways, or as one of them dominating in this way while the other becomes more or less passive. When this is the case, the one who becomes passive will typically attempt to assert his or her will through seeking out external activities, environments, or other people to become involved with that the other knows nothing about.

The power struggle between the two can have several behavioral applications. One of the most common applications is one wherein an individual presents oneself to the other as someone who is totally aware of what the other's issues and problems are. In essence, they set themselves up as a *de facto* therapist or counselor to the other. When this is the operative dynamic, the one playing out the role of the therapist will have the capacity to identify the weakest emotional dynamics in the other. Focusing on those dynamics keeps the other partner dependent. Thus, the counselor unconsciously is trying to guarantee his or her need for security and permanency through the role. The one who is dependent is trying to guarantee his or her need for security by creating a *de facto* parent/child dynamic—"take care of me" is the unconscious voice. The power struggle occurs when the dependent one attempts to either break free from the influence of the counselor, or attempts to actually heal whatever the wounds are. The counselor will resist this since their role is dependent on the dependent one maintaining those wounds. In other cases, each of them will alternate back and forth between the roles of counselor and counselee. Each is invested in maintaining this orientation because of the need for security and power.

Another form that this dynamic can create is one wherein the relationship is reduced to sexual addiction. In this application, the two Souls have a great magnetic attraction to one another without really knowing why. Relative to the desire to merge which is ever-present in the archetype of composite Pluto in the Eighth House or Scorpio, the only way for this to occur is through sexual addiction to one another. Because there is no real basis of mental communication, they do not really know why they are attracted to one another. Because of this, the only way to penetrate each other, in order to know each other, is through sex.

When this is the operative dynamic, it will lead into a very intense sexual relationship that becomes addictive. Relative to power and will issues, one partner may attempt to totally sexually possess and "own" the other—to create a condition of sexual slavery in which the submissive partner is expected to be available for sex whenever the other partner desires it. This will typically occur when the "slave" person is highly insecure, and extremely needy of emotional nurturing as a result of problems in their childhood. Thus, they learn in this type of relationship that these needs can be met as long as they make themselves available in this way. Such a person's emotional nature has been wounded and suppressed in childhood, but they learn that the intensity produced through sexual union unlocks those buried emotions, and they feel alive because of it. Thus, they submit and become addicted to the sexual dynamic. Sex on demand is now the operative dynamic in which the "slave" is expected to give in to any of the sexual desires of the partner. Because of the need to dominate through will in order to feel secure, the dominating one will attempt to possess the other one in every possible way, including anal penetration. The dominating one will be typically attracted to "sexual taboos." In other cases, each of them will alternate between these roles. Because the sexual dynamic is never enough to sustain any couple that desires to be together for a long time, this orientation always leads to termination of the relationship. The termination is based on the sense of lack, which can also motivate one or the other to seek out other people to become involved with. When this occurs, termination of the relationship will soon occur.

In the Consensus state, this placement will correlate to a couple who have mutual desires to confront the existing nature of the limitations that have brought them together in life after life. The common problem is based in traditional gender assignment issues wherein the man has attempted to have power over the woman. The woman in this case has felt deep inner power within her, yet this power has been crushed by the dominating will of the man. This has caused great confrontations to occur as the woman has attempted to assert her own will either directly to him, or to unconsciously work against him through covert activities of one kind or another. The confrontations have produced very hurtful and wounding words that are not resolved. These cumulative wounds become linked with anger and rage, and the need to hurt one another in order to "get back." After the heat of the battle there are cycles of calm in which they both attempt to emotionally renew themselves through gentle words of atonement and deep lovemaking. Obviously, the love/hate dynamic is very active. The man has typically been unfaithful to the woman in many of these lives, and the woman could have been just as unfaithful relative to getting emotional needs met which the husband was incapable of fulfilling. Jealousy becomes a constant problem, and the resulting unconscious memories can cause the projection of these fears in each subsequent life.

They will have a mutual desire to obtain material power from the existing society that they live within. Together they can be very clever, or even underhanded or dishonest in designing ideas or schemes to accomplish this goal. When this has been the case in other lifetimes, it can create a karmic condition in which the desired material security is denied, or it can lead to a great loss of the existing material resources at some point through larger forces or powers that they cannot control. This mutual desire structure can also create a condition in which they become isolated from one another in every way except through the commonality of this shared desire. They will be highly secretive regarding the inner workings and goings-on of their relationship to all others. Highly suspicious, they will create a united front that is difficult to penetrate. Unable to truly trust one another, they find it difficult to trust anyone else.

Sexually, the power problems of past lifetimes can make it very difficult for either of them to become too vulnerable with each other. There is an inner buffer that does not allow for a penetration of the heart or Soul. Yet, because they both desire to be touched or penetrated in this way, their sexual relations can be very physically intense. Sex as power can also be the dynamic, as well as no sex at all—this energy becomes entirely focused on the material goals. In other cases, the sexual dynamic may be the only way that they can truly "merge the Souls"; yet after the sexual event, they both resume their emotionally distant stance toward one another.

In the Individuated state, this placement will correlate to a couple who have come together in many lifetimes in order to empower one another. The basis of the initial attraction in every life has typically been a shared commonality of wounds acquired from other people and circumstances. Both will symbolize to the other some great magnetic power of an undefined nature. Attraction to the power within each creates a hypnotic effect that mesmerizes both of them. The attraction becomes compulsive because of this. As the relationship unfolds in each life, the need to penetrate to each other's Soul begins to uncover the wounds that each has created in the other. As this occurs, unresolved anger begins to manifest between them. This results in a duality of experience together. On the one hand, they experience cycles of incredible connectedness wherein intense emotional communion with one another occurs. In this communion, each lets down their emotional guard, and, in so doing, each shares the depths of the other. Each can be or seem like a true emotional healing balm to the other. Each can feel extremely validated by the other, and each can feel that the other is truly "there" for them. Deep emotional, psychological, and "Soul" work can be accomplished as they confront the nature of their wounds, and truly attempt to heal those wounds together. This can lead them into exploring many knowledge systems together such as astrology, psychology, the occult, the nature of the human condition from many different perspectives, and different ways of being sexual together. On the other hand, the surfacing of wounds that they have inflicted on each other can produce cycles of vindictiveness in which both attempt to get back at one another in various ways. In the worst of cases, this can be truly ugly and sadistic.

Sexually, each will have desires to merge with the other. Both will have attractions to exploring sexuality that go beyond the existing sexual conventions of the society that they are in. Attractions to sexual "taboos" will be active, and an inner power within their relationship will occur by "snubbing their nose" at those conventions. Both will desire an intensity of sexual sensation together which allows the intensity of their emotions to be experienced. The sexual dynamic is typically compulsive, yet can also be used as a way of controlling and manipulating the relationship. Sexual and emotional dishonesty has typically occurred wherein both have had "secret" affairs with others. The karma of sexual dishonesty linked with emotional dishonesty consequently exists. Using each other as sexual objects to work out various sexual desires that exist within each individual is also common, although neither one of them is really conscious of this dynamic. Fulfilling each other's desires in this way creates the illusion of love. Because of the underlying desire to merge their Souls, the sexual energy is intense and permeating. It serves both of their needs for psychological, emotional, and Soul renewal. This is why the hurt is overwhelming when emotional/sexual infidelity occurs. Neither can really forgive the other when this occurs, even though they may attempt to on a mental level. But once trust has been violated with the composite Eighth House Pluto couple, it is almost impossible to recover.

In the Spiritual state, this placement will correlate to a couple who has had mutual desires to allow the power of God to infuse the very essence of their relationship. Over many lifetimes, such a couple has experienced many different forms of spirituality emanating from many different cultures. They have a combined desire and need for the "proof" of God. As such, they have oriented to many different practices and methods that allowed for this proof to occur from within. Using a common spiritual "baseline" as the foundation of the relationship created a necessary strength that allowed both of them to experience the progressive surfacing of the wounds of lifetimes—wounds from many sources, including the wounds that they created for one another. This will be a couple who has traveled a very long evolutionary and karmic journey together, and who have more or less succeeded in staying together despite the temptation to separate in various other lifetimes because of the problems encountered. The desire to merge their Souls has sustained them. The love of their Souls toward one another has been more strong than the potential undermining effect of the various wounds. They have learned to empower each other as a result, and they have learned that the ultimate security for the relationship is found in their mutual commitment to God. As a result, they can be a spiritual powerhouse together. Many other people or couples will be attracted to them for their counsel, and because they symbolize what many other couples desire to become. They will manifest a spellbinding, magnetic effect on other people. Even through they will feel drawn to give to others as necessary, they will still be very secretive and protective of the inner nature of their relationship. Within their relationship, most of the time they will be silent together. They have developed a high degree of telepathic awareness of one another. They will speak only as necessary. Each will feel comfortable with the silence of the other. When issues come up between them, they will focus on them intently, and move through them quickly.

Sexually, they will focus of the sacredness of Tantra, or methods like it. These methods will be used to penetrate each other's Soul, and the divinity within each. Thus, they will penetrate to the Ultimate Divinity together in this way. The intensity of sensation produced in the body will be used to penetrate and remove all blockages within consciousness that prevent experiencing the inner divinity. Tantric practice of this kind will be just as important as meditational or other yogic practices. From this baseline, most of these couples will engage in other ways of being sexual as they both desire a progressive elimination of all other sexual desires so that a rapid evolution of the Soul can occur. They have already realized that sexual desire is one of the main binding forces that keeps the Soul engaged in realities like that of Earth. The attitude that this perspective creates thus allows the desires to be worked out because of the attitude that this perspective creates.

POLARITY POINT IN THE SECOND HOUSE OR TAURUS

The archetypal themes that correlate to the next evolutionary step for the couple with composite Pluto in Scorpio is to realize that each has been mutually responsible for what has occurred with the relationship, whether past and present. It then becomes essential that each forgive the other for whatever has occurred. This understanding is

best realized when both can understand that they have come together to bring to the surface the impurities and limitations in each, and
then to realize that even though there may have been great hurt experienced through one another, that there still is an abiding love that
emanates from their Souls. Orienting to this love will allow the
wounds to be healed.

Within this, it is essential that each learn how to allow the other
to identify and supply their own needs. This will lead to self-reliance,
which allows for true self-empowerment. In this way, the relationship
becomes ever more powerful and metamorphic for each. Each will
learn the difference between wanting to be together simply because
they want to be, versus the addictive compulsion to be together because of what each symbolically represents to the other—the capacities, abilities, resources, etc., that each wants from the other relative
to their perceived lacks. Once this occurs, they have eliminated together the karma of use, manipulation, and the acts of betrayal that
follow once the "use" of the relationship has been outworn. Thus,
they must learn to not be afraid when each of them desires to have
independent experiences, and to subsequently learn a new way of
being secure together. Above all else, they must learn to be totally
honest with each other in every way so that the karma of secrets is
eliminated. Even when honesty creates an "ugly" situation, it will be
the right situation.

In the Spiritual state, it is also important for the couple to understand that they have become spiritually enmeshed and dependent on
each other's strength for their own spiritual progress. Thus, it is vital
that they learn how to be apart at times in order to progress spiritually through their own efforts. Even though God is the binding force that
permeates their relationship, God only wants any of us to be ultimately
dependent on God. Thus, an enforced loss of one another will occur
at some point for this step to be accomplished, unless both realize this
important step when they are still together and take the appropriate
action as a result.

PLUTO IN THE NINTH HOUSE OR SAGITTARIUS

Composite Pluto in the Ninth House or Sagittarius correlates to a couple that has had mutual desires to understand the larger reasons or
meaning for life, the deeper reason or purpose for their relationship,
the psychological or emotional "truth" that exists within the relationship, and to learn the consequences of dishonesty together, including

dishonesty between them, and/or the consequences of being dishonest toward others who are linked with their relationship.

Couples who have composite Pluto in the Ninth House or Pluto have commonly felt deeply drawn to one another in many lifetimes without really knowing why. This has simply been experienced as a strong Soul magnetism toward one another. This magnetism serves as the basis of the attraction. Yet, because there is no conscious understanding of why the attraction exists, they have typically come together initially through the initiation of many discussions of a philosophical or intellectual nature, talking about a wide range of subjects or topics. Interrelating in this way would then evolve into discussions in which they would begin to share their own life stories. They would find points of commonality in their sharing of life stories, and points of intellectual or philosophical agreement relative to the subjects being discussed. Focusing on the point of shared commonality would then serve to deepen their personal connection or attraction to one another, and create a rational basis for the relationship. This has typically included the sharing of life goals or directions. In this way, the couple has created an intellectual or philosophical superstructure or overlay for the relationship.

The problem in this is based on the fact that one or both of the individuals has found it difficult to be emotionally or psychologically honest within themselves relative their own evolutionary journey for various reasons. Consequently, the mutual creation of an intellectual or philosophical superstructure or overlay that serves as the basis for the relationship has been used to mask or hide the actual emotional, psychological, or sexual reality or agenda of one another as individuals, and the agenda for the relationship as a result. Because of this core of emotional and psychological dishonesty within each, the agenda and core dynamics within the relationship are rooted in dishonesty also.

This can be very difficult to understand, or be consciously in touch with. The reason for this is that each can appear to be so very sincere, "real," and honest. This is based on the ability of each of them, as individuals, to create ways of understanding or explaining their own life stories that are not based in truth—stories or explanations that cover up the actual truth. The need to cover up the truth leads them to actually believe the stories and explanations themselves. Because they can believe in the stories or explanations to the point that they become the ersatz truth, the sharing of these stories or explanations can appear to be so very sincere, honest, and real.

In most cases this is done without conscious intent. Each of them has become so ingrained in this pattern over many lifetimes that it simply constitutes the way that they are. It is a compulsive and habitual pattern operating unconsciously. In some cases, one or both will consciously misrepresent themselves to the other, or one or both will create, and hide behind, some pretext that masks the actual reasons or basis for their desire to be together. In all cases, each will symbolize to the other something that each desires from the other even when this something is not consciously known or understood. Because each is unconsciously drawn to the other for that reason, each will do what is necessary in order to discover what it is. All too often this has led to a situation of mutual dishonesty wherein personal misrepresentation, lies, deceptions, exaggerations, and half-truths have been created and presented as the "truth" to one another.

The karma of dishonesty that can exist for such a couple has also caused them to search for the actual truth that exists between them. Thus, in many lifetimes together, there has been an interweaving between cycles or moments of dishonesty and honesty. Relative to Pluto, this interweaving is caused by necessary confrontations. In other words, both at various times would become aware of something that was not true as reflected through one another—something that one or the other has said, presented, or explained about themselves, a situation, or an explanation for some behavior. This would then trigger necessary confrontations that were intended to discover the actual truth. Even though this is the intention of such confrontations, the typical reaction in one or both when confronted in this way has been to defend whatever the lie or dishonesty was about. This need to defend symbolizes a deep-seated fear in one or the other, or both, that is rooted in a need to be something that one is not—a deep-seated inadequacy within that manifests as the need to exaggerate or misrepresent oneself in some way. Fearing exposure of this dynamic causes the person to defend whatever the dishonesty is about. In the process of defending, one or both will attempt to convince or convert the other through some rationalization or explanation relative to the original lie, exaggeration, misrepresentation, or deception. They will attempt to create another view or perspective that has the effect of making the other believe in the truth of the new explanation which, in turn, allows for the original lie to be sustained.

When these have been the operative dynamics (which they commonly are), one or both individuals will have been emotionally and psychologically shocked when the actual truth of one or the other, or both, has been caused to manifest. Through extension, the truth of what the dynamics have been in the relationship is now exposed as well. Because the composite Ninth House Pluto or Pluto in Sagittarius archetypally symbolizes the desire to know the truth of anything large or small, revelation of the truth of one another and the relationship is fated to occur at some point. The causes that lead to this revelation can be any circumstance: a small pinhole in the balloon blows up the whole balloon. Whatever the cause, when this truth is revealed the psychological and emotional reaction of the one who has been lied to, or of each when both have been lied to, is one of massive disillusionment, bewilderment, and betrayal. The reason that this reaction can be so massive is that the one whose untruths have been uncovered can, again, seem so honest, sincere, and real. They can be quite convincing. Thus, the shock is based on disbelief— a suspension of belief directed toward the one who was once believed in so strongly. This produces the karma of dishonesty, and when this is the karma between two people such people will continue to meet, life after life, until this karma is worked out. Their intention is to arrive at a state of absolute honesty with one another no matter what the consequences of that honesty may bring.

Within this archetype, many of these couples have also desired to understand together the larger reasons for life itself, and to understand their relationship within the broader context of these reasons—the "truth" that explains the phenomena of existence. Thus, many of these couples have desired to explore various philosophies, religions, cosmologies, or metaphysical systems which attempt to explain the basis of Creation, and the human being's relationship to that Creation. For many, this mutual desire has led to lifetimes in which they have incarnated in a variety of cultures, east and west, in order to expose themselves to as many philosophies, religions, or cosmologies as possible.

As a result, many of these couples will have a tremendous degree of acquired knowledge together, knowledge that has been inwardly realized through various practices, and knowledge that has been gained through actual experiences relative to the exposure to so much cultural diversity. Such couples will reflect a natural wisdom together as a result. Because of this past-life desire to experience so much relative to different cultural exposures, many of these couples will feel like they are not "at home" in the current culture that they are born into. There can be a deep sense of cultural alienation, and a mutual desire to discover a place in which they feel more "at home." For many, this will manifest as a deep attraction to the land and nature. They are often found living in relatively remote places with some degree of proximity to a town or city. The reason for this is that many such couples have desired to understand the difference between natural law and manmade law. As a result of this mutual desire, many of these couples have spent lifetimes in cultures that were dependent on the land and nature, cultures that understood Nature to be a living consciousness whose parts were interrelated and connected within themselves—the American Indians as an example. When this has been the case, the nature of those prior lifetimes has been linked with nomadic cultures. Thus, such a couple will manifest a deep restlessness together relative to trying to discover where their "home" is.

For many couples who have had this mutual desire to explore various philosophies, cosmologies, religions, etc., it is not uncommon for one or the other, or both, to philosophically manipulate the conceptual understanding of life—the nature and function of one's belief structure. Remembering that what we believe determines how we interpret anything, the conscious or unconscious intention for such manipulation is linked with the psychological, emotional, or sexual agenda. Thus, to have some psychological, emotional, or sexual need or desire met leads to a manipulation of the philosophical superstructure that is serving as the basis of the relationship. Manipulating the conceptual nature of whatever their existing philosophical, cosmological, metaphysical, or religious structure is for the relationship thus changes how one or the other will interpret any given behavior, need, or desire. This creates its own form of dishonesty, as well as the karma that can result from that dishonesty. Within this, it can also be quite common for one to attempt to dominate the other's way of thinking about life, as reflected in the nature of their philosophy or beliefs. When this is the case, it means that the nature of their personal power and security is totally linked with the nature of the beliefs that comprise their philosophy or religion. Thus, the need to convince and convert the other to their way of thinking in order to remain secure and powerful.

In the Consensus state, this placement will correlate to couples who have had a mutual desire to explore the adventure of life together within the framework of the cultural conventions of their native society. They will share a wide range of topics and subjects together which will stimulate a deeper sense of connection between them. There will be a mutual desire to align themselves within a larger religious framework in order to understand life, themselves, and the relationship. This will manifest as an orientation to the existing nature of the religion that defines the mainstream or consensus of their society. How they interpret their relationship, each other, and life will be dogmatically based on this religion. The overlay of this religion is used to mask or hide the reality of their emotional, psychological, and/or sexual dynamics, desires, or needs. One or the other, or both, can attempt to dominate in the sense making each other "toe the line" with respect the tenets of the religion that they are using. Others may simply use the religion as a moral imperative to sustain the relationship even though their intimate interpersonal dynamics may no longer exist. Still others may use their religion together as a form of power to win others to their point of view—to convince and covert.

Some couples within the Consensus state will have no specific desire to understand the larger reasons for their relationship in the sense of dogmatically embracing some religions, however. These are the couples that either blindly go to some church because society expects them to, or couples who are more or less agnostic. In both cases, such couples will manifest a more or less carefree attitude toward life, an attitude that suggests life is just one time around. Because of this, they will be orientated to life in a relatively hedonistic way. Such couples will still discuss many interesting subjects and topics with one another. These are the types that want to perpetually have a good time. Such couples will always be traveling here and there, visiting night clubs, having dinners out, going to discos, and so on. Within this attitude, one or both have had a deep inner orientation to personal freedom, and an attitude that suggests that they can do as they please. Consequently, these types are always open to new experiences, including the possibilities of being with other people when the situation arises. When this is the operative dynamic, some of these types will even have long-distance relationships—relationships with someone else who lives in another place while maintaining the existing relationship, or the couple itself may be living in different places wherein each has "affairs" with others as the desire to do so arises. Thus, there has typically been a lack of personal honesty within the relationship over many lifetimes concerning these matters. When one or the other, or both, has been made aware of such dishonesties in this or other lifetimes, this has resulted in great emotional and psychological pain—a pain born of disillusionment relative to "believing" in the partner, and their integrity. As said earlier, such couples are fated to remeet, life after life, until an absolute honesty is arrived at between them.

Sexually, many of the Consensus state couples will be constrained relative to the nature of the religious doctrines that they are defined by. Thus, the "morality" of sexuality will be a religious imperative that conditions their natural sexual desires and needs. This can promote its own kind of psychological and emotional frustrations. Others, who are not excessively defined by religions, will reflect the spirit of sexual adventure. These types can have great fun, sexually speaking, and are willing to try different ways of being sexual within the context of the current culture—whatever constitutes sexual "liberation" from a current cultural point of view. Many such people may find it difficult to be monogamous with one another, and even more difficult to be honest about this when it occurs. This reflects situational ethics, honesty, and monogamy—in one moment one or the other can "promise" monogamy because of desiring to sustain an existing connection or relationship, and at some other point become attracted to someone else who stirs their curiosity. The spirit of sexual adventure and conquest becomes ignited, and they become involved with someone else despite promises to the contrary. This, of course, sustains or creates a sexual karma with the one who has been lied to, and this karma is an extension of the larger karma of overall dishonesty and personal misrepresentation.

In the Individuated state, this placement will correlate to couples who have had a mutual desire to independently investigate and experience a diversity of cosmological systems of belief relative to the nature of the Creation. Each of them as individuals has evolved to a point where there is a fundamental desire for personal freedom to explore any experience that each deems necessary for their own growth. The individual desire to perpetually grow and evolve independent of the existing cultural system has created a core alienation from society. Couples in this condition have been and will be attracted to one another through their alienation from culture, and through the mutual desire to grow and evolve independent of culture. Together, they will desire to discover the "truth" of who they each are as individuals, and to create a shared philosophical belief system through which the relationship is understood and lived. As a result, they will discuss and have interest in many different philosophies, cosmologies, Eastern and Western religions, metaphysics, psychology, astrology, shamanism, and so on. Relative to the Individuated state, such couples will typically combine different thoughts and ideas from many different systems in order to create a unique system of beliefs that supports their

individual desires and needs. Such couples will come together, life after life. Their initial contact in each life will involve the sharing of their
life stories. These stories are typically not the actual truth. In the telling
they become embellished, exaggerated, or distorted in one way or another. When this occurs, it symbolizes two main dynamics. The first is
that each individual feels a deep sense of inadequacy or inferiority
which is compensated for through the exaggerations, misrepresentations, etc. The second is that each feels highly attracted to the other in
the sense that each symbolizes something that the other wants. This,
in turn, only fuels the personal misrepresentations to one another, because they both feel they must impress the other in some way in order to gain their interest and attention. Thus, the foundation of the relationship is created through dishonesty. Such couples will also be
highly restless together. This restlessness combined with the alienation usually leads such couples into desiring to live close to the land,
away from big cities, and in touch with Nature.

These types of couples have developed a deep way of relating and
communicating with one another. They can talk about many things
with great versatility. Together they will always desire to understand
the "big picture"—of life itself, and of themselves as individuals. Together they will have a disdain for cosmopolitan and sophisticated
lifestyles. They will be very "natural" people as individuals, and as a
couple. They will also share a fine humor together that embraces the
vision of the absurd. Because of the prior-life dynamics of dishonesty
(which neither will be consciously aware of in each life that they come
together), each will typically ask the other never to lie to them. They
will find themselves saying this to one another without really knowing why. Typically, they will understand this in the context of their personal pasts in each life, since one or both has experienced being lied
to by someone else before their relationship has occurred. Each will
promise to one another that they will not. Yet, the lie has already occurred relative to how each other's life stories were related, and neither one knows it. Because the intention of the composite Ninth House
Pluto, or Pluto in Sagittarius, is to arrive at the truth, to become absolutely honest no matter what the consequences, this intention leads
to an element of fate—at some point the dishonesty will become exposed in some way. This produces total psychological shock when it
occurs. Massive disbelief follows. Feeling totally misled occurs. This
dance will continue until such a couple learns the lesson of absolute
honesty with one another.

Sexually, such a couple will feel free to explore the sexual customs and methods of many different cultures. This is an extension of their desire to expand their consciousness and horizons of personal awareness. Thus, they will feel very sexually free with one another. A couple in this condition will be very intuitively aware of one another at all times. Sexually, they will manifest a great degree of intuitive sexual awareness of one another. Thus, they will be highly attuned to one another's sexual energy and responses. The sexual energy will be more or less constant between them. They will make each other feel good. Because they feel highly connected to one another, they will be sexually open to each other. Being sexually open to one another allows for a deep, intense sexual response to one another. Sexual adventures and discoveries will occur together. Many of these couples will desire and enjoy having sex outside in the context of nature. This allows their consciousness to expand and embrace nature as a result. Both will be interested in the sexual history of one another. This interest is an extension of the desire to know the truth of one another. One or the other, or both, can misrepresent or be dishonest about their sexual histories. This can occur because each may fear losing the other if they were honest about their sexual past. Their justification is that the inner need and investment to be with one another supercedes the importance of being honest. When the truth is discovered at some point, this can result in psychological and emotional withdrawal which then affects the sexual relationship. Sexual withdrawal may occur.

In the Spiritual state, this placement will correlate to a couple who has traveled a very long journey together over many lifetimes. They have formed relationships with one another over great lengths of time, spanning many cultures. Their mutual intention has been to expose themselves to as many different spiritual systems and cosmologies as they could. The intention within this has been to discover the cosmological or spiritual system that most perfectly symbolizes the essence of their Souls, and then to commit to that one system as the primary vehicle in order to expand their consciousness together. As a result, such a couple will manifest a deep wisdom together. This wisdom will be of a psychological, philosophical, and spiritual nature. They will be natural teachers together, and for one another. The intuitive element within their consciousness, individually and together, will be totally developed. They will emanate a vibration of "knowingness— of embodying truth. This truth will be the truth they have realized together.

Thus, they will speak as one. Their words and teaching, their knowledge, will appear to be identical. They will be very natural people, both together and as individuals.

Because of their expanded consciousness, one or both will be able to remember the phenomena of past life for themselves as individuals, for their relationship history, and for other people. Consequently, relative to other lifetimes in which there was the dynamic of dishonesty when they were in other evolutionary conditions together, these memories will necessarily surface into conscious awareness. They must surface so that each of them can not only have some final realizations as to why that occurred, but also to forgive one another for the fact that it did. As said earlier, these types of couples will continue to meet and remeet until the ultimate intentions of the composite Ninth House Pluto, or Pluto in Sagittarius, is realized—to arrive at a state in which absolute honesty exists between the two. Thus, evolving into this condition will produce the necessary remembrances in order for forgiveness to occur, and to release the karma created therein.

Relative to the time that we are now living in, many of these types of couples will also feel the energy of restlessness. In this condition, however, this restlessness is caused by much larger forces than their own Souls. Our times are very transitional now with respect the changing of the Ages from Pisces to Aquarius. As such, new paradigms and ways of understanding "reality" are becoming and will continue to become progressively necessary. Other ways of understanding and relating to our planet, Nature, and the universe are becoming essential in order for the survival of the planet and the life forms on it to continue. Many of these couples symbolize and reflect the new "seed thoughts" of these new paradigms, and ways of understanding what is necessary in order to proceed. As an example, the sign Sagittarius correlates to the ancient archetype of the *daemon*—human consciousness united as an equal within the totality of Nature versus being superior to it. As Pluto moves into Sagittarius through transit, this reemergence of an ancient archetype will occur through the circumstantial necessity of the cumulative consequences of human actions within the last two thousand years. As a result, many are being moved and placed in different localities all over the world in order for their knowledge to be shared or disseminated to others in those places. The restlessness within such couples that drives them to wonder where to be, here or there, is actually caused by the universal forces that we can call God. The challenge for such couples is to follow their intuitive sense of guidance to show them where to be, even when this makes no apparent rational sense.

Sexually, such couples will understand that the sexual dynamic is a natural law of creation. They will be free from religious doctrines that suppress this normal and natural function. As a result, their sexual life will be spontaneous and free. There will be a natural attunement to the sexual energy that exists between them, and a harmonization with that energy when it exists. Embracing sacred sexual practices that expand the consciousness will be the foundation for their sexual dynamics. A very few of these couples will have evolved into a state of natural celibacy together.

POLARITY POINT IN THE THIRD HOUSE OR GEMINI

The archetypal theme that this polarity point correlates to is for the couple to learn how to speak to one another in absolutely honest ways at all times— not with "forked tongues." It means that by learning to be absolutely honest within themselves, and with each other, that the circumstances created will always be exactly the right circumstances, even when such circumstances lead to situations or outcomes that are not pleasant, or lead to losing one another.

This polarity point requires an examination of the superstructure of beliefs that the couple is oriented to in such a way as to determine if those beliefs are being used to create interpretations that serve as justifications for psychological, emotional, or sexual agendas that are not being honestly represented to one another. This also requires an honest examination to determine if one or the other is using such beliefs to manipulate the thought of the other for the same reasons. If this is the case, each of them must examine honestly this fact, and make the effort to be more emotionally/psychologically honest about the nature of their desires and needs.

For couples in which one of them is trying to convince and convert the other to their own particular belief structure in order to feel secure and powerful, the Third House/Gemini polarity point requires the one who is doing this to allow the other to independently think for him or herself. In so doing, the relationship will expand because of the increase in knowledge and conscious awareness that the other will now bring into the relationship.

For those in the spiritual condition, the primary challenges are to allow the past-life memories to surface that concern the causes of dishonesty that had existed between them at other lifetimes in their evolutionary journey together so that forgiveness can occur, and to intuitively follow the guidance of the universal forces—God—that wants to have them live here or there so that they can be positioned to share their knowledge with others accordingly.

PLUTO IN THE TENTH HOUSE OR CAPRICORN

When Pluto is in the composite Tenth House or Capricorn, a variety of archetypal dynamics can be in operation. The evolutionary condition for the couple will determine which archetypes are most emphasized. These different archetypal themes include the desire to understand the nature of family dynamics and the impact that such dynamics have on determining the psychological and emotional reality of each person, and how this reality conditions their orientation to relationships, both general and intimate. Within this, there can be a desire to recover and heal the displaced and unresolved emotions of childhood. This, in turn, can lead to one or both partners playing *de facto* parental roles at various points within the relationship in order for the unresolved emotions to be recovered, and the psychological damage to be healed.

Many such couples will actually have been linked to the same biological families of origin in other lifetimes, either as siblings or as parent and child. Some of these would have experienced various degrees of trauma together relative to the impact of family dynamics on them. For some of these, the nature of such trauma will be sexual incest. For others, the nature of the trauma can be linked with the whole family who had power and privilege, and then lost it in some way. Within this, some would have experienced very psychologically manipulative parents who played one family member off another relative to who would inherit the power and privilege. For others, the trauma can be linked with very judgmental, critical, and abusive parents who attempted to control every aspect of their lives. This can also occur when one has been the prior-life parent of the other, which created a fundamental polarization between them. For some, this trauma can be traced to another time in which they were siblings who were banished from the family home.

Couples who have composite Pluto in the Tenth House or Capricorn could have also desired to examine the nature of judgments together—judgments that come from within themselves as individuals, and judgments that emanate from others in general. The question is, what constitutes the nature of judgments? The dynamic of judgment is inherent to consciousness. Judgment is a necessary component of consciousness, because it allows us to make decisions. It allows us to learn about life itself. The issue is on what basis we constitute the nature of our judgments. For most people, the basis of the judgment patterns is determined by the culturally held truths, moralities, religions, and the consensus opinion about anything. Thus, people use as the basis of their judgments that which the consensus decides is right, wrong, good, or bad. Since judgment is inherent to consciousness, the basis of judgment can also be linked with Natural Law. This is judgment in the correct and natural state. For example, if my children want to go play on a highway full of cars, I do not need any religion or manmade morality to tell me this is wrong: it is simply naturally wrong, and I make a natural judgment accordingly.

Thus, many couples have desired to examine the nature of judgment together. The reasons for the mutual desire can include the fact that they have projected negative judgments on one another in other lifetimes, judgments based on consensus beliefs which had the effect of creating real problems or polarization between them. It can include being the recipients of such judgments from other family members in this or other lifetimes, and the effects that such judgments had on them. It can also include, in some cases, both of them being the recipients of judgments projected on them by society itself in this or other lifetimes, and the effects that such judgments created for them. Real devastation has occurred to some who have experienced the weight of such judgments either among themselves, from parents, or from the society. When we are wrongly judged, we first feel guilty or that there is something wrong with us, and then we feel anger. When this is the emphasized dynamic within the relationship of the couple, it means that one or all of these forms of judgments have occurred. The intention on focusing on this is to undo the damage that was created because of it, and to work toward rebuilding a positive self-image in one or both. In so doing, the guilt and anger caused by the wrong judgment can also be purged.

Other couples will desire to understand the nature of "reality" together. What is the basis of what we all call reality? Here again, if enough people call something real then it becomes real. Is there more to reality than most people agree on? Is your reality my reality? Is mine yours? Is the reality of my relationship different than yours? Is the reality of Earth different than the reality of Jupiter? Is the reality of a time/space, cause/effect universe different than a universe that is nonlinear? The point here is that some couples who have composite Pluto in the Tenth House or Capricorn will desire to understand the structural nature of what we commonly call reality. These couples desire to understand the structural nature of consciousness, and the reality that is determined for consciousness relative to the structure that it exists within. In this way, they desire to understand themselves, their relationship, and the "reality" that both exist within.

Other archetypes that exist with the composite Tenth House Pluto, or Pluto in Capricorn, reflect couples who have just recently switched genders together; or this current life could be the life in which this switching is taking place. When this is the case, it means that they must switch these roles in order for their evolutionary journey to proceed, because they had reached a limit together in the old roles. For some, it will mean that they are actualizing the inner male and female together through the alteration of gender roles. Lastly, composite Pluto in the Tenth House or Capricorn can mean, for a relatively few couples, that they are culminating an entire past life history together that has spanned countless centuries and many different ways of being connected. This culmination can presage the fact that they are in the process of ending their journey together on Earth, and/or it can mean that they have simply completed an entire evolutionary cycle which will now lead to a new cycle, and an entirely new way of being together.

In the Consensus state, this placement will correlate to a couple who has had mutual desires for power and status within society over many lifetimes. This will typically reflect a couple who had had some lifetimes previous to this in which they felt a deep sense of powerlessness within society—they felt controlled and dominated by it. Many such couples have employed relatively ruthless means to actualize this desire—the ends justifying the means, in their estimation. Even when they actualized their desire, they still felt threatened by anyone who was perceived to potentially undermine their position, status, or power. This, in turn, caused them to set in motion any manner of strategies to undermine such potential threats. Other couples have been born into families in which the desired social power was inherited. These couples have still felt threatened by others who were perceived to potentially undermine them. Subverting such potential threats has also been the reaction in these couples. In both cases, an accumulation of guilt has occurred because of this, a guilt born of natural judgment because the ends never justify wrong means. Consequently, many of these couples have experienced recent lifetimes in which there has been a karmically determined loss of power, status, and privilege. In this evolutionary condition, such couples do not have the ability to understand why this has occurred. They simply feel a deep inner anger and resentment at "the system," and all others who have achieved status and position through the use of right means, and who are not threatened by others in the sense of doing something ruthless to undermine such others. The great teaching of Capricorn, the Tenth House, and Saturn is to accept the responsibility in one's own actions. Such couples must learn to do this so that this pattern of behavior, and the karma therein, can stop. Couples who have learned this will be couples who use their stature, position, and power to benefit other people: to help others get ahead.

Other couples with this symbolism will simply be ordinary citizens as defined by consensus society. Yet they will also have a mutual desire to "get ahead" within the system. These are usually very good, hard-working people. They will focus on material well-being. This focus can preclude any real emotional interaction as the relationship wears on. Some will walk in the footsteps of their family of origin, and others will attempt to do it in their own way. The impact of their family of origin will be difficult in some way, usually in the sense of families that are highly judgmental of one or both of them. As a result, much of what passes for their emotional interrelatedness with one another will be based on discussions about their families. In all cases, such couples will be highly judgmental types, the basis of such judgments being rooted in consensus-held beliefs of the existing society—the family karma of judgment being passed on.

Sexually, most of these couples will simply adhere to the sexual conventions of the society of origin. The sexual dynamic can be quite complicated, in that each will have a fear of being emotionally vulnerable. This fear of vulnerability is compounded when each of them issues hurtful judgments toward the other, many of such judgments occurring as a reaction to feeling emotionally unfulfilled through one another—anger linked with emotional needs that go unmet. When this is the case, and it goes on for a length of time, the sexual relationship between them can become non-existent. For others, they simply do not have the time for sexuality because of the intense focus on "getting ahead." So much energy is exerted toward this goal that the sexual energy becomes transmuted relative to the goal. When this is the case, it is a reflection of the displaced emotions of childhood resulting from a lack of real emotional nurturing. Learning to suppress their emotional nature as children manifests in their adult life as the fear of being vulnerable, or not even knowing how to be. All the emotional energy within them becomes focused on their material goals.

In the Individuated state, this placement will correlate with a couple who has experienced a tremendous degree of emotional, psychological, and sexual damage from their families of origin, from others in general, and from the various societies that they have been born into. The nature of this damage is based on the use of wrong judgments, persecution, and being used by others as scapegoats for their own displaced anger or frustrations. Such a couple has commonly been in the same family in the lifetimes in which this damage has taken place. Because of their evolutionary condition of the Individuated state, such a couple has not fit into "the system"—neither the family system, nor the societal system. Because they did not fit in, they were judged to be either threatening or simply odd—the "black sheep" syndrome. As such, they served as easy targets for others, including family members, to project ridicule and disdain upon. The effect of this has produced two people who have been fractured and emotionally wounded in various degrees of intensity. Because both vibrate and resonate differently than most other people, they have often looked to one another for comfort, nurturing, and repair.

Disdaining the "system," such a couple has commonly sought to create their own system. Thus, they create an environment and reality through which to close out anyone that could not be supportive of who they were and are. Such a couple has commonly felt like "strangers in a strange land." The only real sense of connectedness to the Earth has been found in the context of Nature, and with a few others who were "different," like themselves. Together they have desired to rebel against the system, to challenge all the most commonly cherished beliefs, customs, norms, and taboos defined by society, and to question and reflect deeply together on the nature of what constitutes "reality." Such a couple will be highly reflective and serious. They will think deeply together, and they will help one another examine the basis of what constitutes their own judgments, and the judgments of all others. In this way, they have been learning to expand their level of consciousness to embrace larger frameworks of reality than those commonly defined by society. In this way, they have been learning to undo the impact of all the hurtful and negative messages that have come into them from many sources. In this way, they have been learning to repair and heal one another. The essence of this healing concerns learning how to be safely vulnerable again, and to create a sense of safety with one another. In this way, they have been learning the difference between manmade laws, judgments, and opinions, and Natural Law—the role of natural judgment, and its correct use.

The challenge for such a couple is to realize that issues of the past—their own individual pasts, and their pasts together—will cyclically come up between them. This is intentional because both of their Souls are attempting to purge their pasts entirely so that a new cycle can begin that is free from that past. This is very important to remember and accept because the past that they share is not pleasant. As such, this past can influence and contaminate their emotional reality; the past never seems to go away. If not understood properly, this dynamic can create a sense of futility and of being defeated relative to making the efforts to be free from that past. This can poison an otherwise wonderful relationship. The challenge, again, is to accept this as necessary for it will lead to freedom from the past.

Because many of these couples have experienced these dynamics for many lifetimes, they have learned about the impact of societal and parental conditioning. As such, many of these couples will desire to help others understand the same thing. Because of this common desire, each one as individuals, and both as a couple, will strive to actualize work that is dedicated to helping others in the context of society. The intention in this work is to help others understand the nature of their own inherent individuality, and how to actualize that individuality. In this way, they can help others "decondition" and "decompress" from the negative impact of their own families and society. Such a couple will have a very real empathy for such people. Others will trust them accordingly.

Sexually, such a couple will have much healing to do together. Both have been wounded and used in this way. Sometimes the nature of these wounds has been caused by other family members. At other times, these wounds have been caused by adult partners who had dishonest sexual, psychological, and emotional agendas. This has occurred because both of them have unresolved emotions linked with childhood. As such, they are intensely emotionally needy—emotionally starved for necessary nurturing. Because of this, each has all too often attracted sexual predators who can manipulate them relative to working out their own distorted agendas. When these two have come together, they have typically found themselves already wounded. The whole orientation in the beginning of their sexual relationship is to heal these wounds. Because of this, they will be very careful and responsible to one another, ever careful to not create any sense in the other of being used, controlled, or violated sexually. As time goes on, their sexual relationship will deepen and mature. As it does so, the depths of their sexual relationship together can actually touch their Souls. Finding safety and comfort with one another allows for their mutual fear of vulnerability to give way to total vulnerability. Touching and holding will be equally as important to them as the sexual act. Relative to the Individuated state, each will not be afraid to challenge the social conventions of the existing society. They will progressively accept that sexual desires and needs are natural for each. Without judgment, they will allow these desires and needs to be acted on.

In the Spiritual state, this placement will correlate with a couple who has desired to be totally free from all conditioning and judgment dynamics that manifest from parental and societal reality. They have desired to create their own system of reality as defined through spiritual laws of one kind or another, one that will serve as the very foundation of the relationship itself. In this way, they have desired to transcend the influence of society and parents so that the impact from each becomes minimized to non-existent. Their new, more real family, so to speak, becomes God and all those that are actively seeking God in their own lives. Their parents become Divine Father and Mother, or Mother Earth and Father Sky. Embracing spiritual reality has thus allowed them to create their own "system" of reality in which the nature of their specific psychological, emotional, and sexual wounds is understood from the point of view of karmic causes, and/or evolutionary necessity. In this way, each has been progressively learning to accept responsibility for their own actions, and to absolutely accept the responsibility for their overall life conditions. As a result of this, each has progressively purged the dynamic and temptation to feel victimized by life in any way. Such couples will take their responsibilities in life very seriously, and will consciously strive to actualize the specific roles that they have in life in the fullest possible way. Each will encourage the development of those roles and responsibilities in one another. Such couples will be perceived by many others as a lighthouse of wisdom, compassion, understanding, encouragement, and salvation. As such, many of these couples will feel naturally drawn to some kind of work in the context of society, and the world, that is focused on healing, counseling, or teaching in some way that involves spiritual principles.

For couples who have just evolved into this state, the underlying dynamics of guilt and negative judgment that have built up over many lifetimes can cause them to embrace very strict spiritual systems that reinforce the sense of guilt and negative judgment from a spiritual point of view. The sense of guilt and negative judgment occurs relative to measuring their "spiritual progress" according to the nature of the spiritual beliefs. Naturally, they never quite "measure up" to what is expected of them relative to the standards of these beliefs, and this is the causal factor in their guilt. Within these types of couples it is also possible that one has attempted to control or judge the spiritual development of the other—to function as a "spiritual authority" to the other. When this is the case, the dynamic of displaced emotions from one or the other's family of origin, due to the primary nurturing that was needed yet not given, is the causal factor wherein one of them is making the other a "divine mother or father figure" that symbolizes ultimate authority. When these are the operative dynamics, it is essential that such a couple deeply examine why they have chosen a spiritual system that reinforces their sense of guilt and negative judgments together. It is also essential to deeply examine why one or the other is playing the role of "ultimate authority" while the other is needing this role to be played out for them. Until the causative factors are understood for these conditions, the couple's evolutionary progress will come to a standstill, both individually and together.

Sexually speaking, most of these couples will have evolved to a situation wherein they have realized that sexual energy and desire is inherent to the human organism. As such, they will be free from societal or religious judgments. They will naturally embrace sexual practices that are linked with a necessary healing of old wounds, and/or practices that are used to expand consciousness itself. Some will even employ specific practices that have the intention of bringing to culmination the sexual karma that they have created with other people in this or other lifetimes. They will allow and encourage the specific nature of one another's sexual desires to be actualized because they each understand that such desires are linked with the evolutionary progression and development of their Souls, leading ultimately to the progressive elimination of all separating desires, including sexual desires. They will understand that each such desire has a reason for being, and will strive to understand this reason. In this way, self-knowledge occurs for each person and the relationship itself. For example, many such couples will have sexual desires to be dominated, or to dominate. In the spiritual condition, such couples will understand that this type of desire reflected the Soul's desire to be consumed and dominated by God. Through one another such couples can "act out" this desire through the employment of specific sexual practices in which this "domination" takes place. Yet this dynamic is understood and expected from a spiritual point of view, rather than from a sadomasochistic point of view.

POLARITY POINT IN CANCER OR THE FOURTH HOUSE

The archetypal themes that correlate with this polarity point involve the need to penetrate to all emotional and psychological causes that have created the fear of vulnerability, the fear of judgment, the fear of loss or abandonment, and the fear of betrayal. The intention is also to focus on the nature of the parental and societal conditioning in the sense of how this created and shaped what "reality" is—the reality of one inner and outer self, and the reality of the phenomenal world as conditioned by consensus or religious belief patterns. The challenge is to create a personal reality and identity for the relationship that is a reflection of who each partner is inwardly: to allow each person's inner being to come out from hiding, and to assert itself without the fear of ridicule or judgment. In other words, to allow the inner reality of each to become the outer reality for both. This will require great courage because it will demand an examination of that which is being repressed in each, and for what reasons. Each person must learn how to do this from within themselves, and to encourage this in the other. In this way, each person within the relationship will learn how to become inwardly secure and emotionally free.

Within this, it is essential that the couple examine the nature of all dynamics that can cause them to attempt to control or manipulate the development or behavior of each other. All dynamics that can cause one to become dependent on the other must be deeply explored, because the evolutionary intention in this polarity point is for both to become secure from within themselves: to eliminate all external causes of dependency linked with emotional and psychological security. It is also essential that the couple learn how to balance their needs of sustaining their worldly obligations and duties with their needs for a deep and active life of an emotional nature that must occur within the context of their "private time."

For those in the more advanced state of evolution, it can also be very important to recognize how to bring to completion the karmic journeys that they have been sharing with others over many lifetimes. Each person within the relationship will have knowledge of the people with whom such sharing has been taking place. Accordingly, each must desire to break the karmic causes and reasons that have kept them bound to whoever has not had their best interests in their own hearts and souls. This can be very possible in the advanced states, because in these states each Soul has already learned to accept responsibility for its own actions. The couple in these states who have the composite Tenth House Pluto, or Pluto in Capricorn, must learn how to do this so that they can bring an entire cycle to completion in this life. In this way, they will begin a brand-new cycle of evolutionary development together that is free from the burdens of the past—a past together that has been full of great emotional pain suffered at the hands of many other people, and who have fulfilled their need to be punished because of their underlying sense of guilt.

PLUTO IN THE ELEVENTH HOUSE OR AQUARIUS

For couples who have composite Pluto in the Eleventh House or Aquarius, a variety of archetypal dynamics could have been oriented to in past lifetimes depending on the evolutionary condition or state of the couple. These themes or dynamics include interacting with one another in order to learn how to stand back from the immediacy of each other's emotional and psychological reality in order to view it objectively. This theme or dynamic could have taken place in the context of being very close friends together, in the context of meeting each other through a group which formed for a shared purpose or reason, or through a group of people who were working together toward a shared social purpose or function—to start a community or commune, or to work within or start an organization that has a specific social or environmental function, for example. Whatever the specific context was in which such a couple has met each other, the intention was to help each other objectify the specific nature of each other's overall circumstantial reality, and the emotional and psychological dynamics that were the causal factors for that reality. For this to be accomplished, each person has helped the other to detach and disengage from the immediacy of their inner and outer life. In so doing, they have helped each other to see in very clear ways the reasons and causal factors or dynamics that were responsible for the specific nature of their overall reality, and the reality of specific circumstances occurring at any specific moment.

The intention within the desire to objectify each other's life conditions through disengagement and detachment has also been to liberate and change any causal dynamic that has created a condition of stagnation and non-growth. In many cases, such people have desired to change or shift their relationship from the context of being very close and like-minded friends to the context of intimacy: to become lovers. This situation has typically occurred because both had reached a point in life in which they desired to rebel against those conditions in order to be free from them. Sharing this common desire to rebel against whatever their existing life conditions were has thus brought them together intimately.

When this has been the case, other circumstantial variables could have come into play. For example, one or the other, or both, could have already been in a committed intimate relationship with someone else in which an existing problem was creating some degree of polarization within the relationship. Finding help for and understanding of this problem through one another could then have led each of them to desire to become intimate with the other. When this has been the situation, it has all too often been kept in secret from the existing partner. In other words, their shared intimacy has occurred while one or the other, or both, attempted to maintain their existing relationship. Karmically, of course, this has created difficulties for one or both partners relative to those existing partners.

In other situations, there may have been no existing partner when the shift was made from friendship to intimacy. In many of these cases, the shift to intimacy has led the termination of their relationship. This has occurred because the shift has changed the dynamic between them from friends who could help each other objectively see the nature of their reality, to intimate partners who subsequently lost that objectivity. The proximity of intimacy created a psychological and emotional compression between them which then collapsed the ability to be objective because of the unresolved emotional and psychological issues that each had as individuals relative to their own intimate relationship issues. These individual relationship issues were operating independently of one another until they became intimate with one another. When this has been the case, a karma has also projected on the other's motivations and intentions for desiring to become intimate that rarely has anything to do with each other's actual reality. Thus, it is a karma of mutual projection. Obviously, this is the opposite of how the original connection was first created—through the ability of each to help the other objectify and see clearly the nature of their reality, and the reasons for that reality.

In some other cases, this dynamic of friends who can help each other clearly see the nature of their individual reality has been arrived at differently. Relative to the evolutionary nature of life, many couples who have composite Pluto in the Eleventh House or Aquarius have recently shifted their relationship from intimacy to friendship. This occurs in evolutionary terms for one of two reasons. In the first case, the couple has become so hopelessly enmeshed psychologically and emotionally that their ability to see and understand each other objectively had become non-existent. Relative to this, the shifting into a friendship dynamic will allow each to progressively develop the ability to understand the other objectively because such a shift is the exact antidote, karmically and evolutionarily, for the breakdown between them that occurred because of intimacy. In the second case, the couple had developed and completed their desire to be in intimate relationships with one another while at the same time desiring to keep connected to one another in subsequent lifetimes. This is simply a natural evolutionary progression from intimacy to friendship reflected in each other's mutual desires to stay connected to one another for many lifetimes. They simply like and enjoy one another, and have created a mutual desire and promise to help one another in future lifetimes in the context of being trusted friends. When this is the case, a karma of mutual dependency is sustained.

Another theme or archetype that could have been in operation prior to this life when composite Pluto is in the Eleventh House or Aquarius involves two people who have desired to work together toward some common life objective or goals. This has typically produced a limited kind of partnership or relationship that has a singularity of purpose. Within the sharing of the mutual goals or objectives there has been a high degree of like-mindedness and focus. A connectedness to one another has occurred because of the mutual desires reflected in the shared objective or goals. Yet, typically, this connectedness is limited to those goals or objectives, and does not include a connectedness to the rest of one another's overall life situation. This situation occurs because the overall life conditions and specific nature of each partner's individual reality is inwardly and outwardly so very different from the other's. As a result, there has been no real way to connect to one another beyond the shared focus reflected in the commonality of some specific objective or goal that has been actualized together in some kind of social context of a non-intimate nature. This dynamic, however, has still allowed each to objectify reality through the other because each is so different than the other. It is because each is so different in a comprehensive way that both must detach from those

individual differences in order for the actualization of the shared objectives or goals to occur. This detachment thus allows a *de facto* acceptance of those differences to occur. In this way, each of them
serves to help the other to expand their consciousness relative to experiencing and accepting the diversity and totality of life itself: to not
limit evolutionary growth simply because something is different or
conflicting with one's existing belief or value systems.

For other couples who have composite Pluto in the Eleventh
House or Aquarius, a very difficult situation has occurred in prior lifetimes which has caused the relationship to not be complete or finished. This situation correlates with the sudden, unexpected loss or termination of the relationship. This loss or termination will have
appeared to "come out of the blue." This kind of situation, of course,
creates tremendous emotional shock, a shock so deep and thorough
that there is no real ability to have any perspective serving as a guide-
post to why this has occurred. Sometimes this lack of perspective precludes resolution of the situation within the lifetime that the traumatic separation took place. When this occurs, it creates its own set of
psychological and emotional problems, and, for some, it can be very
difficult to carry on with the rest of one's life.

There can be several causes or reasons for this sudden, unexpected loss. In the context of being friends, either or both may have had
some secret agenda, motives, or intentions that they have hidden from
the other. When at some point these intentions surface, it is a sudden
surprise and shock to the one who was unaware of their partner's true
intentions. This sudden surfacing has then produced an insurmountable
rift within the relationship leading to its sudden termination. Another
example in the context of being friends involves an excessive co-dependency that has been built up to the point that neither one can function without the other. This excessive dependency has thus become a
causal factor in one of them suddenly dying, or in some way suddenly disappearing from the other's life. The sudden termination of the relationship has then forced one or both of them to learn how to function without the other. If the relationship has been in the context of
intimacy, the reason for this sudden loss involves issues that arise when
the same excessive dependency on one another has also occurred. The
sudden termination or loss of one another has occurred for the same
reason as above—for each to learn how to function without the other.

The condition of sudden loss or termination of the relationship
can always be seen when the following astrological patterns exist:

composite Pluto in the Eleventh House conjunct the South Node; composite Pluto in the Eleventh House and being squared by any planet except the Sun (with the squaring planet being in either the Second or Eighth Houses); or composite Pluto in the Eleventh House and in opposition to any planet (except the Sun) in the Fifth House.

In the Consensus state, this placement correlates to a couple who has come together in friendship or intimacy because of experiencing a mutual frustration with the overall conditions of their lives. This mutual frustration reflects in each a desire to change or liberate from those conditions in some way. As a result, this couple has spent a great deal of time in conversations wherein they have extended mutual support, validation, and empathy toward one another. In this way, they have been learning how to detach from and objectify the nature of the conditions creating the sense of frustration. This has been done through examining the psychological dynamics in each which has served as the causal factors in the frustration. In so doing, a deep self-knowledge has occurred in each through the nature of their connection together. For some, this knowledge has actually been used to try and change those life conditions. These changes have caused both to necessarily terminate and radically alter the nature of their pre-existing relationships. This, in turn, has created many problems for each. These problems occurred through the other people who were part of each other's life prior to the necessary changes. Many of these other people have rebelled or created all manner of problems for these two as the necessary changes were implemented. As this was occurring, the couple continued to support each other so that the changes could be sustained.

For others, these changes have been talked about without actually implementing the knowledge gained through one another which would allow for the changes to be made. When this has been the case, such a couple has continued to live with a high degree of frustration because of not implementing the necessary changes. Typically, as a result, both have then created secret realities that most others in their lives knew nothing about. The nature of those secret realities would be symbolic of the changes that both of them actually wanted to make. In essence, they had created a double reality—maintaining the existing nature of their circumstantial reality because of a fear to change it, while, at the same time, creating a hidden life or reality that most others know nothing about.

Sexually speaking, when there has been intimacy shared in this way, such a couple has desired to embrace new or experimental ways of being sexual. This implies a pre-existing frustration with the ways that they had been sexual, either with themselves or with other people. These new ways will typically have been held in secrecy from all other people except those of like mind. For some who have maintained their connection at a friendship level only, there has been a desire to be sexual with one another that has not been acted on for a variety of reasons. When this has been the case, they have had sex together "in their heads." This unresolved desire from prior lifetimes can become its own causal factor leading to becoming lovers in this or another life.

In the Individuated state, this placement correlates to a couple who has experienced a fundamental estrangement and alienation from normal society together. Accordingly, they have bonded together through this mutual alienation, and served to support and validate one another because of it. In this evolutionary state, they have discussed a wide range of topics that concern the nature of what we all call reality. There has been a mutual desire to detach and stand apart from the mainstream of life. From this vantage point, they have desired to experiment with many different ways of living—to test various beliefs, values, and the lifestyles that these create. They have learned to understand and to see one another in very objective terms, and to facilitate the individual growth needs of each, even when this has meant changing the dynamics in their own relationship. Many, for example, shift from being friends to lovers, back to friends, then back to lovers, etc., over many lifetimes as their individual needs for growth dictate.

The intensity of their bond has occurred through the commonality of their thought processes. The commonality of their thought processes has served to create a magnetism of vibrational like-mindedness. Because of the commonality of mutual alienation from mainstream societies, many of these couples have desired to live together in communities or communes of like-minded Souls—fellow passengers on Earth who have also felt fundamental estrangement from ordinary people. Forming or being in such communities with other people has allowed them to continue in their evolutionary process of individuation, and to feel sustained because of community. Many of these couples, accordingly, have created great works together in one form or another. The nature of these great works has had a transformative impact of the very social systems that they felt alienated and estranged from. Other couples in this evolutionary condition have simply bonded with others in small blocks of people who have experienced this same alienation without creating formal communities—

groups of people who live on the streets, so to speak, or who operate in other group contexts.

Sexually speaking, when there has been this kind of intimacy, such couples have openly rebelled and rejected the prevailing social mores or customs of the existing society. As in the Consensus state, there has been the desire to experiment with any way of being sexual that was in defiance of existing social/sexual mores and customs. The difference here is that this rebellion is open versus being done in secrecy.

In the Spiritual state, this placement indicates a couple who has desired to radically liberate from all the internal and external conditioning factors of life that shape our sense of inner and outer reality. They have done this through an absolute rebellion against all external forms of authority, and through intense spiritual practices that have had the effect of creating a consciousness that is utterly observational—essentially detached from within itself in order to objectively observe the causal factors for any thought, feeling, or emotion. In this way, absolute self-knowledge occurs which then can be used to continue the deconditioning process. This couple has served to facilitate this process together, and, as such, has created a high degree of bonding with one another.

Many have either joined or come together in spiritual communities that have had this intention. Others have simply become a group of two, so to speak. Still others have formed or become part of small groups of like-minded Souls that have had no specific connection to formal spiritual communities. In all cases, the intention of freedom from external conditioning has been the same.

Sexually speaking, almost all couples in this evolutionary condition will have so fundamentally detached their consciousness in order to create the observational effect necessary to self-knowledge, that the sexual function of the body is no longer experienced within their consciousness. As a result, sexual desire has been detached from and not acted on.

POLARITY POINT IN THE FIFTH HOUSE OR LEO

The primary archetypal themes that this polarity point correlates to in order for an evolutionary progression to proceed are relative to the actual context or dynamics that have defined the couple before this life. In the case of friends or lovers who have become too dependent on one another for validation, support, encouragement, and sustainment, the lesson becomes learning how to take full charge of their own lives independent of the other. In essence, they need to learn how to become inwardly self-validating and self-sustaining in such a way as to creatively actualize and to act on the nature of the thoughts that lead to a lifestyle and way of being that are symbolic and reflective of who they actually are on an inner basis. In so doing, they will change their inner vibration and progressively attract people of like mind who will serve to nourish this new development. In so doing, they will learn who their real friends are and are not.

In the case of the individuated Souls who have experienced a fundamental alienation and estrangement from mainstream society, and who have resisted integrating into that society because of the alienation, the lesson becomes one of creatively actualizing and integrating their ideas, values, and ideals, in the context of society in such a way that the uniqueness of their specific works or lives have a transformative effect on the mainstream society itself. Each person within the couple must learn how to do this on their own terms, and in their own ways independent of one another.

For those in the Spiritual state, the primary lesson is to take the tremendous amount of knowledge that they have on the nature of reality from a conditioning point of view, and to creatively actualize specific forms through which to disseminate this knowledge to others. In this way, they can help others become aware of the nature of their own conditioning patterns, and they can help those so inclined to become more liberated from such patterns in order to actualize their own inherent individuality.

PLUTO IN THE TWELFTH HOUSE OR PISCES

For couples who have composite Pluto in the Twelfth House or Pisces, a variety of archetypal themes have been oriented to depending on their evolutionary condition, needs, and karmic conditions. These themes include the mutual desire to help each other expose and understand the causal factors in the nature of their delusions, illusions, fears, and/or phobias of all kinds. Within this, the desire to help each other heal the effects of various traumas and/or to heal the nature of any emotional, psychological, or sexual wound could have defined the intention for their relationship. Such couples have also desired to penetrate to the core of each other's Souls with the intention of helping each other identify the causal factors in each other's psychological reactions to life. The intention within this has been to help each other metamorphose any psychological dynamic that has been inhibiting or blocking necessary growth—to help each other to become as inwardly open, healed, and free as possible.

When this has been the operative archetype or dynamic, such couples will have experienced an extreme psychic sensitivity to one another. This sensitivity has been caused by their mutual desire to penetrate to the core of each other's Souls. Anatomically and physiologically, the Twelfth House, Pisces, and Neptune correlate to the pineal gland within the brain. This gland secretes a hormone called melatonin. This hormone sensitizes consciousness in order to dissolve any boundary or barrier preventing direct connection to the Source of all things: God. Its ultimate function is to help the Soul merge itself consciously with God. Thus, a couple who has had these intentions will automatically magnetize and activate this gland within one another. This mutual activation creates an extreme sensitivity to one another in such a way that each has felt that they are literally and symbolically inside one another at all times. There is no sense of boundaries or separation. The intensity of their mutual sensitivity has created a situation wherein they are always aware of one another at all times in a psychic sense, even when there are thousands of miles of physical distance between them. The mutual activation of this gland has created a condition wherein they psychically osmose each other. As a result, many such couples have the same thoughts, desires, needs, and dreams at the same time.

For many such couples, this condition reflects a mutual desire to merge their Souls together. For these couples, the experience of always being within one another, of experiencing no boundary or separation from one another, is a very desired and joyous experience. These couples have and will feel that they have finally realized their "ultimate" or "perfect" lifemate. Many of these couples, in addition, will have desired to isolate themselves from the overall environment, and to create a reality in which they could simply focus on themselves so that the merging and healing of their Souls could take place. For others, this condition is simply a reflection of their mutual intention to help each other heal a variety of wounds, fears, phobias, traumas, and so on. For some, the situation of feeling that there are no boundaries, that they are always inside of one another, could have been, and can be, quite troublesome because one or the other, or both, can feel that they can never escape or be separate from the other, since a sense of separate life with clear boundaries is non-existent.

Another archetypal theme or dynamic that could have been the causal factor in bringing couples together who have a composite

Twelfth House Pluto or Pluto in Pisces is one in which each has felt a high degree of obligation toward the other, an obligation to help and take care of one another at all costs. Some will understand or feel this in karmic terms, others will simply feel this sense of obligation without knowing why. When this has been the operative dynamic, each has felt that they must sacrifice their own individual needs, desires, and life for the other. For many this has created the very real psychological feeling of being in a symbolic prison with no way out. The causes of this situation can include the following:

- A situation wherein either or both have severely betrayed and violated the trust of the other to the extent that an intense trauma was produced. The trauma itself created a state of psychological disintegration and immobilization.

- A situation wherein either or both have operated as sadistic tormentors in one form or another. Massive and intense abuse of a psychological, emotional, or sexual nature occurred in which an almost absolute destruction of the other's Soul took place

- A situation wherein one person has sacrificed their own physical life in order to save the other. The causes or scenarios in which this could have occurred can be many. The overall signature existing in their mutual synastry charts combined with the composite chart will reveal exactly the scenarios and causes of this situation. The one who had been saved will thus feel the desire to sacrifice their life to the other, subsequent to the life in which they had been saved.

- A situation wherein either or both have misrepresented themselves to the other in extreme ways, which caused an intense disillusionment to occur which, in turn, caused a state of psychological catatonia to manifest.

- A situation wherein either or both has desired to kill (and/or has killed) the other for a variety of reasons usually linked with feeling victimized in severe ways.

Another archetypal theme or dynamic that could have occurred with a couple who has composite Pluto in the Twelfth House or Pisces is the mutual desire to bring to culmination an entire evolutionary cycle of being together as intimate partners. When this has been the operative dynamic, such couples will exhibit an unconditional love, acceptance, and giving to one another. There will be a great peace and silence between them that reflects an absolute knowledge of one another. There will be an almost absolute sense of inner attunement to one another, and they will seem almost as one person. Such couples will be highly reflective together, almost museful. Some who are evolved to the Spiritual state will have the ability to consciously remember their entire or partial prior-life journeys together which have brought them to the point of releasing each other from the desire and need to be together intimately.

Another archetypal theme or dynamic that could have occurred with a couple who has composite Pluto in the Twelfth House or Pisces is one wherein there has been a mutual desire to help one another to learn how to simplify life together, and to only act on that which is essential for life to be sustained. When this is the operative dynamic, it usually correlates to a couple who has experienced previous lives of great turmoil, chaos, crisis, and complexity, individually or together. In those lives, a state of mutual and individual exhaustion had been reached. As a reaction, this type of couple has thus manifested the mutual desire to actualize a life of simplicity wherein only that which was essential for life to be sustained was acted on. As a result, they would have had some very recent lifetimes together wherein they had desired to live in relatively remote or rural environments that were sparse with regard to other human beings. They desired to live close to the land with many animals, plants, and the ability to grow their own food.

In the Consensus state, this placement correlates to a couple whose specific reality depends on what archetypal dynamics have been in place in prior lifetimes. For those who have had the intention to help each other heal various wounds, fears, phobias, and so on, the couple will have lived in relative isolation from others, and will have made a mutual commitment to some guiding religious doctrine. They would have appeared invisible to most other people. The intensity of their deep and quiet life together has produced an invisible bubble in which they operate together. For those who have felt a deep obligation to one another for whatever causes, such a couple will exhibit a deep inner isolation from one another while at the same time constantly taking care of one another, or one will be always taking care of the other. Many will exhibit an unspoken bitterness toward the other. There will be a sense of being tormented through one another. One or the other, or both, may seek escape from this situation through alcohol or drugs, or through a fanatical focus on some religious doctrine.

Those couples who are bringing to completion an entire relationship cycle will live a very well-ordered life of a very simple nature. They will seem like one person in many ways, and will exhibit a love that is simple, natural, deep, quiet, and unconditional. They will have made a mutual commitment to some guiding religious doctrine. They will be generous to others, and desire to help others who are in sincere need. Those couples who have desired to learn how to simplify their lives together will be living in a relatively secluded environment, minding their own business, appearing to be like countless other "normal" people, and sharing a mutual religious commitment.

Sexually speaking, the dynamic of touching and holding will be more important for most of these couples than sexual intercourse itself. Sexual expression, when it does occur, will be an extension of this touching and holding: slow, gentle, and sensitive. There will be no need to sexually experiment, and the sexual expression will be quite conventional according to the sexual norms of the existing society. For others, particularly for those in a condition of obligation, the sexual dynamic is most commonly non-existent. In situations where the dynamic of still trying to hurt the other is present, the sexual orientation can be a sadomasochistic nature wherein each is working out the distortions of these archetypes.

In the Individuated state, couples who have desired to help each other heal various wounds, phobias, fears, etc., will exhibit an intense bonding to one another, and alternate in the roles of saving and being saved. Their mutual attunement toward one another will reflect a conscious awareness of each other at all times. They will also exhibit a deep distrust at many other people, and will be very exclusive of whom they allow into their lives. Accordingly, they will seem very reclusive and unavailable to most others. Their life together will alternate between cycles of intense discussion and communion, and cycles of a deep quietness in which they simply live together fulfilling whatever their specific tasks and obligations are. Their deep attunement to one another can also create a situation wherein each reproduces the unresolved wounds of the other. They will have made a mutual commitment to some eclectic form of psychological, philosophical, or spiritual system of thought. Those couples who have desired to begin the process of remerging or merging their Souls together will also exhibit these same dynamics. Yet these couples will have had an even more intense desire to isolate themselves from life, and their knowledge of one another will be more inclusive and deep.

Those couples in a state of obligation will exhibit an almost total isolation from one another on an inner basis, with each living a life quite removed from the other. Both will attempt to actualize some sort of independent life in the sense of fulfilling some sort of vision that correlates with their own specific individual sense of purpose of life. They will feel intensely tied to one another without necessarily knowing why, or how to change it. Bitter toward one another, they will alternate between cycles of verbal criticism toward one another, and cycles of an uncomfortable silence. Each will project what is occurring in their own subconscious dynamics on the other. Some will escape through drugs, alcohol, or through acting out various fantasies that the other may know nothing about.

Those who have desired to actualize the archetype of simplicity together exhibit the manifestation of a combined vision that takes them to a relatively remote environment in which they can simply focus on making whatever the nature of that vision is come true. They will be highly individualistic people who are deeply creative. A quiet, permeating love will exist between them which will inspire many other people. They will unconditionally support each other in whatever they desire to do or become. They will share a common commitment to some guiding spiritual philosophy, yet apply it in their own individual way.

Sexually speaking, most of these couples would have begun the transition between primary, physical sex to an orientation to sexual practices that have the intention of expanding consciousness together. The mutual attunement to one another's Souls is reflected in their emotional and sexual attunement toward one another. As a result, there typically is a deep sexual harmony between them in which maximum satisfaction can take place. Many will exhibit a desire to be consumed sexually through one another—to symbolically be inside of each other, so to speak. The sexual energy between them can alternate between intense, consuming passion and expression, to gentle and slow lovemaking. Many will encourage the acting out of one kind of sexual fantasy or another. They can be highly creative in a sexual sense. They will be alternating cycles of intense sexual involvement with one another, and cycles in which the sexual involvement does not take place. Many of those in the condition of obligation will not be sexual with each other. Some will seek sexual fulfillment with others, and this will be done in high secrecy in most cases. Others will desire to sexually abuse or ridicule the other in some way. This can also include acting out the sadomasochistic form of sexuality together.

In the Spiritual state, this placement correlates to couples who reflect the desire to merge their Souls together, the desire to unconditionally help each other heal whatever unresolved wounds exist, or the desire to complete a whole evolutionary journey together. The condition of obligation to one another will not exist in this condition as manifested in the other evolutionary states. In this state, this archetype will manifest as feeling obligated to help as many other people as God asks them to help because of the natural wisdom and knowledge that each will have, both individually and together.

Such couples will have committed together to a guiding spiritual philosophy of life. Their entire life will be defined by it, and it will permeate the very essence of their consciousness. They will serve as examples to others because of it. They will exhibit an unconditional love and acceptance of one another, and they will experience inner divinity within themselves and each other because of their relationship. Each will be committed to a work that is dedicated to helping other people in some way, both individually and together. They will seem as if they are one person, and they will have a total awareness of each other at all times. Their thoughts, desires, needs, dreams, etc., will be the same at almost all times. No boundaries will exist between them. When problems do manifest, they will exhibit a patience toward one another that allows the problem to resolve itself. They will speak to each other as necessary, and enjoy great moments of silence together. They will also experience the desire to withdraw from the world as much as possible, yet be highly responsible in fulfilling whatever their specific roles are that involve helping other people.

Sexually speaking, such couples will exhibit a total orientation to sacred sexual practices that are intended to allow each to experience the inner Godhead within themselves and each other. If sexual healing is necessary because of left over wounds from other lifetimes, or wounds created in this life before they met, they will employ the appropriate methods for this to be accomplished. If either has the desire to act out a sexual fantasy, each will understand this to be necessary, healthy, and positive because each will realize that this is the way to eliminate any kind of desire that prevents the Soul from merging back into God. They will manifest a deep sexual and Soul attunement with one another, and will both be aware of what each other needs. Their deepest sense of satisfaction will occur through the satisfaction of the other, so to speak.

POLARITY POINT IN THE SIXTH HOUSE OR VIRGO

One of the deepest archetypal themes that this polarity point correlates to for most of the couples at this evolutionary junction is to learn when to help each other heal the various wounds that most have built up over various lifetimes, and when to let each other resolve or heal those wounds for themselves. Relative to the Twelfth House or Pisces, the desire to always help, to always sacrifice oneself in this way, is a primary orientation. There are, of course, times when helping another actually is a disservice to the other because it does not allow them to do their own essential work. Thus, this polarity point is teaching many of these couples exactly that lesson. When to help, and when not to, can be a very confusing issue for some of these couples. The very best way to know when to help, and when not to, is to simply inwardly attune oneself to the intuitive element within consciousness. The answer will always be there. The challenge is to learn how honor it even while feeling the temptation to help anyway.

This lesson will extend beyond the couple itself, and be included or linked with the other people that the couple feels drawn to help, both individually and together. Again, the answer of when to help, and when not to, will be intuitively felt within their consciousness.

Another primary theme or intention for many of these couples is to learn how to balance their desire, need, and temptation for living a life of relative seclusion from the world, with their evolutionary and karmic requirement to do individual and/or collective work together that has the intention of benefiting others in some way. For those in the condition wherein they have felt a deep obligation toward one another, or one to the other, it is essential to not only complete what the karmic obligation is about, but to strive to learn to accept the responsibility for this condition versus the temptation to continue to feel victimized because of it. If the dynamic of feeling victimized because of this obligation is sustained, then the karma will also be sustained and keep recycling itself until an acceptance of responsibility for this condition occurs. Many who are in this situation will benefit through professional therapy, although the therapist should have the capacity to explore the past-life dynamics responsible for this situation. A past-life hypnotherapist might be the answer here.

Chapter Twelve

Pluto in Sagittarius

Since most of this book was written while Pluto has been in Scorpio, I feel it would be beneficial for most readers if some thoughts were written about Pluto's movement into Sagittarius. In order to accurately understand Pluto's manifestation in Sagittarius, and the future dynamics or events that it will correlate to, it is essential to understand the past which has lead to and created the reality that we are all experiencing now. We must remember that astrology only correlates to reality, it does not cause it. Remember also that astrology only operates relative to the observed and existing reality of anything—societies, world events, and individual people. To accurately understand the past that has conditioned and defined the moment is to understand the probabilities of inner and outer future events. In this spirit and perspective, I would like to begin this understanding by succinctly discussing the historical past that has led to our times.

Beyond discussing Pluto's movement into Sagittarius, it is also important to remember and understand that nothing exists of itself; everything in the Creation is interrelated and interdependent. Thus, in terms of our current context, most astrologers recognize that we have begun the movement into the Aquarius Age. And as we move into the Aquarius Age, it obviously means that the Pisces Age is now beginning to culminate. Anytime an Age comes to culmination, the opportunity and evolutionary intention is for the cycle of history relative to that Age to stop repeating itself. In order for this to occur, all the dynamics that are part of that Age come to a head within a relatively brief amount of time. This phenomena thus creates a period of time in which the psychological experience of reality becomes one of condensed intensity, both individually and collectively. The psychological experience of time being condensed thus allows for the essence of all the dynamics that have defined collective and individual reality to be experienced, and, hopefully, to be understood. This understanding produces realizations that reflect the new times or Age that is evolving into existence. This realization symbolizes and reflects the new paradigms that we must individually and collectively embrace so that growth and evolution can occur in order to stop the cycle of individual or collective history from repeating itself.

From the point of view of thousands of years of history, it is an obvious fact that even when the Ages have gone into transition, the prior cycle of history tends to repeat itself despite the evolutionary intention not to. Why is this? The answer to this question reflects the very essence of the philosophical premise of the *Pluto* books—the four natural evolutionary conditions of the Soul. If we remember that seventy percent of the collective mass of people inhabit the Consensus evolutionary condition, then we can understand why the cycle of history rarely stops repeating itself until some cataclysmic event or events create a reality in which there is no choice but to change. Remember that the Consensus state is a state in which the operative principle is Saturnian: the need to conform to the existing understanding of phenomenal reality as defined by the majority of people in any time or place. As a result, seventy percent of the people anywhere cannot stand back and detach themselves from the time or place in which they live. Because of this, there is no ability to carry forward or apply the lessons learned from any event or dynamic, either personally or collectively. Please remember that just fifty years ago, during the last World War, the collective thought and slogan that followed the insanity of the concentration camps was "This will never happen again." Unfortunately, it has already happened again relative to many current events on Earth—the insanity of the "ethnic cleansing" of the Bosnian War being but one example.

So as we discuss the future possibilities of Pluto's movement into Sagittarius, it is essential that we understand the historical cycles that have conditioned the structural nature of our existing reality. And it is essential, at this point in time, that we embrace the fact that we have entered a time frame in which the transition of the Ages between Pisces and Aquarius is now just beginning. From the point of view of the past, it is critical that we understand that during the last Aquarian Age, 25,000 years ago, that the original matriarchy was firmly established. By evolving into a new Aquarian Age, it would seem essential that we understand, as best we can, what the context was for the last Aquarian Age if we are to apply what was understood and realized then so that a harmonization with what is needed now can take place.

In essence, the matriarchal reality was a reality in which all people lived in harmony with natural laws; the laws of the natural world which are self-evident. Nature was understood to be fully conscious, interrelated, and interdependent, and all created forms of life within nature were seen to be co-equal. Nature reflected on Earth was considered to be God—there were no sky gods at that time. In today 's world, this is what we call Gaia. As a result, the belief systems of that time were directly linked to the self-evident laws of the natural world. As such, all people interpreted phenomenal reality from the point of view of natural laws. In so doing, the matriarchy lived within a total state of balance and equality within the totality of the rest of the manifested Creation. Their teachers were the self-evident laws of nature, and more specifically, the animals and plants around them. Animals and plants were considered to have living spirits within them that could teach and communicate with people, and vice versa.

Within the matriarchy, men and women patterned their own relationships in direct observance of the natural world by observing how the various animals lived within their own realities, and how the gender roles of masculine and feminine were naturally acted out. In this way, it was understood that the source of Creation emanated from the feminine principle, since the act of giving birth and the maintenance of the family units was dependent on the feminine members of whatever tribe or pack of animals they were observing. At the time of the matriarchy, neither men nor women had the intellectual knowledge that both men and women co-equally created a baby. Thus, when a woman conceived a child, this was considered to be a magical act directly linked with the Source of Creation Itself, even though there was no concept for that Source in the way that it is understood today. It is this historical fact that was the reason for the existence of the matriarchy. And because of this fact , the ways in which men and women of that time understood and related to their sexuality was also completely different than today. To have sex with a woman was to have sex with the magical aspect of the Creation. In modern vernacular, it would be stated as "making love with God." Thus, sexuality within the framework of the matriarchy was a sacred dynamic that was in harmony with natural laws.

Within the matriarchy there was no monogamy, there was no nuclear family as we know it, there was no paternity, children were raised on a communal basis, and the male children were typically sexually initiated through specific rituals at puberty in order to teach them about the natural laws of, and proper use of, sexual energy. Because the people of that time lived according to natural law, the women and men lived very differently than in today's world, a world totally dominated by patriarchal beliefs. For example, every women has a naturally dual sexual nature. One the one hand, the woman has the need and desire for what can be called the primary partner type of man. This is the type of man who desires by nature to be a constant partner to the women. On the other hand, each women has a natural desire for what can be called the "wild man," this type of man having the natural nature which is the antithesis of the primary partner type of man—to be totally free, uncommitted, and desiring to plant his "seed" in as many places as possible.

There are two natural laws or reasons for this natural evolutionary and biological law. One reason is rooted in the survival of the species itself. What this means is that because the primary causes for death to the human organism are viruses, bacteria, and parasites, the human organism must have a very strong immune system to fight against these types of invasions. To have a strong immune system, the human organism must be able to evolve or mutate the immune system over time. This evolution or mutation occurs through the biological act of sexual intercourse wherein the sperm and ovum combine to make another person—he pre-existing immune systems of the two people who are exchanging their sperm and ovum combine to make a new person, thus a changed or altered immune system that is produced through the fusion of the sperm and the egg. If reproduction of the human species, or most any other form of life was an asexual act, a cell reproducing itself through splitting itself, then the immune systems within the human organism would remain static or fixed. Thus, as a strategy for survival, the human organism (and most other living organisms) has adopted the strategy of sexual intercourse to sustain its own life form. Long ago when the human population on Earth was very small, this required, relative to natural laws, the woman being available to as many men as she could be, so as to experience as much diversity as possible relative to the instinct within the species to survive. This natural law was also part of the necessity of creating diversity within the gene pool of the human organism. Even with a male's sperm there is are special sperms that evolutionary biologists have called "killer sperms." When a man ejaculates into a women, these killer sperms surround the cervix of the women in order to kill or block other sperms from entering the cervix. Those sperms are actually linked to the immune system of the ejaculating man. Thus, a women would have intercourse with as many of the "wild man" types as possible in order for the natural law of "selection" to occur—to only become pregnant by strong, vital men which would then guarantee the survival of the species.

The other reason is also just as important, and natural. This reason or law is rooted in the fact that all living beings carry their entire evolutionary background, or knowledge, in their sexual fluids. When sexual fluids unite in the act of sexual intercourse an osmosis (Pluto) occurs wherein each person is absorbing into themselves the other's "knowledge." Thus, for a woman to embrace the multiplicity of various sexual unions with different men was to expand her own consciousness through the absorption of as much sperm as possible. Through natural law this was and is a evolutionary imperative. In this way, as her own consciousness expanded, the woman would then have the effect of helping the men evolve as she would release her own fluids to the man during intercourse. When people lived naturally, those natural ways were simply lived without any of the problems that have been created by the patriarchy, such as possessiveness, jealousy, attachment, etc. If you doubt the validity of what I am saying, simply visit a professional evolutionary biologist and ask them these questions. Your patriarchal conditioning may be shocked at the answers, because even these scientists have now come to those same realizations. And these dual archetypes in the women still naturally exist, as does the dual archetype for man; the primary partner type of man, and the "wild man" archetype. This is why the issue of monogamy in our times, naturally speaking, is a free choice issue. In other words, monogamy in the sense of one person just being with one other person, is not yet programmed into the genetic structure of the human organism as it is in, say, wolves or eagles. If it were, then all the problems associated with infidelity would not exist; there would be no desire or impulse to not be monogamous. Even two people who are in the best of relationships, who feel totally committed to one another, can still feel instinctual attractions to others.

This alone should demonstrate the natural laws that we are talking about here.

As a result of all these natural ways of living, there is no historical evidence of any kind that demonstrates wars or sexual violations to women throughout the entire time of the matriarchy! Within this, there were no class differences—all was shared equally. People had personal possessions, yet no one owned land—the land was everyone's on an equal basis. Men and women were considered total equals that had their own natural roles. Given these historical facts, this would tend to suggest that by being in harmony with natural laws, such things as wars, sexual violations to women and children, one gender trying to dominate the other, political struggles for power and dominance, the personal psychology of feeling threatened or jealous of a partner leading to attachment or control, simply do not or cannot exist. Comparing this to our "modern" world, and all the truly horrible things that have occurred for thousands of years now, this would seem the ideal to be re-realized!

So the obvious question becomes this—how, when, and why did this way of living change ? The change began when men began to realize that they had an equal role in conceiving a child. This may sound strange, but it is the actual reason that a slow transition began between the matriarchy and what we now call the patriarchy. For reasons that are not yet clear this created a new sense of power in men. Astrologically speaking, this transition began during the Capricorn sub-age of the Cancer Age—rather interesting symbolism given the fact that both Capricorn and Cancer correlate psychologically to gender definition and assignment as promoted by the consensus of any society! Relative to men's new sense of power, the progressive transition to patriarchal domination began. As such, the nature of belief systems themselves began to change. As a result, how phenomenal reality was interpreted and understood also began to change. Instead of living within the context of natural laws and the beliefs that these laws created, the progressive transition to the patriarchy led to manmade beliefs and laws that were in progressive opposition to natural laws. Progressively, as the patriarchy began to take over and dominate, men created belief systems whose intention and motivation was rooted in the need to create justifications for their superiority over women, and, through extension, Nature itself. This started with the invention of "sky gods" that were a simultaneous reflection of the manmade doctrine that there is an intrinsic or natural conflict between the worlds of spirit and flesh.

Flesh, which represented in essence sexuality, was now presented as a temptation that undermined the world of spirit. Thus, to be a spiritual person, to spiritually evolve, one must suppress and control the natural energies emanating from the body. Woman now represented the world of flesh and the sense life of the body. Thus, she now symbolized temptation, and, if followed, man's spiritual downfall. This belief system created by men is represented in many myths developed during this time in history, including the Garden Of Eden Myth. Thus, as the patriarchy became ever more entrenched, became the mainstream of thought, women became progressively subjugated to men's will, control, and domination. It is also interesting to note that as the people evolved during the matriarchal time, they too finally realized that there was an ultimate Creator for the manifested Creation. The first recorded name for such an ultimate creator was Nammu—a female god, not a male god. Nammu was understood to represent the totality of Nature everywhere, and was understood to also be an evolving force, not something that was inherently perfect.

Essentially, women had two choices for thousands of years relative to the patriarchy. A women could either legally declare herself to be a prostitute, in which case she was allowed to own possessions including land, and to educate herself, or she could declare herself to be a "good woman." This meant she had to become married to a man, and reduce her life to living within a small hovel of a house. She was never allowed to leave that house, was not allowed to own possessions or be educated in any way, and was, of course, expected to produce children with the hope that they would be male children. This was essential for men to have yet more power, because to have power was to own land. To have more power, the husband must be able to pass his land and possessions down to his male children. Because of this need, men had to know who they had had intercourse with in order to know who their children were. This became the basis of the nuclear family, paternity, the requirement and expectation for women to be monogamous, and the suppression of natural laws including natural sexual laws. Thus, the ritualized sexual initiation rites for male children at puberty were suppressed. Again, anything that is natural and becomes suppressed will assume distorted forms. For example, by the time of the early Roman Empire, the middle and wealthy classes of people would send their pubescent sons to professional prostitutes in order for this initiation to occur. Yet this was not the same in any way as compared to the sexual rituals of the matriarchy, with its inherent knowing and understanding linked with natural laws. It became reduced to physical sexuality of a rather gross nature. As the centuries unfolded, sexuality was progressively understood to be a simple act of biological reproduction.

In essence, men created belief systems that conceived of a perfect male god, the essence of whose Creation was imperfect (a contradiction that escaped their intellectual cognition for reasons that must now be obvious), and in which men were not only superior to women, but that humans in general were superior to Nature. Relative to man's need to dominate, control, and subjugate women, this also manifested as man's inherent right to dominate and control Nature and natural laws. Over time, women were conceived to be inherently evil (witness the writing of the First Century Christian writers), and were made to feel guilty for being women, since they symbolized man's spiritual downfall. Relative to the manmade idea or belief that God is inherently perfect, and that to achieve spiritual advancement one had to suppress the life of the flesh, women were made to atone for their inherent guilt. And men were made to feel angry for giving in to the temptation embodied in women. As stated earlier in this book, this is the causal factor for the pathology and psychology now called sadomasochism. Both men and women were now taught not only that all must suffer in order to atone for their imperfection as compared to the perfect male god, but that spiritual growth itself was dependent on circumstantial suffering.

Progressively, natural laws and natural living gave way to manmade beliefs that were in direct contradiction to natural laws. We must remember that anything that is suppressed will become distorted at a subconscious level, and that which is natural when suppressed will become the basis of anger or rage. Thus, as the patriarchy became ever more established, the very opposite reality that defined the matriarchy became the "reality" that we all sadly know today. The heritage of the patriarchy includes wars that cause hideous suffering for those involved (wars all too often having "religious" justifications), economic and political classes of people causing class conflicts (the haves and have nots), the psychological and sexual abuse of women and children, the psychological dynamics of jealousy, possessiveness, and attachment within intimate or marital relationships, the psychology of egocentric ambition or self-interest to get ahead of the next person that breeds competition, ulterior motives, secret or dishonest agendas, and the egocentric feeling of being more important than the next person.

Because of these patriarchal belief systems, Nature itself has become progressively violated by human beings. With rare exception, no longer do human beings live within a consciousness of equality with Nature. When natural laws are simply allowed to exist, Nature is always in a state of absolute balance and harmony. Natural laws are self-regulating and self-correcting. Because of the manmade belief that humans are superior to Nature, which is something to be dominated and used for the human benefit, the human organism is in an almost total state of imbalance relative to the rest of the natural world. The consequences of this fact have come (and will continue to come) to a head within this century, and that to follow.

At this point, it may be very interesting to look at all this through the glasses of astrology. From the point of view of past lifetimes and evolution, it is remarkable that almost all people on the planet today have their South Nodes of the planets Jupiter, Saturn, and Pluto in Capricorn, with, of course, their North Nodes in Cancer. Also, almost all of us have the South Node of Neptune in Aquarius and the North Node in Leo, and the South Node of Uranus in Sagittarius, with its North Node in Gemini. What does this mean ? It means that almost all the people on the planet today have had past lifetimes exactly when the original matriarchy was in place (South Node of Neptune in Aquarius) and lifetimes when the transition between the matriarchy and patriarchy began and picked up momentum (South Nodes of Saturn, Jupiter, and Pluto in Capricorn). With the South Node of Uranus in Sagittarius for most of us, this means that most of us have lived at least a few lives within tribes, cultures, or societies that were defined by natural laws. And now, here we all are at a very precarious time in the history of Earth itself when, in effect, we have a galactic return 25,000 years later to the original matriarchal point!

So why is this collective group of Souls on the planet now? This linkage between this group's past being born at this point in history suggests that this group is now here in order to apply the realizations and lessons from those distant times to our world today, and to the future. It suggests that real spiritualization (Neptune) will occur when we remember our ultimate spiritual root (the South Node of Neptune in Aquarius). Thus, it means to return to how the matriarchy lived, in a state of absolute balance with natural laws and Nature. In so doing, the dissolving (Neptune) of manmade beliefs of a patriarchal nature will occur. From this original spiritual root, the very nature of how we interpret phenomenal reality will also change because the nature of our beliefs will become realigned with Nature and natural laws. This is truly the real meaning of having the North Nodes of Jupiter, Saturn, and Pluto in Cancer—to return to our original origin (Cancer) in terms of our lives on Earth. In so doing, the very nature of our individual and collective self-image (Cancer) will metamorphose (Pluto) by eliminating and dissolving the artificial thoughts and beliefs promoted by the patriarchy (Capricorn).

In essence, we will become realigned with the original and true self-image that has always been there from the beginning of time. In so doing, there will be a realignment of the physical, emotional, and spiritual bodies into a state of natural balance and integration. Spirit and flesh will no longer be interpreted as mutually antagonistic. As a result, the patriarchal beliefs leading to suppression of all that is natural will be removed. Once removed, all the behavioral distortions that occur because of suppression will no longer exist. As a result, the causal factors leading to all kinds of displaced rage and anger will no longer exist. By returning to a collective and individual reality defined (Saturn) by natural laws (the original Aquarian Age) we will return to a state of balance, not only with ourselves as a collective organism, but with the planet itself. With the North Node of Neptune being in Leo, it would seem clear that the Pluto in Leo generation is to be the initial generation that progressively will enunciate this need and vision. Just as the great astrologer Dane Rudhyar pointed out and predicted, this generation will produce key "seed people" in the decade of the 1990s who will initially promote the vision of a new paradigms that reflect the Aquarian Age that is now beginning to manifest. And, evolutionary speaking, this primarily occurs through the dissemination of ideas that can now migrate all over the planet because of the media of print, film, television, and other information technologies, as seen in the South Node of Uranus being in Sagittarius, with its North Node in Gemini, for most people on the planet today.

A simple review of recent history will illustrate the point of the Pluto in Leo generation being the initial generation to promote the need to embrace a new paradigm and vision. During the middle to late 1960s, there was a progressive rebellion by this generation against the prevailing norms, customs, moralities, and religions of the consensus societies of that time. This included a total rebellion against how men and women were expected to relate, including the institution of marriage. There was a total "sexual revolution" as a result (remember the slogan "free love"?). Within this, there was an active search of information or knowledge systems from other cultures and times, and there was a strong focus on expanding consciousness through the use of drugs, and various Eastern spiritual systems as well as forms of Western Magic and Wicca. Environmental issues began as many wanted to re-embrace the sacredness of the Earth. This all occurred as the planet Neptune transited Scorpio, thus causing a transiting T-square to the natal South and North Nodes in this generation's birth charts. At the same time, Neptune was squaring this generation's natal Pluto in Leo. Corresponding with this transit was the transit of Pluto in Virgo. This transit thus created a T-square to the natal South and North Nodes of this generation's Uranus. And, if this were not enough to trigger this generational rebellion, the transit of Uranus was in Libra conjuncting the natal position of Neptune for the entire generation, indicating the total rebellion against gender assignment, and the roles within relationships that this reflects. Keeping in mind that the South Nodes of Jupiter, Saturn, and Pluto are in Capricorn, with their respective North Nodes in Cancer, the Uranus transit conjuncting the natal Neptune of this generation triggered the natural T-square between their natal Neptunes and these Nodes. The women's movement began at this time.

Since that decade, the movements that it spawned have increased to the point of creating a collective awareness of the issues related to the environment, the dissolving of the barriers between races and classes of people, women's and children's rights, and a progressive return of women to positions of power. During the time that Neptune and Uranus have been transiting in Capricorn relative to Pluto in Scorpio, all the dark and hidden secrets of women's and children's sexual abuse have been revealed. The "wounded child" became a buzz word in therapeutic circles. And, during 1992, more and more women became elected to political office. This occurred as the transits of Neptune and Uranus conjuncted all of our South Nodes of Pluto, Jupiter, and Saturn in Capricorn! This has even included the election of women to run patriarchal countries like Turkey and Pakistan.

I do not mean to suggest in this that somehow we will return to a reality in which we are all wandering around in buffalo hides and living in teepees, so to speak. Of course this is totally impossible given the nature of our world today—autobahns, supermarkets, etc. It does mean that we must learn how to apply natural laws in the context of these times and the times to come. *This is the specific challenge and requirement.* If one studies history, and understands the fact that seventy percent of all people are in a Consensus state, it is apparent that the evolutionary necessities reflected in the emerging Aquarius Age will not occur through some sudden collective enlightenment as so many "New Age" writers claim.

Quite the contrary, these necessary changes, in all probability, will occur through circumstantial necessity. Typically, this will manifest as cataclysmic events of varying degrees of intensity until there is no choice left but to change. The greatest danger to our planet remains that of nuclear bombs and the technologies they have spawned. Later on, I will discuss the different ways that this danger can manifest. At this point, you may find it interesting to consider that the planet Pluto, which directly correlates with nuclear fission and related phenomena, was discovered exactly when its movement through the sign Cancer conjuncted its own North Node at 18° Cancer, and in opposition to its South Node. At the moment of discovery, Pluto was also making an exact conjunction to the North Node of Saturn, also at 18° Cancer. For anyone who has debated the relevance of the Nodes of the other planets, this should be your wake-up call!

Within a few years of Pluto's discovery, the wheels were set in motion that led to the invention of the first atomic bomb. The war was the justification for this massively destructive device, but remember that wars have only occurred since the patriarchy began its domination of collective and individual reality. It is also interesting to note that the primary inventor of the atom bomb, Oppenheimer, was a devotee of the Hindu Goddess Kali, who is a female deity (Cancer) of destruction and rebirth. His intention and hope (Pluto) was that if he built such a device, there would never be a threat of war again because of the destructive power of the bomb itself—no one would ever dare use it. Unfortunately, this did not occur. This single invention, of itself, has completely altered the structural nature of our reality (Saturn) for all time. Here again, we see the link to when this transition began, the Capricorn sub-age of the Cancer Age, and the group of people on the planet today. Could there be any other greater danger to the violation of natural laws, and Nature Itself, than the spectacle and tragedy of this invention? The real horror of this potential was, of course, demonstrated during World War II when the United States dropped the atom bomb on Japan. And, yes, this occurred when Pluto was transiting in Leo, and conjunct the North Node of the Moon in the United States' birthchart! This event was the cause of the United States becoming a world superpower, and it radically altered how humanity was to relate to itself (the Pluto transit in opposition to the South Node of the Moon in Aquarius in the United States birthchart). The point here is to understand that Aquarius, Uranus, and the Eleventh House can correlate to a radical altering of existing conditions, and to total and sudden change. Even when the Cuban Missile Crisis came to a head in October of 1962, and everyone on Earth did not know if they would live or die, the transiting Saturn and South Node of the Moon were conjunct the South Node of the Moon in the United States horoscope!

So what is the message and teaching in all of this ? As this "galactic return" begins, the planet Pluto is now moving into Sagittarius. Uranus and Neptune will be traveling through the sign Aquarius for the next eight to ten years and conjuncting the South Node of Neptune. Relative to the context of our existing "reality" what can we expect for our individual and collective future? Let us first agree that no projection or prediction for our future can be an absolute. Individual and collective choices can be made at any moment that will affect or influence subsequent events or phenomena. And, of course, the Aquarian Age will last around 2,500 years— a great amount of time for all the archetypal intention and changes to be affected. So, at best, we can talk about probabilities relative to existing tendencies, individually and collectively. And since so much of our individual and collective future depends on the choices made, we can only realistically talk about future possibilities that cover the next twenty to thirty years at most. It is in this spirit and perspective that I will orient my thoughts about the future.

The intention and archetype of Aquarius and Uranus is to liberate from any pre-existing condition that is preventing necessary growth or change—to radically alter existing conditions so that growth can occur. Relative to Pluto's movement into Sagittarius, this will initially manifest relative to Nature and natural laws. Sagittarius as an archetype is directly connected to the inherent truth or laws that correlate with the apparent mystery of the manifest Creation. Since the manifestation of the patriarchy, a progressive state of imbalance has occurred with respect to the human species and its relationship to the rest of Nature and natural laws. The effects of this in today's world are obvious: the breakdown of our atmosphere (Aquarius) which is allowing increased radiation upon the surface of the planet, the total pollution of our water, air, and earth, the progressive contamination of our food supplies, the horrible spectacle of hundreds of species of different life forms becoming extinct on a daily basis, the raping of the Earth itself relative to cutting down the various forests including the tropical rain forest, and so on. Since Pluto is one our great teachers with respect to acknowledging the limits of anything, clearly we are beginning to reach the limit of this kind of destruction. As a result, Nature will progressively begin to erupt against the human organism in a variety of ways that will necessarily "catch people's attention." And this is intentional from the point of view of Nature, or Gaia, in order to teach the human organism about the effects of its delusionary patriarchal doctrines promoting the human dominance of Nature.

The vehicles that will "catch peoples attention" will manifest through increasingly intense Earth events such as earthquakes, volcanic eruptions, destructive storms including tornadoes, hurricanes, and typhoons (when is the last time you can remember, for example, six or seven hurricanes manifesting at the same time on a repeated basis in the Caribbean.) The progressive warming of the atmosphere due to the "greenhouse effect," which is due to human activities, will in all likelihood produce a two to six-degree rise in temperature on our planet within the next hundred years. The effects to the world coastlines, and the people and industries that live there, will be cataclysmic from their point of view. Add to this the fact that the current hole in the ozone layer is larger than the European continent. The increase in radiation that this creates will cause genetic mutations in many forms of life that are directly exposed to this radiation. This vehicle can also include nuclear accidents such as Chernobyl in the future. And what are the long-term effects of the existing level of contamination because of the nuclear waste that no one seems to know what to do with?

This does not mean, by the way, that somehow the entire west coast of the United States will break off as so many "New Age" writers have been predicting, including Edgar Cayce of all people. For those who have studied geology as I have, this is simply geologically impossible because of the nature of the tectonic plates in that part of the world. Very difficult Earth events will take place in this region, but they will not cause a breaking off, in some sudden event, of the entire west coast. This splitting is already under way through the natural tidal flow of the tectonic plates, but this will take hundreds of thousands of years to be finally accomplished. Beyond the effects to human life, the material cost for such destruction is what will catch people's attention. Within this, the ongoing extinction of hundreds of forms of life on a daily basis will create increasingly cataclysmic disturbances to bio-environments whose balance and integrity is dependent on the varied forms of life that are becoming extinct. These sorts of imbalances of increasingly cataclysmic proportions will set in motion a chain reaction that will affect every other form of life within the total system we call Earth. There are many examples that could be cited about this. For example, in South America there is now an increasing danger to human beings because of an explosion of caterpillars whose sting kills the human being. This explosion has been caused by the virtual elimination of this caterpillar's natural predators, who are becoming extinct due to human activities.

Another major way in which Nature will rebel (Aquarius) against the human organism is through the progressive mutation (Pluto) of the forms of life we call bacteria and viruses. Those who have followed my work over the years, who have attended various lectures and so on, you know that I have been talking about this for a long time. Years ago, when Pluto began its movement into Scorpio, I said that these forms of life would begin to mutate in order to survive. The survival instinct in all forms of life is symbolized in the sign Taurus, and since Taurus is the natural polarity of Scorpio, and all time/space reality operates through polarity, it was a very easy deduction to make. These forms of life had to mutate in order to survive the increasingly intense allopathic drugs, and because of the increasingly horrible imbalances within Nature itself due to the activities of the human being. I also stated that many of these mutated viruses and bacteria would become increasingly life-threatening to human beings in order for Nature to create a necessary culling effect of an overly dominant species so that a re-balancing could occur within Nature. And I stated that the means of transmission from person to person would primarily be through the exchange of fluids in one way or another as long as Pluto remained in the water sign Scorpio. Unfortunately, all this has in fact come to pass.

With Pluto now moving into a fire sign, and Neptune and Uranus moving into an air sign, I will now state that at least three to four of these viruses or bacteria will mutate again, and become airborne. Once airborne, these viruses and bacteria will spread through the common air (atmosphere) that we all share. In our times, this is particularly problematic because of the nature of our modes of transportation, such as airplanes that take people from land to land every single day. This will produce a very intense focus on the medical industry as it attempts to catch up and adjust to this phenomena. New realizations will be spawned because of this, which will primarily involve genetic engineering, new designs in allopathic drugs and medicines, and technologies to minimize these effects relative to the travel industry. It does not take a big leap of imagination to imagine the effects of this upon the human population. Let us remember that Sagittarius is naturally inconjunct Taurus and Cancer—the very survival (Taurus) of the species will be threatened, which will impact not only the global family, but the immediacy of our own families (Cancer), and friends (Aquarius). This will certainly catch people's attention.

The progressively intense impact of these phenomena will necessarily create a crisis in the belief systems or structures of everyone on the planet. Virgo and Pisces are the natural archetypes that correlate with crisis, and Pluto moving into Sagittarius creates a natural mutable Grand Cross that also involves the Sagittarian polarity of Gemini. This crisis is necessary relative to the larger intent of dissolving or eliminating the belief systems that determine how we interpret phenomenal reality as defined by the patriarchy. In other words, at some point, people will increasingly become forcefully aware that Nature is in fact stronger and more powerful than the human organism! The Virgo/Pisces axis relative to Sagittarius will necessarily create a humiliation to the collective human ego that will require total adjustments (the mutable archetype) in the nature of our belief systems, resulting in a return to natural laws, and living in a state of balance with the totality of Nature.

Within this, the fanatical edges of all existing patriarchal religious traditions will become even more fanatical in their effort to force down the throats of the majority of people their very limited moral agendas of a patriarchal nature. We have already seen this, yet it will become even more extreme. Even as of this writing, we see in the United States people who are running for President whose intention, if elected, is to use the Bible as the very basis of their administration. Such people will never win a free election in any land because their agenda does not reflect the will of the majority of the people. Yet, in some countries, because they cannot be elected freely or fairly, the self-righteous inflation of their delusions of grandeur will manifest as trying to force their agendas not only on their own home countries, but also trying to export and force these agendas in other countries. The means used to accomplish this is terrorism—religious terrorism that is self-justifying relative to its beliefs. The real danger in the future, relative to these kinds of groups, is religious/nuclear/biological/terrorism—small groups of religious fanatics who get their hands on various kinds of nuclear weapons or biological agents and essentially hold the planet hostage relative to the implementation of their agendas. This will catch people's attention. And this will necessarily occur in order for the larger evolutionary intention to occur: the elimination and dissolving of patriarchal belief systems which has caused this insanity to occur in the first place. In essence, they will blow themselves up!

Historically speaking, the last time Pluto moved into Sagittarius when Neptune and Uranus also moved into Aquarius directly correlated with the beginning of the revolution in human consciousness that is known as the Renaissance. This revolution reflected a drastic change from the perception of Church and God as all powerful, to the rebirth of humanism. It also directly correlated and manifested as the beginning of the discipline we now call natural science, or the observation of Nature and natural laws. This was also the time of Nostradamus, who had Pluto in the first degrees of Sagittarius. And, of course, Nostradamus issued his famous visions (Sagittarius) that embraced thousands of years to come. His intention in issuing these visions was the hope that the cataclysmic aspects of them would not occur if only people could be forewarned. Unfortunately, his forewarning was not, and has not been, heeded. Accordingly, many of his visions, predictions, have come true. My opinion and view of this same cycle again is that we will now shift from humanism to a focus upon what is called the Gaia—the Earth as a living, fully conscious, interrelated, and interdependent whole, with a reorientation to natural laws as our teachers leading the way.

One potential event that will catch people's attention, if it occurs, may be the actual manifestation on our Earth of life forms from other galaxies or universes. This manifestation will occur to and be witnessed by the collective, not just a few. Imagine the effect this would have on the consensus state of people in all lands. Imagine the effect to the nature of our existing beliefs, (i.e., people like Carl Sagan who voice that we are the only ones), and how we interpret phenomenal reality. Who can say if this will actually occur? I certainly cannot. My intuitive feeling is that it is probable because of the extreme distortion to the balance of nature that already exists. This distortion requires such a cataclysmic shock to the collective Soul. A variation of this theme will occur relative to astrophysics. Sagittarius is the archetype in our consciousness that makes us aware that we are connected to something much larger than just the Earth, such as the stars and galaxies that we can see in the night sky. Aquarius is the archetype in our consciousness that observes life in a detached way. Today, with the Hubbell Telescope in orbit above our Earth, peering into the distant galaxies, new observations will occur that will completely challenge our preexisting views about the nature and structure of "reality" itself. The nature of this challenge will be linked with natural laws— that which is inherent and natural. The point here is that there will be progressive observations of this kind that are linked with "outer space". And progressively, these observations will have the effect of aligning the human being back to a state of being in harmony with natural laws.

In particular, as we observe the transits of Neptune and Uranus becoming ever closer to the South Node of Neptune (i.e., 9° Aquarius), we can anticipate incredible "discoveries" of this kind. And the nature of these discoveries will shatter in many ways our pre-existing ideas about the nature of "reality." Even within our own solar system, this is already occurring. Recently the United States sent a spacecraft called Galileo to the planet Jupiter. This spacecraft is now orbiting Jupiter. It sent a probe into the atmosphere of Jupiter. This probe sent back data that has begun to completely challenge scientists' pre-existing beliefs and ideas about the nature and structure of this giant planet. Even the symbolism of this event is interesting. The mother craft Galileo hovered above the planet in order to observe it in a detached way (Aquarius), and sent a probe to penetrate its atmosphere (Pluto), which has had the effect of confronting (Pluto) the nature of pre-existing beliefs about it (Sagittarius). Since Jupiter rules the sign Sagittarius, is this event just coincidence or synchronicity relative to Pluto moving into Sagittarius at this time? 500 years ago, when this cycle occurred before, the discovery of "new worlds" occurred, with the European nations sending out various sailing boats to discover new continents. This time, this cycle in the context of the emerging Aquarius Age will correlate with the discovery of "new worlds" in space, and the colonization of at least one planet in our own solar system—Mars.

From an individual point of view, Pluto's movement into Sagittarius, relative to Neptune and Uranus moving into Aquarius, will correlate to many interesting dynamics. One of these will be the progressive actualization of each individual's personal truth relative to rebelling or liberating from religious, societal, and parental conditioning patterns. Within this, any of us who have been, or are, wearing false masks or personas that hide who we really are will experience inner and outer dynamics that will remove these false masks.

Our actual reality or truth will be revealed. This can create problematic situations in terms of our existing intimate relationships, friendships, and in our professional relationships. This will be a time of increasing restlessness as the inner desire to grow increases in intensity. This inner restlessness will manifest as an external restlessness for many, reflecting a desire to change one's existing reality dynamics and conditions. For many, this will translate to the desire to live in new places, or to see new places. Collectively, this will manifest as tremendous migrational flows of people from one place to another. This, in turn, will lead certain governments to change their immigration policies in order to control their own borders.

There will also be an increasingly interesting phenomena in which more and more people "tune out" the overwhelming amount of new and information that is progressively bombarding us from all directions. This is a left-brain dynamic (Gemini,Virgo) that the individual Soul will progressively oppose (Pluto's movement into Sagittarius). Pluto's movement into Sagittarius will progressively shift the center of gravity in our consciousness from the left to right brain—from the linear and empirical, to the non-linear and intuitive. In essence, this reflects a need within the collective, and each individual, to deepen (Pluto) their own need to tune into or listen to what is going on within them. Because of this, the collective and the individual will progressively confront and rebel against the Gemini superficialities emanating from any source, including governmental leaders. This is exactly why any governmental leader who is trying to speak to the truth of anything will receive a positive response from the collective, no matter what party affiliation they hold. Conversely, any political leader who says one thing, while meaning or intending another, will be exposed and will experience a fall from power. A perfect example of this point, as of this writing, is the dangerous Newt Gingrich in the United States, and the extreme conservative wing of the Republican Party that he represents. He and his agenda have been revealed despite all the Gemini words reflected in his "Contract (Pluto) with America." When he became Speaker of the House, his popularity was at an all-time high. As of this writing (January 1996), he could now be less popular than former President Nixon at the time of Watergate. He has been exposed, and the people see right through him because of Pluto's movement into Sagittarius—identifying the actual truth of anything. His fall began exactly when Pluto moved into Sagittarius for good in November of 1995, progressively forming opposition to his

Mercury, Uranus, Saturn, and Sun in Gemini. And this same effect, again, will occur to any person or leader who is wearing a false mask.

As each individual progressively tunes out from the bombardment of information from too many sources, accesses his or her own right brain and tunes into it, then the Neptune and Uranus effect in Aquarius will occur—the rapid evolution of the brain through the production of dendrites manifesting as new intuitive realizations or thoughts reflecting the inherent or natural truths of not only themselves, but also that of the intrinsic nature of the Creation Itself. Thus, how each of us has been interpreting the dynamics we call Self, and how we have been interpreting what we call "reality," will necessarily change for the better as we throw off the shackles of patriarchal beliefs. One of the interesting effects of this "tuning out" will be a tuning in to things like the Internet. Here, people find one another in a typical Uranian way—they connect through "like-mindedness." Because the Internet also allows for complete anonymity, this allows people an interesting freedom to explore thoughts, desires, or needs that they would otherwise not act upon. The Internet allows for people to connect to other people worldwide, and it operates more or less beyond any government's ability to control it short of cutting off the electrical supply. Because of this, it may prove to be a vehicle of increasing rebellion and relative anarchy against any government that is excessively dictatorial and restrictive relative to individual rights. Even as of this writing, Germany has attempted to censor some of what is offered on the Internet. Any government can try to do this, yet the people will be able to find ways around it because of the nature of the Internet. In fact, the people of Germany have done just that. In a sense, it may become the new "opiate of the people." With Pluto's movement into Sagittarius, the Internet (Aquarius) will in all probability have another interesting application that concerns how we are educated. Education correlates with Sagittarius and Gemini, thus, it is probable that the Internet will offer opportunities in education that have never occurred before. This will include being able to secure an entire university education over the Internet as more and more universities around the world offer their programs and courses in this way. This can also include the entire home school movement as more and more people "hook up" and combine their resources dedicated to educating their children independent of the normal educational structures of many countries.

I want to emphasize again that we are moving into a 2,500 year evolutionary process. Thus, the necessary evolutionary adjustments will take a long time to accomplish. If one projects into the far future, the very end of the Aquarian Age, using astrological symbolism as the glasses of this projection, it would seem clear that there will be a 200 year period of time, right at the end of the Aquarius Age, that may prove that the "condensed and intense period of time" in which all of these dynamics come to a head will determine the future survival of the human species as we know it, and of the Earth as we know it. This is when the South Node of Saturn shifts to Aquarius, and the South Node of Pluto also shifts to Aquarius. Saturn reaches this exactly at A.D. 2500, and Pluto reaches this at exactly A.D. 2700. Nostradamus predicted for these 200 years a time of worldwide peace in which galactic communities would be firmly established after massive cataclysmic events had occurred. His specific vision is stated in his own words: "There will be a hecatomb which will occur close to the millennium end. Then those who entered the tomb will leave." This 200-year period begins when the South Node of Saturn moves into Aquarius. And on that day, guess what? Pluto will be at 28° Sagittarius (the galactic center), and Neptune and Uranus will once again be in Aquarius. We can only hope that the words of Jesus may then come true: "The last shall come first." My prayer for all of us is that we wake up soon, and make the choices necessary to preclude any unnecessary suffering to those who always suffer first—the weak and the powerless. None of this is fated to occur. The human being has the god-given right and power to make its own choices that affect the very next moment. Let us hope that all of us can tune into the spirit of our own Mother Earth and listen to the guidance therein. God Bless to all of us!

Conclusion

It is my sincere hope that you have found some meaning in this material, and that it will help you understand relationship dynamics in a new way. And for those in the counseling professions, especially astrologers, I hope that you will be able to apply this material in a meaningful and constructive way on behalf of your clients. My deepest hope is that by understanding the nature of all conditioning patterns, especially those emanating from the patriarchy, all of us will be able to help in the absolute need of bringing the pathologies of sadomasochism to a quick culmination. Those who wish to write to me for any reason can do so via Llewellyn Publications.

God Bless,
Jeffrey Wolf Green

Stay in Touch . . .

Llewellyn publishes hundreds of books on your favorite subjects.

On the following pages you will find listed some books now available on related subjects. Your local bookstore stocks most of these and will stock new Llewellyn titles as they become available. We appreciate your patronage!

Order by Phone

Call toll-free within the U.S. and Canada, **1–800–THE MOON.**
In Minnesota call **(612) 291–1970.**
We accept Visa, MasterCard, and American Express.

Order by Mail

Send the full price of your order (MN residents add 7% sales tax) in U.S. funds to:

Llewellyn Worldwide
P.O. Box 64383, Dept. K333-6
St. Paul, MN 55164–0383, U.S.A.

Postage and Handling

- $4.00 for orders $15.00 and under
- $5.00 for orders over $15.00
- No charge for orders over $100.00

We ship UPS in the continental United States. We cannot ship to P.O. boxes. Orders shipped to Alaska, Hawaii, Canada, Mexico, and Puerto Rico will be sent first-class mail.

International orders: Airmail—add freight equal to price of each book to the total price of order, plus $5.00 for each non-book item (audiotapes, etc.). Surface mail—Add $1.00 per item.

Allow 4–6 weeks for delivery. Postage and handling rates subject to change.

Group Discounts

We offer a 20% quantity discount to group leaders or agents. You must order a minimum of 5 copies of the same book to get our special quantity price.

Prices subject to change without notice.

Free Catalog

Get a free copy of our color catalog, *New Worlds of Mind and Spirit.* Subscribe for just $10.00 in the United States and Canada ($20.00 overseas, first-class mail). Many bookstores carry *New Worlds*—ask for it!

PLUTO: Volume I
The Evolutionary Journey of the Soul
Jeffrey Wolf Green

If you have ever asked "Why am I here?"or "What are my lessons?" then this book will help you to objectively learn the answers from an astrological point of view. Green shows you how the planet Pluto relates to the evolutionary and karmic lessons in this life and how past lives can be understood through the position of Pluto in your chart.

Beyond presenting key principles and ideas about the nature of the evolutionary journey of the Soul, this book supplies practical, concise and specific astrological methods and techniques that pinpoint the answers to the above questions. If you are a professional counselor or astrologer, this book is indispensable to your practice. The reader who studies this material carefully and applies it to his or her own chart will discover an objective vehicle to uncover the essence of his or her own state of being. The understanding that this promotes can help you cooperate with, instead of resist, the evolutionary and karmic lessons in your life. Green describes the position of Pluto through all of the signs and houses, explains the aspects and transits of Pluto, discusses Pluto in aspect to the Moon's Nodes, and gives sample charts and readings. It is the most complete look at this "new" planet ever.

0-87542-296-9, 384 pp., 6 x 9, softcover $15.00

To order call 1-800-THE MOON
Prices subject to change without notice.

How to Personalize the Outer Planets
The Astrology of Uranus, Neptune & Pluto
Edited by Noel Tyl

Since their discoveries, the three outer planets have been symbols of the modern era. Representing great social change on a global scale, they also take us as individuals to higher levels of consciousness and new possibilities of experience. Explored individually, each outer planet offers tremendous promise for growth. But when taken as a group, as they are in *How to Personalize the Outer Planets*, the potential exists to recognize accelerated development.

Seven prominent astrologers in *How to Personalize the Outer Planets* bring these revolutionary forces down to earth in practical ways:

- Jeff Jawer: Learn how the discoveries of the outer planets rocked the world
- Noel Tyl: Project into the future with outer planet Solar Arcs
- Jeff Green: See how the outer planets are tied to personal trauma
- Jeff Jawer: Give perspective to your inner spirit through outer planet symbolisms
- Jayj Jacobs: Explore interpersonal relationships and sex through the outer planets
- Mary E. Shea: Make the right choices using outer planet transits
- Joanne Wickenburg: Realize your unconscious drives and urges through the outer planets
- Capel N. McCutcheon: Personalize the incredible archetypal significance of outer planet aspects

0-87542-389-2, 288 pp., 6 x 9, illus., softcover $12.00

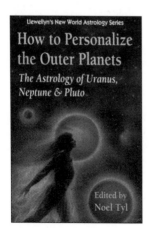

Llewellyn's New World Astrology Series
How to Personalize the Outer Planets
The Astrology of Uranus, Neptune & Pluto
Edited by Noel Tyl

To order call 1-800-THE MOON
Prices subject to change without notice.

Synthesis & Counseling in Astrology
The Professional Manual
Noel Tyl

One of the keys to a vital, comprehensive astrology is the art of synthesis, the capacity to take the parts of our knowledge and combine them into a coherent whole. Many times, the parts may be contradictory (the relationship between Mars and Saturn, for example), but the art of synthesis manages the unification of opposites. Now Noel Tyl presents ways astrological measurements—through creative synthesis—can be used to effectively counsel individuals. Discussion of these complex topics is grounded in concrete examples and in-depth analyses of the 122 horoscopes of celebrities, politicians, and private clients.

Tyl's objective in providing this vitally important material was to present everything he has learned and practiced over his distinguished career to provide a useful source to astrologers. He has succeeded in creating a landmark text destined to become a classic reference for professional astrologers.

1-56718-734-X, 924 pp., 7 x 10, 115 charts, softcover $29.95

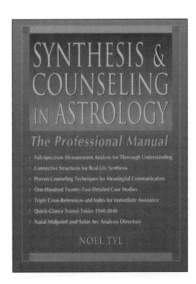

To order call 1-800-THE MOON
Prices subject to change without notice.

Mythic Astrology
Archetypal Powers in the Horoscope
Ariel Guttman & Kenneth Johnson

Here is an entirely new dimension of self-discovery based on understanding the mythic archetypes represented in the astrological birth chart. Myth has always been closely linked with astrology; all our planets are named for the Graeco-Roman deities and derive their interpretative meanings from them. To richly experience the myths that lie at the heart of astrology is to gain a deeper and more spiritual perspective of the art of astrology and of life itself.

Mythic Astrology is unique because it allows the reader to explore the connection between astrology and the spirituality of myth in depth, without the necessity of a background in astrology, anthropology, or the classics. This book is an important contribution to the continuing study of mythology as a form of New Age spirituality and is also a reference work of enduring value. Students of mythology, the Goddess, art, history, Jungian psychological symbolism and literature—as well as lovers of astrology—will all enjoy the text and numerous illustrations.

0-87542-248-9, 382 pp., 7 x 10, 100 illus., softcover $17.95

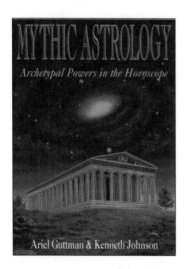

Archetypes of the Zodiac
Kathleen Burt

The horoscope is probably the most unique tool for personal growth you can ever have. This book is intended to help you understand how the energies within your horoscope manifest. Once you are aware of how your chart operates on an instinctual level, you can then work consciously with it to remove any obstacles to your growth.

The technique offered in this book is based on the incorporation of the esoteric rulers of the signs and the integration of their polar opposites. This technique has been very successful in helping the client or reader modify existing negative energies in a horoscope so as to improve the quality of his or her life and the understanding of his or her psyche.

There is special focus in this huge comprehensive volume on the myths for each sign. Some signs may have as many as four different myths coming from all parts of the world. All are discussed by the author. There is also emphasis on the Jungian Archetypes involved with each sign.

This book has a depth often surprising to the readers of popular astrology books. It has a clarity of expression seldom found in books of the esoteric tradition. It is very easy to understand, even if you know nothing of Jungian philosophy or of mythology. It is intriguing, exciting, and very helpful for all levels of astrologers.

0-87542-088-5, 576 pp., 6 x 9, illus., softcover $16.00

Astrology and the Games People Play
A Tool for Self-Understanding in Work & Relationships
Spencer Grendahl

Expand your self-awareness and facilitate personal growth with the Astro-analysis approach to astrology! Astro-analysis is a completely new and unique system that enables you to combine simple astrological information with the three-ring model of basic ego states—Parent, Adult, and Child—used in popular psychology. This easy-to-follow technique makes available to the average person psychological insights that are generally available only to astrologers. Not only is it easy to transcribe your horoscope onto Astro-analysis' three-sphere diagram, but you will find that this symbolic picture provides accurate and meaningful perceptions into the energy patterns of your personality, clearly delineating the areas that may be "overweighted" or most in need of balance. This material is enhanced by examples and explanations of horoscopes of actual people.

Astro-analysis is a powerful self-help tool that will quickly make you aware of the basis for your behavior patterns and attitudes, so you can get a new perspective on your relationships with others and determine the most promising strategies for personal growth.

1-56718-338-7, 224 pp., 7 x 10, softcover $12.95

Sexuality in the Horoscope
Noel Tyl, editor

To empower clients to be more successful and satisfied in every area of life is the astrologer's legitimate aim. You might specialize in relationships or finance, but you cannot ignore the rest of a client's life if you intend to enhance the whole person. You must be willing and able to deal with the private and the often painful, the repressed as well as the blissful.

Sex is a biological drive with a chemical basis, physiological parameters, physical manifestations, emotional and psychological dimensions, and sociological implications. It involves our self-awareness and self-esteem, our capacity for communications, and parental influence. At the most basic physical level, it is friction. At the most spiritual level, it is merging into transcendental oneness.

The experience of sexuality is complex in its manifestation in life and the horoscope. As they explore charts of the famous, infamous, and everyday persons, ten well-known astrologers share insights into these intriguing topics:

- Classic Scenarios of Psychosexual Development – Noel Tyl
- Pluto Pathology: The Dark Side of Human Sexuality – Glenn Perry, Ph.D.
- Relationship Dynamics and Their Sexual Reality – Marion D. March
- Sexual Energy & Creativity – Gina Ceaglio
- Imagination/Fantasy: Sexuality's Escape Valve – John Townley
- Homosexuality in the Horoscope – J. Lee Lehman, Ph.D.
- Freeing the Spirit: Getting Beyond Denial – Ted Sharp
- Integrating the Sexual Profile for Wholeness – Jayj Jacobs
- Sexual Repression – Anthony Louis, M.D.
- AIDS: An Astro-Medical Perspective – B. F. Hammerslough
- Includes the charts of famous personalities

1-56718-865-6, 6 x 9, 336 pp., softcover
$14.95

Ecstasy through Tantra
Dr. Jonn Mumford

Dr. Jonn Mumford makes the occult dimension of the sexual dynamic accessible to everyone. One need not go up to the mountaintop to commune with Divinity: its temple is the body, its sacrament the communion between lovers. *Ecstasy Through Tantra* traces the ancient practices of sex magick through the Egyptian, Greek and Hebrew forms, where the sexual act is viewed as symbolic of the highest union, to the highest expression of Western sex magick.

Dr. Mumford guides the reader through mental and physical exercises aimed at developing psychosexual power; he details the various sexual practices and positions that facilitate "psychic short-circuiting" and the arousal of Kundalini, the Goddess of Life within the body. He shows the fundamental unity of Tantra with Western Wicca, and he plumbs the depths of Western sex magick, showing how its techniques culminate in spiritual illumination. Includes 14 full-color photographs.

0-87542-494-5, 190 pp., 6 x 9, 14 color plates, softcover $16.00

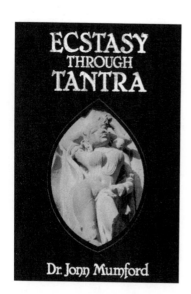